FORGOTTEN BLITZES

Forgotten Blitzes:

France and Italy under Allied Air Attack, 1940–1945

Claudia Baldoli and Andrew Knapp

continuum

Continuum International Publishing Group

The Tower Building
11 York Road
London
SE1 7NX

80 Maiden Lane
Suite 704
New York
NY 10038

www.continuumbooks.com

British Library Cataloguing-in-Publication Data
A catalogue record for this book is available from the British Library.

ISBN HB: 978-1-4411-3109-6
ISBN PB: 978-1-4411-8581-5

Typeset by Fakenham Prepress Solutions, Fakenham,
Norfolk NR21 8NN
Printed and bound in India

This book is dedicated to those unknown victims of bombing whom we glimpsed in scores of air raid reports, too distant from their families as they died, or too disfigured, to be identifiable.

Contents

Preface

This book was written as part of a project, financed by the Arts and Humanities Research Council, on 'Bombing, States and Peoples in Western Europe, 1940–1945'. The project has been an immensely rewarding adventure for both of us since we first applied for it in 2006, and our archival research would have been quite impossible without the AHRC's generous financial assistance. Part of the project was the construction of a web exhibition, including photographs (http://centres.exeter.ac.uk/wss/bombing/index.htm); these, in greater numbers than would have been possible on these pages, serve as the illustrations for this book. In addition, our respective universities – Newcastle and Reading – provided us with leave to write up.

The book also owes much to many individuals. First among these has been Professor Richard Overy, whose inspired leadership of the 'Bombing, States and Peoples' project has made it feel worthwhile, intellectually exciting, and above all fun. The 'bombing team' – the project members, including Vanessa Chambers, Lindsey Dodd, Stephan Glienke, and Marc Wiggam, as well as the project's advisors, Gabriella Gribaudi, MacGregor Knox, Phil Reed, Nick Stargardt, and the group who came together to prepare the project book in September 2009, have all been a great stimulus and encouragement.*

The availability of a network of national and local archives across France and Italy (as well as in the USA and the UK) has been an absolute precondition of this project and we take this opportunity to thank them collectively here. There is not space in a short preface to mention all the archivists who have assisted us, but Caroline Apostoulopoulos (BDIC, Paris), Sylvie Barot (Le Havre), Giulia Beltrametti (Turin) and Marie-Claude Berthelot (Mémorial de Caen) have been outstanding.

Other individuals have furthered our reflection in seminars and other discussions throughout its duration. They include Tommaso Baris, Marc Olivier Baruch, Helen Berry, Stephen Bourque, Susan Castoro, Carlotta Coccoli, Antonella De Palma, Pietro Di Paola, Ruth Easingwood, Patrick Facon, Martin Farr, Paolo Ferrari, Marco Fincardi, Peter Heinl, Amy Hill, Tim Kirk, Simon Kitson, Nicola Labanca, Simone Neri Serneri, Marta Nezzo, Matt Perry, Luigi Petrella, Felix Schulz, Neelam Srivastava and Megan Trudell.

* Cf. C. Baldoli, A. Knapp, and R. Overy (eds), *Bombing, States and Peoples in Western Europe, 1940–1945* (London: Continuum, 2011).

Despite all this excellent advice, we will still have made errors in this book, and they will still be entirely ours.

As always, finally, people close to us – Sara and Viveca Knapp, and Maria, Mario and Giaime Baldoli – have been unstinting in their support and forbearance, and deserve our most profound gratitude.

Claudia Baldoli
Andrew Knapp

Brescia and Reading, August 2011

List of Abbreviations

ACG	Archivio Comunale, Genoa
ACS	Archivio Centrale dello Stato, Rome
AD	Archives Départementales
AD BduR	Archives Départementales des Bouches-du-Rhône
AD LA	Archives Départementales de la Loire-Atlantique
AD SM	Archives Départementales de la Seine-Maritime
ADN	Archivio Diaristico Nazionale, Pieve Santo Stefano
AFHRA	Air Force Historical Research Agency, Maxwell, Alabama
AFM	Archivio Fondazione Micheletti, Brescia
AG	Affari Generali (Italy), *L'Amérique en Guerre* (France)
AM	Amministrazione Municipale (Italy), Archives Municipales (France)
AM BB	Archives Municipales de Boulogne-Billancourt
AM CB	Archives Municipales et Communautaires de Brest
AN	Archives Nationales, Paris
APA	Association pour l'Autobiographie, Ambérieu-en-Bugey
ASB	Archivio di Stato, Bologna
ASG	Archivio di Stato, Genoa

ASLS	Archivio di Stato, La Spezia
ASM	Archivio di Stato, Milan
ASN	Archivio di Stato, Naples
ASP	Archivio di Stato, Palermo
ASTa	Archivio di Stato, Taranto
ASTo	Archivio di Stato, Turin
BDIC	Bibliothèque de Documentation Internationale Contemporaine, Nanterre
BIDP	Bulletin d'Information de la Défense Passive
CA	*Le Courrier de l'Air*
CCIPAA	Comitato Centrale Interministeriale Protezione Anti Aerea
CFLN	Comité Français de Libération Nationale
CLN	Comitato di Liberazione Nazionale
COSI	Comité Ouvrier de Secours Immédiat
DAGR	Direzione Affari Generali e Riservati
DDDP	Direction Départementale de la Défense Passive
DDP	Direction de la Défense Passive
DGPCSA	Direzione Generale Protezione Civile e Servizi Antincendi (Divisione Protezione Civile)
DGPS	Direzione Generale Pubblica Sicurezza
DiCaT	Difesa Contraerea Territoriale
DPP	Divisione Polizia Politica
ECA	Ente Comunale di Assistenza

FDRPL	Franklin D. Roosevelt Presidential Library, New York
FF	Francs Français
GIL	Gioventù Italiana del Littorio
GPRF	Gouvernement Provisoire de la République Française
GU	Gazzetta Ufficiale
ICC	International Criminal Court
IIGM	Seconda Guerra Mondiale
INSMLI	Istituto Nazionale per la Storia del Movimento di Liberazione in Italia, Milan
ISTAT	Istituto nazionale di Statistica
JO	Journal Officiel de la République Française (before July 1940) Journal Officiel de l'État Français (July 1940–August 1944): Lois et Décrets
LC	Library of Congress, Washington DC
MA	Ministero dell'Aeronautica
MEP	Member of the European Parliament
MI	Ministero dell'Interno
MinCulPop	Ministero della Cultura Popolare
NARA	National Archives and Records Administration, Washington DC
OSS	Office of Strategic Services
OVRA	Organizzazione di Vigilanza e Repressione dell'Antifascismo
PCF	Parti Communiste Français
PCI	Partito Comunista Italiano
PNF	Partito Nazionale Fascista

PPF	Parti Populaire Français
PWE	Political Warfare Executive
RAF	Royal Air Force
RG	Record Group (USA), Renseignements Généraux (France)
RNP	Rassemblement National Populaire
SHAA	Service Historique de l'Armée de l'Air
SHAT	Service Historique de l'Armée de Terre
SIPEG	Service Interministériel de Protection contre les Événements de Guerre
SNCF	Société Nationale des Chemins de Fer Français
STO	Service du Travail Obligatoire
TE	Témoignage Écrit
TNA	The National Archives, Kew, London
UNPA	Unione Nazionale Protezione Antiaerea
USAAF	United States Army Air Forces

List of Maps and Tables

Note: Illustrations may be found on the 'Bombing, States and Peoples' web exhibition (http://centres.exeter.ac.uk/wss/bombing/index.htm).

1

Introduction

Italy's surrender to the Allies was announced on Wednesday 8 September 1943 at 5.30 p.m. A few hours earlier, 131 aircraft of the US Twelfth Air Force had attacked the hill town of Frascati, 13 miles outside Rome, home to the headquarters of Germany's commander in the Mediterranean theatre, Field Marshal Albert Kesselring. The raid destroyed half the town and killed about 500 of its civilian inhabitants; Kesselring and his staff, dispersed in a number of villas, escaped unscathed and continued to hold back the Allied advance till the spring of 1945.[1] That night, on the Channel, the French resort town of Le Portel became a target for 252 aircraft of RAF Bomber Command, together with five American B17s. The site of a long-range German gun emplacement, Le Portel was attacked as part of Operation Starkey, a simulated Allied invasion of France designed to draw the Luftwaffe into action on unfavourable terms. The raid left the guns undamaged, but 95 per cent of Le Portel was destroyed, its civil defences overwhelmed, and 500 French civilians killed.[2]

Compared to Operation Gomorrah, which had destroyed much of Hamburg and killed some 37,000 Germans six weeks earlier, these were minor raids, aimed at impeccably military targets. Nevertheless, in the space of under 12 hours, at 800 miles' distance, the Allies had – uselessly, as it turned out – taken the lives of 1,000 civilians, half of whom were officially viewed by the British as 'not only friends, but allies', and half belonging to a nation that had signed its act of surrender five days earlier.[3] Nor were these the worst attacks of September 1943 on either country. In Italy, Pescara, on the Adriatic coast, suffered hundreds of victims in a raid by the US Ninth Air Force on 14 September, while attacks on Bologna took a similar toll 11 days later; in France, two big raids on the western city of Nantes, on 16 and 23 September, claimed nearly 1,500 lives, as well as 2,500 injured, and provoked the spontaneous and chaotic evacuation of about half of the city's population of 200,000. Nor was September 1943, which left close to 3,000 civilian dead from air raids in each country, the worst month of the war for either; Italy had suffered worse the previous August, while France would receive its heaviest raids in the spring and summer of 1944.

The literature on bombing in World War Two has focused, understandably but excessively, on the British and German experiences. The Blitz is woven into Britain's national identity, and has inspired a profusion of accounts, both conventional and critical.[4] The strategic offensive against Germany, which absorbed over half the Allied bombing effort of the European war, was deeply controversial before it ended. The main focus of a major US official survey, of a British official history, and of countless works on the bombers and their commanders and crews, it has recently prompted both searing narratives of the German experience and explorations of the ethics of bombing.[5] Relatively few studies, by contrast, concentrate on

France or on Italy. Local histories abound, and range from the anecdotal to the exhaustive; spectacular episodes like the bombing of Caen or Monte Cassino fall into broader military narratives; but full-scale national accounts are rare.[6] Allied bombing barely features in the historical industry built around wartime France, and sits uneasily with any established narrative. Similarly, in Italy, the national rhetoric of the Liberation after 1945 reduced the bombing experience to a phase of the war in which the Anglo-Americans could no longer be regarded as enemies.

This comparative marginalization is unjustified. Other than Germany, no European countries were more heavily bombed than France and Italy (Table 1.1). By way of comparison, the tonnage dropped on the United Kingdom was less than one-fifth of the Italian total, barely more than one-eighth of the French.

Table 1.1 Allied bombs dropped on Europe, 1939–45, by destination

Region	***Tons of bombs dropped***	***Percentage of total bombs dropped***
Austria, Hungary, and Balkans	185,625	6.7%
France	570,730	20.6%
Germany	1,415,745	51.1%
Italy (incl. Sicily)	379,565	13.7%
Other	218,873	7.9%
	2,770,540	100.0%
(German bombs, including V-weapons, dropped on the UK, 1940–45)	74,172	

Sources: for Allied bombs: United States Strategic Bombing Survey, *Statistical Appendix to Over-all report (European war)*, Washington DC, 1947, Chart no. 1 (http://wwiiarchives.net/servlet/document/113/1/0); for German bombs on UK: R. Overy, *The Air War, 1939–1945* (Washington, DC: Potomac Books, 2005), 120.

For both France and Italy, these figures reflected heavy, prolonged periods of bombardment and substantial casualties (Tables 1.2, 1.3). In France, raids on Channel ports during the invasion scare of 1940 were followed by attacks on Atlantic harbours, home to German surface warships and to growing numbers of U-boat pens, and on industrial and rail targets in northern France. From August 1942, the RAF was joined in these raids by the UK-based US Eighth Air Force. Nearly four-fifths of all raids on France, and some seven in ten of French civilian casualties, came in 1944, when almost the whole country, with the partial exception of the south-west, came under attack. As well as continuing heavy raids against industry, the spring saw attacks on V-weapon sites and a campaign of unprecedented scope against rail centres, in northern France but also the southern coast and the Rhône valley, which were hit from bases in Italy. After the D-day landings on 6 June, these raids were complemented by operations in support of ground forces. This role entailed some of the biggest raids of the war: villages east of Caen received over 5,000 tons of bombs from 942 aircraft of Bomber Command on 18 July, while Le Havre attracted 1,846 sorties and 9,790 tons of bombs between 5 and 11 September.[7]

Table 1.2 Raids and deaths from bombing in France, 1940–5: the postwar figures

	Air raids		***Civilian deaths***	
Year	***No.***	***As % of total***	***No.***	***As % of total***
1940	210*	2.2	3,543*	6.5
1941	450	4.8	1,357	2.5
1942	488	5.2	2,579	4.7
1943	788	8.4	7,446	13.6
1944	7,482	79.3	38,158	69.8
1945	18	0.2	1,548	2.8
Totals	9,436	100.0	54,631	100.0

Sources: Ministère de l'Intérieur, Direction de la Défense Passive, *Bulletin d'Information de la Défense Passive et de la Protection contre l'Incendie*, nos. 25 (September 1944), 26 (October–December 1944) and 27 (February–May 1945); France, SHAA 3/D/322/1, État Major de l'Armée, Bureau Scientifique de l'Armée, 'Étude Général des Effets des Bombardements Aériens Alliés'; Archives Municipales du Havre, H/4/14/4, Reseignements Demandés par M. Brianchon, Secrétaire Général Adjoint, le 16 février 1945.†

Table 1.3 Deaths from bombing in Italy, 1940–5: the postwar figures

	Aerial bombing		***Other bombing***	
	Civilian	**Military**	**Civilian**	**Military**
Pre-armistice	18,376	2,576	754	162
Post-armistice	41,420	1,982	5,154	167
Totals	59,796	4,558	5,908	329

Source: ISTAT, *Morti e disperse per cause belliche negli anni 1940–1945* (Rome: Istituto Centrale di Statistica, Failli, 1957), 26.‡

* Figures include victims of German raids. Victims of Allied raids only were 292 dead and 636 wounded.
† The *Bulletin d'Information de la Défense Pasive* (*BIDP*) has been used as a basic source as it is the only one to offer year-on-year totals based on returns from France's town halls and prefectures. However, it is a contemporary source, begun in April 1942, and it stresses that its figures should be considered as minima. In particular, issue nos. 25 (which note the failure of many reports to come in owing to the prevailing difficulties of communication) and 26 clearly fail to include the big raids on Le Havre in September 1944 in their figures. Local figures for these raids (1,536 killed and 517 missing presumed dead, and 650 wounded) have therefore been added to those in the main source for September 1944. For the years 1941–2, the Bureau Scientifique de l'Armée document has been used for the number of raids only. The *Journal Officiel* of 26 May 1948 gave the somewhat higher overall death toll of 56,896. For a fuller discussion of the difficulty of reaching a reliable figure, see Appendix 1.
‡ As explained in Appendix 1, these figures are underestimated.

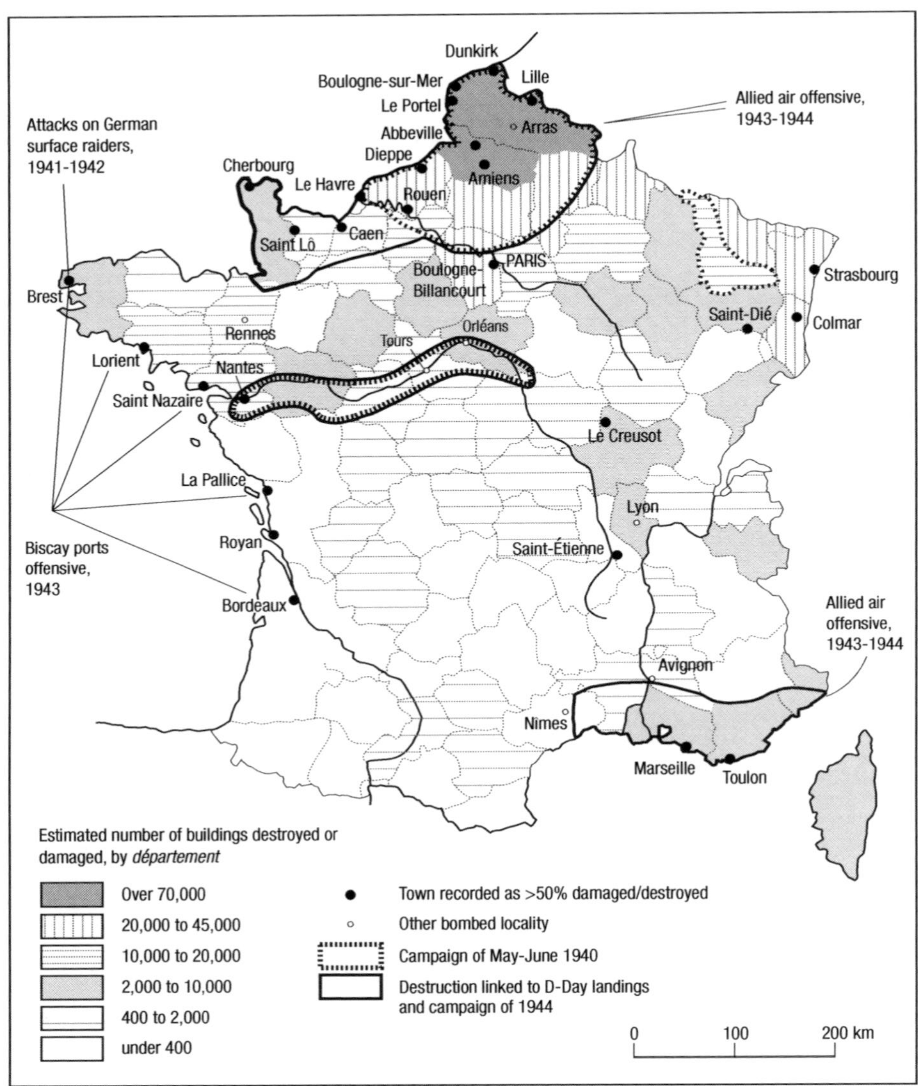

Map 1.1 France: the geography of destruction, 1940–5 (adapted from E. Alary *et al.*, *Les Français au quotidien, 1939-1949* (Paris: Perrin, 2009), 404. © Éditions Plon-Perrin-Presses de la Renaissance, 2009).

Map 1.2 Italy: Main priority targets raided
Map designed by Carlotta Coccoli

French figures drawn up at the end of the war also showed nearly 130,000 wounded in raids since 1940.[8] Of the dead, probably one-third were killed in Normandy in the spring and summer of 1944, with Caen and Le Havre sustaining some 2,000 victims each, Rouen some 1,800, Lisieux nearly 800 and Saint-Lô 500 (though the greatest proportional loss was in the village of Évrecy, which lost 130 of its 430 inhabitants).[9] In absolute terms Marseille suffered the single most lethal Allied raid of the war, when an attack by the US Fifteenth Air Force on 27 May 1944 claimed at least 1,831 victims.[10] With loss of life went immense material destruction. Of France's communes (municipalities) of over 10,000 inhabitants, *most* were classified as *sinistrées* after the war, indicating a level of destruction in excess of 30 per cent.[11] Again, the damage was particularly intense in Normandy: 82 per cent of Le Havre was destroyed, 77 per cent of Saint-Lô, 75 per cent of Lisieux, 73 per cent of Caen, 42 per cent of Rouen.[12] But they were far from alone: ports, in particular – Lorient and Saint-Nazaire, Brest and Boulogne – suffered levels of destruction in excess of 80 per cent. In Nantes, some 60,000 people were reported bombed-out after the raids of September 1943; in the small railway junction of Modane, on the route into Italy, 3,500 people – three-quarters of the population – suffered the same fate[13]; in Lyon, the figure was estimated at 25,000, in Marseille, at 30,000, after the big raids of May 1944.[14] Royan, one of the 'pockets' on the Atlantic coast where German garrisons held out for months after the liberation of the rest of France, had been almost completely destroyed by some 7,000 tons of bombs (including napalm) before it surrendered on 18 April 1945.[15] Post-war surveys suggested that between 10 and 15 per cent of France's total stock of 12 million housing units had been destroyed.[16] The task of reconstruction took a generation, during which tens of thousands of French families lived in all kinds of temporary accommodation, including Nissen huts vacated by Allied troops.[17] And much that was wrecked was, strictly, irreplaceable. If the cathedral of Rouen was saved – having burned for several days after a raid on 30 May – the same could not be said of the less illustrious, but still ancient, urban fabric of dozens of towns and villages in Normandy and elsewhere.

In Italy, meanwhile, the bombing of major cities began barely 24 hours after Mussolini's declaration of war on France and Britain on 10 June 1940, while the last bombs of the war fell early in May 1945, targeting German troops retreating towards the Brenner Pass. During the intervening five years almost every Italian city experienced bombing. Northern industrial centres such as Genoa, Milan and Turin received over 50 raids each, and sustained an area bombing campaign by the RAF, targeting both industry and civilian morale, between October 1942 and the armistice of September 1943. Milan alone suffered some 2,000 victims.

Southern Italy was targeted from the RAF base in Malta between 1940 and the autumn of 1942 in raids aimed both at the Italian navy and at the flow of Axis supplies to North Africa. Palermo was first attacked on 23 June 1940, Naples on 31 October. On 11 November, three Italian battleships anchored at Taranto were seriously damaged by Fleet Air Arm torpedo-bombers. From late 1942 raids on southern Italy were largely taken over by the USAAF based in North Africa; they intensified as part of the preparation for Allied landings in Sicily and, later, on the peninsula itself. As over Germany, the RAF bombed at night, the USAAF by day. But the latter's attempts at 'precision bombing', though less hampered than in other theatres, proved as devastating for the population as those of British 'area bombing' in northern Italy, thanks to the high number, high altitude, and large scale of American operations. Southern cities such as Naples and Messina took over 100 raids each; Naples, in its worst year (1943) lost nearly 6,100 of its inhabitants to bombing.[18]

Two-thirds of Italian civilian casualties, however, occurred *after* the armistice of 8 September 1943. In the north, area bombing ceased but heavy raids continued against industrial and rail targets, now part of an essentially German war effort. In central and southern Italy, meanwhile, communications objectives and areas near the front line were bombed in support of ground operations. As the military campaign moved from the Gustav Line to the Gothic Line (between autumn 1943 and summer 1944), central Italy, entirely spared till spring 1943, became the most bombed part of the country.[19] This situation continued from the breaking of the Gothic Line until the liberation of northern Italy. Although large city centres were no longer targeted, attacks on communication lines continued, hitting residential areas and smaller towns situated along them.[20] These 'tactical' raids inflicted heavy damage on small and medium towns throughout the peninsula: Foggia, for example, lost 75 per cent of its residential buildings, while other localities such as Ancona or Rimini were repeatedly attacked as they found themselves on the front line for months.

It should be added that both France and Italy were also bombed by the Luftwaffe. In France, the campaign of May–June 1940 saw northern towns such as Abbeville and Amiens, and surrounding villages, sustain levels of destruction reaching 75–80 per cent according to the (possibly exaggerated) prefectoral reports of the following month.[21] The Luftwaffe also attacked the Citroën works on the Quai Javel in Paris and targets as far away as Cherbourg and the Loire valley, while the Italian Air Force hit Orléans and Marseille. That summer's raids left some 3,250 civilians dead and 2,000 wounded.[22] Such raids served both to provoke a mass exodus, ensuring that the retreat of the French army would be clogged by civilian traffic, and to warn local authorities of the consequences of resisting the German advance.[23] By the time the Wehrmacht reached western France, many mayors had taken this to heart and did all they could to negotiate a peaceful surrender.[24] Even so, on 17 June 1940 the city of Rennes suffered what was probably France's single most lethal raid of the war, when just three Stukas hit ammunition wagons next to a troop train.[25] Areas of Italy suffered German attacks some three years later, after falling under Allied control. Indeed, southern Italian ports suffered raids from both sides after the Allied landings: in August 1943, the Germans bombed Palermo while the Allies were bombing Taranto and Naples. German bombing continued for several months, although on a much more limited scale than Allied raids, with the last, and heaviest, German attack on Italy occurring on 15 March 1944; targeting Naples, the Luftwaffe killed 278 civilians.[26] The Germans hoped both to wreck military supplies and communications and to disrupt the Anglo-American administration of the territory. Civilians therefore, now had to look to the Allies, their recent attackers, for assistance in facing the raids.

German raids, however, are peripheral to the focus of this book, for reasons of scale, spread and duration. Locally devastating though they were, they involved many fewer tons of ordnance than those of the Allies. Neither France nor Italy suffered a sustained German offensive on the same scale, in time or in space, as the Blitz on Britain. Moreover, the raids on France of 1940 were integrated into a wider *Blitzkrieg* that provoked the collapse, not only of the French war effort, but also of much of the French state, as well as the flight of some eight million refugees (six million of them French) from their homes, all within six weeks.[27] The effects of bombing in such a campaign are virtually impossible to isolate from the general debacle. By contrast, and a few seaborne raids on ports aside, bombing was the *only* type of Allied military action inflicted on France from July 1940 to June 1944, and on mainland Italy from June 1940 to June 1943. The Allied bombing offensive against France and Italy, therefore, can be studied in itself; the German cannot.

COMPARING THE FRENCH AND ITALIAN EXPERIENCES

If the extent of the damage, human and material, justifies greater attention being paid to France and Italy, so too does the two countries' place in Allied bombing strategy. In both France and Italy, the relationship between attackers and attacked differed significantly from the British and German cases. Britain and Germany bombed one another, with few restrictions, in an attempt to destroy military and economic capacity and to break civilian morale. By contrast, British attacks on France were aimed, with greater or lesser accuracy, at specific targets linked to the German occupiers, not at French civilians. Italy was treated like Germany until the armistice of 8 September 1943; thereafter the Allies treated it like France. Both countries, therefore, experienced attacks by 'friends' bearing a promise of liberation, as well as by enemies. This ambiguous and shifting relationship between civilians and those who periodically rained destruction upon them is one justification for a particular study devoted to France and Italy. It also suggests a comparative treatment. Indeed, the Allied staffs themselves compared the French and Italian cases as they defined bombing strategy and the possible restrictions that might be placed on it for political reasons. They also transferred bombing practices from one theatre to the other. The Allies' approaches to bombing France and Italy, both military and political, are the subject of Chapter 2.

Although military events are central to the content of this book, it is not primarily a work of military history. From Chapter 3, the focus shifts to the manner in which states and peoples in the two countries prepared for and faced air attack. There are obvious points of comparison between the regimes of Vichy France and Fascist Italy. Both were right-wing authoritarian regimes that lacked the democratic institutions and free press through which public policy could be openly debated. Both shared, in the body of Prefects, a Napoleonic instrument designed to ensure compliance at territorial level (in each Italian province, in each French *département*) with central government policy. At municipal level, both had replaced (partially, in the case of Vichy) elected mayors and councillors by appointees (who were still subject to prefectoral supervision). Both states monitored public opinion closely by opening mail and tapping telephones, and both understood that failure to protect their populations adequately from bombing could further undermine such legitimacy as they had. Both *also* saw Allied bombing as an opportunity, if maximized by skilful propaganda, to mobilize their publics against the democracies. Both states, finally, were significantly weaker than their British or German counterparts. For at least part of the war they exercised only partial sovereignty over their own territory. Both suffered German occupation: in northern and western France from June 1940; in the former 'free' zone of France, bordering the Mediterranean, from November 1942; in central and northern Italy from September 1943. German occupation meant a demand for labour and resources that hampered both states' efforts to prepare for and cope with the extreme strain of major air attacks. Both states also saw an Allied military presence, in Sicily from 9 July 1943, in mainland Italy from 3 September 1943, and in France from 6 June 1944. Both, too, faced, and fought with increasing but unsuccessful ferocity, armed resistance groups; and in both countries pro-Allied sentiment led a significant sector of the population to view bombing as a painful but necessary prelude to liberation from occupation and fascism.

Alongside these similarities, of course, lie equally significant distinctions. The first concerns the troubled history of regime change in the two countries. France had prepared for the war, and fought its first ten months, under the Third Republic – a democracy, albeit an increasingly authoritarian one from 1938. Only on 10 July 1940, under the impact of catastrophic defeat by Germany, did the National Assembly vote the Republic out of existence and replace it with the French State, led by the 84-year-old Marshal Philippe Pétain and domiciled not in Paris but in the spa town of Vichy. The Vichy regime itself gave way, in August 1944, to General Charles de Gaulle's republican and pro-Allied, though unelected, provisional government, built up from the external and (from September) internal Resistance movements. Italy, by contrast, had been ruled by Mussolini's fascist dictatorship since 1922, and had willingly entered the war against France and Britain on 10 June 1940. On 25 July 1943, under the impact of Allied successes in Sicily and a vote of no-confidence in the Fascist Grand Council, Mussolini was dismissed by King Victor Emmanuel III and arrested. His successor Marshal Pietro Badoglio negotiated the armistice with the Allies. From September 1943 two regimes effectively coexisted in Italy: in the North, the Italian Social Republic (or Salò Republic), a fascist regime led by Mussolini after his rescue from custody by German special forces and collaborating with the Germans; in the South, a pro-Allied government under Badoglio and then Ivanoe Bonomi.

Second, the two authoritarian states differed in their internal structures. In Italy, the Fascist party had colonized the institutions of the state, and remained the dominant channel of political communication and mobilization well into the war. When the party lost the public's confidence, as it clearly had by 1942–3, the state itself was dramatically weakened. By comparison, Vichy France, though far from democratic (the parties of the Third Republic were banned), remained a regime in which discernibly different groups – traditionalists, modernizers, and fascists, in Robert Paxton's triptych – vied for influence: a 'pluralist dictatorship', in the words of Stanley Hoffmann.[28] The fascists' hand was strengthened in 1943–4, but no big fascist party emerged. The fascist groupings that did exist in the northern zone lacked members, and in any case the German occupiers had no wish to see a strong French nationalist force. And for many Vichy officials, service to the state remained as powerful an ideological base as service to the regime.

Third, the role of the Church inevitably differed between France and Italy. In France, while the Third Republic's rigorous separation of church and state was softened, Vichy tried to avoid being labelled as clerical. An unofficial channel of social and political communication of all kinds, the Church only rarely became an open political actor. In Italy, by contrast, the regime had a longer history of collaboration with the Church, and it was inevitable that the Vatican would assume a higher political profile as the Fascist state withered and as Rome itself, hitherto untouched by the war, was directly threatened in 1943.

Fourth, Germany's relations with the two countries were wholly distinct. Fascist Italy was a full, though junior, Axis co-belligerent from 1940, and opposed Allied raids with its own fighters and anti-aircraft batteries as well as passive defences. Even the Salò Republic had co-belligerent status – though increasingly an auxiliary one, as Italian pilots found out when their worn-out aircraft were replaced by German models with German markings. Vichy France, by contrast, sent volunteers to fight with Germans on the Eastern front, kept colonial troops till 1942, but retained largely ceremonial armed forces at home. The Luftwaffe took care of France's active defence, and only with hesitation used Frenchmen as observers and to man a few anti-aircraft batteries; only passive defence was left to the French, who had difficulty negotiating the resources they needed from the occupiers.

A fifth and final contrast lay in the Allies' attitude to France and Italy. France, despite the German occupation and despite periodic imperial hostilities (fighting between Vichy and British, then Allied, vessels and troops occurred at Mers-el-Kébir and Dakar in 1940, in Syria in 1941, and North Africa in 1942), was never quite an enemy. The civilian population was viewed as friendly and de Gaulle's external resistance to Germany was based in London from 1940.

Bombing policy never targeted French civilians. Fascist Italy, on the other hand, as an enemy belligerent, could expect comparable treatment to Germany, with only the Alps and strategic priorities as constraints. Although the armistice of September 1943 gave Italy a broadly comparable status, in the eyes of air staffs, to France, the Allied armies continued to face Italian enemies in the residual forces of the Salò Republic, while the Italian Resistance lacked the quasi-official status of de Gaulle's French National Liberation Committee (CFLN).

The manner in which governments and populations in France and Italy prepared for bombing as war approached is the subject of Chapter 3. During the 1930s, as Europe faced the prospect of a new war in which large-scale bombing was widely expected, both regimes sought to develop a legal and institutional framework for civil defence. Both, too, attempted to create, consolidate, mobilize, and train the civil defence and emergency services – in France chiefly through the apparatus of the state, in Italy through the Fascist party. Evacuation, especially of the school-age population, was also part of the planning process; so, too, were basic civil defence measures such as the distribution of gas masks, the provision of sirens and shelters in major cities, or the definition of blackout regulations. Both countries sought, as well, to enlist civilian co-operation with civil defence measures. Yet preparation for bombing in both France and Italy was frequently both inadequate and inappropriate, its effectiveness limited by three factors. The first was financial cost. Second, preparing for air raids carried a political cost, since it represented both a preparation for the war that every government claimed to be trying to avoid, and an implicit admission that enemy aircraft would be able to bomb the national territory. Third, expectations of future air raids were, understandably, incorrect, with the danger of gas attacks being vastly exaggerated and the destructive power of 'conventional' raids gravely underestimated.

This became clear after air raids had started. Chapter 4 examines how the public authorities in both countries faced the reality of bombing, and adjusted measures taken before 1939. On each main count – the functioning of the institutional framework, the development of civil defence and emergency services, the organization of evacuation, the provision of shelters, the functioning of blackout measures and sirens, and relief for the bombed-out – the authorities in both countries struggled to keep pace with the ever-increasing scale of attacks. The record also suggests, however, that while the Vichy authorities in France continued efforts, however inadequate, to protect the public right up to the Liberation in August 1944, in Italy the state collapsed under the assault, providing the nearest approximation available to an enemy being bombed into submission. This contrast in performance is at the heart of Chapter 4.

Public morale in both France and Italy was explicitly targeted by the Allies, though for different reasons. At the same time, the regimes in both countries tried to use raids to mobilize populations in their own favour and against the Allies. But as Chapter 5 shows, despite considerable efforts to turn the promising raw material of Allied bombing to their own advantage,

Vichy and the Fascist regime (and even more the Salò Republic) failed to win the propaganda war. Three reasons are suggested here. First, Allied propaganda, whether through the European services of the BBC or in the form of leaflets dropped from aircraft, encouraged the view of bombing as a regrettable prelude to an inevitable liberation. Second, Vichy and Fascist propaganda was undermined both by the authorities' mediocre or poor record on air raid protection and by their broader unpopularity. Third, as official propaganda lost credibility, rumour, especially in Italy, took its place; and rumour blamed the raids either on an impersonal fortune or on the Axis powers themselves – not on the Allies.

The unpopularity of governments, however, did not prevent a degree of public mobilization against air raids. For many civilians, cities became symbolic and emotional spaces to be defended. The defence of their hometown *was* the defence of the motherland; mobilization around a locality, even in collaboration with the state authorities, did not necessarily entail support for the regime. Here too, however, France and Italy present a clearly differentiated record. In France, despite the government's near-complete loss of public support, Pétain himself could still attract large and favourable crowds during visits to bombed cities in the spring of 1944. Moreover, as Chapter 6 shows, Vichy remained capable of orchestrating a range of associations within civil society that assisted the victims of bombing. Italy, by contrast, witnessed public demonstrations of anger at the Fascists' failure to organize protection of cities or relief for bombed-out civilians. Chapter 7 explores the shifting and contradictory ways in which civilians coped with bombing. It does so by examining people's own narratives of raids – survivors' descriptions in memoirs and diaries, as well as local authorities' reports on the creation of a world of myth and rumour which challenged the state's, but also sometimes the Allies', propaganda. The chapter also analyses people's perception of both the bombers and their own regimes' wartime regulations. As the raids increased, civilians' attitude towards both the Allies and the regimes that were supposed to defend them from the bombs might change. In Italy more than in France, this meant withdrawal of support from the dictatorship.

The Allied message that bombing was a promise of liberation, though initially welcomed by many in France and even in Italy, became steadily less convincing to the public in both countries as raids became heavier and deliverance apparently more distant. As Chapter 8 shows, the French and Italian resistance movements recognized bombing as a military necessity, and assisted in the protection of downed airmen when they could, but risked losing legitimacy with the civilian population by supporting bombing too obviously. The support of Resistance fighters became increasingly critical as the bombing intensified, applauding raids that hit German-linked targets accurately and minimized civilian casualties, but criticizing those that did neither and appealing to the Allies for a more sensitive bombing policy. The final area of interest concerns relations with the Allies, who occupied many bombed towns in both France and Italy after their liberation. Research as it stands shows a very diverse record, with the Allies resented and fêted in nearly adjacent localities.

The conclusion steps back from the direct experience of bombing to consider two questions. One concerns what their response to bombing shows about the differences between state and society in Vichy France and in Fascist Italy. The French, it is suggested, proved remarkably capable of developing collective responses to bombing, and displaying considerable solidarity, despite the weakness and unpopularity of the regime. In Italy, by contrast, Fascism not only mortally weakened the state; it had also, by 1943, practically hollowed out civil society, making such collective responses much rarer. Second, the conclusion considers the ethics of Allied bombing in these two cases, where the Allies were not fighting the all-out bombing war they waged against Germany, but were still visiting terrible damage on civilian lives and property. In some ways the cases of France and Italy have more contemporary pertinence than the offensive against Germany. An all-out conventional bombing war between two great powers of the kind that occurred between Britain and Germany has been inconceivable since August 1945 because of the availability of the atomic/nuclear option. On the other hand, a more limited bombing war, designed to attack a narrower range of targets allegedly to liberate the population from oppressive rulers (as was the case in Iraq, in former Yugoslavia and in Afghanistan), is altogether easier to envisage in the contemporary world, and the cases of France and Italy may offer valuable lessons.

It is a commonplace that for the contemporary historian, the problem of sources is one of abundance not penury. There remain, it is true, lacunae in the case of the present study. The Cabinet and ministerial papers that are a staple for researchers on the summit of government in the United Kingdom (and which are used for Chapter 2, in particular) are largely lacking for Vichy France and Fascist Italy. But abundance remains the rule. Central government archives supply, not only a steady stream of laws, decrees and circulars, but also some at least of the memoranda and financial and other documentation that underlie them. Opinion research from both countries, in the form of reports on letters opened, telephones tapped, and conversations overheard, is also available nationally. Above all, however, our research has been at the local level, where prefects, mayors, local authorities and the general public confronted the realities of bombing. Local studies exist, impressionistic and popular at some times, scholarly at others. But the book will rely chiefly on the wealth of local archival material including official files, newspapers, pamphlets and posters, as well as the memoirs, diaries and correspondence of officials and ordinary civilians. This study cannot hope to be a complete record; its ambition is to offer a representative slice of the French and Italian communities whose sufferings were part of the price of Europe's liberation.

Notes

1 Discussion on the opportunity of bombing Frascati began as early as January 1942 (cf. TNA AIR 20/5304, W. Freeman to A. Cadogan, 19 January 1942).

2 M. Cumming, *The Starkey Sacrifice: the Allied Bombing of Le Portel, 1943* (Gloucester: Alan Sutton, 1996); AN F/lcIII/1178: prefectoral report, Pas-de-Calais, 3 October 1943.

3 For the official view of the French, see TNA FO 954/23, message from Foreign Secretary Eden to the French people, 14 July 1942.

4 For the former, cf. for example G. Mortimer, *The Longest Night* (London: Orion Books, 2005); for the latter, A. Calder, *The Myth of the Blitz* (London: Jonathan Cape, 1991).

5 The official works are: United States Strategic Bombing Survey, *Over-all report (European war)*, Washington DC, 30 September 1945 (see http://wwiiarchives.net/servlet/document/113/1/0); Sir C. Webster and N. Frankland, *The Strategic Air Offensive Against Germany, 1939–1945* (4 vols: London: HMSO, 1961). Examples of the other categories are: M. Hastings, *Bomber Command* (London: Michael Joseph, 1979); D. Richards, *RAF Bomber Command in the Second World War: the Hardest Victory* (London: Penguin, 2001); J. Friedrich, *The Fire: The Bombing of Germany, 1940–1945* (New York: Columbia University Press, 2006); H. Knell, *To Destroy a City: Strategic Bombing and its Human Consequences in World War II* (Cambridge, Mass.: Da Capo Press, 2003); A. C. Grayling, *Among the Dead Cities* (London: Bloomsbury, 2006).

6 The local studies will be encountered in the rest of this book. The only current national account of France is E. Florentin, *Quand les alliés bombardaient la France* (Paris: Perrin, 1997); the only scholarly account of Italy, M. Gioannini and G. Massobrio, *Bombardate l'Italia. Storia della guerra di distruzione aerea, 1940–45* (Milan: Rizzoli, 2007).

7 M. Middlebrook and C. Everitt, *The Bomber Command War Diaries, 1939–1945* (Leicester: Midland Publishing, 2000), 544, 579.

8 AD Morbihan 7W/4794, Ministère de l'Intérieur, DDP, *BIDP* no. 27 (February–May 1945).

9 C. Prime, 'Les bombardements du jour J et de la bataille de Normandie', in B. Garnier, J.-L. Leleu, F. Passera and J. Quellien (eds), *Les Populations civiles face au débarquement et à la bataille de Normandie* (Caen, CRHQ, CNRS-Université de Caen and Mémorial pour la Paix, 2005), 39, 47; for Rouen, cf. M. Dandel, G. Duboc, A. Kitts, and E. Lapersonne, *Les Victimes Civiles des Bombardements en Haute-Normandie, 1er janvier 1944–12 septembre 1944* (Caen: CRHQ-RED, La Mandragore, 1997), 13–14, 19.

10 AD BduR 76W/121, prefectoral report on raid of 27 May 1944, dated 15 June 1944. The report confirms 1,831 bodies found, and suggests that, with at least 100 still under the wreckage, the death toll would rise to 2,000.

11 D. Voldman, *La Reconstruction des villes françaises de 1940 à 1954: histoire d'une politique* (Paris: L'Harmattan, 1997), 35.

12 Prime, 'Les bombardements', 39.

13 SHAA 3D/44, *BIDP* no. 13, October 1943.

14 AD BduR 76W/121, prefectoral report on raid of 27 May 1944; G. Chauvy, *Lyon, 1940–1947: L'Occupation, la Libération, l'Épuration* (Paris: Perrin, 2004), 235.

15 M.-C. Villatoux, 'Les Bombardements de Royan (janvier et avril 1945)', in M. Battesti and P. Facon (eds), *Les Bombardements Alliés sur la France durant la Seconde Guerre Mondiale: Stratégies, Bilans Matériaux et Humains*' (Paris: Cahiers du CEHD, no. 37, 2009), 125–34.

16 Voldman, *La Reconstruction*, 33, 35.

17 Cf. for example M. Lantier (ed.), *Renaissance et reconstruction de Saint-Lô (Manche), 1944–1964* (Saint-Lô: Université Inter-Ages, 2000); G. de la Porte ed. *Le Havre, Volonté et modernité* (Le Havre: Éditions La Galerne, 1992).

18 A. Rastelli, *Bombe sulla città. Gli attacchi aerei alleati: le vittime civili a Milano* (Milan: Mursia, 2000), 183–5; G. Gribaudi, *Guerra totale. Tra bombe alleate e violenze naziste: Napoli e il fronte meridionale, 1940–1944* (Turin: Bollati Boringhieri, 2005), 161.

19 Gioannini and Massobrio, *Bombardate l'Italia*, 11.

20 *Ibid.*, 494–5.

21 J. Legrand, *Courageuse Abbeville, 3 septembre 1939–3 septembre 1944* (Abbeville: Imprimerie F. Paillart, 1990), 12; AN, F/1cIII/1180, Somme, prefectoral report, 30 July 1940.

22 AD Morbihan 7W/4794, *BIDP* no. 27; SHAA 3D/322/1, France, État Major de l'Armée, Bureau Scientifique de l'Armée, Étude Général des Effets des Bombardements Aériens Alliés, Bilan Général.
23 J. Vidalenc, *L'Exode de mai–juin 1940* (Paris: Presses Universitaires de France, 1957), 101–3.
24 R. Gildea, *Marianne in Chains: Daily Life in the Heart of France during the German Occupation* (London: Macmillan, 2002), 21–30.
25 AM Rennes, 6/H23, Des précisions sur le bombardement de Rennes du 17 juin; Liste des personnes identifiées, victimes du bombardement du 17 juin 1940; AM Rennes 1048/W11, Mairie de Rennes, Service des Pompes Funèbres et des Cimetières, Note du 26 octobre 1946.
26 Gribaudi, *Guerra totale*, 159–60.
27 Figures for refugees are taken from H. Diamond, *Fleeing Hitler: France 1940* (Oxford: Oxford University Press, 2007), 150.
28 S. Hoffmann, 'The Vichy circle of French conservatives' in S. Hoffmann, *Decline or Renewal? France Since the 1930s* (New York: The Viking Press, 1974), 3–4.

2

Purpose and Politics: the Allies and the Bombing of France and Italy

It took the Luftwaffe approximately 1.2 tons of bombs to kill a British civilian. The Allies were noticeably less efficient against the Reich: it required some 3.4 tons to kill a German. An Italian took more still – some 6.3 tons – and a French civilian as much as 10.1 tons.[1] In other words, not only did the Allies drop more bombs on Germany than on France and Italy; they killed more German civilians for each ton they dropped.

The difference between the British and German figures may be put down, in part at least, to superior German civil defence arrangements. But the apparent resilience of the Italians and French cannot be explained in these terms; their civil defences, as Chapters 3 and 4 will show, were mediocre at best. Moreover, France and Italy were easy targets compared with Germany. France was used as an arena to blood the RAF's trainee or freshman aircrews from 1940 until at least 1943.[2] The US Eighth Air Force flew roughly half its first year's sorties (17 August 1942–16 August 1943) against France, with a loss rate per mission of 3.7 per cent, compared with an average of 5.7 per cent.[3] RAF Bomber Command, attacking northern Italy in October–December 1942 and August 1943, achieved average loss rates of 1.8 per cent, and zero for some raids.[4] If the French and Italians, though less well defended, were more likely than Germans to survive each ton of bombs, the obvious explanation is that the Allies did not bomb France and Italy in the same way as they bombed Germany; that they did not target civilians, or not all of the time.

Alone in the book, this chapter considers attacks on France and Italy from the bombers' perspective. It focuses, first, on the actors and processes that defined bombing policy. Second, it examines the range of purposes that bombing was expected to serve in each case. Finally, it analyses the political constraints affecting bombing policy on France and Italy and their weight relative to perceived military necessity.

BOMBING POLICY: ACTORS AND PROCESSES

The strategic bomber forces that attacked France and Italy were the same as those that bombed Germany: RAF Bomber Command and the US Army Air Forces (USAAF), in particular the Eighth Air Force, based in Britain, and the Fifteenth Air Force, set up in November 1943 for use against Axis targets including southern France, northern Italy, and central and south-eastern

Europe.[5] Tactical air forces also bombed both countries. In the Mediterranean theatre, these included RAF Middle East and RAF Malta. These were joined, from 1942, by the US Ninth Air Force, initially assembled on Egyptian bases, and, after the Allied landings in North Africa that November, by the Twelfth Air Force, based in Algeria; these forces then fell under the umbrella of the Allied Mediterranean Air Forces. In Britain, meanwhile, tactical air forces preparing for the invasion of Europe were developed from autumn 1943, and included British groups as well as the US Ninth Air Force, now transferred from the Mediterranean. Northern France and northern Italy, therefore, were bombed by British-based aircraft; southern France and the whole of Italy by (mostly American) aircraft based, first in North Africa, and then in southern Italy.[6]

Bombing policy was decided, in the last resort, at the top: in the War Cabinet in London, by the President in Washington, and at the periodic summits where discussions between the President and the Prime Minister and their staffs and ministers were paralleled by meetings of the Allied Combined Chiefs of Staff. But summit decisions were rare. In practice, in relation to the strategic offensive against Germany, the bombing chiefs enjoyed considerable freedom of action within a framework defined by general directives drawn up under the authority of the British, then the joint, Chiefs of Staff. That was also true, to a degree, in relation to France and Italy, but they were more subject to interventions from the political executive, and to command structures in which bombers could be integrated in combined offensives with ground troops.

For the first half of the war, until early 1943, the major instrument of British, then Allied, bombing policy was RAF Bomber Command. Its Officer Commanding-in-Chief from February 1942, Sir Arthur Harris, saw the systematic destruction of Germany's cities as the key to victory. Sir Charles Portal, Chief of the Air Staff from November 1940 to 1945 (and Harris's predecessor but one at Bomber Command), though less dogmatic in his approach, accepted the bombing offensive against Germany as the centrepiece of RAF strategy for most of the war.

Decision-making processes were complicated by America's entry into the war and the build-up of the USAAF in Europe. Political control of the Allied Air Forces was now exercised jointly by the President and the Prime Minister, advised by the Combined Chiefs of Staff, which set up a permanent organization in Washington; a Combined Targets Committee and a Combined Operational Planning Committee were created to co-ordinate the British and American bombing efforts.[7]

The relationship between the two air forces changed (as it did for ground forces) as the Americans became numerically preponderant. In principle, control of the American strategic bombing forces in Europe – the Eighth and the Fifteenth – was exercised, on behalf of the Combined Chiefs, by Portal. But American forces assumed steadily greater autonomy as they grew, especially when, in January 1944, they were brought under the unified command, as the United States Strategic Air Forces in Europe, of General Carl A. Spaatz.[8]

The Ninth and Twelfth air forces in the Mediterranean, meanwhile, like their RAF counterparts there, would fall, from January 1943, under the command of Air Chief Marshal Sir Arthur Tedder, as Commander-in-Chief of the Allied Air Forces in the Mediterranean (the Fifteenth could also on occasion be borrowed for ground support duties in case of need).[9] Tedder's only superior in the Mediterranean, with whom he built a close working relationship, was the Supreme Commander of all Allied forces there, General Dwight D. Eisenhower. At the end of 1943 both men moved to London, Eisenhower as Supreme Head of the Allied Expeditionary Force (SHAEF), and Tedder as his deputy (Tedder was replaced in the Mediterranean by Lieutenant-General Ira Eaker, who had been moved from the US Eighth). And from mid-April 1944, with considerable reluctance, the strategic bomber forces found themselves placed at the disposal of SHAEF to prepare the D-Day landings and support the ensuing Allied campaign in north-west Europe; they were only released from this task in mid-September.

Making these command structures work was invariably complex, all the more so as the two air forces took different approaches to bombing. Bomber Command had adopted the 'area' bombing of German cities as a general policy after a study of night raids prepared for the War Cabinet in August 1941 (the Butt report) had shown that only one in three RAF bombers got within five miles of its target.[10] The directive of 14 February 1942, in which Bomber Command was invited to bomb 'industrial areas' and 'to focus attacks on the morale of the civil population, in particular industrial workers'[11] implicitly acknowledged the difficulty of finding specific targets – and also signalled, at best, an indifference to civilian lives.[12] By contrast, the Americans, equipped with better-armed aircraft and the Norden bombsight, espoused daylight 'precision' bombing, as being both more effective than area bombing and more in tune with domestic political preferences.[13] As General 'Hap' Arnold, chief of the USAAF, told Eaker in June 1943, 'we want the people to understand and have faith in *our way of making war*'.[14] In practice, the two approaches were run simultaneously. The crucial 'Casablanca' directive, agreed by the Combined Chiefs of Staff on 21 January 1943, listed the specific targets envisaged by the Americans – 'submarine construction yards, German aircraft industry, transportation, oil plants, other targets in enemy war industry' – while adding the much broader aims of Bomber Command: 'the progressive destruction and dislocation of the German military, industrial and economic system, and the undermining of the morale of the German people to a point where their capacity for armed resistance is fatally weakened'.[15] Operationally, the USAAF bombed by day, Bomber Command by night. And with the Norden bombsight's capabilities sharply reduced in cloudy European weather, American Flying Fortresses or Liberators bombing by day from over 20,000 feet proved scarcely more precise than British Lancasters or Halifaxes on night missions.[16]

The strategic offensive against Germany absorbed about half of the bombers' total effort and was their defining task. With the exception of Italian industrial areas in 1942–3, most of the attacks on France and Italy did not, officially, count as area bombing and did not target civilians. But many were carried out by forces that frequently did one or both.

TARGETS

According to the United States Strategic Bombing Survey, strictly military targets, including enemy bases, airfields and aerodromes, and V-weapon sites, accounted for just 20 per cent of the Allies' total bombing effort in Europe. By contrast, 37.4 per cent of Allied bombs were dropped on industrial targets, including aircraft factories, oil, chemical, and synthetic rubber plants, and other manufacturing sites. A further 36.3 per cent hit transport facilities – inland and maritime ports (4.2 per cent) and land transport, chiefly rail (32.1 per cent).[17] All three broad types of target were well represented in both France and Italy. But the balance differed from the averages, with attacks on industry somewhat less important and raids on military and transportation targets rather more so.

Industrial targets and workers' morale

Enemy industry and civilian morale were intimately linked in the minds of the British air chiefs in relation to Germany. Morale was also targeted in attacks on industries in both France and Italy, but in almost opposite ways. Italy was viewed as a country that could be knocked out of the war through air raids that would wreck both industries and the morale of urban populations. By contrast, raids on French factories, at least through the period of Axis victories during 1942, were seen as helping to convince the civilian population of the Allies' continuing commitment to carry on fighting.

The conviction that bombing would have a big effect on morale in a population unlikely to support its country's war effort was a constant of British policy towards Italy until the armistice of September 1943. The War Cabinet considered contingency plans for war with Italy in late April 1940, six weeks before Mussolini opened hostilities. Although there was no certainty that the RAF could spare bombers from Germany, it was 'recognised, however, that even a limited offensive against Italian industry would have a big moral effect in Italy and might, therefore be justified'.[18] Available intelligence indicated that Italians, northern industrialists included, had no desire for war.[19] What Italians feared most and were 'least prepared to combat', in the view of Sir Cyril Newall, Chief of the Air Staff till November 1940, was air attack. For the British, the legitimate targets of such attacks were aircraft factories, and 'many such factories are placed where the effect of air attack will be brought home to the largest portion of the population'.[20] Northern Italy, moreover, was within easy range of southern French bases before the fall of France. Late that May the Air Ministry argued that Italy's northern industrial regions constituted 'a vital area even more important to their war strategy, both morally and materially' than were the Ruhr or London respectively to Germany and Britain; a blow at those industries as soon as Italy declared war, it was suggested, 'might well have a decisive effect'.[21] Again, Sir Anthony Eden, then Secretary of State for War, told Churchill that 'Italy is the weaker partner, and we are more likely to knock her out by air attacks than Germany'.[22]

Industrial areas thus figured prominently among the RAF's Italian targets in 1940 and 1941.[23] Although Germany was always the primary target, in October 1940 Bomber Command was ordered to continue the offensive against Northern Italy whenever weather permitted.[24] In a separate directive the following month to forces based in Malta and the Middle East, the Air Ministry added that 'alternative targets should be in the centres of Italian population'.[25] In December, a War Cabinet meeting stated that Italy did not require 'raids of the Coventry type' as Germany did, since the Italians' emotional temperament meant that smaller attacks would still obtain a great moral effect.[26] Italian 'psychology' was considered 'not suited for war', and the British therefore expected that bombs would have political as well as military consequences – regime change and Italy's elimination from the war.[27]

However based on racial stereotypes, the British view appeared to be borne out – at least partially – on the ground. In March 1941, an intelligence source in Rome observed that 'however limited the real effects of the bombardment of Genoa, its psychological and moral effects in Italy are enormous. People say: it may happen anywhere.' The evident ease with which the enemy passed over air defences that Mussolini had claimed were impenetrable provoked great fear and anxiety among Italians, who 'unanimously accuse Mussolini, as the only one responsible for the war'.[28]

The heaviest raids on Italy, however, only began in late October 1942, to coincide with Montgomery's offensive against Axis armies at El Alamein. Between 22 October and 12 December 1942, six night attacks on Genoa, seven on Turin and one daytime attack on Milan demonstrated to Harris that defences were so weak that the only difficulties were posed by the Alpine barrier and the distance of the target, and these were easily surmounted. Moreover, Harris later noted that although the attacks were still lighter than those on Germany (the Alps dictated smaller bomb loads), 'the effect on Italian morale was enormous and out of all proportion'. He added that 300,000 people, half the population of Turin, had abandoned the city and that panic had probably been even greater after the daylight attack on Milan 'by less than one hundred Lancasters'.[29] Although Eden initially voiced concerns that the raids could reinforce solidarity among Italian civilians as the Blitz had among the British, the dominant British view was that panic, plus skilful propaganda, could persuade Italians that the Fascist government, and not the British, was to blame.[30]

Central to Britain's Mediterranean strategy, as Sir Alan Brooke, Chief of Britain's Imperial General Staff, wrote in his diary on 15 December 1942, was 'pushing Italy out of the war'.[31] By the year's end, following the successful *Torch* landings on 8 November, American bombers joined the campaign from new bases in North-West Africa, complementing British-based RAF attacks on northern Italy with their own raids on the South. The Air Minister, Sir Archibald Sinclair, could assure the War Cabinet that 'all important Italian towns will have been brought within the range of effective attack' and that it would be 'possible to drop some 4,000 tons of bombs a month, an amount comparable with the average weight of attack delivered on Germany in the months before North Italy was made the main target of our heavy bombers'.[32]

Heavy raids on Turin, Milan and Genoa brought workers out on strike and into the streets demonstrating for peace in spring 1943. This was presumably the very type of effect that the supporters of area bombing had hoped for. With the Axis almost defeated in Africa, Eden, now Foreign Secretary, suggested that the majority of the Italian population wished for an Allied victory:

> One of the most striking features about the state of feeling in Italy is the comparative lack of hostility towards the British and the Americans. This attitude does not seem to have been seriously affected by the recent heavy bombing attacks on Italian cities and attempts of Italian propaganda to make capital of the civilian casualties. appear to have been ineffective.[33]

The conviction that support for Fascism was buckling was reinforced during 1943 as the Allies drove Axis forces out of North Africa (by 13 May) and landed successively in Sicily (10 July) and on the Italian mainland (3 September). Air power was viewed as a major contributor to this. Sicily, once taken, would provide new bases for Allied aircraft to attack central and southern Italy, and put 'so much pressure on the Italians that Mussolini would fall and the Axis partner might quit or even change sides'.[34] America's OSS (Office of Strategic Services), set up during the war to supply intelligence assessments to Roosevelt and the military leadership, stated that the 'area bombing' attack on Turin on 12 July 1943 (which provoked 792 civilian victims – more than in any raid on an Italian city hitherto), 'created a critical situation' which the authorities found difficult to control; 'a similar treatment' was therefore recommended for Milan.[35] A report by the 310th American bomber group, which took part in the raids on Naples of 17 July and on Rome on 19 July, supported that conviction, stating that the raids had provoked demonstrations for peace and sabotage activities across Italy.[36] Similarly, British and American commentators described the bombing of Rome of 19 July 1943 as one of the causes of Mussolini's fall. Harris later claimed that the panic caused by Bomber Command's attacks on industrial cities in northern Italy 'did as much as any other single factor' to provoke the fall of Fascism.[37]

Tedder recalled that the fall of Mussolini 'gave hope that Italy might be promptly knocked out of the war', and added: 'in order to provide the Italians with a worthwhile incentive to an early armistice, we began heavy attacks on Naples and other points on the mainland on 1 August'.[38] In northern Italy, meanwhile, Bomber Command hit Genoa, Milan and Turin between 7 and 17 August. The conviction that Italians longed only for peace was so strong that British Intelligence maintained that more bombing would turn them against the new Prime Minister, Marshal Badoglio, as well, leaving him with no choice but to ask for an armistice:

> Momentarily public opinion in Italy is likely to wait on events to see whether in fact Badoglio's policy is to make peace. Italy is so demoralised that any revival of spirit can be excluded. If Badoglio does not in the near future make peace and if a heavy scale of air attack is maintained against Italy, public clamour is likely to be so great as to compel the Italian government to agree even to unconditional surrender.[39]

In August 1943 Bomber Command was studying the most effective ways of destroying the homes of Italian civilians by making a comparison between the structure of Italian and German towns: the problem was that the first were 'as a rule more solidly built and less "burnable"' than the latter. In Italy there were 'hardly any houses in the ordinary sense', but dwelling units made of 'a set of rooms in a large block built round an open court'. The walls were 'very thick, the roofs covered with heavy tiles … and the floors are made not of timber but of marble, tiles or other fire-resisting material'. All this, said the study, made the use of explosive bombs more suited in the Italian case than the use of incendiary bombs – leaving little doubt that the RAF was still targeting Italian civilians even after Mussolini's fall.[40]

Italian morale ceased to be a target after the armistice and the German occupation from September 1943, but Allied raids on industrial targets, now designed solely to wreck productive capacity, continued. Turin, Milan and their surrounding industrial areas were bombed until April 1945 and October 1944 respectively. By then, many of their industries had been relocated to nearby provinces (a process that began after the attacks of winter 1942–3 and that eventually slowed down already patchy production levels). After that, cities along the railway line between Liguria, Piedmont, Lombardy, Venetia and Friuli became new targets.[41] Brescia, for example, was hit in 1944 and 1945 for its marshalling yard but also because an important branch of the Milanese firm Breda produced weapons there.[42] Verona, Vicenza, Padua, Treviso, Udine and Trieste were also repeatedly bombed in 1944 and 1945. Since power stations, gasworks and railway lines were close to city centres, these attacks sometimes caused high casualties: the bombing of Treviso in April 1944 killed 1,600 civilians and hit, among other medieval buildings, the famous *Palazzo dei Trecento*. Two raids on Vicenza killed 56 civilians and hit the cathedral and the fifteenth-century *Ca' d'Oro* palace in May 1944, and killed 317 civilians in November. In Trieste, an attack in June aimed at the oil refineries killed 400 people in the city centre. The attempt to hit the Breda factory outside Milan in October caused 614 civilian deaths, 200 of whom were children of a primary school in the working-class periphery. It is true that the previous month,

General Harold Alexander, supreme Allied commander in the Mediterranean theatre, had invited the Italian partisans to cease acts of sabotage against Italian industries – with a view to preserving some industrial capacity for the post-war period.[43] But raids on these northern cities, mostly by the US Fifteenth Air Force, continued right until the end of the war in 1945, albeit with fewer casualties.

As French industries served German economic and military purposes, they too were attacked. For most of the war some 30–40 per cent of French industrial output was produced for Germany; the armaments, construction, and aircraft industries worked practically full-time for the Reich.[44] Well-known firms like Renault, Hotchkiss, and Citroën were building tanks for Germany by 1941. In Saint-Nazaire, all the major shipyards had received big orders to build naval vessels for Germany by November 1940; in Nantes, 90 per cent of output at the Batignolles locomotive works was going to the Reichsbahn by early 1941, while the Société Nationale de Construction Aéronautique du Sud-Ouest (SNASCO) was building aircraft and aero-engines for Heinkel, Junkers, Focke Wulf, and BMW.[45]

As purely industrial objectives, such concentrations invited bombing, and the Ministry of Economic Warfare fed Bomber Command with a steady stream of (not always accurate) information on industrial targets both within Germany and in German-occupied Europe.[46] In addition, however, the British also expected bombing to affect French civilian morale, but not as it affected that of Italians. As a defeated, non-belligerent power, France could not be 'knocked out of the war'. Regime change was a meaningless aim in a country more than half occupied by Germany; French civilians were viewed as recent allies whose co-operation would be valuable in the eventual liberation of Europe. Morale in France, from the Allied point of view, meant support for and belief in an Allied victory. In order to achieve this, the French must be convinced, by propaganda and if necessary by direct demonstrations of military force, that the Allies were in the struggle to win.

The view taken from 1941 that major raids on industrial targets would benefit the Allies' standing in occupied Europe was forcefully articulated by Air Vice-Marshal Medhurst, Assistant Chief of Air Staff for Intelligence, on 8 January 1942. Optimistically referring to 'the incipient revolt against the occupying forces of which so many signs have recently been perceptible', Medhurst claimed that French morale was better in areas bombed by the RAF, and that failure to attack industrial targets was viewed as a sign of British weakness in the air.[47]

Targets capable of affecting morale were chosen with great care. To deliver political benefits, they needed to be clearly linked to the German war effort, and big enough to be easily identified from the air, so as to minimize civilian casualties. Such considerations inspired the first of the major industrial raids on France, against Renault at Boulogne-Billancourt on 3/4 March 1942. The Billancourt plant had acquired symbolic status before 1939 as the heart of

France's automotive industry. Now it was building lorries for Germany. Harris, appointed as head of Bomber Command two weeks earlier, recorded that in the following months, the weakness of German defences in France allowed daylight attacks, though 'against few or no defences, we were often able to attack by night with equal precision'.[48] This overstated the case. The Renault raid killed 337 French civilians – more than in any raid hitherto on *Germany* – and left 9,548 people bombed out, in a population of just over 80,000.[49] It wrecked buildings, but did less damage to tools than initially thought – a pattern that would be repeated elsewhere. Production restarted within weeks and reached a peak the following September; the factory would be revisited, with other industries in the Paris suburbs, by the US Eighth Air Force twice in 1943.[50]

From the British point of view, the raid was still a major success and a model for future attacks, notably on Poissy and Gennevilliers in the Paris suburbs that spring. In April 1942, Eden, now Foreign Secretary, wrote to Sinclair that:

> Europe this spring needs proof of our activity and hitting power. All our evidence goes to show first, that the Renault raid and those which followed it had a bracing effect on French morale; secondly, that our allies in every occupied territory are crying out for similar raids. Failure to follow up the Renault raid might be regarded as a sign of British weakness in will-power or material.[51]

Two days later, the Defence Committee adopted a programme of propaganda against France, adding that 'raids on the French coast, and effective bombing attacks on targets in occupied France, would have an advantageous effect, from the political point of view, in the near future'.[52] Eden's proposal to publish a list of Bomber Command targets, for propaganda and warning purposes, was rejected by Portal on the revealing ground that it would raise hopes in occupied territories for raids that Bomber Command could not deliver; Eden still argued to Sinclair that the list should be published anyway, and that the French 'want and expect us to bomb the factories in their midst' that were working for Germany.[53]

From late 1942 onwards, however, British planners appear to have lost confidence in the 'psychological' benefits of bombing France. The successful *Torch* landings in North Africa had re-established Allied credibility on the ground, and there was a growing awareness of the negative as well as the positive propaganda value of bombing a supposedly friendly population. The experience of the Schneider works at Le Creusot in October 1942 had showed the limits of Bomber Command's accuracy: industrial targets escaped with minor damage while nearby workers' housing was badly hit.[54] As in Italy, however, 'pure' industrial raids on French targets continued. Late that year the German military command in Paris, faced with a list of 31 damaged factories, organized a 'catastrophe corps' to ensure the timely despatch of specialist repair teams.[55] Targets in 1943 included, for example, the Dunlop factory at Montluçon, gunpowder plants at Angoulême, Bergerac, and Toulouse, aircraft factories in the Toulouse area, and the Toulon arsenal. The accuracy of Allied raids was extremely variable, as a report by the Comité Français de Libération Nationale (CFLN) highlighted in May 1944.[56] The daylight attacks on Rennes in March and May 1943 – described as 'deplorable' by the CFLN – claimed some 300 and 200 civilian lives respectively, for slight damage to the target[57]; the attack on industrial zones of Nantes of 16 September killed some 1,500. By contrast, in a 'model' raid on 8/9 February 1944, Bomber Command's 617 squadron destroyed the Gnôme-Rhône aero-engine works near Limoges, giving the 300 workers time to leave the plant and hitting no housing.[58] This, however, was the work of an elite unit: if Bomber Command's general accuracy had improved by spring 1944, few crews could achieve this level of precision.

Ports

In both France and Italy, ports held numerous attractions as targets for bombers. They were relatively easy to see; they accommodated enemy warships; they were crucial to the enemy's supply lines; and they were often industrial centres as well.

In Italy, ports, aerodromes and naval bases were seen as principal targets, along with northern industry, from 1940. That August, in discussions of possible attacks on Italian ports from Greece and Malta, the War Cabinet listed Bari, Naples, Venice (Marghera), Trieste, Fiume (in present-day Croatia) and Leghorn as key oil transit ports, Taranto as the most important naval base, and Brindisi, Trieste, Pola (present-day Croatia), plus the Sicilian ports of Augusta, Messina, Syracuse and Trapani as additional naval targets.[59] Marghera, Augusta, Trapani and the Sardinian port and aerodromes of Cagliari had already been bombed by August; the Apulian ports of Bari, Brindisi and Taranto were hit in the autumn. The port, marshalling yard, oil refineries and city centre of Naples were hit for the first time on 31 October 1940. Through 1941, southern ports – Naples in particular – were bombed in order to disrupt supply lines to Axis forces in Libya. The following year, the bombing of Sicilian ports intensified as the war in Africa progressed in preparation for the next stage of the Mediterranean campaign. Sicilian ports and Naples were repeatedly attacked throughout 1941, 1942 and 1943, while in northern Italy, Marghera and Genoa in particular came under attack until almost the end of the war in the spring of 1945.

One of the few clear British successes of 1940 was gained on 11 November, when 21 Fairey Swordfish torpedo bombers attacked the Italian fleet at anchor in Taranto, sinking or seriously damaging three battleships and a heavy cruiser and substantially diminishing the Italian threat to British vessels in the Mediterranean. Far more severe, however, from the point of view of civilians, were the persistent raids on Genoa, Naples and Sicilian ports almost throughout the war.

France's Channel ports, meanwhile, were among the closest Axis targets to Britain. Le Havre, 100 miles from the British south coast, endured over 140 raids during the German occupation, or an average of one every ten days; closer ports like Boulogne suffered more.[60] The need to prevent a German invasion of the UK in 1940 involved attacks on the build-up of German shipping and barges in French ports between Calais and Le Havre, as well as on Luftwaffe airfields in France. The most intensive attacks on what became known as 'Blackpool front' – the Channel ports on either side of Calais – took place on 7 September 1940, when the invasion of Britain was seen as imminent.[61] They accounted for most of the 292 French identified as killed in British raids during 1940.[62]

Brest, in Brittany, became a major Bomber Command target because of the German surface vessels – notably *Scharnhorst* and *Gneisenau* – docked there from late 1940. From 4 January 1941 to 12 February 1942, Brest received 25 major raids (of over 50 heavy bombers) and numerous smaller ones – a total of 1,655 tons of bombs. In March and April 1941, indeed, the port attracted over half of Bomber Command's (still modest) effort.[63] The raids did some damage to the German ships and encouraged them to flee. They also, however, killed 207 Brestois, and seriously injured 336, as well as forcing many others away from home at night as bombs destroyed steadily more of their city.[64]

A far more serious menace to Atlantic shipping than surface raiders, however, were U-boats, which began using the Biscay ports of Brest, Lorient and La Pallice (just north of La Rochelle) from mid-August 1940, and Bordeaux and Saint-Nazaire shortly after. Bordeaux and Lorient were attacked on 8/9 December 1940.[65] But the heaviest raids were two years later. Losses of Allied merchant shipping late in 1942 prompted Churchill to create an Anti-U-Boat Committee, which recommended bombing the Biscay ports. On 14 January Bomber Command was ordered to carry out area bombing of Lorient, Saint-Nazaire, Brest and La Pallice; the same day, a telegram spelt out that 'the Secretary of State has ruled that in order to achieve the stated military object of the operation the CinC is at liberty to choose any aiming point even if the resultant bombing causes complete devastation of the inhabited areas of the town'.[66] The pattern that would be used over Germany – Bomber Command attacks by night alternating with daylight visits from the US Eighth – began here. They were among the heaviest Allied raids on any objective hitherto; the eighth raid on Lorient, involving 466 aircraft, was the first to deliver over 1,000 tons on a single target.[67] Both Lorient and Staint-Nazaire were flattened, though the death toll – roughly 100 in each case – was low thanks to timely evacuation. The attacks were scaled down in March, after Harris had denounced the 'futility' of trying to penetrate reinforced concrete several metres thick (the submarine pens still stand).[68] A final series of raids hit the bases (including Brest) in August 1944 – by which time most of the U-boats had been redeployed towards Norway.[69] Other ports, meanwhile, received attention after Biscay. Toulon, for example, was attacked nine times between 23 November 1943 and 6 August 1944.[70]

Three other aims lay behind raids on French ports. One was to destroy port-based industries. Saint-Nazaire was destroyed in the heavy raids of February and March 1943 for its shipyards as well as its submarine pens; the arsenal at Toulon was a major target in the first raid on the city, by the US Fifteenth Air Force on 24 November 1943. Second, the Allies needed to wreck German motor torpedo boats threatening the cross-channel supply routes in the wake of D-day; this led to two big raids on Le Havre and Boulogne in mid-June 1944. Finally, they sought to dislodge German garrisons and take the ports for their own use. In September 1944 – after the liberation of Paris and the overthrow of the Vichy regime – this led to some of the heaviest raids of the war, on Le Havre.

Rail centres and bridges

Railways too were at least as well represented among French and Italian targets as in the overall European figures. The heaviest attacks on rail systems served to prepare and support ground campaigns in both countries, where success or failure could depend on how quickly the enemy could move reinforcements. No area of bombing policy demonstrates greater continuity between the Italian and the French theatres; in both theatres, too, the policy adopted was highly controversial. Marshalling yards were typically in the hearts of cities, surrounded by workers' or railwaymen's housing. The raids nevertheless proceeded in both countries.

Attacks on rail centres had a powerful intellectual advocate in Solly (later Lord) Zuckerman, a zoologist and scientific adviser to Tedder and Eisenhower in the Mediterranean theatre from 1943.[71] Following Operation Husky (the Allied invasion of Sicily), Zuckerman compiled a report, based on aerial photographs, on-the-spot assessments, and prisoner interrogations, which concluded that the Sicilian and southern Italian railway systems had 'become practically paralysed by the end of July 1943 – as a result of attacks on only six railway centres, Naples, Foggia, San Giovanni, Reggio, Messina, Palermo'.[72] Zuckerman's report convinced Tedder that attacks on rail centres held the key to successful bombing.[73]

By the time of Tedder's departure for London at the end of 1943, Zuckerman's thesis had nevertheless attracted critics. Lauris Norstad, Eaker's director of bombing operations, claimed that between October and December 1943 the efficiency of attacks on rail bridges by fighter-bombers was 'six to seven times greater than that of yard attacks'.[74] The yards versus bridges debate raged when the Allied armies stalled at the Gustav Line, but as the Italian campaign progressed, evidence produced by intelligence and operations staffs 'fell more and more on the side of the bridge theory'.[75] Traffic into southern Italy had had to pass through only a few marshalling yards, notably those at Naples and Foggia; but in central and northern Italy, the rail system 'contained so many yards that it would be very difficult to knock out all of them, whereas every important line ran over bridges and viaducts', particularly in mountainous areas. Experience also demonstrated that tracks could be repaired more quickly than bridges.[76] The outcome was a compromise. During Strangle (the operation against Italian communications targets), 'a whole system of bridges, yards, tunnels, defiles, even open stretches of track', came under attack and railway targets represented major bombing priorities.[77] Thus in March 1944, the main priorities of the Strategic Air Forces were as follows: 'Priority 1 – Pointblank targets in Germany; Priority 2 – Selected North Italian railway objectives; Priority 3 – Operations in support of the land battle'. Priorities for the Tactical Air Forces were: 'Priority 1 – Operations in support of the land battle; Priority 2 – Railway objectives in the belt whose North boundary is inclusive Pisa-Rimini and whose South boundary is approximately 100 miles from the present front line; Priority 3 – East coast Italian ports used as supply terminals'.[78]

The strategic air forces, chiefly the Twelfth and the Fifteenth US Air Forces, also took part in the Italian campaign, though their use in attacks on Germany diminished their Italian role between summer 1943 and the fall of Rome in June 1944. In particular, they attacked supply lines, notably yards in central Italy, and the Alpine routes into the north.[79] Rail targets on southern French supply routes into Italy, such as the Cannes-La Bocca marshalling yard and the Anthéor viaduct, were also attacked, though with limited success.[80] Ancona and its province were bombed continuously between October 1943 and July 1944.[81] During the first week of July 1944, a month after the capture of Rome, missions against rail and road targets extended up to the Po Valley via the Pisa-Rimini sector, the Cremona-Bologna area, and the Spezia-Parma-Florence-Leghorn rectangle.[82] In the second week of July, the Milan-Lambrate, Brescia, Verona, and Mantua yards were bombed. In early August, after the bombing of yards at Genoa and bridges in the Bolzano area (disrupting German traffic through the Brenner pass), it became difficult for Kesselring, the German commander in Italy, to supply his troops; at times he was 'virtually isolated from the rest of Europe'. All routes from France and the Tarvisio route from Austria were closed, and between the Po and the Arno there were around 90 breaks in rail lines.[83] Following the Allied *Dragoon* landings in the south of France, the Germans permanently lost the Riviera and Mont Cenis supply routes into Italy, leaving them only four railway routes into the country; the Brenner into northern central Italy and the Tarvisio, Piedicolle and Postumia lines into the north-east. In the four days up to 29 August, the US Fifteenth Air Force dropped over 1,200 tons of bombs on bridges and viaducts along these four lines, and Italian partisans blew up the viaduct on the Piedicolle line, together interrupting railway traffic between northern Italy and Austria and Yugoslavia.[84]

Tedder, meanwhile, took his Italian lessons to London, where as Eisenhower's deputy he began planning the air forces' role in *Overlord* from the start of 1944. 'Concentrated, precise attack upon railway targets scientifically selected', he considered, 'might make all the difference to the success or failure of the long awaited invasion of France'.[85] The strategic bombing of rail centres, he held, would destroy not only track, locomotives and rolling stock, but also repair facilities, crippling the rail network in depth, rendering tactical raids just before and during the invasion itself doubly effective, and preventing the arrival of German reinforcements. By late January 1944 Zuckerman (still

Tedder's scientific adviser) had prepared a list of 76 'nodal points' of the French and Belgian rail systems. This was the basis of what became known as the 'Transportation Plan', which coincided with the temporary transfer of the strategic air forces to the SHAEF orbit from April 1944.

An intense political debate on the plan served only to limit it at the margins.[86] Between 3 March and 5 June 1944, 63,636 tons of Allied bombs were dropped on Transportation Plan targets across almost the whole of northern France. Bomber Command dropped 64 per cent of this total – 40,930 tons, or 40 per cent of its total effort over the period.[87] To these raids were added attacks on southern targets, especially in the Rhône valley, from bases in Italy: Marseille, Lyon, and Saint-Étienne all received their first major raids in this period. This was a scale of attack not yet seen in France. Bomber Command's share exceeded the *total* of 34,426 tons it had dropped on occupied territories (including France) up to December 1943.[88]

The effectiveness of the Transportation Plan has remained the subject of fierce debate. Major disruption to the rail network certainly took place. The Renseignements Généraux, the French internal intelligence services, reported that by the end of June, the SNCF could only use one-third of its normal rolling stock. The number of coal trains supplying Paris from the Nord and Pas-de-Calais fell from 40 in January 1944 to just 2 in June, and railwaymen were threatening strike action to back a 30 per cent pay claim in compensation for their increasingly dangerous working conditions (SNCF management granted a back-dated rise).[89] The provinces too lacked coal; this, plus Allied raids on power stations, dramatically cut power supplies to French industry working for the Germans.[90] According to the detailed French War Ministry report on the raids produced after the Liberation, total traffic on the SNCF network had fallen by half (compared to January) by the start of June 1944 and by three-quarters by July; in northern and western regions, traffic in June 1944 stood at 15 and 10 per cent respectively of January levels.[91] Nevertheless, the French rail network was far from paralysed by 6 June: 393 German troop trains ran in France in June 1944 and 203 in July.[92] Lines cut were quickly repaired. While air raids cut tracks 2,234 times (compared to 1,094 cuts by sabotage) between January and July 1944, repairs to cuts in rail centres were made in a matter of five days at most.[93] Moreover, as Tedder concedes, 'the enemy had been able to maintain military traffic at the expense of all non-military and economic traffic'.[94]

Attacks on bridges had more immediate effect than cutting lines. A first 'line of interdiction', roughly 100 kilometres round the front, included the lower Seine and the Loire: the destruction of bridges ultimately reduced traffic by 97.5 per cent in the Seine sector, 78 per cent in the Loire sector, and 70 per cent between the two.[95] Cloud cover slowed down these raids: as Air Marshal Sir Trafford Leigh-Mallory, in command of the Tactical Air Forces supporting the D-Day landings, observed on 13 June, 'I sometimes think that the Powers above may have Fascist tendencies, so bad has been the weather.'[96] The wider interdiction plans, including bridges between the Seine and the Loire, and those over the Oise, were not completed until early August.[97] However, the Transportation Plan is best considered in the light of its progressive effects on rail traffic in the weeks after the invasion. Tedder's claim that 'by the end of July … the combined effect of air attack and to a lesser extent French sabotage had made the rapid transfer of troops by rail impossible'[98] is borne out by the French War Ministry report, which stresses slow speeds, incomplete journeys and diversions, to conclude that 'very considerable disruption' was caused to German troop transport between May and July 1944. [99] But it was done at a cost of 16,000 French deaths and 25,000 buildings completely destroyed between March and May 1944.[100]

Tactical targets

A major share of raids on France and Italy took place in support of Allied ground forces fighting to liberate the two countries. The raids were especially protracted in Italy, where ground combat was spread out over nearly two years, and briefer but heavier in France. As the Allies ejected Axis forces from North Africa and prepared to land on European soil for the first time since 1940, the USAAF and the Allied supreme command in the Mediterranean agreed on the necessity of air superiority. Throughout May 1943, therefore, the principal airfields of Sicily and Sardinia were bombed often and hard. So were Foggia and the two principal airfields in the Naples area, Capodichino and Pomigliano. The aim was not only to disable Axis air power but, in time, to seize airfields for Allied use. With airfields in Malta saturated, Spaatz proposed capturing the island of Pantelleria, viewed by Eisenhower as a prerequisite to the invasion of Sicily. After a massive bombardment in the first week of June, the garrison of about 12,000, its morale shattered, duly raised the white flag as the Allied troops landed.[101]

Subsequent objectives were the port of Naples, to provide logistical support for the Allied campaign on the mainland, and the Foggia airfield to serve as a strategic base. Between mid-June and mid-August 1943, 2,000 tons of bombs were dropped on ports and bases in Sicily and southern Italy, nearly 7,500 tons on airfields and fully 15,500 tons on communication lines: 'so intense an effort', wrote Tedder, 'certainly helped to undermine Italian morale on the island and to prepare the way for the imminent Italian collapse'.[102] The heaviest attacks hit Catania (yards, repair shops and industrial installations), Reggio and San Giovanni in Calabria (yards, ferry slips and port facilities), Messina and Agrigento (supply lines), Sicilian airfields of the Gerbini complex, Sciacca, Trapani, and Calabrian airfields at Vibo Valentia, Reggio and Crotone. Such a combination of strategic and tactical efforts steadily wore down Axis opposition in Sicily: Palermo fell on 22 July, Trapani the following day, though the Axis only evacuated Messina, their last foothold, on 17 August.[103]

The rapid reinforcement of German forces in Italy made it clear that Allied armies needed air strikes to delay German concentrations. As noted above, in March 1944, operations in support of the land battle were the top priority for the Tactical Air Forces in Italy and the third priority for the Strategic Air Forces.[104] For example, at the time of the German counterattack at Anzio, strategic bombers were enlisted for the Italian campaign, attacking the Anzio area in support of the troops in February, before returning to concentrate on the bombing of Germany. Central Italy, having received raids on rail targets from 1943, was bombed most intensively as the Allies sought to break through the Gothic Line. Bologna was hit 94 times (by the RAF Mediterranean Air Force and the US Twelfth and Fifteenth) at a cost of some 2,500 victims.[105] The attack on Monte Cassino, and the controversy surrounding it, are described below. And the pattern laid down in Allied attacks on Germany, but also the Biscay ports, applied to Italy: the Americans bombed by daylight, the British by night.[106] Both strategic and tactical forces continuously accompanied the Allies' slow progress up the peninsula.

In France, one type of target for which there was no Italian equivalent was the launching sites for German V-weapons, of which the Allies had been aware since late 1943. These appeared in three directives in 1944, twice as a major objective, and attracted heavy attacks on rural Normandy, Picardy and Flanders, where the sites were located, from December 1943 until the liberation of these regions at the end of August 1944.[107] Most sites were in open country and the risk of civilian casualties was therefore quite small. By mid-August, Bomber Command had dropped nearly 36,000 tons of bombs on these targets, coded 'Crossbow', and lost nearly 100 aircraft and 650 crew members in the process.[108] 'Crossbow' targets by Allied air forces from 5 December 1943 to 3 September 1944 received some 2 per cent of all Allied bombs dropped in the war, and provoked Tedder's comment that the policy amounted to using a 'sledgehammer for a tintack'. Much of the effort was wasted, thanks to the Germans' success in maintaining decoy sites. But attacks on supply sites, in particular, significantly reduced the number of successful V-1 raids on Britain before advancing Allied troops removed the sites from German control.[109]

Support for ground forces, in France as in Italy, took many forms: attacks on airfields, ammunition or fuel dumps, coastal batteries, or transport targets, but also direct attacks on enemy positions in support of the Allied armies in Normandy and, in August, in southern France as well.[110] Indeed, the Allied bombing offensive on French territory reached its climax during the three months after D-Day, claiming nearly 20,000 civilian victims.[111]

Three types of attack deserve particular attention. One was the bombing of 'choke points' – villages and small towns situated at crossroads. Destroying these, in the hours and days before and after the first landings, would, it was hoped, stop German reinforcements moving by road. Though civilians were warned to expect these raids, the warning leaflets were so general and so widely scattered that they were not taken seriously, especially in localities where no German forces were based. Norman villages like Évrecy and Condé-sur-Noireau suffered, proportionately, some of the heaviest damage and highest death tolls of the whole war. Second, heavy bombers were given what was effectively an artillery role in support of six major Allied ground attacks in Normandy. In one of these, west of Saint-Lô, bombing materially assisted the American break-out (as well as killing some American troops in the forward lines). On the other hand, the bombing of Caen and its suburbs in operations *Charnwood* and *Goodwood* on 7–9 and 18–21 July failed to do the same for British forces. Some two-thirds of Caen was destroyed and 2,000 of its inhabitants killed in the battle for the city; by cratering large urban areas, the bombing actually hindered the British advance.[112] The use of heavy bombers to support ground operations was often poorly co-ordinated with army planning. With little or no delay between bombing and the ground advance, and against shallow German defences, it could prove effective, as at Saint-Lô; without these conditions, as at Caen, it did not.[113] Third, heavy bombers were used against German fortified coastal positions, to limit potential delays to the Allied advance entailed by long sieges. Their effectiveness in this role was limited.[114] The 9,790 tons of bombs dropped on Le Havre between 5 and 11 September, for example, wrecked most of the city centre and killed over 2,000 civilians, but made less impact than the concurrent artillery bombardment on German ground defences and coastal batteries.[115]

Compared with the strategic offensive against Germany, Allied targeting policy against France and Italy showed a slighter preoccupation with enemy 'morale' (with the chief exception of certain raids on Italy before September 1943), a greater reluctance – again with notable exceptions – to undertake area bombing, and a relatively greater concern to hit precise targets. This was due to political considerations outlined below. But the use of the strategic bomber forces, with a mediocre record of accuracy, for 'precision' raids entailed a high level of what came to be called, in a later age of greater accuracy, 'collateral damage'.

THE POLITICS OF BOMBING

The policy-makers and policy processes were, broadly, the same whether the bombing campaign applied to Germany, France, or Italy. But the political and military considerations that shaped policy were not. France was viewed not as an enemy but as enemy-occupied territory; so was Italy after September 1943. Civilian casualties here were, in principle, an object of concern as they were not in Germany; so too, in the Italian case at least, were monuments, viewed as essential to Europe's cultural and religious heritage. Vigorous arguments about how heavily and indiscriminately these countries should be bombed persisted well into 1944. Military necessity usually won the arguments, but the fact that they took place at all indicated a degree of continuing political constraint.

Rules of engagement

The distinction between different countries as bombing targets was reflected in two general statements of British bombing policy, dated 31 May 1940 and 29 October 1942. These differed from conventional bombing directives in that they defined rules of engagement rather than specific targets. These, and the postscript relating to Italy after the surrender of September 1943, also reflected a progressive, albeit partial, eclipse of humanitarian concerns in bombing policy.

The statement of 1940 was the more restrictive of the two. For all potential targets, including those in Germany, it not only declared the 'intentional bombardment of civil populations' to be illegal, but also stated that in raids on military objectives, '(b) It must be possible to identify the objective, (c) the attack must be made with reasonable care to avoid undue loss of civil life in the vicinity of the target, (d) the provisions of Red Cross conventions are to be observed.' A list of military targets was attached, followed by lists of aerodromes and naval dockyards, factories serving military purposes, and lines of communication.[116]

June 1940 affected bombing policy in two respects. First, Italy became a target when it declared war on France and Britain. Second, the armistice of June 1940 raised the question of the applicability of these rules to France, provoking a debate in the Air Ministry that reflected Britain's ambiguous attitude to Vichy.[117] The discussion was (temporarily) settled by a memorandum from Sinclair, accepted by the War Cabinet on 26 July. This was more restrictive (in relation to France) than the statement of 31 May, further limiting what constituted a legitimate target – although obvious German military objectives in occupied France, plus vessels at anchor in territorial waters, oil installations, lines of communication, and aircraft and aero-engine factories, were all included. The unoccupied southern zone remained off limits.[118]

The second general statement, dated 29 October 1942, established a radical difference, hitherto only implicit, between enemy and occupied territories. Over Germany, Italy and Japan, the enemy's resort to 'unrestricted air warfare' was held to justify attacks aimed, among other things, at civilian morale; the restraint of May 1940 was officially abandoned, area bombing officially endorsed. For occupied territory, on the other hand, the 29 October letter reproduced, word for word, much of the June/July 1940 policy.[119] The statement still applied only to the *occupied* zone of France, but this policy was soon overtaken by events: the move of German and Italian troops into the southern zone on 11 November 1942 meant that all France was now open to attack.

Even without this Axis encouragement, however, the policy in relation to France slipped badly within weeks of October 1942 with the Allied area raids on U-boat bases on the French Atlantic coast. The following year, the extent of the slippage was reflected in another context, when Portal contemplated the consequences for bombing policy of Italy's surrender. In a note dated 15 September 1943, he wrote that:

> My first inclination is to treat occupied Italy in the same way as occupied France, i.e. to warn the Italians that if they work for the Germans they do so at their own risk and they should keep clear of factories and other objectives of military value. It may be that we should also indicate that those cities which adopt an effective system of passive resistance to the will of the Germans will be exempt from bombing while those which countenance a revival of the Fascist regime will not.

By stating that Italian civilians in the vicinity of factories were there at their own risk, Portal's note went against the spirit and the letter of the statement of 29 October 1942. Moreover, his suggestion that anti-Fascist towns should be exempt from bombing was rapidly dropped after a correspondence between the Deputy Chief of Air Staff, Air Chief Marshal Sir Norman Bottomley, and the Deputy Director of Bombing Operations, Air Vice Marshal Sydney Bufton. In his note of 22 September, Bufton argued that:

> If we promised Italian cities immunity from area bombing as a reward for non co-operation with the Germans, we might find ourselves in difficulties if an urgent military necessity arose to bomb precise targets (e.g. marshalling yards) within those cities. The population might well mistake a not very successful heavy daylight attack on a marshalling yard in the heart of their city, for an area attack, immunity from which they had been promised.[120]

Bufton's remarks go to the heart of much of what French and Italian civilians experienced between 1942 and 1945: for the people under the bombs, a second-rate 'precision' raid (and most were second-rate) could resemble an area attack. Such area attacks were viewed as fair punishment for a belligerent, Fascist Italy. But precision bombing was still expected, in principle, from British and American air forces over France throughout the war, and over Italy after September 1943. That in turn reflected a degree of political restraint that applied, in principle, to bombing policy in relation to both countries.

Political constraints: French civilians

Bombing France meant attacking a country that was officially neutral, half-occupied by the Axis (and fully occupied from November 1942), recently an ally, and which had engendered an internal and external Resistance movement with which Britain maintained relations, however stormy. The Vichy government controlled two-fifths of France, the French fleet and most French colonial possessions. These the Allies, and especially Churchill, feared would fall into German hands.[121] The United States, moreover, maintained diplomatic relations with Vichy until November 1942. Britain's interest in preserving Vichy's independence – however threadbare – from Germany, and preventing the worst-case scenario – France's entry into the war alongside the Axis – constrained bombing policy. From 1940 until November 1942, bombing policy could even be discussed, through the indirect diplomatic channels that passed via the Madrid and Washington embassies.

Within the Air Ministry, the question posed from 1940 was whether the maintenance of French neutrality was more important than the destruction of enemy targets on French soil. It acquired new urgency in 1941, when the Air Staff, not yet fully committed to area bombing, aimed to attack economic targets both within Germany and in occupied territory. If factories in occupied France were viewed, in principle, as acceptable targets, Portal's request, in April 1941, for permission to bomb in the southern zone too was far more contentious. General Hastings Ismay, the Military Secretary to the War Cabinet, took the view that unoccupied France was 'in certain senses a neutral country',[122] and Portal's request to bomb the *zone libre* was refused. A year later, Eden saw no reason to change policy until Pétain was 'behaving much worse than he is at present'.[123] Only when the German occupation extended south could the bombs follow.

Bombing the occupied North was subject to restrictions, the detail of which was constantly under review.[124] In June 1941, permission was given in principle for the daylight bombing of factories in the Occupied Zone, and in November Sinclair sought specific approval for the night bombing of four key factories, including Renault at Boulogne-Billancourt. The War Cabinet, however, deferred the decision for a month; by December, with the USA now in the war, but negotiating with Vichy to maintain French neutrality, further delay was ordered.[125]

Bombing policy could also be affected, if marginally, by the steady trickle of French protests to embassies in Washington and Madrid in 1941 and 1942. Many of these got no further than the Air Ministry: municipal councillors of Le Havre, who complained after an RAF raid had wrecked a big department store, were dismissed as 'German nominees [who] do not speak for the population'.[126] Protests from the summit, however, could get more attention. Recent attacks on Lille and Brest were raised at the War Cabinet on 25 August 1941; a message of regret for the loss of life was sent to the French embassy in Madrid and aircrews were instructed to avoid bombing occupied territory if accuracy was doubtful.[127] An October 1942 complaint about overflights of the southern zone led to an investigation as to whether Vichy's neutrality had been violated, though this was abandoned with the occupation of southern France the following month.[128]

In general, however, the year 1942 saw a progressive relaxation of restrictions on bombing. In March, the Boulogne-Billancourt raid, though technically more or less within official policy, was of an unprecedented scale and violence. The same month, it is true, RAF bombers participating in the combined operation against Saint-Nazaire docks refrained from bombing because of poor visibility, in accordance with official policy.[129] By May, however, the poor-weather restriction had been dropped in relation to combined operations, with the agreement of the Foreign Office.[130] The unrestricted bombing and machine-gunning of goods trains by day and of passenger and goods trains by night was authorized in July, in a directive which claimed that French civilians authorized to travel by rail at night 'might normally be assumed to have collaborationist tendencies', and this authorization was confirmed in the general statement of 29 October 1942.[131] Meanwhile hesitations arising from possible American reactions to bombing effectively ended in April 1942, when Laval's return to power provoked a sharp deterioration in relations between Washington and Vichy; the US Eighth Air Force started bombing France on 18 August, and for the next four months France was the target of almost all American raids. The Torch landings of November 1942 won control of North-West Africa for the Allies and led to the German occupation of the South, and to the final diplomatic break between Vichy and Washington. In less than a month, Vichy had lost any capacity it had possessed to restrain Allied attacks. This inevitably facilitated the decision to undertake the area bombing of the Biscay ports in January 1943. Even so, concerns about civilians did not disappear entirely: an Air Ministry instruction to hit two French industrial targets, dated 21 May 1943, stipulated requirements for 'reliable and experienced' crews, good weather conditions, and in general 'every possible effort' to avoid civilian casualties.[132]

The last big political debate over the bombing of France concerned the Transportation Plan, agreed on 25 March 1944 by Eisenhower, Tedder, and (with great reluctance) by the British and American air chiefs. Portal requested authorization for the plan on 29 March, but warned of heavy civilian losses; the following day Ismay quoted to Churchill an estimate of the British Ministry of Home Security that 'between 80,000 and 160,000 casualties might be caused by the bombing, of which a quarter would be killed'.[133] Within the War Cabinet, the possibility of civilian casualties on this scale provoked acute concern, political as well as humanitarian. Eden, notably, feared for the RAF's reputation on the continent, and a loss of support among rail workers, whose co-operation was needed for sabotage operations. Above all, he stressed the Soviet threat: difficult post-war Anglo-French relations 'in a Europe that was already looking more to Russia than we would wish' were not in Britain's interest. The French, he argued, might accept civilian casualties 'in the heat of battle', but not as part of a calculated plan, inviting 'propaganda which suggested that while Russian armies defeated the enemy armies in the east, the British and Americans confined their efforts to killing French women and children'.[134] Churchill's opposition, expressed at no fewer than five late-night meetings of the Defence Committee and three meetings of the War Cabinet in April and early May of 1944, was even stronger.

Their misgivings were overcome, first by news from France, which reported lower casualties from early raids, and less political damage, than expected;[135] second, by the absence of any alternative plan as the planned date for the Normandy landings approached; and third, by Eisenhower's clear statement that the success of D-Day depended on the Plan.[136] The final arbiter was President Roosevelt, whose response gave Eisenhower and the Transportation Plan his unambiguous backing: 'However regrettable the attendant loss of civilian lives is,' wrote the President on 11 May, 'I am not prepared to impose from this distance any restriction on military action by the responsible Commanders that in their opinion might militate against the success of Overlord or cause additional loss of life to our Allied forces of invasion.'[137]

May 1944 marked not only the closure of the debate on the Transportation Plan but also the effective end of political discussions about bombing France. The Defence Committee (Operations), a crucial forum for debate in the spring of 1944, met only twice more in the war, and never to discuss bombing in occupied territories. As for the War Cabinet, its discussions were practically confined to noting routine reports prepared by SHAEF and Bomber Command. Raids of the scope of those on Caen or Le Havre, which would have been discussed at Cabinet level before the Transportation Plan debate, were now decided within SHAEF. In September, the destruction of Le Havre could be reported as a routine operation alongside attacks on German targets.[138]

Eisenhower did, it is true, send a message to the bomber chiefs, for the 'attention of every member of aircrews fighting over Europe' demanding 'scrupulous care to avoid any but military targets'.[139] The record of the following 11 months, however, suggested that military targets were broadly interpreted. One reason for this withdrawal of political control was the 'heat of battle' argument: even opponents of the Transportation Plan, like Eden, had conceded that civilian casualties would have to be accepted once ground operations had begun and Allied soldiers were fighting and dying for the liberation of France. Another explanation was based on observations on the ground, where Allied political agents saw no sign either of the 'hatred' for the Western Allies, or of a surge in support for Russia at the West's expense.[140] By mid-June 1944 in short, the strictly political objections to the bombing of France had all but disappeared.

Political constraints: Italian monuments

The bombing of Italy presented the Allies with political problems of a different kind. Italy was an enemy belligerent until September 1943; neither the Fascist regime nor the Salò republic could use diplomatic back channels to address protests as Vichy had. While British attacks on France were aimed, in principle, at targets linked to the German occupiers, the British identified Italian civilian morale as a target from the start. American concerns about the area bombing of Italy were, it is true, expressed after Mussolini's fall on 25 July 1943: US intelligence, in line with more general American misgivings about area bombing, recommended in August that bombing be limited to 'military objectives outside the thickly populated zones', otherwise 'we risk upheavals against the Badoglio government and premature intervention by the Germans'.[141] But the Germans intervened anyway, and despite disagreements between the Allies about the effectiveness of area bombing, concern over civilian victims was rarely an issue as it was for France.

By contrast, the Allies were embarrassed by criticism from the Vatican, especially if supported by international concern over attacks on Italy's historic cities. Unease regarding the bombing of these cities was expressed from the time of the first area bombing raids on northern Italy. In December 1942 Eden wrote to Churchill that although he was 'all in favour of widening our range of Italian targets', he hoped 'that we shall not feel it necessary to attack cities of great artistic interest such as Florence and Venice'.[142]

The question that provoked most discussion between the two Allies, and between the Allies and the Vatican, concerned the bombing of Rome. Debates continued until the city's liberation on 5 June 1944 and involved the political, military and diplomatic authorities. The decision to bomb the capital of Fascist Italy was based on both military and political considerations and taken after long discussions which reflected worries about 'unfavourable reaction from the Roman Catholic Church, as well as from many artists, architects, historians, and others throughout the world'.[143] Despite several statements from Churchill to the contrary, the Allies were conscious that Rome was not like any other city, and both the Combined Chiefs of Staff and Eisenhower, as Supreme Commander in the Mediterranean, recognized the importance of careful selection and training of aircrews.[144]

In the correspondence between the Vatican and the Allies, doubts about the bombing of Rome were intertwined with the wider question of Marshal Badoglio's unilateral declaration in August 1943 of Rome as an 'open city'. The link between bombing and the special status of Rome (which would eventually be bombed 51 times, with the loss of over 7,000 victims) continued to be raised by Vatican diplomats in attempts to assure the city's immunity. For the Allies, however, Rome was first and foremost the capital of an Axis power. Indeed, the question was never if, but when a raid on Rome would be militarily justified. Before the invasion of Sicily, Rome represented a symbolic target. Afterwards, however, Rome assumed a new strategic importance because of the crucial role of its two marshalling yards, the Littorio and the San Lorenzo, which handled almost all rail traffic between northern and southern Italy. While the Americans worried about Catholic public opinion at home, Churchill – in contrast to his caution about attacks on France – had already told the House of Commons in September 1941 that 'We have as much right to bomb Rome as the Italians had to bomb London last year.'[145] At the Combined Chiefs of Staff meeting in June 1943, just before the Allied landings in Sicily took the ground war to Italian territory, the British were concerned that Eisenhower might oppose the plan, and chose to confront American caution. Citing the bombing of St Paul's and Westminster Abbey, as well as that of churches in Malta, they claimed that 'if the USA had their churches bombed they would have no qualms about Rome'.[146]

Indeed, Churchill showed no understanding of what was so special about Rome. As he told Eden on 1 August 1943:

> I do not understand why, if we are to bomb the cities of Northern Italy, the populations of which are the most favourable to the Allies and the most violently anti-German, we should not continue to bomb military objectives on the outskirts of Rome. Many people think that bombing Rome was the final blow to Mussolini. I do not put it so high, but I cannot see any reason why, if Milan, Turin and Genoa are to be bombed, Rome should be especially exempted.[147]

On 19 July the 'thoroughly briefed' USAAF crews had carried out the mission, with more than 500 bombers hitting the San Lorenzo and Littorio yards and the Ciampino airfields, dropping around 1,000 tons of bombs. As both yards were damaged, in conjunction with the raid of two days earlier on the Naples yards, a gap of about 200 miles in the Italian rail system prevented the southbound movement of Axis troops and supplies by rail for several days.[148]

After the bombing of Rome, the most controversial air operation of the Italian campaign took place on 15 February 1944, when US bombers together with artillery destroyed the abbey at Monte Cassino. Founded by Saint Benedict in the sixth century, the abbey had immense artistic and religious significance. The Germans had men and supplies close by, but as US Army commander General Mark Clark and most Allied leaders in the area knew, German troops were not in the monastery itself.[149] However, General Bernard Freyberg, commander of the New Zealand Expeditionary Force, while preparing to send his troops against German defences along the mountain, asked for the bombardment. As an American division commander, General Fred L. Walker, wrote in his diary the day after the abbey was destroyed, 'this was a valuable historical monument which should have been preserved. The Germans were not using it ... No tactical advantage will result.'[150] Besides damaging the abbey, the operation killed an estimated 250 civilians who had thought it a safe refuge. Having to confront the outcry from the Vatican, as well as resulting German propaganda, Roosevelt was left with no other option than to call the abbey a German 'strongpoint', and to claim that the bombing, although unfortunate, had been a military necessity. Moreover, the bombing of Monte Cassino came only a few days after the bombing of Florence, which had provided the Allies with 'another piece of bad publicity', to such an extent that, in order to help Arnold defend himself against accusations from the press, Eaker sent him an atlas of Italian monuments.[151]

After the Vatican had failed to protect Rome by making it an open city, the Pope's diplomats appealed for other cities to be spared destruction because of their art treasures and religious importance. The Pope was on occasion backed by the British Ambassador to the Holy See, Francis D'Arcy Godolphin Osborne: after the heavy raids of August 1943 on Naples, Genoa, Milan and Turin, Osborne wrote to the Foreign Office that the attacks had been 'directed against the inhabited quarters and centres of the cities rather than against military objectives'. The raid on Naples of 5 August in particular, he claimed, could have been justifiably described as a 'Baedeker raid' since it mostly damaged churches and famous monuments.[152]

As the bombing campaign moved to central Italy in 1944, concern over a number of artistically important cities like Florence, Assisi, Loreto, Siena and Arezzo, provoked more exchanges between the Vatican and the Allies, as well as the Allied publication of manuals locating Italy's treasures for the bombers, so they could try to avoid them. Perhaps the most sensitive target, discussed at a British Chiefs of Staff meeting on 1 March 1944, was Florence, a major rail junction between Bologna, Pisa and Rome, a key marshalling yard, home to Italy's principal locomotive repair shops, and thus, for the Allies, a vital target. But the yards were barely a mile from the famous Duomo. Worries about monuments extended high into the Mediterranean command: Eaker's Deputy Air Marshal John Slessor told Portal of his reservations on 29 February 1944; 'but if it is proved essential', he added, 'it will have to be done'.[153]

The Chiefs of Staff meeting the next day concluded that 'such attacks should be undertaken if they were considered essential from the military point of view', and 'provided that only carefully selected bomber units were employed', and consequently Florence was bombed.[154] The marshalling yards of Rifredi and Campo Marte stations were hit, as well as a locomotive depot; historical monuments were indeed avoided, although bombs fell on a peripheral area and on two hospitals, killing 215 people. Eisenhower wished to protect Europe's history but not at the expense of his soldiers' lives. This view was shared by his successor as Allied Commander-in-Chief, Mediterranean, Sir Henry Maitland Wilson, who issued a directive, which came into force in 12 January 1945, which stated that 'subject to the needs of military necessity the civilian population, cities and cultural monuments should be spared'.[155]

In general, therefore, 'sensitive to charges of barbarism, always concerned about the reputation of the AAF at home', the Allies sought to avoid the indiscriminate destruction of famous buildings.[156] Some commanders, like Slessor, 'felt personal sympathy for the endangered places and artworks'. During a visit to Pisa, heavily damaged by bombing between August 1943 (when more than 900 people had died) and January 1944, Arnold wrote in his diary: 'took photographs of Leaning Tower and visited cathedral – a magnificent building with wonderful paintings'.[157] Zuckerman noted in his memoirs that street maps of Italian towns 'copied from Baedeker's guides and marked to show important buildings to be avoided' were included in the briefing kits for each Italian town likely to be a target. A booklet, *Italian Monuments Preservation*, had also been produced for the purpose.[158]

Debates about the risk of hitting Italy's artistic treasures, particularly among the British, were probably also a result of an elite culture that most gentlemen had shared since the late eighteenth century, the era of the Grand Tour. When Eaker established the MAAF headquarters alongside Alexander in the immense royal palace of Caserta, outside Naples, his *aide de camp* James Parton commented: 'once again we found ourselves occupying a building with unique historic and architectural characteristics'.[159] Spike Milligan, a gunner during the Italian campaign (and very far from being a member of the British elite), filled his diary with exclamations of admiration for the places he saw while moving from Sicily to southern Italy. On 15 October, realizing that the Americans had bombed Porta Ercolano, he exclaimed in disbelief: 'I discovered that the Americans had actually bombed it! ... Bombing Pompeii!!'[160] In December, he was admiring the Amalfi Basilica with sculptures by Michelangelo, and the coast.[161] Similar sentiments were expressed by Alanbrooke, who commented on the beauty of the Sicilian coast, on a villa north of Naples and on Pompeii in December 1943.[162]

Indeed, Allied strategists seemed to show more concern for buildings and artworks than for civilians, even after the armistice of 8 September 1943. The occasional official expressions of regret at civilian casualties had a half-hearted ring. For example, in May 1944 bombs hit the village of Sonnino, half-way between Anzio and the main Italian front, which had become a 'secondary target' – an alternative when visibility was bad over the primary objective. Air Chief Marshal Douglas Evill, the vice-Chief of Air Staff, wrote to Churchill: 'it is of course greatly to be regretted that Italian civilian casualties were caused by this air attack but I am afraid that such instances are liable to occur when the population remains in the tactical area'.[163]

CONCLUSION

The bombing of France and Italy resulted from decisions that were arguably more diverse and complex than those shaping bombing policy against Germany, involving a more frequent participation both from ground force commanders and from political leaders. Each such decision had definite military reasons, but the practice of bombing across these two countries was also highly varied, ranging from extremely small-scale and precise attacks to some of the largest raids of the war.

Neither France nor Italy suffered a Hamburg or a Dresden. Individual towns and villages may have sustained comparable levels of damage and loss of life, but on a smaller scale; no city experienced a firestorm that killed tens of thousands. But if area bombing was the exception not the rule over France and Italy, the more limited mode of bombing the two countries experienced was far from benign. For those under the bombs, the difference between area and precision bombing was often hard to discern. Harris's statement, in the middle of the Transportation Plan raids, that 'the heavy bomber is a first-class strategic weapon and one of the least effective tactical weapons' highlights the fact that many raids, however precise in purpose, were conducted by aircraft designed for strategic use, with the same crews who had received the same training.[164] Viewed from the receiving end, the French air ministry report completed in December 1944, generalizing from the Gnôme-Rhône raid on Limoges (exemplary from the British point of view), observed that the Allies 'obtain the desired result, but with a deplorable level of effectiveness [*rendement*]. They wage a rich men's war, knowing that American industry is behind them.'[165]

Eisenhower's message to the bomber chiefs of 2 June 1944 highlighted the contradiction between the indiscriminate bombing of towns and cities and the humanitarian values for which the Allies said they were fighting.[166] Although the contradiction was most flagrant in the case of the area bombing of German cities, it was largely ignored here because of the peculiar brutality of Germany's own conduct of the war. To do the same in the cases of France and Italy proved harder. France had fought alongside Britain until June 1940; its population was viewed as pro-Allied; Vichy disposed of small but significant diplomatic leverage till November 1942; the CFLN was an accepted interlocutor of the British government. Italy, meanwhile, had a less hideous face as a belligerent than its German ally; after September 1943 it was no longer a belligerent, albeit not quite an ally; it had a unique cultural and religious heritage as the heart of the Roman empire, and was the centre of world Catholicism, with an active papal diplomatic corps, independent of the Fascist regime.

There is evidence that these considerations restrained bombing policy in the earlier years of the war. The southern zone of France was not deliberately bombed until its occupation by Axis troops in November 1942; proposals to subject the French Atlantic ports to area bombing were rejected on political grounds in 1942; Rome was spared till July 1943; attacking the heart of Paris was not even discussed (though its suburbs were heavily bombed). But the idea of a restrained Allied policy in relation to France and Italy requires major qualification, in three respects. First, humanitarian restraints carried less weight than political ones. The British took more notice of complaints from Vichy before November 1942 than of protests from the CFLN after, because Vichy controlled territory and a fleet and the CFLN did not. The intrinsic need to avoid civilian deaths came second, in the debates on the Transportation Plan, to worries about the potential damage to Anglo-French relations, considered vital to the post-war stability of Western Europe; in the debates on Italy, it came second to the damage to the Allies' public image that the wholesale destruction of cultural artefacts and buildings would cause. Second, political constraints were most effective earlier in the war, when bombs and bombers were relatively scarce. RAF Bomber Command dropped just 13,000 tons of bombs on all targets in 1940. This rose, modestly, to 32,000 in 1941 and 45,500 (plus the US Eighth Air Force's 1,561) in 1942; as Churchill observed that year, 'Never was there so much good work to be done and so few to do it.'[167] In 1943, by contrast, these two bomber forces could drop over 200,000 tons, and in 1944 nearly 915,000 tons.[168] Penury dictated great selectivity of targets, giving political constraints (among others) greater weight. By contrast, the pressure on resources relaxed from 1943 onwards, meaning more bombs for everyone. Third, political restraints were regularly trumped by military priorities. Area bombing was used on the French Atlantic ports when the Battle of the Atlantic reached a critical stage, and when Vichy had no further cards to play; Rome was attacked when the Allied invasion of Italy raised its strategic importance as a transport centre and the Allies had bases within easy range; the Transportation Plan was implemented, a few minor adjustments aside, in the name of military necessity.

One aspect in which discussions on the two countries diverged substantially was the link made between bombing and morale. In both France and Italy, Allied strategists believed that the bombing of industrial targets served both to damage the Axis war effort materially and to affect civilian morale, but in radically different ways. In principle, Italy could be subjected to area bombing in the hope of destroying popular support for the war and the regime; France, by contrast, should receive precision raids that would raise public confidence in the Allies' will and capacity to pursue the war. In practice, the distinction was blurred. Distance and the allocation of resources dictated that area bombing on Italy was less massive than on Germany. At the same time, the precision sought in many raids on France was not always achieved, and some attacks could, as in Nantes, provoke levels of panic – a collapse of morale – comparable to those seen in Italy. The following chapters will bring the investigation to the receiving end, assessing the results on the ground and analysing how states and societies prepared for and responded to the bombing campaign.

Notes

1 These figures are obtained by comparing tonnages (for all four countries) in Table 1.1 and deaths in Tables 1.2 and 1.3. See also Chapter 1 (Appendix); the ratio of 6.3 corresponds to an Italian death toll of 60,000; if this were raised to 80,000, the Italian ratio would be 4.7. German (and Austrian) deaths through Allied bombing are estimated at 420,000 (cf. O. Groehler, *Bombenkrieg gegen Deutschland* (Berlin: Akademie-Verlag, 1990), 320), though if an additional estimated 70,000 prisoners of war and foreign forced labourers are included, the ratio drops to 2.8 tons per death. The UK death toll is given at 60,595 in T. H. O'Brien, *Civil Defence* (London: HMSO, 1955), 677.

2 Sir C. Webster and N. Frankland, *The Strategic Air Offensive Against Germany* (hereafter *SAOG*), vol. II (London: HMSO, 1961), 149; vol. IV (London: HMSO, 1961), 128–31 (directive of 30 October 1940); TNA AIR 8/424, Trenchard to Parliamentary Air Cttee, 15 October 1941; TNA AIR 19/218, Sinclair to Portal, 3 May 1943. Bomber Command lost 1,102 aircraft over France compared to 6,570 over Germany (TNA AIR22/203).

3 Figures calculated from R. A. Freeman, *Mighty Eighth War Diary* (London: Jane's, 1981), 9–89.

4 Calculated from Middlebrook and Everitt, *War Diaries*, 318–32, 419–22.

5 E. Py, *Un été sous les bombes: Givors-Grigny-Chasse, 1944* (Saint-Cyr-sur-Loire: Éditions Alan Sutton, 2004), 52. On the prospects for bombing Axis targets in southern Europe, cf. *The United States Strategic Bombing Survey. Over-all Report (European War)* (US Government Printing Office, 30 September 1945), 3; Field Marshal Lord Alanbrooke, *War Diaries 1939–1945*, ed. A. Danchev and D. Tudman (London: Weidenfeld and Nicolson, 2001), 437. Cf. also S. Ambrose, *Wild Blue* (London: Simon and Schuster, 2001).

6 Webster and Frankland, *SAOG*, vol. III (London: HMSO, 1961), 33.

7 Richards and Saunders, *The Royal Air Force 1939–45*, vol. III, 3.

8 Webster and Frankland, *SAOG*, vol. II, 75, 82–3.

9 D. R. Mets, *Master of Airpower: Carl A. Spaatz* (Novato CA: Presidio Press, 1998), 169.

10 *SAOG*, vol. IV, 205; Hastings, *Bomber Command*, 120–9.

11 Sir A. Harris, *Despatch on War Operations, 23rd February, 1942 to 8th May, 1945* (London: Frank Cass, 1995; also in TNA AIR 14/4465), 192.
12 On Bomber Command and area bombing, cf. for example, Hastings, *Bomber Command*, 123–40; Sir A. Harris, *Bomber Offensive* (London: Greenhill Books, 1990), 77.
13 LC, Papers of Ira Eaker, Box 1:22, f. 3, Report 'The Case for Day Bombing', n.d. (1944).
14 R. Schaffer, *Wings of Judgment: American Bombing in World War II* (Oxford: Oxford University Press, 1985), 37; Mets, *Master of Airpower*, 159.
15 Harris, *Despatch*, 196–7.
16 R. Overy, *The Air War, 1939–1945* (Washington, D.C.: Potomac Books, 2005), 109–13.
17 *United States Strategic Bombing Survey*, Statistical Appendix to Over-all report (European War) (Feb 1947) Chart no. 1, http://wwiiarchives.net/servlet/document/113/11/0.
18 TNA CAB 65/6/50, War Cabinet conclusions, 27 April 1940.
19 S. Colarizi, *L'opinione degli italiani sotto il regime, 1929–1943* (Rome-Bari: Laterza, 2000), 308.
20 TNA AIR 20/5304, Note by the C.A.S., 29 April 1940.
21 *Ibid.*, Minutes of 30 May 1940, 'Possible operations against Italy'.
22 TNA PREM 3/242/7, A. Eden to the Prime Minister, 26 August 1940.
23 TNA AIR 10/1657, Intelligence Headquarters, Bomber Command, RAF, 'Operational Numbers Bomb Targets (Italy)'.
24 TNA AIR 19/481, W. S. Douglas, Air Vice-Marshal, Deputy Chief of the Air Staff, to the Air Officer Commanding-in-Chief, Headquarters, Bomber Command, RAF, 30 October 1940, (printed in *SAOG*, vol. IV, 128–31).
25 TNA AIR 2/7397, Air Ministry to A.O.C. Malta and Middle East, 11 November 1940.
26 TNA CAB 65/10/31, War Cabinet conclusions, 30 December 1940.
27 Gribaudi, *Guerra totale*, 48.
28 TNA FO 371/29918, Mr Wszelaki to Foreign Office, 13 March 1941 (report written on 12 February 1941).
29 Harris, *Bomber Offensive*, 140–1. Typical raids on German targets at the time used 200–300 aircraft.
30 TNA FO 371/33228, Memorandum of the Foreign Secretary A. Eden, 20 November 1942, cited in Gribaudi, *Guerra totale*, 79.
31 Alanbrooke, *War Diaries*, 348.
32 TNA CAB 66/32/28, War Cabinet, Memorandum by the Secretary of State for Air, 17 December 1942.
33 TNA CAB 66/36/26, Memorandum by Eden, 24 April 1943.
34 Mets, *Master of Airpower*, 159.
35 FDRPL, Map Room files, Box 72, OSS Bulletins March–December 1943, source from Stockholm to Roosevelt, Report no. 40, 16 July 1943.
36 AFHRA, microfilm B 0229-1859, The Air Echelon from the USA to Iceland, by Lt. Robert R. Thorndike, cited in Gribaudi, *Guerra totale*, 75.
37 Harris, *Bomber Offensive*, 79.
38 A. Tedder, *With Prejudice: The War Memoirs of Marshal of the Royal Air Force Lord Tedder G.C.B.* (London: Cassell, 1966), 452.
39 TNA CAB 79/63, War Cabinet, Report by the Joint Intelligence sub-committee, 27 July 1943, 71.
40 TNA AIR 20/5988, Bomber Command report of 7/8 August 1943. As early as 23 November 1942, the British undersecretary of foreign affairs Sir A. Cadogan recorded in his diary that Harris was 'bored because "Italian towns don't burn as well as German – too much marble and stuff!"' (*The Diaries of Sir Alexander Cadogan, 1938–1945*, ed. D. Dilks (London: Cassell, 1971), 497).
41 This shift had been already discussed by the Allies in summer 1943: cf. TNA WO 106/3911, note by Chiefs of Staff Committee, 24 August 1943.
42 A. Curami, P. Ferrari and A. Rastelli, *Breda. Alle origini della meccanica bresciana* (Brescia: Fondazione Negri, 2009), 48–9.
43 P. Ferrari, 'Un'arma versatile. I bombardamenti strategici angloamericani e l'industria italiana', in P. Ferrari (ed.), *L'aeronautica italiana: una storia del Novecento* (Milan: Angeli, 2004), 414–15; 421.

44 A. Mitchell, *Nazi Paris: the History of an Occupation, 1940–1944* (New York: Berghahn, 2008), 115–16; A. S. Milward, *The New European Order and the French Economy* (Oxford: Oxford University Press, 1970), 277–8.

45 Gildea, *Marianne in Chains* 65.

46 For the general role of the Ministry of Economic Warfare, cf. *SAOG*, vol. II, 214–15; vol. III, 302–3. For a Ministry of Economic Warfare appraisal of one French target, cf. TNA AIR 19/218, Air Ministry memo of 6 November 1943.

47 TNA AIR 19/217, 'Air Policy: Additional Note to War Cabinet (42) 3rd Meeting', ACAS (I), 8 January 1943.

48 Harris, *Bomber Offensive*, 104–5, 142.

49 Archives Municipales de Boulogne-Billancourt (AMBB), 6/H/72: Réponse aux renseignements demandés par Melle Levenez sur les bombardements, 26 January 1945.

50 TNA AIR 19/217, Freeman Matthews to Sinclair, 14 July 1942; Florentin, *Quand les alliés*, 113; Freeman, *Mighty Eighth War Diary*, 111.

51 TNA AIR 8/424, Eden to Sinclair, 15 April 1942.

52 TNA CAB 69/4, Defence Committee (42(11th)) of 17 April 1942.

53 TNA AIR 8/424, Portal to Sinclair, 26 April 1942; AIR 19/217, Eden to Sinclair, 11 May 1942.

54 TNA AIR 19/217, Freeman Matthews to Sinclair, 19 March and 14 July 1942; Middlebrook and Everitt, *War Diaries*, 268, 317, 398–9.

55 Mitchell, *Nazi Paris*, 114.

56 TNA AIR 40/1720, Military attaché report, 30 May 1944, Allied bombing raids over France: original French TNA FO 371/41984 and AN F1/A/3743 (Note sur les répercussions des bombardements anglo-américains sur le moral des populations en France, 17 May 1944).

57 AM Rennes 1048/W/11, Mairie de Rennes, Service des Pompes Funèbres et des Cimetières, Note du 26 octobre 1946. In March, 291 bodies were buried, in June, 196 – but a further 8 and 3 coffins respectively of 'human remains' were also interred.

58 P. Brickhill, *The Dam Busters* (Basingstoke: Pan Macmillan, 1983), 155–7.

59 TNA PREM 3/242/7, War Cabinet, joint Planning Staff, report signed by Daniel, Playfair and Slessor, 31 August 1940. On Pola cf. Raul Marsetič, *I bombardamenti alleati su Pola, 1944–1945. Vittime, danni, rifugi, disposizioni delle autorità e ricostruzione* (Rovigno-Trieste: Centro di Ricerche Storiche di Rovigno, 2004).

60 As early as November 1940, the Prefect of Pas-de-Calais reported that 800 buildings in Boulogne (whose total peacetime population was 22,000) had been destroyed and 2,000 badly damaged. AN F/1cIII/1177/62, prefectoral report, Pas-de-Calais, 20 November 1940.

61 D. Richards, *Portal of Hungerford* (London: Heinemann, 1977), 161; Richards, *RAF Bomber Command*, 64.

62 SHAA 3D322/1, Bureau Scientifique de l'Armée, Bombardements aériens en territoire français.

63 S. Roskill, *The War at Sea*, vol. I (London: HMSO, 1954), 291–2; Middlebrook and Everitt, *War Diaries*, 115–22, 139–234; Florentin, *Quand les alliés*, 44–5.

64 J.-Y. Besselièvre, 'Les bombardements de Brest (1940-1944)', in Battesti and Facon (eds), *Les Bombardements Alliés sur la France durant la Seconde Guerre Mondiale: Stratégies, Bilans Matériaux et Humains*' (Paris: Cahiers du CEHD, no. 37, 2009), 106–14; Archives Municipales et Communales de Brest, 4/H/4/25, monthly reports, March 1941–February 1942.

65 Roskill, *War at Sea*, vol. I, 349, 352.

66 TNA AIR 19/217, Anti-U-Boat Committee, 13 and 18 November, 9 and 23 December 1942; Eden to Sinclair, 18 December, and Sinclair to Eden, 22 December 1942; First Sea Lord to War Cabinet, 10 January 1943; Sinclair to Eden, 12 January 1943; ACAS (Ops) to Officer Commanding-in-Chief, Bomber Command, 14 January 1943; Air Ministry to Bomber Command HQ, 14 January 1943. TNA CAB 65/37, WM43(6th) conclusions, War Cabinet meeting of 11 January 1943.

67 Middlebrook and Everitt, *War Diaries*, 343–55.

68 TNA AIR 19/217, Memorandum on Bombing of Biscay ports, 30 March 1943.

69 TNA AIR 41/74, RAF, Air Historical Branch, *The RAF in Maritime War*, vol. V, 30.

70 J.-B. Gaignebet, 'Incertitudes de la paix, cruautés de la guerre (1929–1944)', in M. Agulhon ed., *Histoire de Toulon* (Paris: Privat, 1980), 355.
71 S. Zuckerman, *From Apes to Warlords: The Autobiography (1904–46) of Solly Zuckerman* (London: Hamish Hamilton, 1978), 183; A. Villa, *Guerra aerea sull'Italia (1943–1945)* (Milan: Guerini, 2010), 49–55.
72 Tedder, *With Prejudice*, 441–2; Zuckerman, *From Apes to Warlords*, 210.
73 Tedder, *With Prejudice*, 503.
74 J. F. Kreis, ed., *Piercing the Fog: Intelligence and Army Air Forces Operations in World War II* (Washington DC: Air Force History and Museums Program, 1996), 187.
75 *Ibid.*, 188; LC, The Papers of Ira Eaker, Box 1:26, f. 3, Eaker to Gen. Jacob Devers, 1 April 1944.
76 W. F. Craven and J. L. Cate (eds), *The Army Air Forces in World War II*, vol. 3: *Europe: Argument to V-E Day, January 1944 to May 1945* (Washington DC: Office of Air Force History, 1983), 372–3.
77 *Ibid.*, 376.
78 TNA WO 204/930, Allied Force Headquarters, Inter-Services Supply Committee Paper, 3 March 1944.
79 TNA CAB 122/313, Air Ministry, Annex to report of 26 July 1943; TNA AIR 14/730, Air Staff, report of 23 August 1943.
80 P. Castellano, *Chronique d'un bombardement manqué aux conséquences tragiques: attaque de la gare de triage de Cannes-La Bocca fin de soirée du 11 novembre 1943* (Ollioules (Var, France): Éditions de la Nerthe, 2000). Brickhill, *The Dam Busters*, 132–3, 158–61. Cf also NARA, RG 226, Box 107, Caserta files, Report by the Allied Force Headquarters, 18 December 1943.
81 On Ancona, cf. C. Caglini, *Bombardamenti su Ancona e provincia, 1943–44* (Ancona: Cassa di Risparmio, 1983).
82 TNA WO 204/930, Allied Force Headquarters, Office of Assistant Chief of Staff, Memorandum, 4 July 1944.
83 Craven and Cate (eds), *The Army Air Forces*, vol. III, 406.
84 Richards and Saunders, *The Royal Air Force 1939–45*, vol III, 220.
85 Tedder, *With Prejudice*, 489.
86 See below, p. 36.
87 TNA AIR 20/2799, Transportation Targets Attacked from UK during Week to Sunrise 5th June 1944.
88 Harris, *Despatch*, 44.
89 AN F7/15299/27, Direction des Renseignements Généraux, 2e section, notes, 17 June 1944, 19 June 1944, 28 July 1944, 14 August 1944.
90 Gildea, *Marianne in Chains*, 299.
91 SHAA, ref. G1309, Ministère de la Guerre, Bureau Scientifique de l'Armée, *Les Bombardements Aériens des Chemins de Fer Français de Janvier à Août 1944* (Paris, 1945), 189.
92 *Ibid.*, 188.
93 *Ibid.*, 35.
94 Tedder, *With Prejudice*, 610, and graph facing 541.
95 SHAA, Ministère de la Guerre, *Les Bombardements Aériens*, 35, 70.
96 TNA AIR 37/784, Allied Expeditionary Air Force: daily reflections by Air Chief Marshal Sir Trafford Leigh-Mallory, KCB, DSO, 24.
97 SHAA, Ministère de la Guerre, *Les Bombardements Aériens*, 87, 90–3.
98 Tedder, *With Prejudice*, 579, and graph facing 541.
99 SHAA, Ministère de la Guerre, *Les Bombardements Aériens*, 188.
100 Ministère de l'Intérieur, DDP, *BIDP*, nos. 20–22.
101 Zuckerman, *From Apes to Warlords*, 18; Mets, *Master of Airpower*, 160.
102 Tedder, *With Prejudice*, 453.
103 Craven and Cate (eds), *The Army Air Forces*, vol. 2: *Europe: Torch to Pointblank*, 458.
104 TNA WO 204/930, Allied Force Headquarters, Inter-Services Supply Committee Paper, 3 March 1944.
105 F. Manaresi, 'I bombardamenti aerei di Bologna', in C. Bersani and V. Roncuzzi Roversi Monaco (eds), *Delenda Bononia. Immagini dei bombardamenti 1943–1945* (Bologna: Pàtron, 1995), 47.

106 A. W. F. Glenny, *Mediterranean Air Power and the Second Front* (London: The Conrad Press, 1944), author's foreword, 7.
107 For the concerns raised in the War Cabinet and the British General Staff after the first V1 attacks, see Alanbrooke, *War Diaries*, 558–63.
108 Tedder, *With Prejudice*, 584.
109 S. Darlow, *Sledgehammers for Tintacks: Bomber Command Confronts the V-1 Menace, 1943–1944* (2002), 199–201. For details on destinations of the raids, see Florentin, *Quand les alliés*, 210–11, 215–16, 220, 243, 401, 403.
110 Florentin, *Quand les alliés*, 425, supplies a table of targets attacked in August.
111 The initial French figures for June to August 1944 were 19,232 killed and 27,011 wounded (Ministère de l'Intérieur, DDP, *BIDP*, nos. 22–24).
112 W. I. Hitchcock, *Liberation: the Bitter Road to Freedom, Europe 1944–1945* (London: Faber and Faber, 2008), 26–31; TNA AIR 37/661, 'Overlord: Report on Bombing of Caen', 7.
113 I. Gooderson, *Air Power at the Battlefront: Allied Close Air Support in Europe, 1943–45* (London: Frank Cass, 1998), 132–6, 143–8.
114 *Ibid.*, 137–8.
115 A. Knapp, 'The Destruction and Liberation of Le Havre in Modern Memory', *War in History*, 14.4 (2007), 477–99.
116 TNA CAB 66/10, Annex II to WP (40) 186, 31st May 1940.
117 *Ibid.*, WP (40) 204, Sinclair, 'Bombardment Policy in France', 22 July 1940; AIR19/217, comment on WP (40) 284, minute by Melville, 24 July 1940.
118 TNA CAB 66/10, Memorandum by Secretary of State for Air, WP (40), 284, 22 July 1940; TNA AIR 19/217, WM (40) 213th Conclusions, 26 July 1940.
119 TNA AIR 2/7757, Assistant Chief of Air Staff (Policy) to all Commands, 29 October 1942.
120 TNA AIR 2/7757, Portal to Bottomley and Bufton, 15 September 1943; Bottomley to Bufton, 17 September 1943; Bufton to Bottomley, 22 September 1943.
121 R. T. Thomas, *Britain and Vichy: the Dilemma of Anglo-French Relations 1940–42* (London: Macmillan, 1979), 61–2, 91; D. Johnson, 'Churchill and France', in R. Blake and W. Louis (eds), *Churchill* (Oxford: Oxford University Press, 1993), 41–55; 54.
122 TNA CAB 80/27/42, CoS (41) 242, 16 April 1941, Portal, 'Air Bombardment Policy in France'; CAB 79/10/37, CoS (41) 242, 17 April 1942.
123 TNA FO 954/8A, Eden to Portal, 9 April 1942.
124 TNA CAB 66/10, WP (40) 204, Sinclair, 'Bombardment Policy in France', 22 July 1940; TNA AIR 19/217, extract from WM (40) 213, 26 July 1940; TNA CAB 80/27/42, CoS (41) 242, Portal, 'Air Bombardment Policy in France', 16 April 1941; TNA AIR 19/217, extract from WM (41) 104, 20 October 1941.
125 TNA CAB 65/18, WM (41) 62, 23 June 1941; FO 371/28451, Sinclair, 'Air Policy', for discussion at War Cabinet meeting 6 Nov. 1941, WP (41) 260; AIR 19/217, WM (41) 111, 11 Nov. 1941.
126 TNA FO 371/28541, Declaration of the Municipal Council of Le Havre, 26 August 1941; Piétri to Hoare, 27 September 1941; minute by Speaight, 17 October 1941.
127 *Ibid.*, Piétri to Hoare, 18 August 1941; minute by Mack, 24 August; Sykes to Mack, 1 September 1941; Hoare to Piétri, 23 September 1941.
128 TNA FO 371/32000, Hoare to Foreign Office, 28 October 1942; Henry-Haye to Hull, 28 October 1942; British Embassy Washington to French Department of the Foreign Office, 6 November 1942; Grimes to Balfour, 10 November 1942; minute by Speaight, 12 November 1942.
129 Cf. TNA ADM 1/20019.
130 C. E. Lucas Phillips, *The Greatest Raid of All* (London: Pan Books, 2000), 1–2; TNA FO 371/32000, Ismay to Churchill, 19 May 1942; minute by Speaight, 22 May 1942; minute by Cadogan, 23 May 1942; minute by Eden 24 May 1942.
131 TNA AIR 19/217, Sinclair to Churchill, 25 July 1942; extract from WM (42) 96th, War Cabinet conclusions, 27 July 1942; Bottomley to Harris, 30 July 1942.
132 TNA AIR19/218, Air Ministry to AOC-in-C Bomber Command, 21 May 1943.
133 *Ibid.*, CAS to Prime Minister, 29 March 1944; Ismay to Prime Minister, 30 March 1944.
134 TNA CAB 69/6, Defence Committee, 3 May 1944.
135 *Ibid.*, Bombing Policy in Connection with Overlord. Note by the Chief of Air Staff, 13 April

1944. Churchill had requested that the Transportation Plan incur no more than 10,000 civilian deaths. French figures (in Ministère de l'Intérieur, DDP, *BIDP*, nos. 19–21) indicate a total of 16,082 deaths during the three months of the plan (March–May 1944), though not all of these will have been killed in raids on transportation targets.

136 Tedder, *With Prejudice*, 529; TNA AIR 37/1116, 85–7, Eisenhower to Churchill, 2 May 1944.

137 TNA FO 371/41984, Churchill to Roosevelt, 7 May 1944; Roosevelt to Churchill, 11 May 1944; W. S. Churchill, *The Second World War, vol. V: Closing the Ring* (1952), 466–8.

138 TNA AIR 37/1118, SHAEF Air Staff meeting, 12 September 1944; CAB 65/43 and CAB 66/56, Summaries of Bomber Command operations presented to Cabinet, 11 September and 18 October 1944.

139 TNA AIR 37/1012, Eisenhower to Air Commander-in-Chief, AEAF, Air Officer Commanding-in-Chief, Bomber Command, and Commanding General, USSTAF, 2 June 1944. See also below, p. 250.

140 TNA FO 371/41862, Report of the SHAEF, 13 June 1944; TNA FO 371/41863, Report by Major K. Younger, 5 September 1944; TNA FO 371/41864/Z6752, Report by Major D. Morton, 29 September 1944, circulated to the Cabinet 3 October 1944.

141 FDRPL, Map Room files, Box 72, OSS Bulletins March–December 1943, source from Berne to Roosevelt, Report no. 52, 17 August 1943.

142 TNA AIR 8/1149, Eden to the Prime Minister, 12 December 1942.

143 Craven and Cate (eds), *The Army Air Forces*, vol. 2, 463–4.

144 Cf. also U. G. Silveri and M. Carli, *Bombardare Roma. Gli Alleati e la 'città aperta' (1940–1944)* (Bologna: Il Mulino, 2007).

145 TNA AIR 20/2565, Churchill's speech to the House of Commons, 30 September 1941. Fascist propaganda had trumpeted Italy's role in bombing when Britain seemed near defeat – although none of Italy's semi-obsolete aircraft actually reached London. Cf. the listings of CAI's (Corpo Aereo Italiano) bombing and fighter patrol missions over Kent, Sussex and Suffolk in N. Arena, *La Regia Aeronautica 1939–1943*, vol. I (Rome: Stato Maggiore Aeronautica, 1981), 228–32.

146 TNA AIR 20/2565, RAF Delegation to Air Ministry, 26 June 1943.

147 TNA PREM 3/14/3, Churchill to Foreign Secretary, 1 August 1943.

148 Craven and Cate (eds), *The Army Air Forces*, vol. 2, 464.

149 Schaffer, *Wings of Judgment*, 50.

150 Quoted in *ibid.*, 51.

151 *Ibid.*, 52.

152 TNA WO/106/3911, F. D. G. Osborne to Foreign Office, 21 August 1943.

153 TNA AIR 8/1149, Telegram, Slessor to Portal, 29 February 1944.

154 TNA CAB 79/71/12, Chiefs of Staff 71st meeting, 1 March 1944.

155 TNA AIR 23/1610, Headquarters MAAF, Operations Instruction no. 97, signed C. Cabell, Brigadier General, USA, Director of Operations and Intelligence, command of the Air Commander-in-Chief, 12 January 1945.

156 Schaffer, *Wings of Judgment*, 52.

157 In *ibid.*, 53.

158 Zuckerman, *From Apes to Warlords*, 211.

159 J. Parton, *Air Force Spoken Here. General Ira Eaker and the Command of the Air* (Bethesda, Md: Adler & Adler, 1986), 355.

160 S. Milligan, *Mussolini: His Part in My Downfall* (London: Michael Joseph, 1978), 50–1.

161 *Ibid.*, Entries for 27 and 28 December, 221; 234.

162 Alanbrooke, *War Diaries*, entries for 13, 16 and 18 December 1943, 498, 500, 501.

163 TNA AIR 20/2566, D.C.S. Evill, Vice-CAS., to Prime Minister, 6 May 1944.

164 A. Harris, speech at Headquarters 21 Army Group, 15 May 1944, quoted in H. Probert, *Bomber Harris: His Life and Times* (London: Greenhill Books, 2001), 293.

165 SHAA 321/1, République Française, Ministère de l'Air, Direction Technique et Industrielle, *Rapport sur les bombardements aériens en territoire français* (Paris, December 1944), vol. I, Limoges, 19.

166 See below, p. 250.

167 TNA AIR/8/424, Churchill to Portal, 29 March 1942.

168 Calculated from Harris, *Despatch*, 44; *SAOG*, vol. IV, 454–5.

3

Preparing for Cataclysm, 1922–1940

Every European power expected an air war in 1939. Barely 15 years after the Wright Brothers' first powered flight, World War 1 had already seen aircraft bomb Paris (claiming 226 victims by 1918), and London (with 162 civilians killed in a single raid on 12 June 1917). All belligerents had developed heavy bombers by the war's end. The imperial powers – Britain, France, Italy and Spain – all used bombs against subject peoples, chiefly in the Middle East and North Africa.[1] The Japanese air force had bombed China since 1932. Both Germany and Italy lent air support to Franco's Nationalists in Spain; if the bombing of Guernica in 1937 caught the world's, and Picasso's, imagination, the Italian raids on Barcelona in March 1938 were more deadly, killing at least 2,000 civilians.[2] The pioneering theorist of air power, the Italian general Giulio Douhet, confidently asserted in 1921 that the next war would be 'frightful', with international conventions and agreements disregarded, bombs and gas used massively against civilian populations, and victory going to the power with the greatest offensive capability.[3] Douhet's *The Command of the Air* was being read in translation by specialists across Europe ten years after its first publication in 1921. Stanley Baldwin's November 1932 statement to the House of Commons that 'the bomber will always get through' acted as a (no doubt unintentional) popularization of one of Douhet's central tenets, and corresponded to received wisdom in both Britain and France in the 1930s.

Expectations of an air war were not the same as an accurate forecast of the precise air war that occurred. Neither the French nor the Italians expected to be bombed primarily, or at all, by British and American aircraft; nor could they anticipate the vast tonnages dropped by the Allies from 1942–3. The Italians expected a war with Britain but underestimated the RAF's capacity to retaliate against Italian strikes on British Mediterranean positions. Instead, by May 1940 they had come to overestimate the threat posed by the French air force, especially on north-western industrial cities.[4] The French expected attack from Italy, but believed they could repel it; they were (justifiably) more frightened of the Luftwaffe.[5] In both London and Paris, the destructive power of 1930s air forces was much overestimated. In 1937, Britain's Committee of Imperial Defence expected, on the basis of 50 casualties per ton of bombs and 600 tons dropped daily, that 60 days' bombing of Britain would kill 600,000 civilians and injure a further 1.2 million.[6] British and French behaviour at the time of the 1938 Munich crisis was affected by fears of an overwhelming German air attack in the event of war, including the use of poison gas, outlawed by the Geneva Protocol of 1925. Similarly, General Alfredo Giannuzzi Savelli, President of

Italy's National Committee of Anti-Aircraft Defences, warned in 1931: 'the air weapon has now an ally: chemicals'.[7] This particular threat did not materialize – a rare instance of mutual deterrence working to ensure the respect of an international treaty. But no such outcome could be guaranteed.

Organizing civilian protection against cataclysm from the air, however inaccurately forecast, faced states with a challenge of unprecedented complexity, involving a level of management of civilian life going far beyond the co-ordination of war production undertaken in World War One. A system of look-outs had to be organized, blackout provisions arranged, and an audible network of sirens installed. Shelters had to be built, gas-masks supplied, the evacuation of (at least) children, the infirm and the elderly planned. Emergency services had to be greatly expanded, and complemented with air-raid wardens, rescue and clearance teams, and anti-contamination squads. Little money was forthcoming for these tasks. In the Europe of the early 1930s – stricken by Depression but not, as yet, immediately threatened by war – civil defence was a low priority for governments seeking balanced budgets. At the decade's end, civil defence had to compete for resources with rearmament. Civilians also needed to be prepared psychologically. While propaganda insisted that the air threat was real and the population had to be ready for it, it also tried to avert any inclination to panic.

Four options were available to protect civilians from bombing, all indispensable, none satisfactory in itself. The first was to rely on active defences – anti-aircraft guns and air forces – to intercept and destroy enemy aircraft, or, better, to carry the bombing war to the enemy. The second was to black out towns and cities. On the well-founded assumption that not all raids were preventable, however, passive defence suggested two other possibilities: the mass evacuation of civilians from likely urban targets, or the provision of shelters close to homes and places of work. The two were complementary (the more civilians were evacuated, the fewer would need shelters) but almost equally challenging, evacuation because of its logistical complexity and shelters because of their cost. Neither the French nor the Italian governments had resolved these issues by the outbreak of war. In all probability, too, they would have failed to counter the threat that never came, of gas attack.

This chapter compares civil defence preparations in Third-Republic France and in Fascist Italy. Opening with the legal and institutional framework developed by the two regimes, it considers basic civil defence preparations – evacuation plans, shelters, gas-masks, sirens, and blackout – before assessing the mobilization of French and Italian populations behind their states' respective policies.

THE LEGAL AND INSTITUTIONAL FRAMEWORK

Effective civil defence demands both close co-ordination between different national ministries (most obviously Defence, Interior, and Air, but also, for example, Health, Education, or Public Works) and a close articulation between national and local government. An adequate institutional framework was therefore a necessary (though not sufficient) condition of civil defence, and governments in both France and Italy tried to develop one. The major difference was that whereas in France, the partnership of prefects and mayors could act as a local transmission belt for central government policies, in Italy, Fascist hyper-centralization had left local government emasculated – though this would change through force of circumstance during the conflict itself.

It is a commonplace that the French Third Republic's chronic ministerial instability hampered effective policy-making. In the case of passive defence,[8] however, this was palliated by the personal interest taken by some of the foremost figures of interwar French politics, and by underlying continuities in their preferences. Legislation was filled out by a growing avalanche of decrees, circulars, notices and instructions, which were then implemented with more or less success locally.[9]

It was André Maginot, during his first period as War Minister, who issued France's first interwar passive defence text, destined for government rather than the general public. Maginot's Instructions of 1922–3, largely based on World War One experience, identified major passive defence needs and went into some detail on issues of sirens, blackout measures and shelters, focusing particularly on the protection of administrative centres, factories and rail links.[10] Maginot stressed the importance of adequate peacetime preparation, but appeared to mean stocking adequate materials (such as blue paint for blackout purposes). The War Ministry would safeguard military installations, businesses would be expected to protect their employees at work, and local authorities would be responsible for the general public; no major administrative reorganization or increase in spending was proposed.

The Maginot text was superseded in November 1931 by a new Practical Instruction on Passive Defence against Air Attack drawn up under Pierre Laval, who combined the offices of Premier and Interior Minister. The previous February, less than two weeks after his appointment, Laval had signed the creation of France's General Inspectorate of Air Defences and the appointment of its first Inspector-General – the 74-year-old Marshal Philippe Pétain, who had just stepped down as Inspector-General of the Army. The Inspector-General was charged with 'investigating the relative importance of the various means of active and passive defence' against air attack.[11] The two central figures of Vichy France were thus also central to France's early civil defence policy.

Like its predecessor, Laval's Instruction was more 'practical' for the administration than for individuals.[12] But it was more systematic than Maginot's. It outlined a civil defence structure, running from central government (the Interior Minister, assisted by a High Committee for Passive Defence), to France's 90 *départements*, down to towns and cities. Here, urban committees (which prefects might create on their own initiative), chaired by the mayor, were to bring together representatives of key local services and establish planning subcommittees on blackout or evacuation, for example. The Instruction also tried to prioritize general security measures (look-out, alarms, and blackout), preventive measures (shelters, evacuation and propaganda), and curative measures (fire-fighting and anti-gas services). It recognized both the state's responsibility to protect its own administration and major public services, and the possible contribution of voluntary associations. Laval's Instruction placed civil defence firmly onto the agenda for France's prefects and mayors. But it brought no legal force and no budget credits. Local authorities, on whom much of the burden would fall, were left to finance new measures themselves. Few did.[13]

The legal force, but little money, was supplied by the Law Organizing Passive Defence on Metropolitan Territory, passed under the Pierre-Étienne Flandin ministry on 8 April 1935.[14] For the first time passive defence was made a requirement across metropolitan France. The need for additional personnel was recognized, and provision made to recruit volunteers and military reservists. A clearer division of responsibilities was set out, with, for example, *départements* in charge of evacuation and the protection of their own services while municipalities organized look-out and blackout arrangements, rubble clearance, and disinfection after gas attacks. The state's responsibility for protecting services of 'national interest' such as the telephone network was reaffirmed. But the law of 1935 was still more focused on safeguarding essential services than on protecting the public. Financial provisions depended on whatever was available in national budgets. While prefects could now require municipalities to undertake essential measures, the extra spending they could demand was tightly limited. And although the law officially gave the interior minister an overall co-ordinating role, it also extended the military's authority over passive defence if a state of siege was declared. The spate of subsequent decrees did nothing to clarify matters; by 1937 passive defence was being pulled between the ministries of Air, War, and Interior.[15]

Many of these issues were resolved by the long-awaited Law on the General Organization of the Nation for Wartime of 11 July 1938, and a flurry of linked passive defence decrees over the following year.[16] Henceforth, responsibility for co-ordinating passive defence lay with the Ministry of National Defence. The minister was Édouard Daladier, who had also been France's Premier since 10 April. The Defence ministry was given a new Passive Defence Directorate, and his decree of 29 July placed the protection of civilians and property at the heart of passive defence. The decree of 12 November, crucially, established that central government would cover capital spending, including, for example, blackout systems for urban lighting, sirens, and above all shelters. This general principle suffered two exceptions: business premises previously identified as responsible for their own protection were not included, and municipalities were allowed to undertake urgent spending themselves. The recruitment of passive defence workers from among municipal employees, volunteers, reservists, and members of the armed forces was covered in a decree of 30 January 1939; a census of urban cellars for possible use as shelters was required in one of 24 February. Decrees in the spring of 1939 gave assistance to firms to cover their spending, allowed expropriations for passive defence needs, set the price and distribution system for gas-masks, required arm bands for passive defence personnel and set out a pay structure for them. Passive defence classes became compulsory throughout the education system from May 1939, and towns were required to organize regular exercises.[17] A detailed *Instruction Interministérielle Relative à l'Organisation Administrative de la Défense Passive* codified the main dispositions six weeks before war began. It demanded a propaganda effort through the radio, the cinema, specialized reviews, special trains, press articles, notices and leaflets, stands in exhibitions, and local lectures, as well as the teaching of schoolchildren.[18] This was paralleled by a new and comprehensive Practical Instruction replacing Laval's of 1931 and including, for example, a detailed chart setting out the passive defence organization expected in a typical *département*, and the composition of Urban Passive Defence Committees.[19]

By September 1939, then, France possessed – on paper – a comprehensive system of civil defence developed over nearly two decades. Integrating all levels of government in the centralized manner of the Jacobin Republic, it also reflected the energy that Daladier brought to war preparations, especially after Munich. Every aspect of the problem was covered by at least one text, usually several and often in great detail.

Italy, as a power which planned for war, might have been expected to take air defences very seriously. Legislation was straightforward to pass, given the destruction of Italy's democratic institutions between 1925 and 1927; no longer discussed in Parliament, as in France, laws were decided by the Fascist Grand Council. And indeed the Fascist regime began early passive defence preparations. A law on war discipline promulgated in 1925 stated in rather broad terms that all citizens had to take part in the moral and material defence of the nation.[20]

This was followed by more practical measures. In August 1928 the government issued a decree on the preparation for war of the Red Cross. Although not assigned the principal role in air raids, its first aid and social duties would continue, in the event of bombing; and despite its notional independence, it would come under War Ministry control in any conflict.[21] The decree became law in December 1928 and laid down a project for the protection of the whole country against raids with conventional bombs or gas attack, and establishing how the Red Cross in each province must achieve this.[22] Although by 1936 little had been done in terms of resources, the Red Cross had been reorganized around the central task of air raid protection, and local first aid posts, triage stations, sites for specialized treatment, and sites for the decontamination of human beings and materials had been set up.[23] Under a decree of September 1931, meanwhile, all cities of over 40,000 inhabitants had to organize emergency fire brigades.[24] The following year saw Italy's first specific law on air-raid shelters, regulating the construction of new tunnels in major urban centres to ensure their availability as shelters in wartime. This was followed, eight years later, by the law of May 1940 for the organization of the nation at war, which recognized the urgency of shelter provision in buildings of older construction (the vast majority of private buildings).[25] Under a law drafted by the Air Ministry from 1939, meanwhile, the protection of industrial sites, whether privately or publicly owned, became compulsory; concerned parties were required to prepare a passive defence plan within three months of the passage of the law, and implement the plan within three years of its approval – that is, by 1943. The War Ministry was charged with ensuring implementation.[26] Industrial buildings were classified into four categories, from essential sites, working directly for the military, whose protection was to be wholly covered by the state, to two intermediate categories where costs were to be shared between government and owners, to other industrial and commercial buildings the protection of which was entirely the owners' responsibility.[27]

These sectoral civil defence measures were paralleled by administrative reorganization. Italy, like France, faced the problem of fragmented administrative competences. In 1931 the War Ministry was given responsibility for air raid alarm systems and air defences – except for airports, defended by the Air Forces, and ports protected by the Navy – each answering to its own ministry. In 1932 passive defence came under the control of the War Ministry, although prefects, who remained responsible to the Interior Ministry, had to apply its directives. All this created overlapping responsibilities, confusion and conflicts.[28] These in turn provoked efforts at co-ordination. The War Ministry was to be aided by the Central Interministerial Committee for Anti-Aircraft Protection (CCIPAA), which brought together representatives of every ministry, of the Red Cross, of the Committee for Civil Mobilization, of the military chemical branch, and of the National Fascist Union of Engineers.[29]

A second, crucial, co-ordinating body, was the National Union for Anti-Aircraft Protection (UNPA), founded in August 1934.[30] Its statute, approved by law in May 1936, established UNPA's headquarters in Rome under War Ministry direction, and its principal task as disseminating knowledge of the dangers of air war throughout Italy. It was to produce propaganda, prepare the individual protection of the population, collect donations, oversee the construction of shelters for private citizens, distribute gas-masks (and ensure that firms purchased them for their employees), and organize volunteer groups to collaborate with the police, the Red Cross and the fire services. Propaganda took the form of courses in schools and institutions, public lectures, publications, posters, films, and the organization of 'days of anti-aircraft protection'. The UNPA had to persuade private landlords to build shelters and to show them how. Its volunteers were to secure public compliance with regulations, including blackout rules and general air-raid discipline, and assist in removing debris and restoring normal life after raids.[31]

However different their perspectives on the coming air war, therefore, democratic France and Fascist Italy had both, by 1939, established legal frameworks for passive defence, and had attempted to tackle problems of co-ordination. There were important differences, however, in the application on the ground of centrally decided measures. In France, the evidence suggests that the formal structures set out by law and decree were indeed created at local level, though at varying speeds, across the country. In the *département* of the Nord, with its experience of German occupation from 1914 to 1918, a passive defence committee was created on 15 June 1932 in line with Laval's 1931 Instruction.[32] In Seine-Inférieure, which included France's biggest Channel port (Le Havre) and a major industrial and rail centre (Rouen), the prefect convened a committee in June 1929.[33] Brest, France's major Atlantic naval port, had a city committee by June 1929, Lyon in 1930, Rouen in 1931, Nantes – with Saint-Nazaire, the major industrial centre of the Atlantic coast – by 1933 at latest. In the Nord, fully 56 municipalities had set up committees by early 1934.[34] By contrast, the prefect of Calvados waited until July 1935, the city of Rennes till 1936.[35]

The first task of a new committee was to draw up a passive defence plan, dividing the town or city into sectors, programming shelters, command posts, first-aid posts, and emergency teams in each, and taking city-wide measures such as blackout arrangements and sirens. Early starters received encouragement from Pétain. The Marshal inspected Rouen and approved its plan in 1931, and chaired a meeting of the Seine-Inférieure committee in 1933; he commented (generally favourably) on Brest's plan submitted the following year; he lectured to an invited audience in the central industrial city of Saint-Étienne in 1931 or 1932.[36] Attentions from the summit continued after Pétain's departure in 1934. Édouard Herriot, mayor of Lyon, former Prime Minister, and President of the Chamber of Deputies, aspired to make his city, and the *département* of Rhône around it, a model of passive defence preparation. On 20 February 1939, General Maurice Gamelin, Commander-in-Chief of the French Army, chaired a special meeting in Lyon that included General Daudin, Director of Passive Defence at the Defence Ministry, and the prefects of the Rhône and of the neighbouring departments of Ain and Isère.[37] The systematic character of national legislation, then, appears to have given France a fairly comprehensive network of local passive defence bodies by 1939. The impression given to the British General Staff in 1938 was that 'France's passive defences were far more advanced than our own, although probably less complete than those of Germany'.[38]

In Italy, as in France, prefects were central to policy implementation. Responsibility for evacuations, alarm systems, shelters, and every other aspect of passive defence, lay chiefly with them. For example, the co-ordinating role of the CCIPAA was meant to be replicated by provincial committees, convened and presided over by prefects. These would include the podestà (government-nominated officials who had replaced elected mayors as municipal government heads), civil engineers of the Genio Civile, delegates from the three armed forces, local industrialists, and managers from railways, fire brigades, and utility companies.[39] It does not, however, appear that these committees functioned as regularly as their French counterparts. Nor did France's local passive defence plans have any equivalent in Italy. Only in war conditions were the powers and spheres of intervention of local administrations extended, not formally but in practice, as they took on tasks which the Fascist state had centralized for almost two decades. Then, the regime's failure to impose 'totalitarian' control on Italian life from above meant that local administrators had use their own initiative – often without any pre-established scheme.[40]

PROTECTING THE POPULATION: EVACUATION, SHELTERS, GAS-MASKS

The obvious defence against bombing was to leave the danger zone. Both French and Italian governments viewed evacuation as an, if not the, essential form of civilian protection. But it could never suffice; towns and cities were targets precisely because they concentrated industries and services vital to war, which needed people to work them. At least these essential persons, and those who serviced their needs, required protection on the spot. Evacuation on the one hand, and shelters plus masks on the other, were therefore complementary. But both expedients challenged governments. Transplanting millions of people in acceptable conditions presented enormous logistical and political difficulties; shelters and gas-masks cost money.

In France, Maginot's 1923 Instruction firmly stated that 'There is no case for generalizing the construction of bomb-proof shelters' – even in hospitals.[41] Direct hits, said Maginot, were rare; trenches, or reinforced cellars, or disused quarries, or natural features such as caves offered adequate, cheap protection against blast or splinters; full protection for all was an impossible fantasy. Eight years later, Annexe 7 to Laval's 1931 instruction added that if civilians could not be sheltered, they might at least be evacuated – sealing the link between the two aspects of civil defence policy.[42] The main thrust of Italian policy was comparable. From the early 1930s, the CCIPAA began studying schemes for civilian protection against air attack, but soon realized that financial constraints precluded a fully effective system. General Giannuzzi Savelli admitted in 1931 that the safest measure would be to reduce the number of people needing protection – by removing as many as possible.[43]

Evacuation plans

The need for evacuation plans, then, was recognized early in the 1930s in France and Italy. Even before the logistical issues were confronted, however, the first difficulty lay in deciding who needed evacuating and who should stay put.

In France, the eastern frontier and the Paris region were earmarked for large-scale, permanent evacuation (*éloignement*) to western *départements* as a matter of course. In addition, however, Annexe 7 to the 1931 Instruction noted that while enemy aircraft could reach any point on French territory, other 'sensitive areas' were vulnerable. As sheltering the whole civilian population of such areas would be 'materially impossible', large-scale evacuation (*dispersion*) was needed here too. Mayors were to divide the population into three categories: non-essential personnel to be permanently evacuated; artisans, shopkeepers or administrative employees to be evacuated by night, but kept at work in the city by day; and essential personnel permanently needed in the city. Prefects would then assign destinations to the first two categories, preferably within the same *département*. The remaining population however, should be protected; in no case should more people than could be sheltered remain in a sensitive area in wartime.[44]

If Annexe 7 appeared to guarantee shelter to residents of 'sensitive areas', therefore, it limited the number expected to need it; large-scale evacuation was placed at the centre of passive defence. Mayors across France soon took Annexe 7 as a formula to massage local shelter requirements downwards. Brest, distant from Germany but vulnerable as a naval base, expected 11,000 of its 61,000 inhabitants to be mobilized, 5,000 to leave voluntarily, 20,000 to be evacuated and 16,000 to disperse at night into nearby villages, leaving just 9,000 permanent residents. Prefect Bollaert of the Rhône planned for the departure of roughly half of Lyon's population of 570,000. Lorient's Passive Defence Committee expected to shelter just one-third of the town's 40,409 inhabitants. Rennes planned 66,777 evacuees, nearly half the population, Saint-Étienne 60,000 evacuees out of 190,000 inhabitants. The *département* of Seine, including Paris and its suburbs, programmed the evacuation of 423,874 French schoolchildren (the non-French were to remain with their parents). Even small towns in rural Normandy such as Bayeux or Honfleur prepared evacuation plans.[45]

Such calculations rested on a number of assumptions. Evacuation would need to be complete for all concerned; it would require adequate transport arrangements to clear destinations. The Paris Prefecture of Police, in a pamphlet closely imitated across the French provinces, advised all persons who could to leave major cities in case of danger.[46] An Interior Ministry instruction of 1938 set out a model evacuation train, well-policed and chiefly composed of converted goods wagons.[47] Destinations were clearly defined. Each eastern border *département*, from Nord and Pas-de-Calais down to Var and Alpes-Maritimes, had a corresponding reception *département* in the rural centre and west.[48] The *département* of Calvados possessed a timetable for the transport of evacuees from particular *arrondissements* of Paris to Norman towns in the first days of mobilization.[49]

Nevertheless, the plans, and their implications for shelters, as outlined in Annexe 7, were flawed. In the first place, some urban populations could hardly be expected to drop. Military or industrial installations, the defining feature of a 'sensitive area', would expand in wartime. Moreover, for calculations about evacuation and shelters to work, all persons selected for evacuation had to leave. This required compulsion. Not explicitly stated in Annexe 7 of the 1931 Instruction, compulsion was certainly implied by its distinction between voluntary evacuees and others. But the means of compulsion were never created. Its status, as mayor Métayer of Rouen reminded his prefect in 1938, was very uncertain.[50] The ambiguity persisted into summer 1939. On the one hand, the Interministerial Instruction of 20 July maintained a restrictive notion of populations to be 'maintained' in cities: public service personnel, workers for defence industries, passive defence personnel, plus service personnel such as shopworkers or artisans.[51] On the other hand, in May Daudin had told Prefect Angeli of Finistère that 'there is no legal text compelling an individual to abandon his home in towns submitted to *dispersion*'; the best way to achieve evacuation was to educate the civilians concerned and provide free transport and suitable accommodation.[52] How the latter was to be done was unclear, especially as another central government communication, from the Interior Ministry to the Prefect of Calvados, had stressed that details of accommodation for evacuees were to be kept secret, and especially that householders should not be told of possible requisitioning measures.[53] The absence of any measures to requisition private transport would also hinder the success of any evacuation.[54] Daudin's statement to Angeli was reaffirmed by the Practical Instruction of 26 June 1939:

> Evacuation (*dispersion*), whose main aim is to diminish the density of the population of a conurbation by spreading it across a limited perimeter within the *département*, only applies, in principle, to those inhabitants who have expressed the wish to take advantage of it, and with the reservation that the latter are not requisitioned for any reason linked to the defence or the functioning of their locality.[55]

On the eve of war, therefore, the main basis on which French mayors had been invited to calculate how many city-dwellers to evacuate and how many to shelter was undermined; and evacuation when real hostilities began was unimaginably chaotic.

In Italy, meanwhile, Fascist rhetoric dictated (predictably) that evacuations had to take place with order and discipline. A census in 1931 sought to establish how many might evacuate under their own steam (people who normally left cities during holidays), how many were required to stay during wartime, and how many needed to be moved compulsorily. For the latter, it was necessary to organize transport, and to find hosting communes in the provinces. To minimize transport difficulties, evacuation had to precede military mobilization. The 1931 census put the population to be evacuated from all cities of over 100,000 inhabitants at 5 million. The population of towns with fewer than 20,000 inhabitants, where evacuees were to be hosted, was 30 million. The hosting communes, Giannuzzi Savelli calculated, would thus see their population rise by one-sixth.[56] But neither central nor local government in Italy attempted to translate these figures to the local level as the French had.

Standards issued between 1934 and 1939 for evacuation of civilians from cities with over 100,000 inhabitants had no precise plan, simply suggesting that part of the population needed to move to the surrounding countryside, preferably during the evenings and with the help of relatives, so as to minimize costs to the state.[57] This was partly due to the Italian administration's centralized character, a feature that would change abruptly with the war. But all Giannuzzi Savelli's 1931 calculations were to prove unrealistic when mobilization began.

In the days after the outbreak of war in September 1939, the regime issued a series of measures, including a communication published by all major newspapers inviting women, children and elderly people living in large cities in Piedmont, Lombardy, Liguria, Tuscany, Lazio, Campania, Sicily and Sardinia to move to smaller towns or the countryside if possible.[58] This public statement is an example of the ambiguity of Italy's 'non-belligerence' policy. Although not ready to bring Italy into the conflict, Mussolini had no intention of staying neutral permanently; society therefore had to be prepared for war before the regime declared it.[59] It is also an early example, among very many, of the regime's uncertain and piecemeal military and civil directives on evacuation.[60] At the same time, however, efforts were made from a propaganda perspective, with the staging of civil defence exercises which included mock evacuations. In 1939 the prefects organized exercises in cities likely to become targets and divided citizens into those who would stay, those who acted as voluntary evacuees, and those who pretended to require compulsory evacuation. The first were given a 'permanence card', the second moved under their own transport after informing their *capo fabbricato* (the UNPA's 'block leaders' in each apartment block), and the last pretended to bring with them up to two pieces of luggage weighing no more than 25 kilos. An itinerary was fixed towards host communes, although the 'evacuees' stopped short of completing the journey and were returned to their homes. Meanwhile, caretakers looked after homes left empty.[61] As in France, evacuations were envisaged not only for industrial cities but also for border areas: Piedmontese villages were prepared for evacuation from February 1940.[62]

A few days before Italy entered the conflict, the War Ministry drew up two lists of cities from which voluntary evacuation could begin. The first list, of 28 localities, included industrial, frontier and port cities, and cities of artistic importance like Venice, Florence and the capital, where evacuations could take place within 20 days of mobilization; the second listed 27 localities considered at lower risk, where evacuations could be postponed. However, no compulsory evacuation was envisaged.[63] In May 1940 it became clear that the transport demands of evacuation clashed with those of mobilization. Trains, trams and other types of public transport were all commandeered by the military, leaving evacuation to start after the mobilization period.[64]

If Italy's practical experience of evacuation after the start of hostilities was indecisive, that of France turned to disaster. The initial evacuation of September 1939 went relatively smoothly, both from the frontier *départements* (thanks in part to the assistance of the army, as yet not militarily engaged) and from Paris. Some 550,000 Parisians, chiefly voluntary evacuees plus officially evacuated schoolchildren, about one-fifth of the capital's population, left. But many returned when the expected massive German air raids failed to occur, and when stories of neglect and mistreatment of children in reception centres began to circulate. That those who sought refuge with their families, rather than in officially assigned centres, were not entitled to free transport was another source of grievance.[65] By early 1940, therefore, the return of evacuees was officially tolerated, schools were reopened, and evacuation plans for defence industries in frontier zones held back.[66]

When mass evacuation did occur, in the face of the German onslaught of May 1940 (including air raids on Holland, Belgium, and the towns of North-Eastern France), advance planning failed altogether. By mid-June some 10 million French refugees were on the road. Few experiences could be further removed than France's *exode* of 1940 from Annexe 7's insistence that evacuation plans needed to be fixed in detail in peacetime, and executed in a calm and timely manner.[67] Not only did the *exode* signal the bankruptcy of France's pre-war evacuation policy; its confusion, with accompanying levels of looting and insecurity, were a caution against evacuation for the rest of the conflict.

Shelters

The challenge of protecting people against bombs and gas was as great as that of moving them about in their millions. In France, Annexe 7 to the 1931 Instruction required shelter for everyone remaining in 'sensitive areas'.[68] This was ambitious, even supposing the success of large-scale evacuations. Annexe 4 to the 1931 Instruction, published in 1932, had, it is true, reiterated some of Maginot's earlier caveats: complete defence against bombs was a chimera, and reinforced-concrete underground shelters impossibly expensive. Basic, cheap protection should be achieved by using disused quarries, mines, natural caves, or tunnels; reinforced cellars; or trenches.[69] Municipalities, therefore, needed to assess shelter space already available (chiefly in cellars); to arrange reinforcement where necessary; and to allocate space and stock materials for digging trenches. Increasingly detailed standard requirements covered the dimensions of shelters, the size of bomb they should resist, the number of entrances, proofing against gas, and distance from buildings.[70] Later Notices, however, balanced these both with cost ceilings and with a new sense of urgency, suggesting that provisional trenches and cellar reinforcements might need to be done quickly, even with lowered standards.[71]

Financial constraint prevented the universal provision expected in Annexe 7. Although the law of 1935 made shelters for the public a municipal responsibility and empowered prefects to require local authorities to commit spending, there is no evidence that this power was exercised. In France, local authorities viewed passive defence as a national need which should be financed from national funds. Only with the law of July 1938 and the following November's decree was the principle adopted that the national budget should pay for passive defence investments. Thus while different mayors might plan shelters at different speeds, little spending was committed before 1939; even then, the money available was limited and projects had to respect technical specifications to win grants.

Brest and Rouen were both early starters in passive defence. Brest, by March 1933, had completed the basic work required by the instruction of 1931, and received Pétain's blessing. The police had listed available cellars; plans had been made, and labour and materials allocated, for digging trenches.[72] By the outbreak of war, however, these measures had been revealed as inadequate: in the winter of 1938–39, plans to shelter 4,239 primary school children consisted simply of grouping them on the ground floors of their schools.[73] Rouen's municipality, meanwhile, had also involved Pétain in its planning, from 1931; but on the eve of war, no more than 10 per cent of the city's population of over 120,000 (in addition to some 110,000 suburban residents) could be sheltered.[74]

Lyon should, in principle, have presented an exemplary record. Prefect Bollaert's account of passive defence in the *département* of the Rhône, which Lyon dominates, showed that cellars for 130,000 people, out of a total population of some 570,000, had already been listed by late 1936.[75] A national centre for trade fairs, Lyon held a big Passive Defence Exposition in the autumn of 1938. Herriot boasted that foreign governments would take notice of the Lyonnais' 'determination to face any eventuality' when they started building trenches, and that his city's Passive Defence Building had no equivalent in all France.[76] Yet Lyon's tally at midsummer 1939 was modest for a city of over half a million people: 7,864 cellars visited, 6,604 approved as suitable, 1,495 complete plans established, and 1,195 notices of work issued to landlords. Just five public shelters, and five for administrative staff, had been completed. And Herriot faced a barrage of questions in the city council in September about neighbourhoods with no shelters at all.[77]

In Marseille, traditionally Lyon's rival for the status of second city of France, a mere 117 cellars had been identified as suitable by November 1939. No more than 10 per cent of the population of some 600,000 had any serious shelter provision by late 1939.[78] In Nantes, the secretary-general of the prefecture berated the municipal engineers' failure to get a grip on the issues; but the prefecture itself could not say how many civilians would be dispersed into the *département*.[79] Nantes had some 24,000 places in shelters (for a population estimated at 180,000) by the end of 1939, 7,000 of them in the most summary trenches.[80] In Lorient, meanwhile, with an obvious target in its naval shipyards, shelter provision before mid-1938 had been negligible; a shelter programme had barely started by the defeat of 1940.[81] In Saint-Étienne, a major centre of France's arms industry, the passive defence committee meeting in March 1937 noted that an 'infinitesimal' number of cellars surveyed were suitable as shelters, but suggested no remedy.[82] By January 1940, the town had a well-protected 'command' shelter below the Town Hall; but in the south-east canton, housing nearly a quarter of the city's population of 190,000, just 425 places were available in reinforced cellars.[83]

Rennes, finally, was a low-priority town where an attack was considered unlikely. On 30 September 1939, the prefect of Ille-et-Vilaine informed mayor François Château that out of his request for FF25 million, only FF200,000 would be forthcoming that year.[84] Central government was more generous in 1940, with credits of FF421,885 announced for trenches that April. An intensive digging programme followed.[85] The fall of France halted it. Rennes was bombed on 17 June.

On the eve of the defeat of 1940, then, few French towns could shelter more than one in ten of their inhabitants, some many fewer.[86] The quality of shelters, moreover, was often poor. As early as December 1939, for example, assistant-mayor Thiéfaine of Nantes requested finance to help re-line flooded trench shelters.[87] Central and local government had grasped the issues clearly – and taken tardy, limited action. The relative abundance of one national budget, in 1939, when FF820 million were allocated for passive defence, compared with total defence spending of FF92.7 billion, only partially compensated for the lean years. Moreover, to build deep shelters, like the small number made available in Paris, would have cost FF46 billion simply for the population expected to remain in the capital.[88] France's population in 1940 was inadequately protected even against the raids of the 1930s, let alone those inflicted by the Allies after 1942.

In Italy Giannuzzi Savelli admitted in 1931 that extending passive defence measures to all Italian cities would be impossibly complex and costly. Italy's policy, in principle, was to be selective. Priority was given to industrial cities and surrounding areas, transportation nodes, marshalling yards, major bridges, dams, and power stations.[89] State workers also needed protection. In April 1935, the Ministry of Public Works requested that Finance Ministry branches across Italy produce shelter construction plans. The same year saw plans produced for shelters in prefects' headquarters, police stations and provincial administrations. Prisons, under a Justice Ministry decision of 1935, were also to have shelters. Harbour offices in port cities (*capitanerie*) also needed them. The Taranto *capitaneria*, for example, queried the Genio Civile in August 1938 about plans for air and gas shelters in its basements.[90]

New buildings, too, were supposed to incorporate shelters. The law of 1932 required new railway, road, metro and funicular tunnels to be bomb-resistant and to possess multiple entrances, an air chamber between external and internal entrances, artificial ventilation, and independent lighting. A decree of 1936 added requirements on air filtration and 'accessory equipment', such as a first-aid area, toilets, drinking water, fire-fighting equipment, and a telephone. Costs were to be met by firms commissioning the tunnels.[91] In September 1936, the regime also required all new homes to be equipped, at developers' expense, with air-raid shelters; a subsequent law prescribed building materials (mostly reinforced concrete).[92] Another law of 1939 added further details on materials and prescribed the withdrawal of building permits if shelter requirements were not met.[93]

Yet at the local level nothing practical seemed to be undertaken, especially for private citizens. In September 1938, the president of the Turin branch of UNPA threatened to resign because he no longer wanted to deceive the population about the effectiveness of existing protection. Not only were old buildings (the overwhelming majority) unsafe, but even new ones were dangerous because their shelters lacked ventilation.[94] In 1939 only 259 public shelters existed throughout Italy, with a total capacity of 72,000; a further 415 shelters for industrial buildings could host 43,000 employees – for a total population of 44 million.[95] As the War Ministry was aware, no resources existed to implement the 1939 plan to protect industrial buildings; when the requirement of 740 million lire was brought to Mussolini's attention in July 1939, the Duce explained that the money was not currently available. Simply to protect those industries most at risk would require 160 million lire and two more years.[96] As for privately owned industrial buildings, the project fell foul of the 'negligence' and 'reluctance which animates private owners when they have to sustain expenses for constructions that are not lucrative either immediately or in the future'.[97] Luigi Gambelli, president of the Central Committee for Anti-Aircraft Protection, complained in November 1939 that many industries were not co-operating, that he was still awaiting plans, and that there was little comprehension of air-raid precautions.[98]

Historic cities also required protection of their cultural heritage. Writing on the protection of Rome in 1938, Giannuzzi Savelli stressed the need to 'proceed to a rational, ordered evacuation of everything that is possible to be transported, according to a predisposed plan and to suitable destinations, chosen with care'. Everything else should be protected with sandbags.[99] However, most preparations to protect art galleries and monuments were only made hurriedly once the war had started, even in a city like Venice.[100]

The imminence of hostilities did, it is true, concentrate official minds. The law of May 1940 for the organization of the nation at war recognized the urgency of the provision of air-raid shelters in older buildings.[101] In Genoa, a city clearly at risk, the prefect required all private landlords to provide a shelter wherever they had at least one room that met minimum specifications for an 'emergency shelter'. Landlords and administrators of apartment blocks were to provide UNPA, no later than 30 November 1940, with a list of suitable rooms, on forms available from the Fasci headquarters; the city council would meet costs.[102] In Italy, in short, serious, local-level attention to shelters effectively began with the declaration of war and the first RAF raids on northern cities.

Gas

Fortunately for both countries, the threat of gas attack failed to materialize. Of course the two governments took the danger seriously. Gas, including the gas-proofing of shelters, featured strongly in pre-war French propaganda for passive defence. Gas detection and decontamination teams were part of every passive defence plan. But a shelter policy that relied so heavily on trenches could never afford much protection against gas. And the sole means of individual protection, the gas-mask, was practically unavailable *en masse* until after the decree of November 1938. A decree on the distribution of masks (stating that recipients should pay for them) appeared only in March 1939; tobacconists were to issue tickets for masks, and their reward (50 centimes per ticket) was only fixed in May.[103] By 1 July 1939, Lyon had just 2,478 masks for the emergency services and 10,000 for the public, with 30,000 more awaited.[104] Neither Nantes, nor Brest, nor Rennes, had received masks in significant numbers by autumn 1939, though Nantes had 15,000 (enough for about one-tenth of the population) by the year's end.[105] These western towns might, it is true, be considered as low-priority areas. But Boulogne-Billancourt, a likelier target, was still distributing its masks in April 1940.[106]

Italy too expected a chemical war against cities. The potential of chemical weapons and their likely use featured in pre-war scientific studies at all levels, and in a 1935 high-school textbook for chemistry and mineralogy courses, prepared under the Education Ministry programme of 1933. While individual defence, it said, would come mostly from gas-masks, gas shelters would provide collective defence; but their complicated system of air filters and ventilation equipment would be too expensive to be installed in every major centre.[107]

In July 1938, two Italian engineers visited shelters in Berlin and reported that while some technical equipment, such as air-raid sirens, was more powerful in Germany, most preparations in the two countries were not dissimilar. However, greater attention was paid by the Germans to chemical-weapon defence, and German shelters were built as gas shelters. Airlocks were required for German shelters but left out of Italian regulations.[108] Like the French, then, the Italians fell back on gas-masks. A 1938 radio advertisement reminded citizens to contact UNPA and acquire a mask. Not only did a mask ensure personal safety; from a national, patriotic perspective, it offered 'an increased resistance of the country within anti-aircraft protection plans'.[109] In 1938 a law extended compulsory gas-mask use to all industrial and state workers ('the distribution of masks to employees of any field of industry must be totalitarian'), with the expenses borne by industrialists and the local state administration respectively. The time-scale, however, was a long one, stretching over ten years from July 1938.[110] Nor were masks provided free; in July 1939 they were listed at 32 lire in shops in Turin, after an Interior Ministry request to prefects that citizens not listed for evacuation must buy one.[111] In Milan, the prefect ordered that landlords provide tenants with masks, but Fascist informers reported that although landlords had paid large sums to UNPA, the masks did not materialize. Rumours began to spread: 'no mystery is made of the fact that no one knows where the money has gone, a natural inference since when those concerned were asked, the UNPA offices had not been able to provide full explanations'.[112] In June 1940, after the first raids on Turin, UNPA recommended that 'those who could afford it buy a gas mask'; no advice was given to those who could not.[113] Contrary to Douhet's predictions, the inadequate precautions of French and Italians were never put to the test.[114]

EDUCATION, PROPAGANDA AND MOBILIZATION

A public policy issue, civil defence also demanded the mobilization of the population. Douhet, while insisting on the importance of offensive air warfare, had stressed the need for a population morally and materially prepared for the worst and able to '*take it*'.[115] A successful blackout required civilian co-operation; reinforced emergency services would require volunteers prepared to risk their lives under bombs. In peacetime, such mobilization presented political difficulties: it entailed an acceptance that war would come despite every government's claim to seek peace, and that enemy aircraft could penetrate national air defences. Publicity, too, though essential to educate and mobilize the population, ran the risk of causing alarm or betraying preparations to potential enemies. Mobilization took numerous forms, of which the most obvious were securing compliance with blackout measures and recruiting passive defence personnel.

The approaches of democratic France and Fascist Italy to mobilization might be expected to have differed strongly. Douhet's views, though influential in the French Air Ministry, were far from uncontested; in Italy, by contrast, he almost had the status of an official theoretician. France's doctrine of air warfare, like the rest of French military doctrine, centred on the defence of national territory; Italy waged offensive air warfare on the Spanish Republicans from 1937. The French Third Republic, even under Daladier's relatively strong government, had to mobilize through persuasion within civil society; in Italy the Fascist Party was central to any task of mobilization. In practice, however, the challenges the two regimes faced were comparable; so were many, though not all, of their approaches – and their limited success in achieving their goals.

In France, official presentations of the threat of air attack, and of war generally, suffered from an obvious contradiction. The Maginot Line stood as a symbol, ever-present in newsreels and even feature films, of a promise that whatever happened, the French were protected and would be spared the horrors of the dearly-bought victory of 1918.[116] Yet as the Instruction of 1931 acknowledged, 'active defence, no matter how well developed, cannot completely protect the population and public services'.[117] From the early 1930s on, a crescendo of posters, brochures, radio broadcasts and press articles detailed official information, regulations and recommendations, on all aspects of passive defence including evacuation, cellar surveys, or gas-proofing a room. The government issued increasingly specialized guidance, for example to the metal and the oil industries. The French had huge numbers of passive defence brochures to choose from, whether official or produced by weeklies like *L'Illustration*. They made clear that, however good French air defences were, air raids would be far heavier, and more extensive, than those of 1914–18. Though all conveyed much the same advice – to leave towns and other vulnerable locations if possible at times of international tension, and to take elementary precautions (such as locating shelters, spreading sand in lofts, keeping a gas-mask, respecting blackout requirements) if obliged to stay put – the level of detail and illustration varied considerably, with the more ambitious offering advice on strutting cellars and digging trenches.[118] The government, however, wanted more. Daladier asked prefects to enlist mayors in the propaganda effort; the Maritime Prefect of Brest asked cinema managers to put out a message on blackout regulations to encourage a compliance so far lacking; the prefect of Finistère wrote to the mayor offering a series of passive-defence films for loan.[119]

Successive governments also enlisted the contribution of voluntary groups. Associations appeared in Laval's *Instruction Pratique* of 1931; their role was reiterated in that of 1939, when a National Passive Defence Co-ordination Committee was founded in Paris under Daladier's instructions to co-ordinate their activities.[120] Associations in France had been lobbying for better air defences for a decade before the war. In January 1930, for example, mayors received a letter from the newly formed Comité Français pour la Propagande Aéronautique, which aimed to sensitize French opinion to the danger of bombing and to provide against surprise raids at the start of a future war.[121] The Union Nationale pour la Défense Aérienne et pour la Protection des Populations Civiles was active in Nantes and in Lyon, where its local branches published bi-monthly magazines; the Lyon union also took part in passive defence training programmes from 1935–6, and claimed credit for lobbying for a passive-defence directorate within the Defence Ministry.[122] The Centre de Documentation pour la Protection des Populations Civiles contre les Bombardements Aériens produced digests of current legislation interspersed with short articles on foreign experiences.[123] A women's organization, the Assistantes du Devoir National, organized national passive defence congresses in Paris on 22 January 1938 and 4 February 1939. Louise Weiss, an activist for women's suffrage (later a *résistante* and later still a Gaullist MEP) founded a centre in Paris to educate the public in civil defence, running stands at the Salon d'Aéronautique in 1938 and at France's Ideal Home Exhibition. She later claimed that her organization taught some 500,000 women how to protect their homes.[124] Private business, meanwhile, maximized the dangers of air raids in order to sell products such as gas-masks, fire extinguishers, concrete, steel, or wooden reinforcements for cellars, or indeed life assurance, advertisements for all of which crowded into the passive-defence brochures.

Fascist Italy, by contrast, glorified war in the air. Official propaganda sought the creation of a national myth of air forces and of air defences, often described as the 'most fascist' weapon. Two figures came to symbolize the legend of the air forces in Italy in the 1930s: Douhet and Italo Balbo, pilot, reorganizer of the air forces and Air Minister between 1929 and 1933. Balbo's successful transatlantic flights in massed Savoia-Marchetti flying boats, and clever use of propaganda in the press and schools, contributed powerfully to Italy's air myth.[125] Douhet established the primacy of the air force (whose capabilities he exaggerated) over the army and the navy. He attached great importance to civilian reactions to bombing; populations would, in his view, turn against their own governments and demand surrender if not adequately defended. However, Douhet also believed that air defences required greater resources than bomber squadrons, and that bombing should therefore be carried to the enemy. Civilians at home, meanwhile, must be prepared for the worst, because a population that was 'led to believe in the efficacy of aerial defence would be frightened and their morale lowered if they found out that it did not protect in practice.'[126] Douhet's 1921 analysis and the myths propagated by Balbo in the 1930s encapsulate the worst feature, from a military viewpoint, of the Fascist regime: the gap between an expansionist foreign policy and the military preparation supposed to underpin it.[127] This was particularly the case as the increase in military expenditure from 1935 was directed, not to rearmament or to the preparation of society for war, but to the conquest of Ethiopia and to intervention in Spain.[128] Spending on active air defences fell vastly below what was identified as necessary: in February 1940, four months before Italy's entry into the war, the Supreme Defence Commission reported to Mussolini that fewer than one-third of the necessary anti-aircraft guns were available, and another third could not be ready before the end of 1942.[129]

Italian passive defence propaganda was disseminated by UNPA, in agreement with the Fascist Party, through the radio, newspapers and specific publications. In 1938 the War Ministry published a book of passive defence instructions, divided into separate files. The first covered the organization of passive defence, with appendices for prefects on practice exercises. The second gave detailed descriptions of explosive, incendiary and chemical bombs, with an extra chapter on germ warfare. Subsequent files explored alarms, blackout levels, shelters, camouflaging targets, and evacuation. Protection from attack focused on gas-masks, the reclamation of land polluted by chemical weapons, preventive measures against fire and fire-fighting operations, and the protection of the country's artistic and cultural heritage. The book ended with information on air-raid precautions in private homes, the tasks of the anti-aircraft police, and bomb disposal. The book was addressed to prefects, factory owners, heads of apartment blocks, fire brigades and other public defence units, and ordinary citizens. Civilians were told that while air defences could not offer full protection from attack, active defences could hinder the enemy's progress towards its targets, and passive defence would re-establish normal life after raids; none of these defences, however, could work without the 'strong collaboration of the population'.[130] Readers were instructed to observe air-raid precautions, to move calmly ('at a fast pace, but without running or screaming') towards shelters (or else towards any available tunnel or arcade) when the alarm sounded, and to respect the blackout (partial throughout the war, total during alerts) at home and on cars and bicycles. Only peacetime preparations, the War Ministry warned, would ensure the rapid blackout of entire provinces when war came.[131]

Another book on civil defence, published in 1938 and reprinted twice before May 1940, was written by the vice-president of the CCIPAA for inclusion in the primary and junior school curriculum, as required by a decision of Italy's National Education Ministry taken at the beginning of 1939. Future wars, the author predicted, would mostly be fought from the air, and would turn all civilians into combatants, obliging them to know how to protect themselves.[132] As well as providing advice on air-raid precautions, the book showed pictures of Spanish cities bombed by Italian and German aircraft, indicating what Italy had been able to inflict upon others. An image explaining the effects of mustard-gas on the human body showed the legs of a black person – possibly an Abyssinian victim of the Italian aggression of 1935–6.[133] Schoolchildren also received propaganda material on air-raid exercises; trenches were dug near school buildings to enable their participation.[134]

How far were the Italian and French publics mobilized? For maximum effectiveness, the public needed to feel that precautions were necessary, that governments could be generally trusted in relation to the war, and that they were doing everything possible to deliver adequate defences. Perceptions, in each case, were linked to public views of the war as a whole in 1939–40. The French entered the war in a state of moral and political confusion, shaped by bitter but also shifting political confrontations since 1934; the Italians were increasingly apprehensive at being dragged into Germany's war of choice.[135] Neither context was very favourable to large-scale mobilization for war; the desire for self-preservation was not enough to ensure full co-operation with civil defence precautions. This was reflected in responses both to government propaganda generally and to civil defence measures like the blackout.

While France, as we have observed, saw significant activity within civil society, it also reflected fractures within it. Indeed, closer examination of air defence associations reveals their close links with the military, with the France of well-entrenched notables, and with the anti-Republican Right. The official patron of the Passive Defence congresses was Pétain. The president of the Comité Français pour la Propagande Aéronautique was Marshal Lyautey and its vice-President the tyre magnate André Michelin; its Air Defence Committee was chaired by Colonel de la Rocque, founder of the far-right *Croix de Feu*. The Union Nationale pour la Défense Aérienne had similar links with the military, and with local business organizations. The Assistantes du Devoir National was launched in 1931 by the Union Nationale des Officiers de Réserve (UNOR), with Marshal Foch's widow as its patron; though later open to all comers, it was initially a movement of officers' wives.[136] In the divided France of the late 1930s, such organizations were inevitably linked with the militarist Right, at a time when much of the Left was still pacifist.[137] Even Weiss, who had worked for Franco-German reconciliation before 1933, was accused by schoolteachers at the Salon de l'Aéronautique in 1938 of indoctrinating children with militarist ideas.[138] And her passive-defence demonstrations in hotels and factories met with 'mockery as we put on our masks and protective clothing'.[139]

Despite the threat of war, indeed, many people found it hard to take passive defence seriously. The press in Brest reported an anti-gas exercise as a spectacle, in which oilskin-clad firemen were followed by more elaborately dressed disinfection teams, 'à la grande joie des curieux'.[140] A course of public lectures on passive defence in Nantes in 1938–9 was poorly attended (although the opposite was claimed for neighbouring Saint-Nazaire).[141] Moreover, it was hard to convince the public until the authorities did more. A brochure drafted by the mayor of Rouen in spring 1938, for example, reminded the Rouennais that the city's defence plan had Pétain's approval, but all references to shelters and medical posts were in the future tense.[142]

The blackout offered another yardstick of the public's active co-operation. But getting blackout policy right was itself not straightforward. The Maginot Instruction of 1924 identified blackout, already used against night raids in World War One, as central to passive defence, but industry and essential services could not keep running in complete darkness.[143] Laval's 1931 Instruction, and the Instruction of 1939, therefore planned a 'normal' wartime regime of dimmed lighting with total or near-total blackout on military order when a raid threatened. [144] But the texts were surprisingly vague about precise measures. The Instruction of 1939 stressed that blackout measures could 'save a town from being bombed', but added that 'general rules were difficult to formulate' and that 'simple, effective solutions needed to be found for each case'.[145] Understandably, then, French towns addressed the issue at variable speeds. The city of Rouen began to consider it in July 1931, though its main decision then was to seek advice from the prefecture on the implications of power cuts. For gas lamps, conical shades and blue paint – widely adopted elsewhere – were favoured. Four years later, the Passive Defence Committee took the 'total blackout' demanded by the prefect for practice purposes to mean lighting at 5–10 per cent of normal strength.[146] Saint-Étienne, meanwhile, waited until March 1937 to conclude that the switch to wartime dimmed lighting might be achieved by disconnecting two streetlamps in three, over three days if the skilled personnel were available.[147]

Cost helped explain the local authorities' caution. Switching from 'normal' dimmed lighting to blackout in an alert required remote-control devices – the Actadis system – to cut lighting quickly without interrupting the electricity supply. By the outbreak of war, most French towns had acquired the necessary equipment and were ready for wartime lighting.[148] This did not, however, guarantee an effective blackout. Actadis proved unreliable, and mayors were urged to enjoin the police or air-raid wardens to notify failures and to receive training in the unsatisfactory system of cutting off the current.[149] More important was the lack of public co-operation, already clear during pre-war exercises. It was perhaps unremarkable that in 1935, with no war scare, the Brest public barely heeded blackout injunctions during an exercise.[150] More surprisingly, though, co-operation was no better for similar exercises early in 1939.

From 1 September 1939, through posters and the press, France's mayors announced blackout measures to apply to the administration, businesses, vehicles and households.[151] But official policy was relaxed after a few weeks.[152] In Brest, the Maritime Prefect complained to the mayor of laxity among the town's larger shops. Overflights revealed haloes of light over Brest and nearby towns.[153] Boulogne-Billancourt prepared a stock of 500 letters to send to recalcitrant householders.[154] The city of Rennes was still visible from over 100 kilometres away on the night of 5 September – and military personnel in requisitioned schools were failing to blackout most lights properly. The mayor used the local press to demand greater public co-operation, requested overflights to observe his town, and wrote in exasperation to the head of the main post office – still well-lit on 17 May 1940, a week after the German invasion.[155] The police chief in the Lille suburb of La Madeleine, one of the closest points in France to the front line, claimed on 24 April 1940 that British troops were treating the blackout as a joke and failing to respond to repeated warnings; when the military failed to set an example, he added, civilians would not comply.[156]

France's difficulties with the blackout were not chiefly due either to the authorities' insouciance or to the public's recalcitrance. Local government did take blackout measures, and even critical overflight reports stated that the blackout was well observed *in general*.[157] But a handful of stray lights could betray a town, and the French measures failed to achieve complete compliance from the authorities, the military (including the British) or the general public. In the event France was defeated in May/June 1940 without facing heavy night attacks. But these were uncertain foundations on which to build future public co-operation.

Italy, meanwhile, saw air-defence exercises particularly from early 1939: sirens were tested and people asked to practise blackout procedures. But as Fascist informers frequently reported, instead of co-operating, people undermined mobilization by spreading negative comments about the country's preparedness for air war. A daytime alert in Turin in January 1939 was 'not taken seriously by the population', and sirens seemed too feeble. *Capi fabbricato*, however, did obtain a blackout of most during the evening alarm.[158] During a similar practice the following October, the police presence was reinforced to prevent 'subversive or anti-national elements' from using the situation to express anti-regime views.[159] Even when exercises worked, and the blackout was observed, as in Padua in April, people discussed them with apprehension. The common feeling was: 'let's hope that it won't be needed, let's hope there will be no war'.[160] In nearby Venice that June, tests faced a complete lack of public co-operation. People stayed on the streets following daytime alarms (only foreigners were 'ready and disciplined'); at night, boats moved about fully lit.[161] In July, the Genoese showed a mixed reaction to the alerts, complying partly with the blackout but commenting widely on the lack of shelters: the four public shelters were tunnels accessible only from limited parts of the city, and private shelters only existed in a very few new houses.[162] Even informers showed scepticism. In September 1939, one asked if it was really necessary to recommend evacuation of children and the elderly – since it was well known that 'zone by zone our system of alarms constitutes an extraordinary degree of safety'.[163] During an exercise in Bari that month, with a similar mix of optimism and carelessness, cars and buses continued to circulate fully lit, with most of the city blacked out; the local informer described the practice as a piece of 'buffoonery'. A month later, an 'UNPA day' in Bari drew public attention as UNPA members in uniforms and gas-masks paraded through the city centre – but complaints when they tried to collect money.[164]

In Milan, an exercise in October 1939, the first since March, degenerated into a shambles. About 15 minutes before the all-clear, one vehicle moved slightly, persuading everyone that the alarm had finished; traffic began circulating with lights on, pedestrians reappeared in the streets, and neither the inexperienced UNPA volunteers nor traffic wardens tried to stop them. When the all-clear finally sounded, many took it for a new alert, and shops began closing their shutters. As usual, people said that proper passive defence required decent shelters and a mask for every citizen; but there was 'no-one who did not see how serious such an incident would be in case of war'.[165] As the threat of war loomed larger in Italy in 1939–40, moreover, the public reacted increasingly negatively towards exercises. The Turin public, like the Milanese, focused on the lack of shelters or free masks. Many people believed practices were conducted 'for foreign policy interests rather than for reasons of internal security'.[166] Again, people in Florence commented that civil defence measures had remained purely theoretical, with no shelters, no protection for monuments and galleries, and overpriced gas-masks.[167]

Industrialists, too, increasingly criticized civil defence measures. In Viterbo province they observed that most plans to camouflage factories and power stations were not practical; anti-aircraft guns were needed instead. When camouflage work began on hydro-electric power stations in the area, rumours circulated about what was happening. People passionately followed everything related to air protection, the informer reported, demonstrating the absence of 'that intimate sense of tranquillity in individuals' souls which derives from the certainty that everything possible had been done to protect the life of the masses'.[168]

Apprehension was mixed with curiosity, another obstacle to the discipline recommended by UNPA. In May 1940, during a daytime alert in Turin, most cars stopped and pedestrians left streets and squares; but many soon emerged to look. During the evening alert many stayed on their balconies.[169] As in 1939, the police were deployed to check not only compliance with passive defence regulations but also political behaviour.[170] Brindisi and Rome saw complaints (from women in particular) that there were no shelters and that innocents would die like mice trapped in their buildings; in Rome, rumours and protests threatened 'to assume remarkable proportions'.[171] The Milanese, meanwhile, had come to regard anti-aircraft exercises as spectacles, continued to ignore alarms, regarded civil defence recruits as simply out to escape conscription, and refused to 'digest' any restriction on the use of light.[172]

A final challenge to both governments was that of recruiting and training personnel for passive defence services as diverse as look-out, trenches and shelters, evacuation, police, fire, medical assistance, personnel and transport. The numbers involved were, potentially, considerable – about 1.5 million people in the UK at the start of the war, including 320,000 full-timers.[173] France, with its smaller urban population, was still viewed as needing hundreds of thousands of recruits; for Lyon, for example, the figure of one regiment plus 7,000 civilians was cited at the meeting with Gamelin in February 1939.[174] The law of 1938 set out four sources of recruits: local authority personnel, requisitioned men free of military obligations, volunteers, and finally second-rank reservists from the military. Personnel had to be available for up to 72 hours annually for exercises and training sessions. It was made clear, however, that the armed services' needs came first.[175]

Recruitment therefore still presented difficulties. In Brest, attempts to attract volunteers in the mid-1930s met with indifference or even hostility.[176] In Nantes in December 1938, the head of the municipal hygiene bureau considered the official recommended total of medical personnel (1,800) as unattainable.[177] Recruitment probably improved after the outbreak of war. In Saint-Étienne, 289 volunteers, 92 of them women, volunteered as building wardens (*gardiens d'immeuble*) in autumn 1939. But many will have been the *concierges* of the buildings concerned.[178] Of the 1,559 passive defence personnel in Nantes at the outbreak of war, 523 were municipal employees, 326 (chiefly firemen) were military, and 710 were 'volunteers or requisitioned men'. But the latter were often medically unsuitable, or changed residence: of ten potential recruits, only four or five finally joined passive defence teams.[179]

Efforts were also made through the 1930s to train personnel.[180] The law of 1938 prescribed regular exercises, including gas attacks, finding and neutralizing dummy 'bombs', blackout, evacuation preparations, and telephone liaison. The Interministerial Instruction of 20 July 1939 required prefects to design annual passive defence training programmes, covering all categories from senior officials to the public.[181] The DDP at the Defence Ministry produced model lectures from 1938, and trainees' efforts were rewarded with certificates at different levels.[182] France began the war with a core of passive defence officers with some training. However, this did not extend to all ranks, and had certainly not reached the general public, as the uncertain responses of the French when faced with real air raids were to show.

Recruitment was a constant problem in Italy, too. UNPA could not recruit men between 20 and 45, as they were liable to conscription, though it could recruit women. The key figure in Italy's civil defence personnel was the *capo fabbricato*, responsible, in the building where he resided (and where he had to remain for the duration of the war) for ensuring blackout compliance, observance of alerts, and discipline inside shelters, as well as fire prevention, first aid and the removal of debris. Appointed directly by the Fascist Party, the *capo fabbricato*, like UNPA members, had to be a Party member. However, many volunteers for the post, like UNPA members, did not quite believe that war would really come; when the situation became dangerous, they sought to withdraw. This was not simply due to excessive optimism or cowardice, but also to poor training, especially compared to that of fire-fighters or the Red Cross. Recruitment restrictions also meant that many UNPA volunteers were over 45, or else – as a story by Italo Calvino tells – adolescents, who imagined a moment of adventure during the 1940 summer holidays but were unprepared for a real war.[183] As for the public's view, the Turin UNPA leadership branch wrote in September 1938 to central office in Rome that most people viewed UNPA as a bluff, only good for pocketing people's money.[184]

Adequate funds were never available for proper training; the collaboration of prefects and other authorities was limited. UNPA membership remained low, at 150,000 in 1937, against 11 million for its German counterpart – while in Britain a single campaign in 1938 brought half a million recruits in just a few months. More money came only in 1939, to help UNPA organize days of mobilization and anti-aircraft exercises. As we have seen, however, these never breached the Italians' scepticism.[185] The February 1940 report by the Supreme Commission of Defence confirmed that the DiCaT (Anti-aircraft Territorial Defence) lacked one-third of the necessary personnel, and that the Red Cross and the fire brigades were similarly afflicted.[186] Numbers of fire-fighters were dramatically insufficient. Turin, Italy's most industrial city, had just 188 at the beginning of 1940; they took their first casualties as early as 14 August 1940 thanks to an unexploded bomb near Alessandria in Piedmont.[187] Both in France and Italy, the emergency services entered the war undermanned, especially by comparison with their British and German counterparts, and undertrained.

CONCLUSION

A 1938 French Air Ministry pamphlet argued that passive defence mobilization in both Nazi Germany and the Soviet Union served not only to reinforce air-raid precautions, but to maintain a 'war psychosis' that was 'only possible in a totalitarian state'.[188] The argument that a state's passive defence preparations reflected its deeper characteristics and its relationship with civil society could certainly apply to Italy and France. But any contrast between 'totalitarian' Italy and 'democratic' France would be far too simple. France's preparations, though flawed in many respects, drew some strength from the solidity of the administrative system and, in the final year, the determination of the Daladier government. Italy, on the other hand, suffered from the functional drawbacks of a totalitarian state – especially the lack of systematic discussion of policy – without achieving corresponding advantages in terms of public compliance.

The governments of both countries were sensitive to the air threat, but from opposite perspectives. In France, it was perceived within a globally defensive approach to war, but also within a tradition that included national defence as part of every citizen's responsibility.[189] In Italy, passive defence was enveloped within government propaganda presenting air power as an advanced technological achievement of the regime. A major consequence was the absence of any critical debate on the roles of active and passive defences against bombing if war should come. There was little opportunity for the evaluation of results, for discussions between central and local administrations, or meaningful comparisons with what was done abroad.[190]

Both countries had legislated massively on passive defence by the outbreak of war. In both France and Italy, however, policy was flawed in two major respects. First, both governments, quite understandably, overestimated the danger of gas attacks, and underestimated the quantity of high explosive and incendiaries that could be rained upon their countries from 1942. Second, their reliance on evacuation, unbacked by either compulsion or logistical preparation, proved unrealistic. Financial resources, moreover, barely followed the policy.

Two important points distinguished France from Italy in the making and implementation of policy. First, the French state possessed the means, in its elected mayors and councils under prefectoral supervision, to develop passive defence locally. By September 1939, French local government had, with prefectoral encouragement, set up committees and engaged actively (if not always effectively) with passive defence issues. In Italy, the centralization of power and the de-vitalization of local politics resulted in frequent turnover of prefects and of local Fascist Party cadres.[191] Local authorities were incapacitated, but the state was unable to substitute for them. For this reason, no detailed defence plans were drawn up in Italian cities as they were in French ones. Second, the sharp rise in passive defence spending (and defence spending generally) in France in 1939 compensated, however modestly, for years of penury. If shelter construction, gas-mask supply, or the constitution of trained passive defence teams were far from complete by the outbreak of war, they were underway. To have sheltered, more or less effectively, some 10 per cent of the urban population was scarcely worse than the level achieved in Britain.[192] The same could hardly be said of Italy, where no comparable spending surge took place before 1940. The inadequacy of preparations was clear from the first air raids in 1940, and local authorities soon began to worry about the moral and political consequences, particularly in industrial areas. [193]

In France and Italy, passive defence propaganda was channelled through all available media, as well as the schools. In neither country, however, did results reach expectations, whether measured by co-operation with passive defence exercises, blackout observance, or recruitment. The problem was not that the French or Italian publics were oblivious to the bombing threat. The uncensored

French press offered plenty of coverage of the danger. [194] In Italy, Fascist informers observed a 'very depressed' general climate in the winter of 1938–9. There was no enthusiasm for annexing Albania, and Italians – the majority – who did not share the regime's imperialist ambitions could not ignore that with each step towards their realization, a war they deeply feared drew closer.[195]

But these worries did not, in general, attract people into civil defence preparations; public reactions more frequently displayed a mix of curiosity, apprehension and non-cooperation. In France, it is true, air-defence associations did surface, but never as mass phenomena. Deep political divisions in the late 1930s meant that passive defence initiatives within civil society were more readily associated with one or another political camp than with the common good; as Laborie has observed, the scope for national consensus in the France of 1939 was limited by 'social antagonisms, ideological barriers, a permanent climate of vengefulness' – none of them propitious to volunteering for civic duties.[196] And while the Daladier government commanded broader support than its predecessors, it inspired obedience more than enthusiasm. In Italy, despite (or because of) an almost twenty-year long totalitarian experiment, trust in the state was less solid. Italian historiography has generally agreed that support for the regime peaked in the mid-1930s and fell off thereafter, not least due to the threat of war and the German alliance. A few months after the Munich conference (celebrated with relief by the masses as Mussolini's personal triumph in preserving peace), anti-French demonstrations staged by the Fascist Party throughout Italy met with indifference, while anti-German comments openly increased.[197] This was clearest in the north-western regions (the closest, both culturally and economically, to France), where the first evacuation exercises were staged before 1940, and where mobilization began. Here, passive defence revealed the gap between government propaganda and reality on the ground; poor levels of compliance reflected the public's lack of support for the regime's war aims or confidence in its capacity to defend its subjects.

Both in France and Italy, there were signs by 1939 of the 'war psychosis' characterized in the French Air Ministry pamphlet as typical of a totalitarian society. But it did not, by and large, produce strong passive defences; nor did it bind the general population to the state by new ties of solidarity.

Notes

1 J. S. Corum, 'The Myth of Air Control: Reassessing the History', *Air and Space Power Journal*, XIV.4 (Winter 2000), 61–77.

2 J. S. Corum, 'Airpower Thought in Continental Europe between the Wars', in P. S. Meilinger (ed.), *The Paths of Heaven: the Evolution of Airpower Theory* (Maxwell Air Force Base, Alabama, USA: Air University Press, 1997), 162.

3 G. Douhet, *The Command of the Air* (Washington, DC: Office of Air Force History, 1983 (1st Italian edn, 1921)), 189–90.

4 M. Knox, *Hitler's Italian Allies: Royal Armed Forces, Fascist Regime, and the War of 1940–1943* (Cambridge: Cambridge University Press, 2000), 71; J. Gooch, *Mussolini and his Generals: The*

Armed Forces and Fascist Foreign Policy, 1922–1940 (Cambridge: Cambridge University Press, 2007), 40.

5 A. Adamthwaite, *France and the Coming of the Second World War* (London: Frank Cass, 1977), 239, 254.

6 R. M. Titmuss, *Problems of Social Policy* (London: HMSO, 1950), 13; T. H. O'Brien, *Civil Defence* (London: HMSO, 1955), 96. The real casualty rate per ton of bombs dropped on the UK between 1939 and 1945 was roughly 19 times lower than this prediction.

7 A. Giannuzzi Savelli, *Conferenza di propaganda per la protezione antiaerea del territorio nazionale e della popolazione civile – Anno 1931-X* (Rome: Istituto Poligrafico dello Stato, 1934), 6.

8 The term 'passive defence', which may be used interchangeably with 'civil defence', highlights the contrast with 'active defence' – anti-aircraft guns and fighters.

9 Between 1922 and 1 September 1939, the French government issued at least 2 laws, 4 decree-laws, 34 decrees, 109 circulars, 29 instructions, 18 arrêtés (ministerial decisions) and 11 notices relating to passive defence. A further 4 decree-laws, 13 decrees, 9 circulars and 2 instructions followed before the defeat of 1940.

10 AD BduR, 77/W/1, Ministère de la Guerre, Instruction provisoire concernant la protection individuelle contre les bombardements aériens, mise à jour au 2 mai 1924.

11 ACM Brest, 4H/4/5, Decree of 9 February 1931, quoted in *Procivil* 1, April 1939, 7.

12 AM BB, 6H/3, Ministère de l'Intérieur, Instruction pratique sur la défense passive contre les attaques aériennes, 1931.

13 A. Hardy, 'La défense passive à Rouen et dans son agglomération', mémoire de Master d'Histoire Contemporaine, Université de Rouen, année 2005–6, 20.

14 Loi du 8 avril 1935, *JO*, 8 April 1935.

15 Hardy, 'Défense passive', 20–1; Décret du 26 mars 1936 (Ministre de l'Air), *JO*, 27 March 1936.

16 Loi du 11 juillet 1938, *JO*, 13 July 1938.

17 See in particular Décret du 29 juillet (Défense passive), *JO*, 30 July 1938; Arrêté du 24 septembre (Direction de la Défense passive), *JO*, 27 September 1938; Décret du 12 novembre 1938 (Défense passive), *JO*, 15 November 1938; Décret du 13 mars 1939 (Participation financière de l'État), *JO*, 17 March 1939; Arrêté du 15 avril 1939 (Vacations horaires), *JO*, 20 April 1939; Décret du 7 mai 1939 (Enseignement, Défense passive), *JO*, 7 May 1939; Décret du 26 mai 1939 (Taxe locale de sécurité), *JO*, 27 May 1939.

18 Instruction interministérielle du 20 juillet 1939 (Défense passive), *JO*, 20 July 1939.

19 AD Manche, 2Z/373, Instruction pratique sur la défense passive (et annexes), 26 June 1939.

20 Law 969, 8 June 1925, *GU*, 23 June 1925.

21 On the Red Cross in Italy during the Second World War, see S. Picciaredda, *Diplomazia umanitaria. La Croce Rossa nella Seconda Guerra Mondiale* (Bologna: Il Mulino, 2003), 151–81.

22 Decree 2034, 10 August 1928 (*GU* 19 September 1928) and law 3133 of 20 December 1928. An Italian province is a territorial division roughly equivalent to the French *département*, and presided over by a prefect as the central government's senior official.

23 ASG, Prefettura, b. 129, *La protezione sanitaria antiaerea e antigas*, no date, but probably 1943.

24 Giannuzzi Savelli, *Conferenza di propaganda*, 122; decree 1175, 14 September 1931.

25 Law 415, 21 May 1940.

26 ACS, MA, AG, 1939, b. 33, fasc. 24, vol. II: 'Schema di disegno di legge che detta norme per la A.A. degli stabilimenti industriali', n.d. (summer 1939).

27 *Ibid.*, vol. I: 'Promemoria', Air Ministry meeting, n.d. (June 1939?); decree 1672, 5 September 1938.

28 Gioannini and Massobrio, *Bombardate l'Italia*, 64.

29 Giannuzzi Savelli, *Conferenza di propaganda*, 10.

30 Decree 1539, 30 August 1934.

31 Decree 1062, 14 May 1936, *GU*, 18 June 1936, 1971.

32 AD Nord 25/W/38184, Commission Départementale de la Défense Passive, 9 July 1932 and 28 December 1933.

33 AM Rouen 4H/52, Arrêté du Maire, 30 March 1938.

34 ACM Brest 4H/14, Note sur la Défense Passive, n.d.; AM Rouen 4H/51, Mayor of Rouen

to Prefect of Seine-Inférieure, 31 July 1931; AM Lyon 1127/WP/09, Rapport Général sur l'Organisation de la Défense Passive, Département du Rhône, n.d.; AM Nantes, H/4/Défense Passive, Ville de Nantes, Travaux Publics, Défense contre les Attaques Aériennes, 20 novembre 1933; AD Nord 25/W/38184, Commission Départementale de la Défense Passive, Nord, 9 July 1932 and 28 December 1933.

35 AD Calvados M/11772/2, Arrêté du Préfet, 1 July 1935; AM Rennes, 6H/20, Ville de Rennes, Arrêté du maire, 14 February 1936.

36 AM Rouen, 4H/64, Ville de Rouen, draft brochure on passive defence, 1938; Hardy, 'Défense Passive', 30; ACM Brest 4H/4/14, Prefect of Finistère to mayor of Brest, 25 August 1932; AM St-Étienne 5/H/65, Maître Courbis to mayor of St-Étienne, 24 November 1934.

37 AM Lyon 127/WP/08, Réunion du 20 février 1939, tenue à la Préfecture sous la présidence de M. le Général Gamelin.

38 O'Brien, *Civil Defence*, 116.

39 Giannuzzi Savelli, *Conferenza di propaganda*, 10.

40 L. Baldissara, 'Il governo della città: la ridefinizione del ruolo del Comune nell'emergenza bellica', in B. Dalla Casa and A. Preti (eds), *Bologna in guerra, 1940–1945* (Milan: Angeli, 1995), 103–31.

41 AD B-du-R 77/W/1, Ministère de la Guerre, Instruction provisoire, mise à jour au 2 mai 1924, Introduction.

42 AD Manche 2Z/373, Instruction Pratique sur la Défense Passive, Annexe 7: La Dispersion, juin 1935.

43 Cf. Giannuzzi Savelli, *Conferenza di propaganda*, and *Offesa aerea. Mezzi di difesa e protezione* (Milan: Martucci, 1936).

44 AD Manche 2Z/373, Instruction Pratique, Annexe 7, 5.

45 ACM Brest 4H/4/35, Ville de Brest, Annexe 7: Plan de Dispersion, note de l'Adjoint au Maire, n.d. (1936); AM Lyon 1127/WP/09, Rapport Général, Défense Passive, Département du Rhône, n.d.; AM Lorient 5/H/8, Ville de Lorient, Commission Urbaine de Défense Passive, 3 June 1938; AM Rennes 6H/20, Ville de Rennes, Questionnaire de 2e urgence; Liste des communes dans lesquelles la dispersion pourrait être faite; AM St-Étienne 5/H/65, Ville de St-Étienne, Conseil Municipal du 31 mars 1939; AM BB 6H/7, Boulogne-Billancourt, Bulletin Municipal Officiel, December 1938; AD Calvados M/11773, Prefect of Calvados to Président du Conseil, 17 October 1936.

46 AM BB 6H/3, Préfecture de Police, Secrétariat général permanent de la défense passive, n.d. (1936), 1, 12; AM Lille 5/H/3/1, 'Lille et sa région sous les gaz' (Paris: Étienne Chiron, n.d.); La Revue Familiale, *Petit Guide de Défense Passive*, September (1939?).

47 AD Calvados M/11773, Ministère de l'Intérieur, Bureau de la Défense Nationale, Instruction Générale à l'usage de Messieurs le Préfets sur les Mouvements et Transports de Sauvegarde, 1 July 1938.

48 AD Calvados M/11773, Département du Calvados, T.XXIII.II, reçu le 10 janvier 1938, (reproduced in H. Diamond, *Fleeing Hitler: France 1940* (Oxford: Oxford University Press, 2007), 19); J. Vidalenc, *L'Exode, mai-juin 1940* (Paris: Presses Universitaires de France, 1957), 17.

49 AD Calvados M/11773, Département du Calvados, Éloignement de la population du Département de la Seine en cas de mobilisation.

50 AM Rouen 4H/52, Mayor of Rouen to Prefect of Seine-Inférieure, 13 July 1938.

51 Instruction interministérielle sur l'organisation de la défense passive, Article 40, *JO*, 20 July 1939.

52 AMC Brest 4H/4/35, Daudin (for Président du Conseil) to Prefect of Finistère, 19 May 1939.

53 AD Calvados M/11773, Interior Ministry to Prefect of Calvados, 12 October 1938.

54 Vidalenc, *L'Exode*, 32.

55 AMC Brest 4H/4/35, Ville de Brest, Adjoint-Maire délégué à la Défense Passive to Prefect of Finistère, 31 May 1939; AD Manche 2Z/373, Instruction pratique sur la défense passive (et annexes), 26 June 1939, 23. Authors' italics.

56 Giannuzzi Savelli, *Conferenza di propaganda*, 16–17.

57 Cf. also E. Cortesi, *L'odissea degli sfollati. Il Forlivese, il Riminese e il Cesenate di fronte allo sfollamento di massa* (Cesena: Il Ponte Vecchio, 2003).

58 *Il Popolo di Roma*, 30 August 1939.
59 Cf. E. Di Nolfo, R. Rainero and B. Vigezzi (eds), *L'Italia e la politica di potenza in Europa, 1938–1940* (Milan: Marzorati, 1985).
60 R. Lucioli, 'Sfollamento, mobilità sociale e sfaldamento delle istituzioni nella provincia di Ancona', *Storia e problemi contemporanei*, 15, April 1995, 49.
61 ASTo, Prefettura, I versamento, b. 513, poster produced by the prefect of Turin, 15 March 1939.
62 ASTo, Prefettura, b. 515, Military Command, Turin zone, to prefect of Turin, 12 February 1940.
63 ACS, MA, AG, 1940, b. 83, fasc. 13, Ministry of War to Italian prefects, to PNF, UNPA, and Carabinieri, 3 June 1940.
64 ACS, MA, AG, 1940, b. 83, fasc. 13, War Ministry, Under Secretary of State Soddu to the Supreme Commission of Defence, General Secretary, 2 May 1940; *ibid.*, Air Ministry, Ufficio di Stato Maggiore, Head of Stato Maggiore of the Air Forces Francesco Pricolo to Supreme Defence Commission, 18 May 1940.
65 Diamond, *Fleeing Hitler*, 24–5; L. Dodd, '"Partez partez", again and again: the efficacy of evacuation as a means of protecting children from bombing in France, 1939–44', *Children in War*, 6.1, February 2009, 7–20; Vidalenc, *L'Exode*, 38–9.
66 Vidalenc, *L'Exode*, 55–6.
67 AD Manche 2Z/373, Instruction Pratique, Annexe 7, June 1935, 7.
68 *Ibid.*, 5.
69 AM Marseille 408W/1, Instruction Pratique sur la Défense Passive, Annexe 4, Des Abris, 13 April 1932, 2. Bomb-proof shelters were, of course, built for ministries (cf. AM Nantes, H4/DP, Mairie de Nantes Bureau d'Hygiène, Défense Passive, Conclusions sur le Stage Effectué à Paris, 6 December 1938).
70 AM Lyon 1127WP/09, Ministère de la Défense Nationale, Notice Provisoire relative à la mise à l'abri de la population, no. 671/DP/3, 24 December 1938.
71 AD Ille-et-Vilaine 1203W/32, Ministère de la défense nationale, DDP, Notice provisoire relative à la réalisation en temps de guerre des installations de mise à l'abri, no. 671-DP3-B, 1 March 1940.
72 AMC Brest 4H/4/19, Mayor of Brest to Mayor of Nantes, 21 March 1933; 4H/4/20, Mairie de Brest, Défense Passive, Note, 1st April 1935.
73 AMC Brest 4H/4/14, Mairie de Brest, Plan de mise à l'abri des écoles primaires, 9 December 1938.
74 AM Rouen 4H/52, Ville de Rouen, Plan de défense passive, 1935, Chapitre III, Liste des abris existants dans des immeubles privés; Mayor of Rouen to prefect, 13 July 1938; Antoine Hardy, 'La défense passive à Rouen', *Études Normandes*, 57.1, 2008, 61–70; 64.
75 AM Lyon 1127/WP/09, Rapport Général, Défense Passive, Département du Rhône, n.d.
76 AM Lyon 1127/WP/08, Ville de Lyon, Comité Consultatif Urbain de la Défense Passive, 18 April 1939; AM Lyon, 1127/WP/09, Conseil municipal, 28 September 1939.
77 AM Lyon 1127WP/09, Ville de Lyon, Conseil municipal, 28 September 1939; AM Lyon 1127WP/19, Défense Passive, Recensement des caves, août-septembre 1939; AM Lyon 1127WP/08, Département du Rhône, Commission départementale de défense passive, 1 July 1939.
78 AM Marseille 408W/1/1, Préfecture des Bouches-du-Rhône, Service Tranchées-Abris, report, 21 November 1939; AM Marseille 408/W/1/10, Préfecture des Bouches-du-Rhône, Services des Abris et des Tranchées, report, 12 April 1940.
79 AM Nantes H4/DP, Préfecture de la Loire-Inférieure, Conférence du 14 mars 1939 sur les mesures propres à assurer la défense passive de la ville de Nantes.
80 *Ibid.*, Ville de Nantes, Défense Passive, note, 22 January 1940.
81 AM Lorient 5H/8, prefect of Morbihan to mayor of Lorient, 14 February 1940.
82 AM Saint-Étienne 5H/62, Ville de Saint-Étienne, Commission pour l'Organisation de la Défense Passive, 13 March 1937.
83 AM Saint-Étienne 5H/65, Ville de Saint-Étienne, Conseil Municipal, session d'avril 1938, affaire supplémentaire no. 73; AD Loire 7W/53, Ville de Saint-Étienne, Défense Passive, Canton Sud-Est, Caves Aménagés au 1er janvier 1940.
84 AM Rennes 6H/22, Prefect of Ille-et-Vilaine to mayor of Rennes, 30 September 1939, 23 April 1940; Ville de Rennes, Services Municipaux de la Voirie, note de l'ingénieur, 12 June 1940.

85 *Ibid.*, Prefect of Ille-et-Vilaine to mayor of Rennes, 23 April 1940.

86 Boulogne-Billancourt was one municipality that claimed more – over 50,000 places (43,000 of them in cellars) for a population of 93,000 (cf. AM BB, 6H/6 DP, Ville de Boulogne-Billancourt, Recapitulation des places disponibles). The city of Lille's records include two claims, dated 15 November 1939 and 28 June 1940 (both in AM Lille 5H/3/3/PD), which vary by a factor of 1 to 10.

87 AM Nantes H/4/DP, Thiéfaine (adjoint, Défense passive), to Prefect of Loire-Inférieure, 5 December 1939.

88 AM Toulon 5H/III/11, Ville de Toulon, La Question de la défense passive, n.d. (1939?).

89 Giannuzzi Savelli, *Conferenza di propaganda*, 10.

90 ASTa, Genio Civile, Nuovo versamento, b. 1468, 23 September 1935; Intendenza di Finanza to Genio Civile of Taranto, 2 April 1937; Ministry of Justice to Director of Taranto Prison, 9 August 1935; Capitaneria of Taranto to Genio Civile, 24 August 1938.

91 Law 1915, 20 December 1932, *GU* 4 January 1933; decree 1553, 25 May 1936, *GU* 27 August 1936.

92 Decree 2121, 24 September 1936, *GU* 21 December 1936; law 1527, 10 June 1937, *GU* 14 September 1937. France had published regulations on shelters in newly constructed public buildings on 20 December 1935.

93 Law 1102, 6 June 1939, *GU* 10 August 1939.

94 ASTo, Prefettura, I versamento, b. 513, UNPA Provincial Delegation of Turin to General President of UNPA, report on the 25th meeting, 30 September 1938.

95 Gioannini and Massobrio, *Bombardate l'Italia*, 88.

96 ACS, MA, AG, 1939, b. 33, fasc. 25, War Ministry to Air Ministry, 13 July 1939.

97 *Ibid.*, fasc. 24, vol. II, Ministero della Marina, Ufficio Leggi e Decreti, Under Secretary of State for Navy Domenico Cavagnari to War Ministry and other relevant ministries, 12 September 1939.

98 *Ibid.*, Luigi Gambelli to War Ministry, other relevant ministries and to all Italian prefects, 5 November 1939.

99 A. Giannuzzi Savelli and G. Stellingwerf, *Protezione anti-aerea di Roma* (Rome: Istituto di Studi Romani, 1938), 6–7.

100 Cf. P. Callegari and V. Curzi (eds), *Venezia: la tutela per immagini. Un caso esemplare dagli archivi della Fototeca Nazionale* (Bologna: Bononia University Press, 2005).

101 Law 415, 21 May 1940.

102 ACG, AM, b. 1138/1, Disposition by the prefect of Genoa, 7 November 1940.

103 Décret du 20 mars 1939 (Masques à gaz), *JO*, 22 March 1939; Arrêté du 30 mai 1939 (Débitants de tabac), *JO*, 3 June 1939.

104 AM Lyon 1127/WP/08, Ville de Lyon, Commission Départementale de Défense Passive, 1 July 1939.

105 AM Nantes H4/DP, Ville de Nantes, Défense Passive, Situation au 11 octobre 1939; Ville de Nantes, Rapport sur la Défense Passive, 22 December 1939; AM Rennes 6H/20, Ville de Rennes, Conseil Municipal, 31 October 1939; ACM Brest 4H/4/15, Ville de Brest, mayor to city architect, 20 February 1940.

106 AM BB 6H/6/DP, Ville de Boulogne-Billancourt, poster of 15 April 1940.

107 C. Bongiovanni, *Corso di chimica e di mineralogia per gli Istituti Magistrali* (Rimini: Stabilimento Tipografico Garattoni, 1935), 157; 160.

108 C. Chiodi and F. Mariani, *Relazione sulle visite ad alcuni impianti di protezione antiaerea in Germania* (Milan: Industrie Grafiche Italiane Stucchi, July 1938). German public shelters did have this anti-gas facility but the informal conversions generally did not.

109 ASTo, Prefettura, I versamento, b. 513, EIAR (Italian Institute for Radio Auditions Communication, n.d. (1938)).

110 Decree 1429 of 27 July 1938, GU 19 September 1938.

111 *Gazzetta del Popolo*, 8 July 1939; ASTo, Prefettura, I versamento, b. 513, Interior Ministry to prefects, 1 July 1939.

112 ACS, MI, DGPS, DPP, b. 211, fasc. 1, sottofasc. 'UNPA', Informer's report, Milan, 14 September 1939.

113 ASTo, Prefettura, I versamento, b. 513, UNPA communication, 18 June 1940.
114 The main exception occurred on 2 December 1943, when the Luftwaffe bombed Bari harbour and hit the American vessel *John Harvey*, which contained 100 tons of mustard gas. The explosion killed over 1,000 civilians and military. Cf. A. Villa, *Guerra aerea sull'Italia* (1943–1945) (Milan: Guerini e Associati, 2010), 188–204.
115 Douhet, *Command of the Air*, 241–2. Original italics.
116 L. Dodd, 'Are we defended? Conflicting representations of war in pre-war France', *University of Sussex Journal of Contemporary History*, 12, 2008, on http://www.sussex.ac.uk/history/1-4-1-1.html.
117 AM BB 6H/3, Ministère de l'Intérieur, Instruction pratique sur la défense passive, 1931.
118 Cf. for example AM BB 6H/3/DP, Manuel de défense passive (brochure), 1939; AM Rennes 6H/20, ABC de la défense passive, brochure, n.d. (1938); ACM Brest 4H/4/5/DP, La Défense Passive, brochure for *La Petite Illustration*, 15 July 1939; AM BB 6H/3/DP, Préfecture de Police (Seine), Ce que le public doit savoir en matière de défense passive (1939).
119 AD Calvados M/11772/2, Daladier to prefect of Calvados, 5 December 1938; ACM Brest 4H/4/14/DP, Vice-Admiral Traub to directors of cinemas in Brest, 27 February 1939; Prefect of Finistère to Mayor of Brest, 19 July 1939.
120 Instruction Interministérielle Relative à l'Organisation Administrative de la Défense Passive, *JO*, 20 July 1939, article 78.
121 AM St-Étienne, 5H/66, Lt-Col de la Rocque to mayor of St-Étienne 20 January 1930.
122 AM Nantes IZ/7, *L'Alerte*, 1938–9; AM Lyon 1127/WP/09, *La Sirène*, December 1937 and December 1938/January 1939; Rapport Général sur l'Organisation de la Défense Passive dans le Département du Rhône, n.d. (early 1936?).
123 ACM Brest 4H/4/5/DP, Bulletin Documentaire Procivil, no. hors série 1939.
124 L. Weiss, *Mémoires d'une Européenne* (Paris: Payot, 1970), vol. III, *1934–39*, 221, 225.
125 G. Rochat, *Le guerre italiane, 1935–1943. Dall'impero d'Etiopia alla disfatta* (Turin: Einaudi, 2005), 224–7; cf. also M. Di Giovanni, *Scienza e Potenza. Miti della guerra moderna, istituzioni scientifiche e politica di massa nell'Italia fascista* (Turin: Zamorani, 2005).
126 Douhet, *Command of the Air*, 241–2.
127 Rochat, 'Il fascismo e la preparazione militare al conflitto mondiale', in A. Del Boca, M. Legnani and M. G. Rossi (eds), *Il regime fascista. Storia e storiografia*, (Rome-Bari: Laterza: 1995), 159.
128 Rochat, *Le guerre italiane, 1935–1943*, 157.
129 Gioannini and Massobrio, *Bombardate l'Italia*, 59, 64–5.
130 Ministero della Guerra, *Istruzione sulla protezione antiaerea* (Rome: Istituto Poligrafico dello Stato, 1938), Fascicolo 1, 'Organizzazione della A.A.', 7.
131 *Ibid.*, Fascicolo 3, 'La segnalazione dell'allarme', 14–15; Fascicolo 4, 'L'oscuramento delle luci', 6–11.
132 General A. Bronzuoli, *La protezione antiaerea delle popolazioni civili* (Naples: Editrice Rispoli Anonima, 1940, 3rd edn – 1st edn 1938), 7–8.
133 *Ibid.*, 31.
134 *La Gazzetta del Popolo*, 21 April 1939.
135 P. Laborie, *L'opinion française sous Vichy: les Français et la crise d'identité nationale, 1936–1944* (Paris: Le Seuil, 1990), 205–11; R. Overy with A. Wheatcroft, *The Road to War* (London: Random House, 2009), 232.
136 Hardy, 'Défense passive', 40.
137 J. Girault, 'Le Syndicat des instituteurs', in R. Rémond et J. Bourdin (eds), *La France et les Français en 1938 et 1939* (Paris: Presses de la Fondation Nationale des Sciences Politiques, 1978), 199.
138 Weiss, *Mémoire d'une européenne*, vol. III, 221.
139 *Ibid.*, p. 207.
140 AM CB 4H/4/15, *La Dépêche de Brest et de l'Ouest*, 1 July 1938.
141 AM Nantes H4/DP, Préfecture de la Loire-Inférieure, Conférence du 14 mars 1939, défense passive.
142 AM Rouen 4H/64, Le Maire de Rouen à ses concitoyens, 31 May 1938.
143 AD Bouches-du-Rhône 77W/1, Ministère de la Guerre, Instruction provisoire, 1924.

144 AM BB 6H/3, Ministère de l'Intérieur, Instruction pratique, 1931; AM Rennes 6H/20, Ministère de l'Intérieur, Annexes à l'Instruction pratique sur la défense passive: no. 1, Guet, Alerte, Extinction des Lumières (Paris: Berger-Levrault, 1932); Instruction interministérielle (Défense passive), *JO*, 20 July 1939.

145 Instruction interministérielle, *JO*, 20 July 1939, 26.

146 AM Rouen 4H/51, Rouen, Commission de Défense Passive, 31 July 1931; AM Rouen 4H/52, Rouen, Commission de Défense Passive, 2 October 1935.

147 AM St-Étienne 5H/62, Ville de St-Étienne, Commission pour l'Organisation de la Défense Passive, 13 March 1937.

148 Cf. for example AM BB 6H/6/DP.

149 AM BB 6H/6/DP, Prefect of la Seine to mayors, 22 November 1939.

150 ACM Brest 4H/4/14 DP, Ministère de l'Intérieur, Sûreté Générale, Ville de Brest, Commissaire Central to Mayor of Brest, 17 April 1935.

151 Cf. for example AM Rennes 6H/20, Ville de Rennes, Arrêté du maire, 1st September 1939 (poster); ACM Brest 4H/4/14, Ville de Brest, mayoral *arrêtés* in *La Dépêche de Brest*.

152 See examples of Rennes, Lyon and the Loire: AM Rennes 6H/21, Ville de Rennes, Secrétaire de la Défense Passive to Préfecture de l'Ille-et-Vilaine, 3 November 1939; AM Lyon 1127/WP/09, Ville de Lyon, Commission Générale du 3 décembre 1939; AM St-Étienne 5/H/66, *Le Mémorial de St-Étienne*, 26 October 1939.

153 ACM Brest 4H/4/14, Aéronautique 2e region, Base d'Aéronautique Navale de Lanvéoc-Poulmic, vol de nuit du 26 septembre 1939; Aéronautique 2e region, Centre des Ballons Captifs, surveillance de la Défense passive effectuée le 3 novembre 1939; Vice-Admiral Traub to Senator-Mayor of Brest, 21 November 1939.

154 AM BB 6H/6/DP, Ville de Boulogne-Billancourt, letter dated 12 January 1940.

155 Cf. AM Rennes 6H/22: correspondence of September 1939 between mayor of Rennes and General Marasse, regional military commander; Mayor of Rennes to Editor of *Ouest-Éclair*, n.d. (September 1939); mayor of Rennes to general commanding air forces in Rennes, 5 February 1940; mayor of Rennes to regional director of PTT, 17 May 1940.

156 AD Nord 25/W/38134, Commissaire de Police de La Madeleine to Capt. A. C. Crawley, British Army, 4th division, 24 April 1940.

157 The report in ACM Brest 4H/4/14, Aéronautique 2e region, Base d'Aéronautique Navale de Lanvéoc-Poulmic, vol de nuit du 26 septembre 1939, mentions that the blackout was well observed *in general*, especially in smaller towns; but larger towns were betrayed by local infringements.

158 ACS, MI, DGPS, DPP, b. 210, Informer's report, Turin, 25 January 1939.

159 ASTo, Prefettura, I versamento, b. 513, Chief of Police to prefect of Turin, 28 October 1939, 'Esperimento di protezione antiaerea'.

160 ACS, MI, DGPS, DPP, b. 210, Informer's report, Padua, 14 April 1939.

161 *Ibid.*, Informer's report, Venice, 9 June 1939.

162 *Ibid.*, Informer's report, Genoa, 13 July 1939.

163 *Ibid.*, Informer's report, Rome, situation of Genoa and Naples, 13 September 1939.

164 *Ibid.*, Informer's reports, Bari, 13 September and 15 October 1939.

165 *Ibid.*, Two Informers' reports, Milan, 25 October 1939.

166 *Ibid.*, Informer's report, Turin, 15 November 1939.

167 *Ibid.*, Informer's report, Florence, 28 February 1940.

168 *Ibid.*, Informer's report, Bagnaia di Viterbo, 2 February 1940.

169 ASTo, Prefettura, I versamento, b. 513, Chief of Police, Turin to prefect of Turin, 23 May 1940.

170 *Ibid.*, Chief of Police, Turin to prefect of Turin, 20 May 1940.

171 ACS, MI, DGPS, DPP, b. 210, Informers' reports, Brindisi, 17 May 1940, and Rome, 9 June 1940.

172 *Ibid.*, Informer's reports, Milan, 23 May and 1 June 1940.

173 O'Brien, *Civil Defence*, 340–41.

174 AM Lyon 127/WP/08, Réunion du 20 février 1939, sous la présidence de M. le Général Gamelin.

175 Loi du 11 juillet 1938, art. 11, *JO*, 13 July 1938.
176 ACM Brest 4H/4/14/DP, Défense passive, n.d. (1937?).
177 AM Nantes H/4/DP, Mairie de Nantes, Bureau d'Hygiène (Directrice), 6 December 1938.
178 AM St-Étienne 5/H/68, lists of volunteers.
179 AM Nantes H4/DP, Ville de Nantes, Défense Passive, Situation au 11 octobre 1939.
180 See for example Lyon and Nord: AM Lyon 1127WP/09, Rapport Général, Défense Passive, Département du Rhône, n.d. (1936?). AD Nord 25W/38056, Département du Nord, Instruction des Cadres Civils de la défense passive, Programme d'ensemble des séances pour l'année 1935.
181 Loi du 11 juillet 1938, JO, 13 July 1938; Instruction interministérielle, arts. 73–8, *JO*, 20 July 1939.
182 AM Lille 5H/3/2/DP, Direction de la Défense Passive, Le Danger Aérien, Conférence d'Information Générale Réservée aux Cadres Supérieurs de la Défense Passive, n.d. (1938?).
183 I. Calvino, 'Le notti dell'UNPA', in 'L'entrata in guerra', *Romanzi e racconti*, vol. I (Milan: Mondadori, 1991), 525–45.
184 ASTo, Prefettura, I versamento, b. 513, UNPA Provincial Delegation of Turin to General President of UNPA, 30 September 1938.
185 Gioannini and Massobrio, *Bombardate l'Italia*, 80.
186 *Ibid.*, 59. The role of the DiCaT was, as explained in a decree-law of 1935, to predispose in peacetime, and to operate in wartime, the defence of the country from enemy air or naval attacks (Decree 181, 21 January 1935, *GU*, 16 March 1935).
187 Gioannini and Massobrio, *Bombardate l'Italia*, 83.
188 AM BB 6H/3/DP, Préfecture de Police (Seine), Ce qu'il faut faire pour vous protéger en cas d'attaque aérienne, n.d. (1937?); ACM Brest 4H/4/5 DP, Ministère de l'Air, *La Défense passive en Allemagne*, (Paris: Imprimerie Nationale, 1938).
189 J. Howorth, 'The Defence Consensus and French Political Culture', in M. Scriven and P. Wagstaff (eds), *War and Society in Twentieth-Century France* (Oxford: Berg, 1991), 167–8.
190 G. Rochat, *Italo Balbo. Lo squadrista, l'aviatore, il gerarca* (Turin: UTET, 2003), 137.
191 S. Lupo, *Il fascismo. La politica in un regime totalitario* (Rome: Donzelli, 2000), 316–19.
192 O'Brien, *Civil Defence*, 189–90.
193 ASTo, Prefettura, I versamento, b. 513, Prefect of Turin to Ministry of Interior, 1940, n.d. but probably autumn.
194 Cf. AM BB 6H/3 DP, 'Alerte au gaz! nous ne sommes pas prêts' *Je sais tout*, June 1934; AM Saint-Étienne 5/H/65, Maître Courbis to mayor of St-Étienne, 24 November 1934; AD Nord 25W/38184, *Le Réveil du Nord*, 29 July 1935; AM St-Étienne 5/H/62, *Le Mémorial*, 18, 19, 22 and 30 March 1938; AM BB 6H/3 DP, *Le Cri de France*, 9 March 1939.
195 S. Colarizi, *La Seconda Guerra Mondiale e la Repubblica* (Turin: UTET, 1984), 62.
196 Laborie, *L'Opinion française sous Vichy*, 207.
197 S. Colarizi (ed.), *L'Italia antifascista dal 1922 al 1940* (Rome-Bari: Laterza, 1976), vol. II, 432.

4

States and Bombing, 1940–1945

Neither Fascist Italy nor Vichy France had prepared for bombing on anything like the scale that they experienced after 1940. But both regimes risked being fatally undermined if they left their people unprotected: in Italy, the unity of party and people lay at the heart of Fascism; in France, Vichy justified its existence by its claim to shield the French from the worst effects of the war.

This chapter concerns how the two regimes' pre-war preparations were reinforced, adjusted, reversed, or overwhelmed under the impact of bombing. Part of the record is about institutional changes, and efforts to co-ordinate the work of (at least) the ministries of war, interior, public works, national education, and finance, as well as (in Italy) corporations, and the armed forces. Part of it is about the articulation of central and local government, with prefectures serving as links between the two as they tried to secure implementation of laws, instructions and norms on civil defence decided in Rome or Vichy or Paris. These efforts aimed to reinforce anti-aircraft defences, to develop evacuation and civil defence measures, to deliver shelters to the vulnerable and allowances to the victims, to protect historic buildings and works of art, and to pay for it all. This chapter, then, covers not only the structure and process of government but also its policy outputs.

The ability to deliver, even partially, on these various counts may be seen as one yardstick of the survival of a state of sorts in each country. Neither regime, however, faced the Allied onslaught alone; in France, and increasingly in Italy as well, policy-making was framed by a formidable ally/occupier.

THE GERMAN PRESENCE

Officially the occupying power in France from June 1940, Nazi Germany was also present in Italy from early on. In both countries, the Germans controlled industrial production and workers, although in Italy they did so only after the September 1943 armistice, when the Reich Minister of Armaments and War Production Albert Speer was granted full powers to exploit northern Italian industry. This entailed control over Italian war production (and thus mediations with Italian industrialists), sending workers to German labour camps, and requisitioning machinery from northern Italian factories – an activity defined by Lutz Klinkhammer as a far-reaching 'sack' of Italy by the Salò Republic's German ally.[1] The Italian experience in this area, however, was still limited compared to that of France. Here, the four-year German occupation, partial then total, constituted a ferocious economic constraint on every aspect of public policy, forcing the massive export of capital, labour, food, raw materials and industrial production to the Reich.[2] By 1943, over 40 per cent of French industry was working for the Germans, along with as many as 57 per cent of Frenchmen aged from 18 to 50. Products of obvious military value – vehicles and aircraft – were almost exclusively for German use. But so, for example, was most of France's production of railway material of all kinds, clocks and watches, and razor blades.[3] Meanwhile French production as a whole, thanks to labour shortages, declining productivity, and the Allied blockade, fell by about one-third during the Occupation.[4] Vichy governments thus faced a 'permanent negotiation'[5] with an ever more rapacious occupier as France was bled white.

Germany's participation in Italy's war effort, and later its presence as an occupier force in central and northern Italy, provoked mixed feelings among the population. They assisted Italy with air defences, and, sometimes, offered emergency services after air raids; but they also requisitioned buildings and shelters. In April 1941 Germany provided Italy with its first radar in Sicily, at Syracuse; the Luftwaffe helped defend southern Italy against RAF attacks from Malta. Early 1943, as Anglo-American control over North Africa tightened, in the Reich's own interest, German radars were placed all along the coastline and anti-aircraft guns brought into northern Italy. These, however, were mostly withdrawn late in 1944 to reinforce German defences and to strengthen the Ardennes offensive. During the Salò Republic German soldiers also worked during and after air raids on Italy, helping clear rubble, and often dying alongside Italian soldiers, Red Cross personnel, fire-fighters and civilians. The ambiguity of Germany's role as ally and occupier was indicated by the common practice of holding separate funerals for Italian and German victims.[6]

The role of occupier, however, was most clearly demonstrated through requisitions. From the summer of 1943, the Wehrmacht's build-up of forces in Italy, particularly the north, contributed to a housing shortage.[7] In Liguria this was exacerbated in the autumn when German-occupied buildings were needed for evacuees from towns situated along the railway.[8] For example, in November 1943 the *podestà* (or state-appointed mayor) of Bogliasco Pieve told the province head (as prefects were called in the Salò Republic) of Genoa of difficulties finding accommodation for 1,200 people living close to the railway: the German military had forced inhabitants out of many buildings.[9] In December, the province head of Turin wrote to the Salò Republic's Interior Minister Guido Buffarini Guidi that German control on already insufficient resources had made it even harder to build new shelters.[10] In Turin province in 1944, German troops again occupied buildings which had housed evacuees – for whom *podestà*s had to seek other destinations, protest proving ineffectual.[11] In Bologna, as the chief of police reported in May 1944, German soldiers sometimes shared houses with evacuated families. In the hope of avoiding German requisitions, civilians wrote letters of protest to province heads.[12]

In France, air-defence policy experienced the more direct attentions of the occupiers. First, the Germans ran active defences – fighters and flak – in the occupied zone from June 1940, throughout France from November 1942. With few exceptions, the French were relegated to a marginal role, though their co-operation was still required. Second, as well as controlling active defences, the Germans claimed the right to control passive defence as well. The extreme formulation of this position was that France had no need for a passive defence directorate within central government; all that was required was for local authorities to carry out German instructions.[13] Though they did not press this, the Germans did insist that passive defence be transferred to a 'civilian' ministry (the transfer from the War Ministry to Interior took place on 16 March 1942), and German supremacy was clearly asserted by decree in the official German bulletin of 3 April 1943.[14]

Third, the Germans intervened directly in many specific areas of passive defence. They constantly demanded better blackout enforcement; after November 1942 they required better fire protection and the formation of mobile Passive Defence Battalions of fire-fighters in major cities; they insisted on their exclusive right to operate alarms and sirens; they instigated the construction of shelters where they considered it in their interests, as at Lorient, home to Admiral Dönitz's headquarters and major submarine base, but could block shelter construction elsewhere.[15] Evacuation policy was similarly subject to German control, exercised with similar capriciousness. The Germans evacuated sectors of French towns when it suited them (in Le Havre and Toulon, for example, as well as the notorious case of Marseille, where the Vieux-Port quarter was emptied and then destroyed).[16] Elsewhere, on the contrary, they demanded the return home of workers who had fled after raids.[17] From October 1941, moreover, a belt of 10–20 kilometres along France's coastline from Dunkirk to Biarritz was classified as a 'forbidden' zone, with entry banned for non-residents.[18]

Fourth, French passive defence efforts were hampered by German requisitioning. This was true not only of labour and raw materials but also of completed shelters, which were regularly built for French civilians only to be taken over by the German military.[19] Fifth, the Germans took a direct interest in passive defence personnel. This was marked by further uncertainty: they wanted efficient, well-trained French passive defence units, but were suspicious of any French body organized on quasi-military lines, even unarmed and part-time. In June 1943 they demanded that the police chief in each town should also run passive defence, before being persuaded that the French police lacked the necessary expertise.[20] At the same time, the Germans required information in each locality, not only on numbers available for passive defence duties but on the names, ages, and professions of all personnel from neighbourhood chief level up.[21] Suspicion could occasionally lead to arrests, among both street-level and senior passive defence personnel.[22]

Finally, as in the Italian case, the occupiers sometimes worked directly with French passive defence forces during and after raids. German troops and ambulances gave assistance after an RAF attack on a train near Blois in August 1942;[23] they supplied bomb disposal teams in several towns (though another technique was to use prisoners to do this job in exchange for remission of sentence – if they lived); German and French fire-fighters worked closely together in the raids on Nantes of September 1943.[24] They helped clear debris in Saint-Quentin in December 1942 and Le Creusot in June 1943;[25] they offered hospital accommodation and space for the wounded in Rennes in July 1943 and Toulon a year later;[26] they shared the deep Sadi-Carnot shelter with French civilians during the siege of Brest in August 1944.[27] This collaboration was assiduously reported (and sometimes exaggerated) in the press.

ACTIVE DEFENCES: ANTI-AIRCRAFT PROTECTION AND ALARMS

In no area was the Germans' role stronger than in that of active defences – fighter aircraft, anti-aircraft weapons and alarms. In France, the occupiers all but monopolized this task, calling on French assistance only from 1943; in Italy, the beleaguered regime relied on German help as the inadequacy of its own preparations became clear. Compared to the Reich, however, both countries remained relatively safe places for Allied bombers to attack.

Italy, at the outset, relied on its own extremely primitive defences. To detect enemy aircraft, instead of radar, a system of 'aerophones' – acoustic listening devices – was put in place, often operated by blind people, who were considered to have better hearing. Aerophones were linked to information-gathering centres, themselves connected to the DiCaT command, which sent the order to open fire. Anti-aircraft batteries were equally antiquated, most dating from World War One; no funds had been found before 1940 to update either detection or weapons. German help, frequently requested, was sometimes forthcoming but often too little and too late.[28]

Another unresolved question concerned alarms. Many were false because the system for detecting enemy aircraft was imprecise. On other occasions, however, alarms only sounded when the bombs were already falling, resulting in high casualties and badly damaging morale, as Chapter 7 will show. Outside the cities, church bells often replaced sirens, since the alarm system was not audible everywhere. Even in the cities, bells were considered as a fall-back in case the system failed.[29]

Malfunctioning anti-aircraft and alarm systems affected industry as well as ordinary civilians. The lack of resources devoted to anti-aircraft defence became noticeable locally within the first months of Italy entering the war. In August 1940 the president of the Macchi Aeronautic factory in Varese (a town of about 50,000 people some 55 kilometres north-west of Milan) warned the Air Ministry that vital war factories like his, though obvious targets, were left defenceless through almost nightly alerts.[30] But no weaponry was available to protect them, the Air Ministry told the War Ministry.[31] In November, a law ordered anti-aircraft protection for all industrial buildings, whether state-owned or private; prefects were meant to ensure that preparations were in place within two months. But the law included no detailed requirements and expected the owners to foot the bill; it was thus practically doomed to fail.[32] In December, the War Ministry compiled a list of major industrial buildings, which showed how many were located outside main cities, a reminder that the bombing of industries was not solely an 'urban' phenomenon.[33] Macchi's problem was common to other crucial war industries, including Italy's premier aircraft manufacturer: the Savoia-Marchetti (later SIAI) plant at Sesto Calende, north of Milan, was still unprotected in February 1941 despite requests for anti-aircraft defences. The enemy, as Mussolini knew, 'could arrive quite peacefully from the sky, destroy everything, and leave undisturbed'.[34] Varese's factories were vital for the Italian air force: they included Macchi, SIAI, Caproni, Agusta, Mona (which made almost all Italy's aero-engine carburettors), and the Taino gunpowder warehouse. Airfields, plus a number of electric- and water-powered stations, were spread around the province. Yet, as late as July 1943, a few days before Mussolini's fall, the area remained virtually unprotected; on the night of 16–17 July British planes flew over the area undisturbed, taking photographs and hitting a power station with precision.[35]

In August 1942 an Air Ministry meeting discussed camouflaging factories. Artificial fog to hide bombing objectives had already been planned for the port of Genoa, for example, in July 1941, but the prefect was worried about reduced visibility for traffic and breathing problems for the population, especially as any wind would have spread the fog to other areas.[36] In any case, resources were too scarce and the system too complex for general use. To disguise entire industrial buildings would also have been too expensive, the creation of fake objectives even more so. Camouflage was, therefore, the only viable option, but was only applied in a few among the many potential buildings to be covered.[37]

Following the area bombing of northern industrial cities in late 1942, a Ministry of Corporations circular of January 1943 told industrialists to improve protection of their buildings to ensure continued production. Again, however, it provided no specific instructions, and asserted that, 'independently of those measures', the functioning of industrial activity was entrusted to 'the sense of discipline, of conscious responsibility and loyalty of all employees': 'it is above all on this spirit of sacrifice that the Ministry of Corporations relies, in order to neutralize or reduce the impact of enemy offences'.[38]

The protection of industries was extended, in principle, to industrial workers. Norms for the protection of industrial buildings established that when the alarms sounded, production was to be halted and workers sheltered or moved away from danger; on 22 March 1941 the Duce had stated that safeguarding workers was essential to continuity of production. War industries were required to prepare a list of essential tasks that must be carried out despite raids, and to make sure that workers performing them were sufficiently protected.[39]

Industrialists, however, complained at the frequent false alarms, claiming that daytime alarms were useless as they were never followed by protective action, and only damaged production by making workers nervous.[40] Industrialists and ministries discussed the issue from the start of area bombing in 1942, and finally reached agreement in August 1943, after the fall of the regime: as they decided that morale would be damaged more by a surprise raid, however small, than by false alarms, the problem was left intact.[41]

The ineffectiveness of Italy's air defences is reflected in low losses among Allied bombers. At the height of the offensive against Germany, Bomber Command typically lost about 5 per cent of aircraft despatched in a raid.[42] By contrast, over Genoa, Milan and Turin, Italy's industrial heartland, only 60 Bomber Command aircraft were shot down in 3,054 sorties between 1940 and 1943, a loss rate of 1.94 per cent.[43]

France's air defences in 1940, though less hopeless than predicted two years earlier by the Chief of the French Air Staff, were unable seriously to hinder the Luftwaffe's daylight bombing; they were then overwhelmed in the more general debacle.[44] From the armistice of June 1940, active defences in the northern zone passed into German hands. The south remained under French control, with a small air force plus anti-aircraft defences numbering some 12,500 officers and men.[45] Their effectiveness, however, was never seriously tested, as the south remained almost unbombed until its occupation by the Germans in November 1942.

German air defences over France fell, for most of the war, under the responsibility of Luftflotte (Air Fleet) 3, which managed anti-aircraft batteries and fighter units as well as bombers and ground attack aircraft operating from French soil. Defending French cities was not Luftflotte 3's highest priority. Its resources served to escort bombers to Britain (especially in 1940), to protect U-boats operating from the west coast, to form the left wing of the so-called 'Kammhuber line' of Reich air defences and, from 1944, to repel the long-awaited Allied landings.[46] The resources available for these tasks, whether in fighters or in flak batteries, were rarely adequate. The occupation of southern France from November 1942 stretched German air defences further; in November 1943, when anti-aircraft batteries were requested in anticipation of an invasion, just two regiments were moved from the Reich.[47] Air Fleet 3's aircraft were 'taxed far above their numbers', according to Boog, when confronting the Allied air offensive over France in spring 1944: a mere 50–100 fighters opposed the D-Day landings on 6 June.[48] The planned transfer of fighter units from Germany to France then turned to disaster, thanks to fuel shortages, damaged airfields, and insufficiently-trained pilots. By August, combat losses and fuel shortages led to an order to restrict Air Fleet 3's activities to a minimum, and by the month's end Luftwaffe units were being withdrawn to Belgium, effectively ending German air defences over French territory.[49]

The relative weakness of German air defences is demonstrated, again, by the Allies' loss rates. US Eighth Air Force sustained average losses of 5.7 per cent in its first year, but 3.7 per cent over France.[50] Among Allied four-engined bombers in 1943, losses there were 2.4 per cent.[51] By the summer of 1944, with Allied air superiority over France largely assured, the figures approached Italian levels – just 1.8 per cent for Bomber Command sorties between May and August 1944.[52]

Weak air defences and the low priority accorded to defending French targets caused friction between Vichy and the occupiers. This was especially clear after the Boulogne-Billancourt raid of 3/4 March 1942, which caught the Germans by surprise: no alarm had been given, and just one Wellington was lost of the 235 aircraft that attacked the Renault factory.[53] Admiral Darlan, then the second figure of the Vichy regime, noted that the bombers had 'flown at low altitude without being seriously troubled either by ground-based defences or fighter aircraft', and asked Fernand de Brinon, Vichy's chief representative in the northern zone, to intercede with the Germans 'to ensure an effective protection for industrial areas and the safeguard of working-class families who labour, in great part at least, for the benefit of Germany'. De Brinon replied that the Germans were committed to reinforcing air defences and giving civilians a 10-minute warning of raids, but were also determined to keep full control of alarm systems.[54]

Air defences were indeed reinforced – somewhat – after the Renault raid; alarm systems would remain the object of contention between the French and the occupying forces throughout the war. In Cherbourg, for example, the passive defence services complained that raids were usually signalled only by anti-aircraft fire; during an attack on Saint-Nazaire in April 1942, the town sirens sounded after those at the submarine base, denying civilians time to shelter.[55] But the Germans insisted on all sirens, including all those in the southern zone from 1943, being activated by their systems alone.[56] This caused delays. Colonel Cornillon, France's liaison officer at the Secretariat-General for Air Defence, reported that no alert had reached Montluçon before bombs started falling on 15/16 September 1943; the Germans refused, in March 1944, to guarantee a 15-minute warning for attacks on Nantes; the same month Cornillon again appealed to the Germans to allow sirens to be sounded on French initiative, but to no avail.[57] His superior, General Moniot, told the prefect of Haute-Savoie, after a raid on Annecy in June, that sirens could only be sounded there if the Germans gave permission from Lyon, 100 kilometres away, or if bombs were already falling; no alarm at all was given for the raid on Marseille of 15–16 August 1944.[58]

The Germans also, however, tried to palliate their own personnel shortages by enlisting French manpower in support of Luftflotte 3. After the occupation of the southern zone and the dissolution of France's residual armed forces on 27 November 1942, Hitler agreed to the constitution of a 'new French army', for the 'defence of Europe'. Air defences were to take priority in this enterprise.[59] French collaboration with the Germans on active defences reached its peak in 1943, when some 2,000 officers and men from the former French air force were assigned to rail-mounted anti-aircraft batteries. The experiment was not a success. Poor accommodation and worse food, the disagreeable experience of serving under direct German command, the non-co-operation of French railwaymen and the hostility of the public (resulting in at least one group of French demonstrators being fired on), all led to plummeting morale, rising desertions, and growing German suspicions of officers and men. The units were disbanded by the end of 1943.[60]

Somewhat more durable were the French observer companies in the southern zone. By early 1944, France possessed an Air Protection Service numbering some 4,200 officers and men, while the Alert Service counted 450 men and 299 women.[61] They too were integrated into a wholly German-controlled system, to which they provided raw information.[62] However, there were signs by late 1943 that the Resistance had infiltrated these services.[63] By the summer of 1944, moreover, they had become subject to increasing attacks and other forms of pressure from the Resistance, to low morale, and to desertions.[64]

In both France and Italy, therefore, active defences were considerably less formidable than over the Reich. In Italy they suffered from underfunding and antiquated equipment, in France from the low priority assigned them by the Germans, and, on the French side, from poor morale linked to the taint of collaboration. Both countries came to depend on the protection of the Germans, whose prime concern was not the defence of the civilian population. The burden falling on passive defences was all the greater.

GOVERNMENTS AND PASSIVE DEFENCE

In June 1940, Fascist Italy tried to ratchet up its passive defences; the Vichy authorities almost decommissioned them. The chief reason for the contrast was that whereas Italy entered the war on 10 June 1940, France's government signed an armistice just 12 days later. An RAF raid on Turin on 11 June, albeit on a symbolic scale, left little doubt in Italy of the nature of the conflict; in November 1941, the southern town of Brindisi was bombed seven times, with at least 107 deaths in a single raid, following which about 70 per cent of the population evacuated.[65] By contrast, the Vichy authorities persisted for months in the illusion that they had left the war, with the obvious corollary that new passive defence measures were unnecessary.

Differing perceptions of the bombing threat between France and Italy were to some extent reflected in law-making: Italy's flurry of legislation from 1940 to 1942 contrasted with France's more limited record. On 21 May 1940, Italy's preparations were laid out in a law on the 'organization of the nation for war'. This defined 'civil mobilization' as the transition from the state of peace to the state of war on the part of public administrations, industries and institutions that were necessary to the resistance of the nation. Citizens not eligible for military service had a duty to take part in the defence of the nation 'in the same spirit of devotion and sacrifice as the combatants'; they could be included in civil mobilization and were subject to military discipline.[66] Civilian service, another law added three days later, consisted in employing people's intellectual and manual activity in the service of the public administrations or institutions necessary in the defence of the nation at war.[67]

A law of 1 November 1940 was devoted to the appointment and duties of the *capi fabbricato* (block wardens), previously only specified in the 1936 law on UNPA. A *capo fabbricato* was required in every office, bank, hotel, education or religious institute, as well as private apartment blocks. S/he was nominated by UNPA, subject to Fascist Party ratification. Once the alarm sounded, s/he had to take full responsibility for the building's defence. While the landlord was required to provide adequate shelter and gas-masks, the *capo fabbricato* had to ensure that regulations were respected and masks issued to residents. S/he had to be over 21, or, in the case of men eligible for military service, over 48. With legislation went significant institutional reorganization. In particular, responsibility for most air protection moved from the War Ministry to the Interior in March 1941. The Air Protection section of the Italian Red Cross also came under Interior Ministry orders, while a decree of 5 May both brought UNPA under the Interior Ministry and set up a Directorate-General for Anti-Air Protection Services.[68] The War Ministry was left with residual control over the transmission of the alarm by DiCaT to provincial air-protection bodies, the protection of military buildings, and bomb disposal.[69]

Newly responsible for civil defence, the Interior Ministry rapidly began reorganizing it on the ground. On 18 April 1941 a circular stated that buildings under multiple occupancy in cities of more than 100,000 inhabitants required a caretaker as well as a *capo fabbricato*.[70] At the end of the year, a law brought fire brigades under a new Directorate-General of Fire Services within the Interior Ministry. The ministry organized a central school to train fire personnel; local-level organization was entrusted to committees which included representatives of the prefecture, the provincial administration, the *podestà* and a fire chief.[71]

More institutions under Interior Ministry control were created in 1941 and 1942. At the end of 1942, a decree replacing that of 5 May 1941 established a Directorate-General for War Services within the ministry. Its role was to supervise civil mobilization, evacuations, extraordinary assistance for those affected by bombing, and road traffic discipline.[72] Another decree mobilized caretakers, in accordance with the law of 24 May 1940 on civilian discipline in wartime.[73] While no significant laws were promulgated between then and the fall of the regime, after the armistice of September 1943 the government in the German-controlled part of Italy continued to cope with the impact of bombing; and in the liberated southern regions with reconstruction. In June 1944, Mussolini issued a decree empowering the Salò Republic's *podestàs* to force men between 14 and 60 years of age to work alongside the German forces repairing buildings, bridges and railway lines.[74] Meanwhile the Kingdom of the South, which was not bombed after the last German raid on Naples in March 1944, promulgated a law in November 1944 aimed at beginning reconstruction. The

Ministry of Public Works was required to start repairs to damaged buildings to accommodate bombed-out households; financial help was also offered to private owners who also began repairing urgently needed buildings. The maximum for state assistance was fixed at 150,000 lire, with a bonus of 10 per cent if repairs were completed by 30 June 1945. Mortgages were authorized for expenses above 150,000 lire, and some state help provided for repayments.[75]

Most of Italy's important legislation was thus enacted in the first two years of the war. This reflected the subsequent disaggregation of Italy's state machinery. As air raids intensified from 1942, and their consequences became harder to tackle, decisions were increasingly left to the local level, with periodic emergency orders from the ministries or from Mussolini.

In France, by contrast, the perception of having left the war, and the German preference for dealing with local authorities, meant that a new nationwide passive defence policy only developed slowly. At the same time some of the reorganization at the top, notably the move of passive defence to Interior and the creation of an interministerial co-ordinating body, resembled the Italian record with a time-lag of about a year.

Vichy's early record on passive defence is one in which apparent indifference competed with incapacity. The remains of the Direction de la Défense Passive (DDP) had fetched up after the Armistice in the picturesque Dordogne town of Sarlat; its staff was cut by four-fifths. With early RAF raids largely confined to the Channel ports, joined by Brest in early 1941, the minority of French citizens exposed to bombing were reported as feeling 'abandoned' by the rest of France; their mayors formed an association, the Conference of Municipalities of Coastal Towns, to lobby an apparently indifferent government for better protection.[76] The DDP had, it is true, relocated to Lyon by February 1941 (and thence, in May 1943, to Paris).[77] But its head from December 1940, General Sérant, still complained in September 1941 that passive defence had sunk into indifference across France.[78] His central staff at the time amounted to just 31 people including typists, 28 in Lyon and three in Paris.[79]

Civil defence received greater official attention after the Boulogne-Billancourt raid of March 1942. Within two months, the DDP's position had been reinforced. Moved from War to the Interior on 18 March, it fell a month later under the responsibility of Pierre Laval, who returned to office (after being sacked by Pétain in December 1940) as head of government and Interior Minister from 18 April. It was Laval who had signed the Practical Instruction on passive defence when he had held the same posts 11 years earlier.[80] His delegation of responsibility for policing and public order to the rising young prefect René Bousquet placed passive defence in the hands of one of Vichy's ablest figures (as well as one of the most notorious, owing to Bousquet's involvement in the round-up and deportation of Jews). Even so, as late as early 1943, Sérant would again complain that basic air-raid precautions were unknown not only to the public, but even to many passive defence authorities.[81]

A second parallel with Italy was the creation, in February 1943, of the

Interministerial Protection Service Against War Events (SIPEG) and the subsequent setting-up of similar structures in the *départements*. Placed under a prefect, Jean Lacombe, and directly responsible to Laval, the SIPEG was intended 'to stamp unity of direction' on bodies responsible for ensuring 'the security of persons, the safeguard of property, the functioning of public services, and the continuation of economic activity' in bombed areas, as well as to keep Laval 'personally informed of all measures taken and of their execution'.[82] The SIPEG also had a highly visible presence in the shape of two trains equipped with operating theatres, catering facilities, medical personnel and social workers, as well as food, clothes and medical supplies, designed to bring speedy succour after raids.[83] A further reorganization in September 1943 gave SIPEG the 'command' of the Refugees Directorate, the Fire Protection Directorate, and the DDP, the last two being placed under a General Civil Protection Directorate within the Interior Ministry.[84] With Bousquet's forced resignation at the end of 1943, this then fell within the General Secretariat for the Maintenance of Order under Joseph Darnand from January 1944. Although Darnand, head of Vichy's Milice, was one of the regime's outright fascists, the SIPEG itself remained relatively untainted and survived the Liberation at least into November 1944.[85]

This reflected the relative continuity of French passive defence policy across the regime changes from the Third Republic to Vichy to the post-war Provisional Government.[86] There was also continuity in legislation. The core text, Daladier's Law on the General Organization of the Nation for Wartime of 11 July 1938, remained in force, empowering Vichy, for example, to requisition buildings and conscript persons for civil defence. The Instruction Pratique of 1939 remained the key text in passive defence policy during 1942–3; Vichy passive defence legislation was validated, in turn, by the Liberation governments in 1944.[87]

Continuity did not, however, preclude activity and innovation. The Vichy governments, especially under Laval, devoted considerable efforts not only to co-ordinating passive defence, but also to gathering and diffusing information and to building adequate manpower. Information-gathering, initially limited to routine police reports, was reinforced from March 1942; an attack like the Boulogne-Billancourt raid both demanded speedy remedies and offered lessons to passive-defence teams across the country. From July 1942, a roneo-ed 8–12-page *Bulletin de Renseignements* (information bulletin) was sent every two months to senior passive defence personnel. Confidential, technical, and free of propaganda, the Bulletin outlined major raids (numbers of aircraft, types of bombs, human and material damage, shelter performance, the successes and failures of passive defence teams), and included a nationwide table (updated the following month as final details arrived) of bombs dropped, buildings destroyed, and casualties. Cazes, appointed as Director to succeed Sérant in September 1943, soon demanded that prefects supply basic information within two hours of any major raid to allow needs for reinforcements in personnel or equipment to be assessed.[88] The *Bulletin de Renseignements* became a printed

Bulletin d'Information, aimed, as Cazes wrote, to ensure that 'bombed regions should give the benefit of their experience to regions favoured hitherto' in areas such as rescue, clearance, the organization of passive defence services, or the reliability of shelters and trenches.[89] It included new government regulations and reprinted articles from the foreign (Axis or neutral) press. Like Cazes himself, the Bulletin survived the Liberation; the last number appeared in May 1945. Although coverage broke down from July–August 1944 (with the big raids on Le Havre in September, for example, going unrecorded in its pages), the Bulletin before then provides a remarkably precise account of major raids on France.[90]

In contrast with Italy, this record suggests an almost frenetic acceleration of legislative or quasi-legislative activity as the bombing intensified. While results on the ground did not necessarily follow at the same pace, the texts themselves were generally practical, specific and well-considered. In Italy too, prefects sent information to the Interior Ministry, after raids, on casualties and damage to infrastructure, industry and communication lines, and Italian local archives contain vast numbers of such reports. However, no effort was made at the centre to collate them or to circulate the results internally.

In purely institutional terms, therefore, the challenge of real air raids led to passive defence becoming a key preoccupation of central government in both France and Italy. If legislation and institutional reorganization had been all that was required, both countries would have been well defended. The French record, however, suggests a more continuous effort to meet the challenge, where Italy increasingly resorted to ad hoc measures.

This is also reflected in the delivery of services on the ground. Despite their highly authoritarian character, both Vichy France and Fascist Italy found that implementing passive defence and social assistance required the co-operation both of different state bodies and local authorities (via the prefects), and also of a wide range of para-public entities that retained a degree of independence from the state and were present, in varying degrees, at the grass roots. These will be covered in more detail in Chapter 6. However, the clearest difference between the organization of passive defence in the two countries is the stronger lead given by central government in France. Here, all localities of 10,000 inhabitants or more had a passive defence service of sorts, and could expect assistance from the prefecture, the field services of main ministries within the *départements*, and, from 1943, the SIPEG, if they needed it. In Italy, by contrast, local authorities were left to organize defences for themselves to a far greater extent, with highly variable results.

In the 'totalitarian state' of pre-war Italy, the communes had been largely confined to routine administrative tasks; in wartime, by contrast, they assumed a central role in managing city life during emergencies. The *podestà*s were required to supervise the work of a range of institutions at commune level, including the Communal Institutes of Assistance (ECAs), the fire brigades, and the local branches of the Red Cross. The predominance of communal institutions over the Fascist Party was established by an Interior Ministry circular of May 1943, which limited the role of the Party in dealing directly with air raids. The Party would only provide help to people whose houses had been completely destroyed, while assistance in all other matters was entrusted to the Communes.[91] On the other hand the Fascist Party and its associate organizations (female groups and youth groups in particular) helped organize evacuations, in co-ordination with the UNPA and centres for the assistance of bombed-out households. Meanwhile the Questura (central police stations in each city) and the Carabinieri (a branch of the armed forces with police duties) were responsible for public order; and the army was employed locally to help cope with the worst consequences of the raids (for example, rescuing people trapped under debris, or clearing streets after exceptionally heavy attacks).

In France the old republican partnership between prefects and mayors remained more or less intact. Each figure was, in principle, at the top of a pyramid. Mayors (or heads of 'special delegations' in cases where the whole council had been dismissed) commanded front-line municipal services ranging from road-building to schools to social assistance. Most passive defence personnel fell under municipal control. Prefects were (in theory at least) at the head of a body of field services that carried the work of central ministries and directorates – Interior or Education or Public Works, for example, and (in wartime) Refugees – to the territorial level of France's 90 *départements*. Mayors were expected to report on their activities to prefects, and relied on prefects for essential resources, particularly central government finance. Prefects would enforce (and sometimes negotiate) the norms and standards under which municipalities operated and supply technical expertise where needed. To implement central government policy, moreover, prefects needed the mayors' active co-operation; their relationship, adversarial at times, was perforce often collaborative. Vichy, in principle, made it more hierarchical, enhancing the prefects' role at the expense of elected local bodies (the councils for the *départements* were abolished in 1940, municipal elections ended, and dissident mayors and councillors dismissed). And a new tier of regional prefects was created in 1941.[92] But the prefectoral corps remained, with some exceptions, a career body, with many of the reflexes of the old regime (to the frustration of the Germans, who engineered a major purge in May 1944).[93] Mayors, meanwhile, sought to retain their legitimacy by 'concentrating on the most basic everyday concerns of the population'.[94] Prefects and mayors were both, it is true, challenged by the fascist parties that developed, with German encouragement, in occupied France: the Rassemblement National Populaire (RNP), the Parti Populaire Français (PPF) and the Francistes. These, however, lacked the organization, the social roots, and the presence of Italy's fascists; moreover, they quarrelled amongst themselves. Where France, despite the occupation, retained an articulated partnership at local level, which was at least partly able to resist politicization, in Italy the roles of local government officers were both less well defined and subject to interference by the Fascist Party.

PASSIVE DEFENCE IN MICROCOSM? THE PROTECTION OF MONUMENTS AND WORKS OF ART

How well did the machinery of government developed by the two regimes cope with bombing? One small indicator can be found in steps France and Italy took to preserve historic monuments and works of art. There is a sense in which these measures represented a microcosm of measures to save lives: without them considerably more art treasures would have been lost, yet they could not hope to preserve historic buildings, or all works of art, against heavy bombing. Moreover, the movement of the war, especially in Italy, meant that safe havens could be transformed within days into battle zones, entailing multiple evacuations.

In France, an interministerial instruction of 12 August 1937 on the conservation of monuments and works of art was implemented from August 1939 by the National Museums Directorate and the Historic Monuments Service. Some 18,000 square metres of stained glass, including the windows of the Sainte-Chapelle in Paris or cathedrals such as Rouen, Bourges or Chartres, were stored on the initiative of the Historic Monuments Directorate; the practice run undertaken during the Munich crisis in 1938 speeded the operation. Flammable materials were cleared out of attics and sand spread in them.[95] Statuary could be removed from facades, and buildings themselves given protection with scaffolding and sandbags, though these were in short supply. The case of St Vincent's church in Rouen illustrates what such measures could, and could not, achieve. Nothing could save the church from destruction by Allied bombs on 31 May 1944 (80 French churches or cathedrals were wrecked or damaged), but the stained glass was preserved and now adorns the modern church of St Joan of Arc. Meanwhile artworks from the Louvre and other museums were put into cases and evacuated to supposedly safe areas. From 27 August 1939, 37 convoys of lorries from France's 23 national museums left for the Loire valley with their precious crates (preferred locations were châteaux and abbeys).[96] Provincial galleries and museums, too, undertook a comparable evacuation. In Bouches-du-Rhône, for example, nearly 400 packing-cases containing material from the museums, libraries, archives and religious buildings of the *département* and of the towns of Marseille, Aix-en-Provence and Arles, were sent for safe-keeping by the chief librarian of Marseille to an abbey and a château north of Aix.[97] Some at least of these objects, however, were returned to Marseille and Aix after the 1940 armistice, before a further evacuation took place, this time to the Château of Laval in the Basses-Alpes, from 1943. A new evacuation was ordered in the spring of 1944, this time to the town of Busset, near Vichy.[98] Even in the fluid situation of 1944, as Karlsgodt observes, a combination of well-chosen safe sites, sound storage methods, and luck achieved a broadly successful preservation operation.[99] That did not prevent total wartime damage to monuments and works of art estimated at FF10 billion, compared with an arts budget, in 1944, of FF424 million.[100]

In Italy, the sheer density of monuments and art treasures, and the movement of the front (and the bombing) up the peninsula, posed even greater problems. On 6 July 1940 the Minister of National Education, Giuseppe Bottai, signed a law stating how superintendents in the provinces were to protect the country's artistic, cultural and historical heritage.[101] In fact, superintendents had already received orders a month earlier to evacuate works of art. Although various local reports demonstrated a total lack of preparation, wherever possible works from museums and private collections began to be packed up, and some of the most famous public monuments were covered.[102]

When the air war on Italy became heavier from 1942, national decisions and resources were insufficient for the protection of invaluable works of art under threat and local resolutions had to be taken case by case. For example, as raids over Sicily increased in March 1942, the Education Ministry set up a commission to safeguard the ancient temples of the Agrigento valley. The commission concluded that while protection was impossible from either shrapnel or direct hits, the only practical precaution – as for most buildings – was to reinforce the temples' foundations. Indirectly, the risks could be limited by removing military targets from the surrounding area; the War Ministry thus ordered that all military services be moved at least 500 metres away.[103]

By summer 1943, however, little could be done at local level to protect monuments. For example, the four raids on Milan in August 1943, aggravated by water shortages, unleashed a week-long fire that devastated many of the city's buildings. The southern provinces of Apulia and Campania, bombed by both the Allies and the Luftwaffe in the summer of 1943, suffered most. The church of Santa Chiara in Naples, for example, was gutted by incendiary bombs which destroyed the frescoes, pictures and sculptures, none of which had been removed. As the war continued, works of art were constantly shifted from place to place in chaotic conditions, subject to both Allied bombing and German theft during the army's northwards retreat.[104] Perhaps the best symbol of this was the appearance, in front of two British reporters who went to interview Indian troops in a villa outside Florence, of Botticelli's Primavera lying unboxed on the floor, among soldiers making tea and within half a mile of German tanks.[105] Besides being a consistent subject of diplomacy between the Allies and the Vatican (and at different times, between the Allies and Badoglio and even the Resistance), the bombing of artistic cities became one of the main subjects of Fascist propaganda, as later chapters will show.

The challenge to Italy had been significantly greater than that to France; the density of historic art was greater, less of it was readily movable (especially if it took the form of frescoes), and the battle raged all over the country. If protecting monuments and art was difficult, protecting people was to prove much more so, calling as it did on financial and political resources beyond the capacity of either regime.

PROTECTION AND PENURY: FINANCING PASSIVE DEFENCE AND WELFARE

Pre-war preparations in both France and Italy had established how limited resources were in relation to the task of giving even basic protection against bombing. From 1940, moreover, war-making took up a growing share of the Italian budget; France, though relieved of the need to fight, had to divert half its spending to the Reich.

Pre-war discussions between Mussolini and military leaders had shown that funds were lacking for both active and passive defences – a point Mussolini chose to ignore as he took Italy to war in June 1940. The military efforts of 1935–7 left little opportunity for further investment in the war economy.[106] In August 1940, Italy's Finance Ministry allocated just 50 million lire to air protection.[107] However, by December it was obvious that hundreds of millions would be needed to protect schools alone. Since such sums were not available, the ministries of war and national education requested that at least schools in key coastal areas be protected. This alone would require 30 million lire.[108] It was also clear by February 1941 that funds were insufficient to reimburse auxiliary institutions for civil defence works; prefects had so far received 250,000 lire, and asked that the sum be doubled.[109]

The difficulties of meeting necessary expenditure, especially on shelters, became ever clearer as Italy's war progressed. For example, following the raid of 9–10 July 1941, the director-general of the Naples air-defence services outlined his shelter needs to Buffarini, then undersecretary at the Interior Ministry: 4.2 million lire was needed for shelters at the port, 21.5 million for the city, 3.5 million for schools – a total of over half the previous year's allocation of 50 million for the whole country. In addition, while the alarm system had been newly upgraded with a grant of 36,500 lire, the raids had hit the siren network.[110] The report suggested that either the funds were insufficient for the defence of the public or they had been improperly distributed, since the inadequacy of the city's active and passive defences was undermining the population's resistance.

In France too, spending lagged behind needs, though probably less drastically than in Italy. In February 1942, on the basis of studies undertaken in 1939, Sérant evaluated investments necessary for France's passive defence needs at about FF8.6 billion, including FF4.1 billion for shelters, FF680 million for medical facilities and ambulances and FF1.5 billion for gas-masks.[111] Less than a quarter of that had been invested in the four years to the end of 1941, with a sharp decline after the peak year of 1939 (Table 4.1); only running costs had risen because passive defence teams had to be paid their hourly rates during raids and alerts. Sérant proposed raising spending to FF920 million a year for three years and FF760 million a year for a further seven years, initially targeted at 27 vulnerable (mostly coastal) *départements* (16 in the northern zone, 11 in the south). With hindsight, his plans appear as ambitious given the record since 1939, but conservative in the light of the future scale of Allied raids. In the event, a budget of FF320 million was expected for 1942 when the DDP was transferred to the Interior.[112] Nevertheless, larger sums became available as the raids intensified. The passive defence investment budget for 1944 was FF600 million; and one of Vichy's last budgetary acts, the following July, was to double that sum, authorizing FF1.2 billion for the year.[113] Sérant's smooth ten-year spending programme might have yielded excellent results if begun in 1930; instead, French passive defence expenditure developed irregularly, in response to the urgency of the situation, but never meeting needs as Sérant had defined them.

Table 4.1 Spending by French central government on passive defence (millions of francs), 1938–41

	Investments				Running costs
	Ministries and other public services	***Seine (Paris and surrounding area)***	***Provincial* départements**	***Total***	
1938	10	45	49	104	0.5
1939	172	210	680	1,062	50
1940	25	137	312	474	180
1941	83	50	117	250	160
Total	290	442	1,158	1,890	391

Source: SHAT 2P/20, Rapport sur l'état d'avancement du programme de la Défense passive à la date du 31 décembre 1941, 14.

Money, however, was not the only problem. In both countries, raw materials were increasingly rare. The lack of iron, lime, concrete, wood and bricks meant that in Italy shelter construction was inadequate even in industrial areas. This was clear in France too: by the end of 1941 the construction of huts for bombed-out households was hampered by shortages of wood, cement and steel; Darlan was inviting prefects to seek 'alternative materials' for shelters; and lack of raw materials was constraining the national investment budget.[114] Early in 1943, Bousquet observed that iron and cement were almost unobtainable, and that it had become impossible to synchronize allocations of credits and of raw materials.[115] In March 1943 the sub-prefect of Saint-Nazaire complained of a lack, not only of raw materials to build shelters, but of coal, wood, candles and oil for lamps.[116] By June 1944 Marseille's *Directeur de la défense passive* reported that lack of fuel made it hard to move materials.[117] Well documented nationally, penury was all too tangible on the ground.

Also crucial to budgets was the growing demand for welfare payments to evacuees and bombed-out households. In Italy, giving immediate assistance to bombed-out households was a task for the ECA in each commune. For example, following a raid on 8 August 1943, the *podestà* of Genoa reported to the prefect that the commune had assisted 3,252 families (10,098 people): food or money to be spent in restaurants was provided. This form of help aimed at coping with an emergency: it stopped after five days, but could be renewed for up to ten. It would then be replaced by a 'normal' level of assistance;[118] the ECAs were required to give families the means to evacuate with their possessions. Bombing victims at the end of their emergency allowances were provided, again by ECAs, with up to 1,500 lire for the head of the family and 500 lire for each remaining family member.[119] In order to avoid fraud, beneficiaries were asked to provide a declaration signed by the municipal police that their homes were uninhabitable, and not just lightly damaged. Allocations were in theory generous: the average annual salary of an industrial worker was around 4,000 lire, and that of a white-collar worker around 12,000.[120] However, particularly from early 1943 and in southern Italian cities, records show that ECAs were encountering increasing difficulties meeting these entitlements.

In France, the welfare system was rather more developed. Vichy marked an important step in the transition between the patchwork of welfare institutions existing in inter-war France and the more comprehensive welfare state that emerged after the Liberation.[121] It also saw a slighter reliance on the municipal authorities and a greater role taken by the state. This was done both directly through the Refugees Directorate or, as 'extreme emergency aid' (*secours d'extrême urgence*), through the prefects, and indirectly through organizations like the Secours National, a para-public body financed by the state and by private and business donations, which behaved more like a charity than a state body. The aid regime was developed and enlarged from 1940 to 1944, following inflation (with a time lag) and aligning benefits for refugees and evacuees.[122] Benefits depended on two important variables: whether the claimant was classified as 'needy' and, for evacuees, whether the evacuation had been voluntary or forced.

The official definition of needy, presented in a SIPEG brochure of May 1944, was relatively generous, and (unsurprisingly for Vichy) very family-oriented: a monthly income (wages and any allowances) of below FF1,600 – a miner's wage – for single persons, but below FF3,470 for a family of four, or under FF4,800 if separated by evacuation.[123] The definition of needy, though fairly restrictive, was not synonymous with destitution.[124]

To receive state aid, evacuees had to produce a *fiche d'évacuation* (evacuation ticket), the bombed-out an analogous *carte de sinistré*. Evacuees needed, first, to live in an area considered at risk. In the wake of the Boulogne-Billancourt raid of March 1942, the Refugees Directorate refined the notion of a danger zone to include sectors of cities, rather than whole *départements*.[125] To obtain their *fiche d'évacuation*, persons wishing to leave would normally agree to go to an official destination for their city or *département*. Compulsory evacuees and the needy would then be entitled to a one-off payment of FF750 per person, plus free transport with up to 150 kgs of baggage plus 200–300 kgs of furniture per person, within the limits of available rail services. Voluntary evacuees not qualified as needy were merely given a promise of assistance from the Refugee Service, though incentives to leave danger zones – including a (means-tested) allowance of up to FF300 per dependent – might be available to assist with additional costs such as rent. Laws of 1 September 1942, 13 May 1943, and 6 January 1944 provided for daily allowances for needy refugees (initially between FF10 for dependent children and FF15 for a head of household, rising to FF15–FF19 from January 1944), as well as provisions for moving costs and rent, heating and lighting allowances.[126]

Victims of air raids – *sinistrés* – were also entitled to free medical treatment if wounded; funeral expenses were covered to a maximum of FF1,000 per person. The *carte de sinistré* was obtainable on a simple declaration following the raid: its holders were entitled to emergency assistance of FF1,000 per person, plus an extra FF500 if the dwelling was completely destroyed; to a daily housing, heating and lighting allowance of FF7 for a household of three; to moving expenses of FF750; and to variable furniture replacement costs. Bombed-out employees who found themselves unable to return to work and were classified as needy were entitled to daily allowances of FF19 for heads of households and FF15 for dependents for three months, falling to FF15 and FF12 in subsequent months or until alternative employment was found.[127] Alongside this assistance regime, designed both to save evacuees and *sinistrés* from destitution and to make voluntary evacuation a materially acceptable option, the government also allocated FF10 million to *Secours d'extrême urgence* in the 1943 budget. This amount was doubled to FF20 million in September, after the Nantes raids, and was intended for deserving cases, designated by committees convened for the purpose.[128]

Vichy's assistance to the victims of bombing is open to several criticisms. First, means-testing excluded many victims. Second, it was complex and bureaucratized, which led to difficulties when, as at Lorient, bombing caused the dispersion both of the recipients and the distributors of aid, or when a direct hit destroyed records.[129] Third, the promise of assistance with removals, designed to encourage evacuation, depended on the presence of transport facilities which were rarely available. Fourth, the levels of assistance were themselves modest.[130] Yet the victims of air raids could expect a more than symbolic level of assistance from the Vichy state. By 1944, national spending directly occasioned by bombing represented nearly FF5.5 billion, or 3.63

per cent of the total state budget; of this, FF4.7 billion, or 3.12 per cent of the budget, was assigned to various welfare functions – looking after child evacuees, refugees and *sinistrés*.[131]

Some of this money, at least, reached its intended recipients in good time: in both Toulon and Saint-Étienne, for example, thousands of bombed-out households were receiving FF1,000, or slightly more, per person, within some 48 hours of reporting their loss after raids in 1944.[132] Unlike Fascist Italy, therefore, Vichy France appears to have managed to keep benefits flowing roughly according to plan until within weeks before its collapse.

SHELTERS

Shelters were the most costly and the most politically salient feature of civil defence. Pre-war preparations in both countries had been inadequate; both attempted to improve them; neither spent enough money, though France's allocations appear to have been the greater. Gauging the success of shelter policy presents difficulties, however: French and Italian local authorities were inclined to overstate the numbers of places by including, for example, cellars that had not been surveyed or reinforced, or trenches fallen into disrepair.

Inadequate finance did not stop Italy's government from issuing a battery of regulations on shelters during the first year of the war. On 5 December 1940 the War Ministry ordered that a sign be placed at the entrance of every shelter (public, collective or domestic) indicating maximum capacity on the basis of two people every square metre. *Capi fabbricato* were responsible for ensuring that these limits were respected.[133] Six days later the War Ministry warned that they were often being exceeded, and that overcrowding could lead to serious problems, especially a lack of air. In the same document, employers were ordered by the Ministry of Corporations to let workers leave their posts if the alarm sounded during working hours, and to pay them for time spent in the shelters.[134] On 29 March 1941 the Interior Ministry issued a circular aimed at ensuring public access to shelters in school buildings, which provincial directors of education had tried to restrict. Especially at night, said the circular, they should be treated as public shelters like any others.[135]

Prefects, meanwhile, were to ensure that laws and decrees on shelters were applied locally. For example, in reference to the law of 21 May 1940, reports from the Genoa commune prefect's commission established that landlords must inform UNPA regarding the adaptability of parts of their property for shelters by 30 November 1940. UNPA had to check with technicians; then the prefect's commission had to take a final decision on the suitability of the premises. Compulsion could be used against obstructive landlords. Necessary spending was to be anticipated by the commune.[136] This was reinforced in January 1941, when the prefect, referring to the decree of September 1936, the law of June 1939, and the War Ministry circular of 30 December 1940, decreed that every block of flats must have a shelter strong enough to resist the collapse of the block. Engineers and architects should assess projects and landlords should bear the expense.[137] Fines for non-co-operation were also set out in ordinances of 7 November 1940 and 14 January 1941.[138]

In practice little was done. Even where enough shelters appeared available, their quality was often unacceptable. In Naples, the Anti-aircraft Protection Directorate warned in 1941 that existing shelters had narrow entrances through which only two people at a time could enter; an orderly queue during an alert was unlikely. Shelters were also wet, being underground and lacking proper flooring. Many owners had not removed their possessions, including bottles, from shelter areas, leaving little room and increasing the danger in case of a direct hit or simply of blast: 'in three-quarters of the shelters', the report noted, 'the required conditions are not observed'.[139]

A visit to Naples by the general director of UNPA, after the raids of October 1941, nevertheless produced a remarkably complacent assessment. While there was room for improvement, it stated, the city's shelters were more or less sufficient and the population was resisting well. During the October raids, industrial areas on the east of Naples were targeted, and there had not been many victims. The prefect had promised new proposals if attacks continued. The UNPA director recommended improvements to shelters such as benches, flooring, or the writing of patriotic slogans on walls, and advised the head of the Fascist party in Naples to be among the people during alarms.[140]

The very next day, however, a commander of the army section of Naples anti-aircraft protection, General Luigi Gambelli, told a radically different story. There were almost no public shelters in areas between the port and industrial sites, his report stated; the private ones could do very little to protect the population; in some blocks people stayed at home during alerts because the alternative was not much safer; and the nearest public shelters were often too far for elderly people or people with children to reach in time. Proper shelters, Gambelli wrote, were needed immediately. This was crucial in terms of the regime's resistance: it was a chance that should not be missed to show that the regime cared about the people. Gambelli consulted with the prefect, who said he would pass the information to the *podestà*, and recommended the improvement of private shelters rather than the building of public ones, which were too costly and difficult to build because of the lack of raw materials.[141]

Gambelli reinforced his conclusions after a raid on 17 November. In Naples as in the rest of Italy, he stated, public shelters 'had just the minimum required level of comfort to make it bearable to spend a short amount of time there. Having to stay there for entire nights, however, was distressing, particularly in those caves ... very humid and with no ventilation.'[142] This problem was aggravated as raids intensified. Cases of people fainting in crowded shelters because of insufficient air became common by 1943, as, for example, explained in a Carabinieri report from La Spezia after a raid in June.[143]

In Milan, too, shelter provision, considered sufficient for night raids, was not considered adequate by the air-protection authorities after the start of daytime attacks, particularly at rush hour, from 24 October 1942 (Table 4.2). Now, despite the fall in population due to evacuation, shelters for 40–50,000 more people were needed in Milan's city centre, within the Navigli, and the same number in the periphery. A programme was set out for the construction of 180 shelters, later raised to 300, at a cost of 150 million lire. It was only partially realized, however: 178 cellars were requisitioned in the centre to shelter 42,000 people, but from these, only 55 shelters were actually created, with a capacity of 18,000. In the periphery, 27 cellars were requisitioned with the aim of creating shelters for 6,700 people. Moreover, the use of incendiary bombs in the raid of 24 October necessitated improvements to the technical specifications of shelters.

Table 4.2 Shelters in Milan, October 1942

Public shelters in schools (available to public outside school hours: number)	203 for 96,710 people
Public shelters in public and private buildings (number)	90 for 37,420 people
Trenches (useful against shrapnel only: linear metres)	9,500 for 43,000 people
Protected arcades (useful against shrapnel only: linear metres)	1,100 for 10,000 people

Source: ACS, MI, DGPCSA, b. 106, report by the prefect of Milan, 4 March 1943.

In June 1943, work was also under way constructing shelters for the 630,000 inhabitants of Turin. According to the prefect, public and private shelters could host about 70,000 people, while work was in progress for sheltering about 100,000. Generally, at least two-thirds of the population could find refuge only in cellars, which were unsafe. Again, a shortage of workers, raw materials and transport hindered the construction of viable shelters.[144]

Similar considerations affected the protection of industry. For example, the city and province of Milan contained around 12,000 industries, with around 600,000 workers. Shelters and trenches, of a sort, had been built for 349,172 workers, concentrated in the industries considered most likely to be targeted. The main problem, as in other cities (and France), was the lack of raw materials, compounded by inadequate means of transport.[145]

In southern Italy, shelters remained unfinished until the end of the war and posed a problem in the liberated regions while the Italian campaign was moving north. In Taranto, the construction of a public shelter, considered urgent in April 1943, was still incomplete in March 1944, as the Commune had not found a company ready to build it for an 'acceptable' price. A report from the provincial administration of Taranto shortly after the end of the war explained that, for reasons of public hygiene, the Allies had requested a return to the pre-war condition of areas disturbed by uncompleted shelter construction.[146]

While the south began to deal with issues of reconstruction under Allied control, the centre and the north under the Salò Republic continued to face heavy raids between 1943 and 1945, with shelter provision that was often desperately inadequate. An inspection of Turin's 102 school shelters reported that only 9 were approximately effective. Nearly all Turinese schoolchildren were therefore in danger, and it was proposed to concentrate classes in three days a week in order to shorten their time in such unsafe premises.[147] A report on Genoa's emergency plan at the end of January 1944 showed that despite evacuations, 516,109 people needed to be sheltered (including evening evacuees). Such conditions made the rule that shelters must provide one square metre of space for every two people utterly unrealistic; the local administration therefore raised the figure to three per square metre. Despite this, an attached list suggested that shelters in most areas of Genoa were not adequate. Moreover, the shortage worsened 'whenever the German command decided to use any of these, either totally or partially, for the armed forces'. As for private shelters, which were supposed to be built at the landlords' expense, there was 'no point talking about them as they are simply shelters created by reinforcing cellars with wood'.[148]

France, too, suffered from a lack of shelters, money and materials, and from German demands. There was, however, an attempt to get to grips with the problem nationally. Sérant's report of early 1942 observed that work had almost ceased in the months after the Armistice, that there had been doubts about its continued necessity, and that many of the rudimentary trench shelters built in 1938–9 had deteriorated beyond use. Sérant estimated that 8 million shelter places were available nationwide, a shortfall of 9.4 million against the 17.4 million required. The programme for 1941, as yet incomplete, would cover just 4.5 per cent of this – 420,000 additional places (265,000 in the occupied zone, 155,000 in the 'free' South).[149] A year later, Bousquet reduced the total estimate of places required to 13 million, and put the shortfall at 6 million. He added, however, that inspections had shown that many shelters officially counted had disappeared, or had been abandoned or requisitioned by the Germans. The way forward, he suggested, was an unspecified number of small shelters in trenches or cellars, using minimal raw materials.[150] Like the shortage of raw materials, the national inadequacy of shelter provision was fully reflected on the ground. Brest and Lorient, subjected as naval bases to heavy and repeated Allied raids but equipped with at least some deep shelters on German orders, were very much the exceptions; few French towns had this type of provision.[151]

Paris was, in principle, well protected. Official figures for the *département* of the Seine in 1943 gave 5,115,800 shelter places, enough for virtually the whole population. Of these, however, the great majority (3,260,000 in Paris itself and 700,000 in the suburbs) were simple cellars without reinforcement; 280,000 were in strutted cellars, 450,000 in trenches, 350,000 in the Paris metro, and 70,000 in various quarries, leaving some 6,000 in purpose-built consolidated shelters.[152] The detailed figures, moreover, suggest somewhat less thorough coverage. Boulogne-Billancourt, for example, had shelter for about half the population at the time of the March 1942 raid, with 43,286 places in cellars and 4,500 in trenches for 99,500 habitants.[153]

The second and third cities of France, both in the southern zone, were less well protected. In Lyon, a report in early 1942 counted 270,000 places in the whole of the Rhône *département* – enough for about one in four of the population, and most of them in rudimentary trench shelters. A year later, the Lyon conurbation offered 197,220 places for about 600,000 inhabitants, but again, about 170,000 of these were in basic trench shelters.[154] Only by the spring of 1944 had the total apparently improved, with some 370,000 places, or shelter for one inhabitant in three, in the whole of the Rhône *département*.[155]

In Marseille, meanwhile, Sérant complained to the Prefect of Police that shelter facilities in the Bouches-du-Rhône *département* were 'very incomplete', that Martigues, with 10,000 inhabitants, had no shelters at all, and that the authorities had only committed FF15,000 of the FF1.5 million allocated to their passive defence needs.[156] At the end of 1943, Marseille could shelter a quarter of a population estimated at 800,000, but many of its shelters were prone to flooding or otherwise unserviceable; their number had barely increased in the previous year.[157] That August a Mme Émile, living at the dock end of the Boulevard National, had written personally to Pétain asking why a car equipped with a loudspeaker exhorted people to use non-existent shelters: 'If it were permitted' she added, 'for a Frenchwoman to have an opinion, M. le Maréchal, I would say that it was more worthwhile to organize subscriptions to avoid there being victims than to assist victims', as the latter resembled closing the stable door after the ass had bolted.[158] Criticism spread after the big raid of 27 May 1944. Weeks later, for example, an energetic young warden was complaining that communicating walls between cellars were still not pierced, and belongings such as coal or bottles had not been removed from them.[159]

Comparable situations, or worse, were found in provincial towns and cities across France, where a first major raid routinely revealed shortages of shelters. Their condition and signposting mattered, too: the public might be ignorant of where shelters were, or reluctant to use them because they were dirty or unlit.[160]

The lack of trench shelters, for example, was blamed for the 274 deaths in Rennes on 8 March 1943; the prefect allocated FF900,000 and ordered the mayor to start an urgent remedial programme.[161] In Nantes, the heavily censored official press was authorized to query inadequate shelter provision: in October 1943, mayor Orrion felt obliged to offer a public answer to several articles covering the issue.[162] But even by the war's end, according to Paul Caillaud, the former Passive Defence Director of Nantes, there were at most 75,000 places for nearly 200,000 inhabitants.[163] Le Creusot, despite having sustained one heavy attack in October 1942, still only had shelters for one-sixth of the population by the time of the second raid in June 1943.[164] In the southern *département* of Var in April 1943, the newly-appointed Passive Defence Director, Captain Marloy, reported just 30,750 places for 220,500 people in the whole *département*, with 19,500 places for a population of 120,000 in Toulon and a mere 500 for the 27,000 inhabitants of the neighbouring port of La Seyne.[165] By the year's end, he could claim a total of 47,700 for Toulon, with 4,500 more under construction. That was still not enough to prevent public dissatisfaction after the raid of 24 November.[166] Ironically, Marloy was ready to declare the shelter position satisfactory, thanks in part to galleries dug into the hills, just as the Occupation, and the air raids, were ending.[167] In Saint-Étienne, an industrial city of nearly 200,000 inhabitants, the head of the shelters service reported to the mayor as late as 23 October 1943 that once German requisitions were taken into account, only 4,136 shelter places were available. A report of a year later – after the Liberation – claimed 34,466 places, but of these 24,000 were in cellars without reinforcement.[168] Here, as in the Lyon suburb of Vénissieux, or the Norman town of Avranches, records show not only that shelters were lacking, badly-positioned, or both, but that they were poorly maintained, degraded from bad weather, dirty, full of rubbish, lacking in amenities such as benches, lighting, or toilets, or even locked or inaccessible.[169]

Rouen had shelters for 42,110 out of its 91,000 inhabitants by April 1944, but its suburb Sotteville, a major target as a rail centre, had some 5,000 places for a population of 20,000.[170] The raid of 19 April 1944 killed over 850 people across the conurbation.[171] During the siege of Caen, where air raids were compounded with shelling in June, as many as 20,000 of the city's 60,000 or so inhabitants took refuge in nearby quarries, wholly unequipped as shelters, for periods of up to six weeks.[172]

Even as the Allied bombing campaign reached its climax in the summer of 1944, therefore, France's population was badly under-protected. Again, however, Vichy's record, inadequate though it was, can be defended on four counts. First, the shelters that there were undoubtedly saved lives. Useless against a direct hit, the humble cellar and the humbler trench were lifesavers against near misses; more robust shelters were better still. For example, a post-war analysis of raids on the Lyon conurbation, which claimed some 1,500 victims from March to August 1944, estimated that without shelters, the death toll would have been 10,000.[173] In Besançon, strutted and roofed trenches resisted bombs of 250 kg exploding 3–10 metres away.[174] Of over 1,000 victims of the American raid on Saint-Étienne of 26 May 1944, none was in an official trench or cellar shelter. In Tours on 20 May, a public shelter for 100 people survived the collapse of a 7-storey building on top of it. In Marseille a week later, a public shelter for 800 people saw a single death – a woman killed by bomb blast when she drew too close to a vent to get a breath of air.[175]

Second, the DDP continued to press for improvements right up to the Liberation, urging prefects to commission regular inspections of doubtful shelters, to press forward with piercing interconnections between cellars to increase both capacity and safety, to streamline procedures for tendering on shelter work, to stop using chalk-based concrete, which had proved unreliable, and to encourage the digging of do-it-yourself 'family shelters' with a subsidy of FF50–FF200 per person protected.[176] Third, while the figures are not fully reliable, protection was improved. Where a shelter of some sort had been available to perhaps one in ten inhabitants of major cities in 1940, it was probably extended to between one in six and one in two by 1944. Fourth, as we have seen, efforts to improve passive defence were undertaken in extremely difficult conditions. Despite its growing oppressiveness in other areas, which intensified in parallel with the Allied raids, this was not a regime that abandoned the French to their fate.

By contrast, the attitude of the Italian regime had been one of irresponsibility from the very start. At a War Cabinet meeting in February 1940, when it was acknowledged that less than 1 per cent of the Italian population could be protected in shelters, Mussolini stated that it was pointless to try and reach impossible targets: shelters could have been made in new houses, but people who lived in old buildings should simply rely on the cellars, or reinforce ground floors with sandbags. Linked to this, spending on improvements to the alarm system was not considered necessary. According to the Duce, it was a problem that would be solved 'on its own' since citizens' hearing in time of war became 'supersensitive', and the most sensitive inhabitants of building blocks would be able to warn their neighbourhood. To this, Marshal Badoglio added that the use of alarms would have been damaging when there were no shelters.[177] Little improvement was made even a few months before Italy entered the conflict; the desperate local attempts to improve the situation during wartime were then obstructed by the lack of resources.

CONCLUSION

The unprecedented strains caused by the Allied bombing campaigns left the governments of both Vichy France and Fascist Italy struggling to keep up. They had to redesign their political and administrative structures, to find unexpectedly large amounts of money, to cope with raw material shortages, to ensure an adequate flow of information, to shelter the public, and to assist people who had lost homes, family members, or both. These things, moreover, had to be done under the constraint, for some or all of the period, of German occupation. Neither country did them very well. Shelter provision was inadequate; welfare assistance was parsimonious, or on occasion absent.

Parallels can be drawn between the two countries' efforts. Both, for example, co-ordinated passive defence and refugee services, through the Directorate-General for War Services in Italy and the SIPEG in France. But the evidence suggests that Vichy France, after an uncertain start, fared less poorly than Fascist

Italy. What survived in France was a state structure in which information flowed from the localities to the central DDP, instructions were transmitted, and new measures considered almost to the fall of the regime. Allocations, especially for welfare, grew in the national budget and were distributed with some efficiency on the ground. Shelter provision, though far from adequate, improved thanks to a reasonably sustained effort from 1941 and (especially) 1942. Few of these things can be said of Italy. At the national level, rhetoric and bluster were too often a substitute for policy, leaving localities to improvise. Budgetary allocations were risible from the start. Welfare was left to local authorities that lacked the necessary resources. Where shelter provision improved, it did so thanks to a flurry of activity in certain towns rather than a national programme.

In the larger context of the conflict, each regime's policy was based on an illusion; in Vichy's case, that an armistice with Germany could end France's war, in that of Fascist Italy, that starting a war alongside Germany could bring an easy victory. In each country, Germany would prove a fatal encumbrance, pillaging the local economy and, above all, attracting the Allied bombers, in France from 1940 and in Italy from 1943, while concentrating its active defences on its own installations and robbing civilians of their shelters. Vichy's illusion, however, probably proved the less pernicious. Nothing in the Vichy record, not even in Pétain's speeches, quite equalled the fatuity of Mussolini's claim that 'supersensitive' hearing would deal with air raids, or the Ministry of Corporations' claim to rely, in case of enemy offences, on employees' 'spirit of sacrifice'. Faced with the reality of big raids, Vichy's policymakers restored and built upon a passive defence programme that broadly continued that of the Third Republic; in Italy, Mussolini's three-year pursuit of a chimerical military victory took priority over the defence of civilians. In Vichy France, as the continuity of personnel showed, passive defence was to a large extent separated from the regime's politics; in Italy it was subject to the intervention of the Fascist Party. And curiously, although the Fascist Party existed to mobilize public support for Mussolini's regime, when it came to engaging with and mobilizing the population to defend itself against air attack, the Vichy state could prove at least as effective.

Notes

1 L. Klinkhammer, *L'occupazione tedesca in Italia, 1943–1945* (Turin: Bollati Boringhieri, 2007), 72. By the end of World War Two, 600,000 Italians were working in labour camps in Germany.

2 Sauvy estimates France's total cash transfers to Germany from 1940 to 1944 at FF862 billion, or, in total, about 2.5 times France's national income in 1938. To that figure, Milward adds a further FF155 billion of pillage in kind: cf. A. Sauvy, *La Vie économique des Français de 1939 à 1945* (Paris: Flammarion, 1978), 78, 238; A. Milward, *The New Order and the French Economy* (Oxford: Oxford University Press, 1970), 81, 283. Daily cash transfers represented 400 million francs, falling to 300 million in May 1941 but rising to FF500 million in December 1942 (J. Jackson, *France: the Dark Years 1940–1944* (Oxford: Oxford University Press, 2001), 169). In October 1936, the pound sterling was worth 100–115 francs; from 1945, the rate was 480 francs to the pound. Before 1939, the pound sterling was worth between 90 and 150 Italian lire; from

1943, the rate was 480 lire to the pound. The franc's value against the German reichsmark was fixed at 0.05 (20 francs to the reichsmark) from June 1940. The lira's value against the reichsmark was fixed at 0.10 (10 lire to the reichsmark) under the Salò Republic. In relation to the German currency, therefore, the lira was worth 2 francs, although in the immediate pre-war and post-war periods the French and Italian currencies had nearly the same value as one another against the pound and the dollar.

3 A. Mitchell, *Nazi Paris: the History of an Occupation 1940–1944* (Oxford: Berghahn, 2008), 5; Milward, *New Order*, 132–4.

4 Sauvy, *Vie économique*, 145.

5 P. Burrin, *La France à l'heure allemande* (Paris: Éditions du Seuil, 1997), 136–49.

6 Cf. for example ASG, RSI, Prefettura Repubblicana di Genova, b. 27, Fascio of Genoa to Province Head, 6 December 1943.

7 ASG, Prefettura, b. 157, *Podestà* of Genoa to Prefect, 20 August 1943.

8 ASG, RSI, Prefettura Repubblicana di Genova, b. 28, Genoa Province Head to *Podestà* of Recco, 11 November 1943.

9 *Ibid.*, *Podestà* of Bogliasco Pieve to Genoa Province Head, 19 November 1943. See also, in the same file, similar documents regarding other towns, like Zoagli and Sori, situated near the railway line, in the early months of 1944.

10 ASTo, Prefettura, b. 524, Head of Turin province to Interior Ministry, 17 December 1943.

11 ASTo, Prefettura, b. 515, *podestà* of Mati (Turin province) to director of local schools (which housed evacuees and Germans), 31 October 1944.

12 ASB, Prefettura, 1944, Serie I, Cat. 16, b. 1, Questura of Bologna to province head, 29 May 1944.

13 SHAT 2P/20, Col. Foerster to French delegation to Armistice Commission, note 392/40-Q, 1940.

14 Loi no. 394 du 16 mars 1942, *JO*, 24 April 1942; AD Morbihan 7W/4794, Ordonnance du 3 April 1943 sur la Défense passive, *Verordnungsblatt des Militäbefehlshabers in Frankreich* (VOBIF), 5 April 1943.

15 SHAA 3D/44/1, Laval to prefects, 21 September 1943; SHAA 3D/473, General Mohr to Secrétariat d'État de la Défense, 9 June 1943; Captain Böhm, liaison officer, to Secrétariat d'État de la Défense, 12 June 1943. On German demands for shelters in Lorient, see AM Lorient 5H/9; on restrictions on shelter construction in nearby Saint-Nazaire, cf. AD LA 1694W/62, Sub-Prefect of Saint-Nazaire to Prefect of Loire-Inférieure, 28 November 1942.

16 AD SM 51W/69, RG Le Havre, Report, 16–22 January 1944.

17 SHAA 3D/48, Lt-Col Henri Laporte, Note 118HL; AD LA 1694W/61, Avis aux ouvriers de Saint-Nazaire, 3 December 1942.

18 AN AJ41/342, Von Stülpnagel to de Brinon, 6 October 1941.

19 Material on requisitioning of shelters may be found in AD SM 51W/254 *passim* (towns in Seine-Maritime); AD Manche 2Z/283, Sub-prefect Cherbourg to Manche DDP, 4 June 1941 (Cherbourg); AD Ille-et-Vilaine 47W/7, Col. Meyer to Prefect-Delegate of Ile-et-Vilaine, 12 October 1942 (Rennes); AM Le Havre H4/14/6, Ville du Havre, Direction des Travaux Communaux, État des prestations de défense passive ayant profité aux formations occupantes, 5 June 1945. In Cherbourg, five shelters, with a total capacity of 900, were reserved for the Germans (Michel Boivin, *Les Manchois dans la tourmente de la seconde guerre mondiale, 1939–1945*, vol. IV (Marigny (Manche): Éditions Eurocibles, 2004), 110).

20 AN AJ41/357, Première ordonnance d'exécution, du 26 juillet 1943 (Défense passive); SHAA 3D/44, Ministère de l'Intérieur, DDP, circulaire relative au décret du 10 novembre 1943 modifiant et complétant l'ordonnance du 26 juillet 1943, 7 January 1944.

21 Cf. SHAA 3D/473, 'Note pour le Colonel Von Mehrhart', 19 November 1943; AM Lyon 1188/WP/6, État Major de Liaison de Lyon, Section I.A, to Prefect of Rhône, 12 February 1943.

22 AD Rhône 182W/66, Chef du Secteur Part-Dieu to Chef du Service des Secteurs, 24 March 1943.

23 AN F7/14901, Prefect of Loir-et-Cher to head of govt., 29 August 1942.

24 M. Schmiedel, 'Les Allemands et la défense passive en France: le cas de Nantes', in M. Battesti and P. Facon (eds), *Les bombardements alliés sur la France durant la seconde guerre mondiale* (Paris: Cahiers du CEHD, no. 37, 2009), 49–56.

25 AN F7/14901, Secrétariat Général à l'Information et à la propagande to Information Ministry, 17 December 1942; AM Lyon 1129W/P10, Ville de Lyon, Corps des Sapeurs-Pompiers, Rapport du Commandant Rossignol (Le Creusot), 22 June 1943.

26 AD IetV 4W/8 Directeur, Service Santé Xe region to Prefect of Ille-et-Vilaine, 17 July 1943; AD Var 1W/64, Prefect of Var to SIPEG, 6 July 1944.

27 The Sadi-Carnot shelter exploded when a drunken German soldier dropped a lantern on a stock of munitions placed there by the Wehrmacht; 373 French civilians were killed (F. Péron, *Brest sous l'occupation* (Rennes: Ouest-France, 1981), 121).

28 Gioannini and Massobrio, *Bombardate l'Italia*, 171; N. Della Volpe, *Difesa del territorio e protezione antiaerea, 1915–1943* (Rome: Ufficio Storico dello Stato Maggiore dell'Esercito, 1986), 38–9.

29 ASG, Prefettura, b. 155, Report of the Comando XV Corpo d'Armata, Uff. Operaz. Sez. D.C., 31 August 1943.

30 ACS, MA, 1940, b. 86, fasc. 37, President of Aeronautica Macchi, Varese, to Air Ministry, 20 August 1940.

31 *Ibid.*, Air Ministry, head of Cabinet Gen. A. Urbani, to War Ministry, Stato Maggiore per la Difesa, 18 September 1940.

32 Law 1841, 28 November 1940, *GU* 16, 21 January 1941.

33 ACS, MA, 1940, b. 85, War Ministry report, 2 December 1940.

34 ACS, MA, 1941, b. 51, fasc. 13, MA, Head of Cabinet Gen. A. Urbani to Regia Aeronautica, 19 February 1941, based on note of 10 February by Mussolini's Secretary Osvaldo Sebastiani.

35 ACS, MA, 1943, b. 55, Air Ministry note of 18 July 1943.

36 ACG, AC, b. 144, Prefect of Genoa to party secretary, *podestà*, head of police and provincial UNPA command, 16 July 1941.

37 ACS, MA, 1942, b. 45, Interior Ministry to Air Ministry, 12 August 1942; *ibid.*, b. 46, fasc. 16, Air Ministry to Cabinet, 14 July 1942.

38 ASTo, Prefettura, I versamento, b. 521, Ministry of Corporations to Fascist Confederation of Industrialists and Workers of Industry, 13 January 1943.

39 ACS, MA, 1941, b. 51, fasc. 10-I, Air Ministry and Interior Ministry, signed Buffarini, to prefects, 3 June 1941.

40 ACS, MA, 1942, b. 46, fasc. 20, 'Promemoria', 30 novembre 1942.

41 ACS, MA, 1943, b. 52, fasc. 5/1, vol. 2, reply to above, Supreme Command I Reparto to Stato Maggiore R. Aeronautica, 11 August 1943.

42 M. Hastings, *Bomber Command* (London: Michael Joseph, 1979), 261–7. This could, of course, vary considerably. Cf. H. Boog, 'The Strategic Air War in Europe and Air Defence of the Reich', in H. Boog, G. Krebs, and D. Vogel, *Germany and the Second World War*, vol. VII (Oxford: Oxford University Press, 2006), 90, 98, 171, 300.

43 Figures calculated from Middlebrook and Everitt, *The Bomber Command War Diaries*.

44 Cf. R. J. Young, *In Command of France: French Foreign Policy and Military Planning, 1933–1940* (Cambridge, Mass.: Harvard University Press, 1978), 162; E. G. Kiesling, *Arming against Hitler: France and the Limits of Military Planning* (Lawrence, Kansas: University Press of Kansas, 1996), 176–7. France had just five anti-aircraft regiments in 1940 to the Luftwaffe's 72 (A. Horne, *To Lose a Battle: France 1940* (London: Macmillan, 1969), 84). For the Paris raid of 3 June 1940, cf. Lt-Col. Sainte-Péreuse, 'Le bombardement de la région parisienne, le 3 juin 1940', *Forces Aériennes Françaises*, 72, September 1952, 737–62; on Tours, C. Morin, *La Touraine sous les bombes* (Chambray-lès-Tours: CLD Éditions, 2000), 56–74.

45 In October 1942, French air force personnel numbered some 4,800 in mainland France and 6,000 overseas; 1,477 pilots were authorized by the Germans. Of French anti-aircraft forces in mainland France, 9,949 were attached to the army, 1,565 to the navy, and 996 to the air force. Significant numbers were also stationed in France's African empire. Cf. AN AJ41/630, Commission allemande d'armistice (Lufwaffe II 2041/2) to French delegation, 19 October 1942.

46 Boog, 'Strategic Air War', 212; Air Ministry (United Kingdom), *The Rise and Fall of the German Air Force* (Air Ministry Pamphlet, London, 1948; reissued, London: Public Record Office, 2001), 75–7, 190–1.

47 Air Ministry, *Rise and Fall*, 148.
48 Boog, 'Strategic Air War', 301, 328.
49 Air Ministry, *Rise and Fall*, 335.
50 Figures calculated from R. Freeman, *Mighty Eighth War Diary* (London: Jane's, 1981), 9–89. See above, p. 16.
51 Boog, 'Strategic Air War', 212.
52 Sir A. Harris, *Despatch on War Operations* (London: Frank Cass, 1995), 42–7. The figures refer to the 1,098 aircraft that went missing in 59,308 sorties over German-occupied territory.
53 Middlebrook and Everitt, *Bomber Command War Diaries*, 245.
54 AN F60/379, Darlan to de Brinon, 9 March 1942.
55 AD Manche 2Z/283, Défense Passive de Cherbourg, Mise à l'Abri de la Population Scolaire, n.d.; AD LA 1694W/62, Prefect of Loire-Atlantique to de Brinon, Ingrand, and Regional Prefect, Rennes, 22 April 1942.
56 SHAA 3D/473, Captain Böhm to Secrétariat d'État de la Défense, 12 June 1943.
57 SHAA 3D/43, Cornillon to Mehrhart, 28 September 1943; AD LA 1694W/61, Feldkommandant Nantes to Prefect of Loire-Inférieure, 28 March 1944; SHAA 3D/473, Gal. Cornillon to special delegate of Luftflotte 3, 16 March 1944.
58 SHAA 3D/44/1, General Moniot to prefect of Haute-Savoie, 28 June 1944.
59 AN AJ41/633, Le Chef de Gouvernement, Secrétariat Général, Ordre de Mission, 22 February 1943. Cf. also SHAT 1P/58, Historique de la DCA et de la Sécurité Générale de juillet 1940 à novembre 1942, Vichy, le 30 juin 1943; and Claude d'Abzac-Epezy, 'Le Secrétariat général de la Défense aérienne (1943–1944), une "armée nouvelle" dans la France occupée', *Revue Historique des Armées*, 188, September 1992, 79–89.
60 Cf. SHAA 3D/395, and SHAT 1P/58, especially Neubronn to Laval, 27 November 1943.
61 SHAA 3D/43 *passim*; SHAA 3D/473, Situation des effectifs, Défense Passive et Service d'Alerte, 1er février 1944.
62 Cf. for example SHAA 3D/400, Plan du sous-sol des PTT à Montpellier où fonctionne le Centre d'alerte.
63 SHAA 3D/43, Böhm to Cornillon, 18 November 1943.
64 SHAT 1P/20, Secrétariat Général à la Défense Aérienne, Rapport sur la situation à la date du 30 juin 1944 des formations de la Sécurité Aérienne Publique et du Service d'Alerte, 18 July 1944, 11; General Moniot to Secrétaire d'État à la Défense, 12 August 1944.
65 ACS, MI, DGPCSA, b. 104, General Director of Anti-Aircraft Defences to undersecretary of state, 12 November 1941.
66 Law 415, 21 May 1940, *GU*, 24 May 1940.
67 Law 461, 24 May 1940, *GU*, 30 May 1940. A later decree of February 1942 added that the Fascist Party was responsible for the supervision of civil service duties (Decree 82, 26 February 1942, *GU*, 3 March 1942).
68 Decree 410, 5 May 1941, *GU*, 30 May 1941.
69 ACS, MI, DGPCSA, b. 16, War Ministry to prefects, to General Command of UNPA, Central Committee of the Red Cross and General Directorate of Fire Services, 1 March 1941.
70 Interior Ministry Circular, 18 April 1941, *Collezione celerifera, Anno 1941* (Rome: Stamperia Reale, 1942), 649.
71 Law 1570, 27 December 1941, *GU*, 3 February 1942.
72 Decree 1566, 16 December 1942, *GU*, 12 January 1943.
73 Decree of the Duce, 22 December 1942, *GU*, 25 January 1943.
74 ASB, Prefettura, 1944, Serie I, Cat. 7, Decree by Mussolini of 18 June 1944, and telegram from Interior Minister Buffarini to province heads of Forlì, Bologna, Parma and Ravenna, 9 July 1944.
75 Decree 366, 17 November 1944, *GU*, 12 December 1944.
76 AN F60/407, Situation des Villes Côtières du Nord et du Pas-de-Calais, 12 mars 1941; AM Nantes 4H/103, Conférence des Municipalités des Villes Côtières, 28 February 1942.
77 This reflected a steady return to Paris by many ministries during the Occupation, though ministers and their staffs stayed at Vichy (M. O. Baruch, *Servir l'État français. L'administration en France de 1940 à 1944* (Paris: Fayard, 1997), 84.)

78 AM Toulon 5H/III/11, War Minister (signed Sérant) to prefects, 24 September 1941.
79 SHAT, 2P/20, Tableau de la Composition de la Direction de la Défense Passive en 1941.
80 Cf. Chapter 3 for the 1931 Instruction. Both the transfer of the DDP to Interior and Laval's return to office were at the Germans' behest.
81 AM Lorient 5H/10, Head of Government (signed Sérant) to prefects, 6 May 1943.
82 AN, F7/14901, Laval to prefects, 13 February 1943, AD Var, 1W/64, Prefect of Var to mayors and senior officials in Var, 21 August 1943.
83 AM Lyon 1188WP/14, DDP, Bureau de liaison, note du 5 mai 1943; Head of Government (signed J. G. Lacombe, chef du SIPEG), to prefects and sub-prefects, 1 July 1943; Head of Government (signed Lacombe) to DDP Rhône, 4 September 1943.
84 Loi du 20 septembre 1943, *JO*, 25 November 1943.
85 AD LA 1690W/141, Prefect of Loire-Inférieure to Interior Minister (SIPEG), 23 November 1944. Cf. also D. Voldman, *La reconstruction des villes françaises de 1940 à 1954: Histoire d'une politique* (Paris: L'Harmattan, 1997), 29.
86 AM Le Havre H4/14/7, Interior Minister (signed Cazes) to Prefect, Seine-Inférieure, 23 February 1945. Sérant's predecessor, General Daudin, had been appointed under Daladier but remained in office till his retirement in December 1940.
87 SHAT 2P/20, Ministère de la Guerre, DDP, Note pour le cabinet militaire, Travaux à exécuter en 1941, 8 February 1941; SHAT 2P/20, Head of Government (signed Bousquet) to prefects, Lyon, 10 May 1943; SHAT 3P/121, Ministère de l'Intérieur, DDP, Première réunion des chefs de la défense passive, 28 April 1944; GPRF, Ordonnance du 18 juillet 1944 (Défense passive), *JO*, 29 July 1944.
88 AD IetV 502W/3, Head of Government (signed Cazes) to Prefects, 25 November 1943.
89 SHAA, 3D/44, Ministère de l'Intérieur, DDP, *BIDP* no. 13, October 1943.
90 AD Manche 127W/1, Ministère de l'Intérieur, Répertoire des principales Notes, Instructions et Circulaires émanant de la Direction de la Défense Passive de 1938 jusqu'au 1er novembre 1944.
91 Baldissara, 'Il governo della città', 104; 113. On the pre-war period see A. Aquarone, *L'organizzazione dello stato totalitario* (Turin: Einaudi, 1995), in particular chapter on 'Il regime'; E. Gentile, *La via italiana al totalitarismo. Il partito e lo Stato nel regime fascista* (Rome: Carocci, 2008), 112–24.
92 Baruch, *Servir l'État français* 228, 249.
93 *Ibid.*, 339, 545, 560; S. Mazey and V. Wright, 'Les préfets', in J.-P. Azéma and F. Bédarida (eds), *Vichy et les Français* (Paris: Fayard, 1992), 267–86.
94 N. Wouters, 'Municipal government during the Occupation (1940–45): a comparative model of Belgium, the Netherlands and France', *European History Quarterly*, 36/2 (2006), 240–1.
95 E. C. Karlsgodt, *Defending National Treasures: French Art and Heritage under Vichy* (Stanford, Ca.: Stanford University Press, 2011), 105; P. Tanchoux, 'La protection monumentale en 1939–45', unpublished paper given at the conference 'Guerres, œuvres d'art et patrimoine artistique à l'époque contemporaine', University of Picardie, 16–18 March 2011, 6.
96 Karlsgodt, *Defending National Treasures*, 71. Cf. also G. Fonkenell ed. *Le Louvre pendant la guerre: regards photographiques 1938–1947* (Paris: Musée du Louvre Éditions, 2009).
97 AM Marseille 71R/1B, Bibliothèque de la Ville de Marseille to Prefect of Bouches-du-Rhône, 22 August 1940.
98 Cf. correspondence in AM Marseille 71R/1A-C.
99 Karlsgodt, *Defending National Treasures*, 85.
100 *Ibid.*, 117.
101 Law 1041, 6 July 1940, *GU*, 8 August 1940.
102 M. Nezzo, 'The Defence of Works of Art Against Bombing in Italy During the Second World War', in Baldoli, Knapp and Overy (eds), *Bombing, States and Peoples*, 105.
103 ACS, MA, 1942, b. 45, Ministry of National Education to War Ministry, 11 March 1942, and War Ministry to Command of 6th Army, 15 March 1942.
104 Nezzo, 'The Defence of Works of Art', 110–14.
105 L. H. Nicholas, *The Rape of Europa. The Fate of Europe's Treasures in the Third Reich and the Second World War* (London: Macmillan, 1994), 260.
106 M. Legnani, 'Guerra e governo delle risorse. Strategie economiche e soggetti sociali nell'Italia

1940–1943', in Fondazione Micheletti, *Annali. 5. L'Italia in guerra, 1940–1943* (Brescia: Fondazione Micheletti, 1991), 349.

107 ACS, MI, DGPCSA, b. 63, Finance Ministry to Interior Ministry, 27 August 1940.

108 *Ibid.*, Interior Ministry to Finance Ministry, 19 December 1940.

109 *Ibid.*, Report by Committee for anti-aircraft defence to Interior Ministry, 28 February 1941.

110 ACS, MI, DGPCSA, b. 106, note by general director of anti-aircraft services for undersecretary of Interior Ministry Buffarini, 24 July 1941.

111 SHAT 2P/20, Rapport sur l'état d'avancement du programme de la Défense passive à la date du 31 décembre 1941, 3–4. Sérant rounded up the figure to FF10 billion to take account of investments already undertaken in the *département* of Seine, around Paris. By way of comparison, France's national budget amounted to FF105.6 billion (*JO*, 1 January 1942, États annexes, 32a); and a month's occupation payments to Germany would, raw materials permitting, have realized Sérant's whole programme (above, n. 2).

112 Loi no. 394 du 16 mars 1942, *JO*, 24 April 1942.

113 *JO*, 1 January 1944, États annexes, 11a; AN F60/379, Loi du 20 juillet 1944 (*JO*, 23 July 1944).

114 AN F60/407, Note pour le cabinet civil du Maréchal, 8 December 1941; AD Manche, Darlan to prefects, 31 January 1942; *JO* 1 January 1942, 3.

115 AM Lorient 5H/10, Bousquet to prefects, 23 January 1943, 5.

116 AD LA, 1694W/66, Sub-prefect, St-Nazaire, to Prefect of Loire-Inférieure, 11 March 1943.

117 AD BduR, 76W/127, Rapport sur l'activité de la DP, 15 mai au 15 juillet 1944.

118 ASG, Prefettura, b. 153–154, letters from *podestà* of Genoa to prefect, 18 and 19 August 1943. When food at restaurants was no longer available, military rations of meat and bread were provided by the Comune (*Ibid.*, *podestà* to prefect, 8 August 1943).

119 ASG, Prefettura, b. 153–154, circular of *podestà* of Genoa to ECA's employees, 9 August 1943.

120 V. Zamagni, *Dalla periferia al centro. La seconda rinascita economica dell'Italia (1861–1990)* (Bologna: Il Mulino, 1993), 402–3. See also D. Bigazzi, 'Gli operai nell'industria di guerra (1938–943)', in V. Zamagni (ed.), *Come perdere la guerra e vincere la pace. L'economia italiana tra guerra e dopoguerra, 1938–1947* (Bologna: Il Mulino, 1997), 212–13.

121 Cf. P.-J. Hesse and J.-P. Le Crom (eds), *La protection sociale sous Vichy* (Rennes: Presses Universitaires de Rennes, 2001).

122 L. Dodd, '"Relieving Sorrow and Misfortune"? State, Charity, Ideology and Aid in Bombed-out France, 1940–1945', in Baldoli, Knapp and Overy (eds), *Bombing, States and Peoples*, 82.

123 The minimum monthly wage in 1944 was FF1,100; a miner received FF1,600, and a worker on a German building site FF3,000; cf. É. Alary, with B. Vergez-Chaignon and G. Gauvin, *Les Français au quotidien, 1939–1949* (Paris: Perrin, 2006), 728.

124 AM St-Étienne 5H/40, SIPEG, Sinistrés, Évacués, Réfugiés, Ce Que Vous Devez Savoir, May 1944.

125 AD IetV 4W/8, Direction des Réfugiés (signed Rivalland), circular 115, 3 April 1942; AD Manche 2Z/106, Ministère de l'Intérieur, Direction des réfugiés, Les différents aspects de l'évacuation, circular 148, 1 February 1944. The notion of a priority *département* survived, but *départements* were reclassified as the war progressed. By 1941, the rating of 32 eastern *départements* had been downgraded against pre-Armistice days, while the same number in the north and the west coast had had their priority raised. Cf. SHAT 6N/338, Programme établi concernant la défense passive (February/March 1940), 5; SHAT 2P/20, Rapport sur l'état d'avancement du programme, 22.

126 Cf. Dodd, 'Relieving Sorrow?', 82–3; Bibliothèque Nationale de France, 8F/Piece 8411, Chef du Gouvernement (SIPEG), Ministère de l'Intérieur, Direction de Réfugiés, Instructions aux Maires concernant les secours, 5 July 1944.

127 AM St-Étienne 5H/40, SIPEG, Sinistrés, Évacués, Réfugiés, May 1944.

128 AM Lyon 101WP3, Commission spéciale des secours d'extrême urgence, 1er mars 1944 à 15 heures.

129 For Lorient, see correspondence in AD Morbihan 9W/38. An example of a dysfunctional refugee office appears in AD SM 51W/250, Note to Director of Prisoners, Deportees and Refugees, 17 December 1944; Note de la Direction Départementale des Prisonniers de Guerre, Déportés et Réfugiés, au Cabinet de M. le Préfet, 12 February 1945.

130 Dodd, 'Relieving Sorrow?', 78.
131 Cf. *JO*, 1 January 1944, États annexes, 12a–13a.
132 AD Var 1W/64, Département du Var, Rapport succinct sur le bombardement du 4 février 1944, 7 February 1944; AD Var 1W66, Préfecture du Var, Service des Réfugiés, Compte-Rendu d'Activités, 18 March 1944. AM St-Étienne 5H/40, Prefect of Loire to mayor Guyot of St-Étienne, 27 May 1944; AM St-Étienne 5H/37, conseil municipal, 8 June 1944. In St-Étienne the prefect was able to commit FF3 million the day after the raid.
133 Communication of 5 December 1940, *Collezione celerifera, Anno 1940* (Rome: Stamperia Reale, 1941), 907–8.
134 Communication of 11 December 1940, *Collezione celerifera, Anno 1940*, 866.
135 Interior Ministry Circular, 29 March 1941, *Collezione celerifera, Anno 1941* (Rome: Stamperia Reale, 1942), 650.
136 ACG, AM, b. 1138, Prefect of Genoa, Decree, 7 November 1940.
137 *Ibid.*, Prefect of Genoa, Decree, 14 January 1941.
138 *Ibid.*, Prefect of Genoa, Decree, 30 January 1941.
139 ACS, MI, DGPCSA, b. 106, unsigned report, but probably by local direction of anti-aircraft defences, Naples, n.d. (1941).
140 *Ibid.*, General Commander of UNPA Giuseppe Stellingwerff to prefect of Naples and Interior Ministry, 27 October 1941.
141 *Ibid.*, General Inspector of Anti-Aircraft Luigi Gambelli to Interior Ministry, 28 October 1941.
142 *Ibid.*, Gambelli to Interior Ministry, 25 November 1941.
143 ASLS, Prefettura, b. 159, report by La Spezia Carabinieri, 7 June 1943.
144 ASTo, Prefettura, I versamento, b. 524, prefect of Turin to Interior Ministry, 26 June 1943.
145 ACS, MI, DGPCSA, b. 106, report by prefect of Milan, 4 March 1943.
146 ASTa, Genio Civile, nuovo versamento, b. 490, Ministry of Public Works, Genio Civile of Taranto to Prefect, 9 April 1943; *Ibid.*, Prefect of Taranto to Provincial Administration, 4 March 1944; *Ibid.*, report of Provincial Administration of Taranto, 21 July 1945.
147 ASTo, Prefettura, b. 519, director of schools to province head, 22 December 1943.
148 ACG, AC, b. 144, Città di Genova, Report on Emergency Plan, 29 January 1944.
149 SHAT 2P/20, Rapport sur l'état d'Avancement du programme, 4–6.
150 AM Lorient 5H/10, Bousquet to prefects, 23 January 1943.
151 For Lorient, cf. correspondence in AM Lorient 5H/14.
152 AN F1/A/3780, CFLN, France-Politique, Organisation de la Défense Passive, 29 July 1943. By 1939, 28 metro stations were officially identified as shelters (Archives de Paris (AP) 1103W/81, Préfecture de Police, Secrétariat Général Permanent de la Défense Passive, Ce que le Public doit savoir en matière de défense passive, 1939, 5). This number had been increased to 55 by 1943.
153 SHAT 2P/18, DDP, 2e Bureau, Bulletin de Renseignements relatif au bombardement de la région parisienne ouest dans la nuit du 3 au 4 mars 1942.
154 AD Rhône 182W/5, Note sur la défense passive dans le Département du Rhône, 18 February 1942; 182W/66, Réponses aux questions posées par l'état-major de liaison de Lyon dans la note du 12 février 1943.
155 AD Rhône 3958W/9, Rapport sur l'Organisation de la Direction Départementale de la Défense Passive, 20 April 1944.
156 AD BduR 77W/1, Sérant to Prefect of Police, Marseille, 4 May 1942.
157 AM Marseille 408W/1/10, Préfecture des Bouches-du-Rhône, État de la population abritée au 31 décembre 1942; AM Marseille 29/II/4, Réunion du service de Coordination de la Protection Contre les Événements de Guerre, 11 December 1943.
158 AM Marseille 408W/1/10, Mme Émile to Pétain, 28 August 1943.
159 AD BduR 76W/129, RG Marseille, Information, 1 June 1944; AM Marseille 27II/49, Jean Cherpin, chef du 4e sous-secteur, to DUDP, 5 August 1944.
160 AM Lorient 5H/10, Laval (signed Sérant) to prefects, 6 May 1943.
161 AD IetV 502W/4, Ville de Rennes, Bombardement aérien du 8 mars 1943: Compte rendu relatif au fonctionnement de l'ensemble des services de la Défense Passive; AM Rennes 6H/22, Prefect-Delegate of Ille-et-Vilaine to mayor of Rennes, 14 April 1943.

162 AM Nantes 4H/107, *Le Nouvelliste*, 25–26 Sept 1943; *Ouest-Éclair*, 2 and 6 October 1943, *Le Phare*, 7 October 1943.

163 P. Caillaud, *Nantes sous les bombardements: Mémorial à la Défense Passive* (Nantes: Éditions du Fleuve, 1946), 155.

164 AD Loire 134W/70, Département de la Loire, Compte rendu sur les renseignements recueillis au Creusot après le bombardement du 21 juin 1943.

165 AD Var 2W/59, Capt. Marloy, Rapport de prise de fonctions, 30 April 1943.

166 AD Var 1W/64, DDP Var, Compte rendu du bombardement de Toulon du 24 novembre 1943, 18 December 1943; *Le Petit Var*, 27 December 1943; 1W/21, RG Toulon, 22–28 November 1943.

167 *Le Petit Marseillais*, 4 August 1944.

168 AM St-Étienne 5H/69, Head of shelters service to mayor, 23 October 1943; Head of shelters service to City DDP, 29 November 1944.

169 AD Loire 7W/26, RG Saint-Étienne, Note d'Information, Saint-Étienne, 7 June 1944; AD Rhône 3958W/75, Département du Rhône, Défense Passive, Chef du Secteur de Grange Blanche, Rapport relatif à l'alerte du 23 mars; AD Manche 127W/25, Directeur de la défense passive, Arrondissement d'Avranches, to DDDP Manche, 5 December 1944.

170 Antoine Hardy, 'La défense passive à Rouen', *Études Normandes*, 57.1, 2008, 61–70; 64; Paul Le Trévier and Daniel Rose, *Ce qui s'est vraiment passé le 19 avril 1944: Le Martyre de Sotteville, Rouen, et la Région* (Saint-Germain-en-Laye: Comever, 2004), 110.

171 AD SM, *Journal de Rouen*, 1–2 May 1944; E. Florentin, *Quand les alliés bombardaient la France* (Paris: Perrin, 1997), 290.

172 L. Dujardin, and D. Butaeye, *Les réfugiés dans les carrières pendant la bataille de Caen, juin-juillet 1944* (Rennes: Éditions Ouest-France/Mémorial de Caen, 2009), 136.

173 AD Rhône 3958W/87, Défense passive pour l'agglomération lyonnaise, Effets salutaires des mesures de DP, 23 November 1945.

174 AD IetV 502W/3, *BIDP* 11, 16 August 1943.

175 AD Manche, 127W/1, *BIDP* 21, June 1944.

176 AD Manche 127W/2, Cazes to prefects, 14 June 1944; AD Var 2W/59, Cazes to prefects, 24 June 1944; AD Manche 127W/1, Cazes to ministers and prefects, 8 August 1944; Ministre de l'Intérieur (signed Folliet, Directeur Général de la Protection Civile) to prefects, 1 July 1944.

177 The minutes of the meeting are in Della Volpe, *Difesa del territorio*, 39–40; 213–18.

5

The Propaganda War

Like every other aspect of the conflict, bombing was the object of a propaganda war. For the governments of Vichy France and Fascist Italy, Allied bombing was potentially a propaganda gift, a life-size demonstration of their enemies' wickedness. This was a message they could develop with the full resources of censorship and the state-controlled media. Any difficulties they had in doing so arose from the shakiness of their own credibility. For the Allies, conversely, air raids were a challenge. Materially, they had to pierce the enemy's defences with their own weapons, chiefly radio and leafleting. Morally, although they started with the favours of French opinion, and stood to benefit in Italy from the growing unpopularity of Mussolini's war, they had trouble justifying the suffering they visited upon civilians. For each side a significant stake was involved: for Vichy and for Fascist Italy, the recovery of some public support, or its complete loss; for the Allies, the threat of being viewed not as liberators but as wanton destroyers. The war of words and images was correspondingly intense, with each side struggling to confront the other's propaganda and to shape civilians' perceptions of bombing.

NARRATIVES OF CATACLYSM: VICHY FRANCE AND FASCIST ITALY

Although they were on the same side and had broadly the same raw material of experience to work from, the propagandists of France and Italy approached their work from fundamentally different starting-points. Vichy's founding act was an armistice with Germany, intended to take France out of the war. Vichy France under Allied bombs was a constant victim, unable to organize active defences, still less any form of riposte. Fascist Italy, by contrast, was out to win the war at Germany's side. In defeated and conquered France, constancy of misfortune allowed the development of a consistent narrative, omitting and distorting truths but seldom needing to use outright lies. Italy's headlong transformation from strutting belligerence to humiliating surrender, and then (under the Salò Republic) to a patently subordinate partnership with the Nazis, led to an incoherent (and mendacious) account. Early denials of air-raid damage were followed by claims that civilians were united behind the regime's war effort and indifferent to losses; these in turn gave way, especially under the Salò Republic, to the same type of wallowing in tragedy (and hatred for the enemy) that Vichy had deployed from the start.

Tools of propaganda

Each regime enjoyed a near-monopoly of media with which to tell their stories about bombing: a censored press, radio broadcasts, newsreels, leaflets and posters, as well as heavily-reported public occasions such as funerals, and official visits to bombed areas. In each case, control was exercised from the highest level. Italy's Minister of Popular Culture, Alessandro Pavolini, sent daily directives to the press, after checking them, till May 1943, with Mussolini in person; under the Salò Republic, Pavolini would become head of the Republican Fascist Party.[1] On 15 June 1940, he recommended – ironically in the light of what followed – that comments on raids should underline that 'as always, the regime tells the truth': to win the propaganda war, the regime needed firstly to be believed.[2] In France, the regime's first information minister, Paul Marion, developed a centralized censorship apparatus at Vichy, though the German authorities also issued directives to editors in the occupied zone. Both used their control over allocations of paper – always in short supply – as a tool of control.[3] Directives censored (for example, by delaying news of a raid, or at least of the town attacked), but above all, they prescribed. Thus newspapers had to cover the second raid on Billancourt on 3 April 1943 on five columns of the front page, with a specified headline ('After the criminal raid by the Anglo-American air forces'), and chosen phrases from Finance Minister Pierre Cathala's speech; a 'personal' editorial condemning the raid was also required.[4] Marion's successor from January 1944, Philippe Henriot, was both more extreme (as a member of the loathed Vichy Milice) and more modern, grasping the opportunities offered by newsreels and, above all, by the radio, which he used to give twice-weekly personal 'editorials'.[5]

For both regimes, it was also important to show the authorities' closeness to the population's sufferings on the ground. Pétain, confined by the Germans to the (initially unbombed) southern zone, despatched ministers or personal representatives to bombed towns: Colonel Bonhomme, in particular, toured towns in Brittany and Normandy in the spring of 1943.[6] Comparable visits were made in Italy by local dignitaries, ministers from Rome or members of the royal family. Princess Maria José of Piedmont, married to the King's son Umberto, was particularly popular – and avidly reported by the press – in Naples, where she lived.[7] Aldo Vidussoni, the Fascist Party's young National Secretary, visited bombed areas of Milan after the raids of 24 October 1942, accompanied by the Minister of Public Works and local councillors. *Corriere della Sera* reported that the population felt 'deeply and proudly' the Party's closeness.[8] A few days later, National Education Minister Giuseppe Bottai inspected damage to the city's university and to a number of schools.[9]

In both countries, too, press coverage was complemented by posters, leaflets, and brochures. Italy's Salò Republic, in particular, produced huge numbers of posters and illustrated pamphlets. Pamphlets published lists of civilian dead, churches, schools and hospitals destroyed, together with pictures of ruined churches and violated statues of the Madonna;[10] one image of Churchill and Roosevelt holding guns over wrecked cities was juxtaposed with an Italian woman carrying a dead child and surrounded by ruins.[11] The cover of a book by the British pacifist Vera Brittain, *Seed of Chaos*, was enlisted as a cover for a pamphlet entitled: 'Those who started it'.[12] France's Information Ministry, meanwhile, printed 250,000 copies of a leaflet entitled 'The Anglo-Americans are delivering France by bombing her.'[13] It also commissioned illustrated magazine-style brochures, in 15,000–30,000 copies, called *Nos villes dans la tourmente* and covering some 20 heavily bombed towns and cities such as Le Creusot, Nantes, Montluçon, Lorient, Rouen and Le Portel. They typically presented a historic pre-war locality, gave a terrifying account of the raid, and finally depicted official visitors, or the SIPEG train, or both, bringing succour and comfort to the victims.[14] But it was the posters, in both countries, which offered the most compelling images. One Italian poster showed Stalin laughing as British and American bombs fell on St Peter's Square;[15] another depicted Roosevelt laughing at the sight of ruined houses, piles of dead bodies, and a young woman sitting on the rubble with a small child in her arms, with the legend: 'President Roosevelt has just been informed of the latest brave achievements of his pilots against the unarmed civilian centres of Italy.'[16] In France, the most striking among many superimposed Joan of Arc in chains over the burning city of Rouen (where she had been burned at the stake, by the English, in 1431). 'Murderers', read the caption, 'always return to the scene of their crime.'[17]

French ceremonies, and raids generally, received systematic newsreel coverage. Whatever the quality of the commentaries and speeches, the images of ruined towns, grieving families, shrouded corpses, and the coffins of adults and children brought the human tragedy of the raids to cinema-goers across France.[18] Fascist Italy had a thriving official cinema industry (the Cinecittà studios were founded in 1937). However, newsreels showing the effects of bombing on cities to criminalize the enemy were rare (with a few exceptions, for example for the cases of Genoa and Milan in 1942) until after Mussolini's fall, becoming frequent from August 1943 and especially during the Salò Republic.[19]

Three significant differences, however, distinguished the propaganda tools of Vichy from those of Fascist Italy. First, France favoured grand, sombre public funerals. These proclaimed not only the authorities' complicity in mourning, but also that of the occupying authorities, with second-row pews in church typically reserved for German officers; and they reinforced Vichy's characteristic association between ecclesiastical authority and the state. The first such occasion was held after the first Billancourt raid, during the day of national mourning on Saturday, 7 March 1942.[20] Other big funerals followed, at Lille in January 1943, in Rennes the following March, in Paris after the second Billancourt raid that April, or in Lyon and Saint-Étienne in June 1944.[21] Italy, too, organized funerals, bringing together local Fascist authorities and the Catholic Church.[22]

But they were on a more modest scale and sometimes went wrong, highlighting tensions between Fascists and people, or Church and regime. On 24 July 1941, for example, the burial of two Fascist air-raid victims in Melito, near Naples, produced such a confrontation; the priest ended up sitting in his church, along with the parish association of Catholic women, rather than cede precedence to the Fascist Party at the funeral procession.[23]

Second, when the Germans let him, Pétain made official visits to France's bombed towns. In May 1944, the Marshal took in Nancy, Épinal, Dijon, the Paris region and Rouen, before departing for Lyon and Saint-Étienne in early June. The visit to Paris, on 26 April 1944, had the highest profile and drew a large crowd that was sympathetic if not precisely enthusiastic.[24] His last public appearance before his post-war trial was at Saint-Étienne, whence he returned to Vichy on 6 June, newly alerted to the Normandy landings.[25] In Italy, by contrast, Mussolini did not tour bombed cities; his regime's loss of credibility was too great.[26]

Finally, although official radio in both countries was viewed (even officially) as being greatly outclassed in levels of public interest by the BBC, this changed in France, at least partly, with the arrival of Henriot, probably the regime's best orator.[27] Italy had no equivalent to this dark but compelling figure.

Despite having had two decades to develop an effective propaganda machine, therefore, Fascist Italy did not deploy it to greatest effect in the coverage of air raids. The effectiveness of Vichy propaganda should not be overstated; it quite failed to check the public's alienation from the regime.[28] But it did allow the development of a consistent message about bombing.

The message

One of the strongest tributes to Vichy propaganda came in an anxious report by the French National Liberation Committee in Algiers, dated May 1944. It detailed the political damage done by Allied raids, and observed that Vichy had contributed by developing a coherent and credible narrative of them.[29] Perfected under Henriot's guidance, the bases of the narrative had been laid down earlier, after the Billancourt raid of 1942.

Its first component was human misery. Newsreel coverage of the Billancourt attack set the tone: it showed bodies in shrouds, coffins large and small, mourners in black overcome by tears, and at one point what appears to be a dead baby. To this was added Pétain's message for the day of mourning, evoking 'streets blown away, neighbourhoods flattened, families decimated, mothers driven mad, children thrown from their cradles into their graves.'[30] A year later Archbishop Clément Roques offered a similar discourse ('in their fury, the monsters sowed ruin and death') at Rennes. [31] Henriot's speech after the April 1944 raids on Rouen and the Paris suburbs talked of the 'grey dawn of despair', attacked delayed-action bombs, dropped so that 'no-one should remain alive and no house standing', before striking a pathetic note: 'Little houses, modest homes with their lovingly tended little gardens, have found what it costs to be classified as a military target by Mr Churchill.'[32] There might be praise for emergency workers or for assistance to bombed-out families, via a Secours National lorry or, better, the SIPEG train.[33] But this did little to dilute the core message of suffering – and, closely linked to it, of fear. 'It's only just beginning, you know', argued a May 1944 newsreel, adding that 'the list gets longer day after day, with thousands of dead added to other thousands.' To a close-up of a blazing block of flats, the commentary warns that 'This building, burning like a torch, is not just a building in Lyon, it is the home of a Frenchman. Tomorrow it might be yours.'[34]

Though hardly the stuff of defiance – there was no 'France can take it' message – the focus on suffering was a persuasive basis for the second argument, the criminal nature of bombing. The Billancourt raid of 1942 was a 'monstrous and odious crime', declared *Le Moniteur*; for Charles Maurras, *doyen* of the French far Right, it was 'immorality matched by pure cowardice'.[35] 'Let us not be afraid of words', ran the May 1944 newsreel on the Lyon raid: 'this is murder.'[36] Where possible, the Church was enlisted to reinforce the moral argument. On 10 May 1944, France's cardinals – bishop Liénart of Lille, Archbishops Suhard of Paris and Gerlier of Lyon – as well as Archbishop Chollet of Cambrai appealed to the British and American episcopate to intercede for an end to the bombing: their appeal was broadcast and reproduced in the press, though the removal from it of a brief allusion to the German bombing of Britain provoked a protest from Suhard.[37] Similarly, the bishop of Saint-Étienne's proclamation of June 1944, that 'when [war] massacres, mutilates, starves, or drives from their homes old people, women, defenceless children in their thousands, viciously sacrificed, it is more than inhuman; it is the shame of humanity' was printed in 20,000 copies.[38]

The third stage of the Vichy narrative was to deny, conceal, or minimize the existence of legitimate targets. Renault's production of vehicles for Germany, widely known to the public, appeared nowhere in newsreels or the press.[39] When Churchill told the Commons in March 1943 that submarine bases had been attacked, *Le Moniteur* replied that no U-boat had been seen in Rouen, Amiens or Rennes.[40] No military or industrial objective lay within a ten-kilometre radius, claimed *France-Actualités* after the Easter 1944 bombing of the Paris suburbs.[41] The Allies' clumsiness reinforced the argument that they cared nothing for French lives. 'Allies fly to the help of France', proclaimed a 1943 leaflet giving the death toll for each city.[42] Claims that the Americans' choice of a Sunday to come to Billancourt in April 1943, or the use of delayed-action bombs, were meant to minimize civilian casualties, were fiercely mocked. [43] So was the RAF's boast that 'we know our business', or the supposed remarks of aircrews returning from Billancourt in 1943 ('splendid weather, fine sport').[44]

With legitimate targets discounted, Vichy's propagandists expounded the 'real' reasons for the raids. Traditional Anglophobia was enlisted in this cause:

allusions to Joan of Arc, or in one case, a claim that the British had bombed Lorient in revenge for a defeat there in 1746.[45] Recent references, though, were more common: the 'desertion' of France by the British (and especially the RAF) in May 1940, the attack on the French fleet at Mers-el-Kébir, or the Syrian conflict of 1941. The same British aircraft which had withdrawn to Britain in 1940, said a brochure entitled '1940–1942' and printed in 2.4 million copies, were now used to bomb France. France offered an easy target for an ally that had deserted her and was not at war with her.[46]

The strongest explanation of the raids, however, was that the 'Anglo-Saxons' aimed to eliminate an economic competitor: 'One town less in France, one port less in France, means so much the less competition, tomorrow, for the shipping lines, the industrialists, the bankers of the City.' [47] This account had many attractions. For the anti-capitalist left it had an obvious superficial plausibility.[48] For the conservative right, claims of the Allies' materialism could be extended to include blindness or hostility to Europe's spiritual and cultural values; hence the destruction of cultural artefacts in France, Italy and Germany.[49] Henriot's elegy for Rouen's 'incomparable law courts, prodigious cathedral, theatre, prefecture, picturesque old quarters … now mutilated, collapsed, ablaze, as delayed-action bombs continue to explode on all sides' gave compelling expression to this line.[50] Anti-capitalism, finally, could be extended, especially by France's fascists, to anti-Semitism. In a spoof Disney cartoon, a stereotyped Jew broadcasts worthless promises of the Allies' imminent arrival as Popeye and Mickey Mouse bomb France.[51] A brochure entitled 'Alert!' linked the destruction of Europe's cultural artefacts across to a 'Jewish war' offering lucrative reconstruction contracts to Jewish business.[52] A spoof edition of the main American propaganda leaflet, *L'Amérique en guerre*, claimed that the 'international Jewish war machine' had been represented at the 1943 Tehran conference.[53] The Franciste party blamed American Jews for raids, and called for collective executions (as if France was not already facilitating them).[54]

What followed from the Allies' economic aims, and their indifference to Europe's civilians and their culture, was that the 'squadrons of liberation', as Henriot ironically called them, could only bring misery, famine and ever-greater destruction to France.[55] 'I warned last 30 December that Italy gave the model of what was destined for us' said Henriot after the bombing of Rouen, adding 'Tomorrow, no doubt, you will need more mourning veils than flags, more flowers for wreaths than bouquets for the victors.'[56] Though hardly optimistic, this message could connect to the anxieties of a people hoping for liberation but suffering from an unprecedented bombing offensive.

Although Italy's propagandists used some of the same interpretations of the raids, their starting-point was quite different, their message far more changeable. Pre-war Italy had been 'air-minded'. In spectacular feats such as Italo Balbo's transatlantic flights, its pilots and aircraft had won world records and international acclaim; air force victories in Ethiopia and Spain appeared in books for Italian children; by the late 1930s coverage in newspapers and films was underpinned by at least half a dozen specialist aviation journals. The air force was a 'mirror of the Fascist regime' that revealed its mythical essence, rituals and scenography.[57]

Not surprisingly, then, early coverage of the air war focused on Italian feats of arms, particularly in the Mediterranean and on southern England. Italian aircraft were reported as racing one another over the *mare nostrum* while harassing British ships.[58] A 1942 pamphlet carried images of aircraft bombing British battleships, of Italian pilots smiling and loading aircraft with bombs; 'Axis aviation dominates unchallenged the battle in the sky', it claimed, with a map representing a successful Axis attack on a Malta-bound convoy off Sardinia.[59] Films like *I tre aquilotti* (by Mario Mattoli, 1942) or *Gente dell'aria* (by Esodo Pratelli, 1943) encouraged Italian youth to enrol in the air force, celebrating not only the pilots' heroism but also the advanced technology of Italy's aircraft industry.[60]

Italians were also told that their air force had bombed Britain (aiming only at military objectives).[61] Italy's efforts in the Blitz were described as equal to Germany's, and conducted in 'perfect *cameratismo*'. These largely imaginary raids, barely discernible to British city-dwellers, served, as Marco Fincardi observes, to boost Italian spirits for a short period in 1940–1.[62] According to *Il Giornale di Sicilia*, Italian pilots with their deep blue uniforms brought Mediterranean colour to grey northern regions, as well as 'solar qualities' and 'Latin instinct' to flying; they returned from raids smiling, their aircraft barely scratched by British fighters.[63]

Glorification of the Italian air force was paired with reports of British raids on Italy early in the war, where it did not replace them. But by 1942 Italy had run out of boasts about non-existent raids on England. Coverage of the bombing war perforce turned to Italy itself. In June 1940, Pavolini had been confident about this. He wanted precise information given on enemy raids, including numbers and even names of the victims. 'The truth' was the best arm against defeatist rumours; the RAF might drop leaflets on northern Italian cities, but they were so laughable that it would do the Italian public good to see them.[64] Even then, though, there was a note of caution: reports on raids should avoid 'sensitizing' readers excessively.[65] Early publication of lists of people who had broken the blackout, aimed at publicizing penalties, was halted – almost certainly because they demonstrated widespread non-compliance.[66]

These precautions turned to outright lies in the face of three successful British attacks on Italian naval ports: the Fleet Air Arm raid on Taranto November 1940, which seriously damaged three battleships; the bombing of Naples harbour that December, damaging a further warship; and the Royal Navy's bombardment of Genoa in February 1941, which sank or damaged over 20 warships and hit nearby industrial and residential buildings, killing 144 civilians and injuring 272. In each case the press denied damage to Italian vessels, reporting that Allied forces had failed to penetrate Italian defences, or had taken hits. This policy of denial had a disastrous effect as the truth spread. News of Taranto travelled across Italy as soldiers were moved to military bases elsewhere.[67] After the Naples raid people in Tortona, nearly 500 miles away in Piedmont, gathered in one square and were reported as declaring, 'when our radio says that only one of our aircraft has not returned, there are instead two or three. Of 15 of our aircraft that left for London not one has made it back.'[68] Mendacious reports of the Genoa raid in the daily *Il Secolo XIX* provoked a furious response from Genoese citizens, enraged by the lies and a sense of being left without defence. A collective letter accused *Il Secolo XIX*, and all the Fascist press, of cheating the people: 'where were the ships that were supposed to fight the British?', it asked. Readers also wondered why indignant articles about the attack on Genoa sat alongside others praising the bombing of Coventry. Others blamed provocation of the enemy: 'After you boasted that the British failed to bomb Berlin and you insulted Churchill, they came to get their revenge on our Genoa!'[69] Despite the damage to the credibility of the official media, however, Pavolini's line barely changed. Newspapers and war bulletins reported Allied raids without comment, and emphasized Axis victories, especially against Malta. Newspapers were told not to report Public Works Minister Luigi Gorla's inspection of air-raid damage in Naples, and were criticized for reports considered 'pietistic' or likely to 'sensitize' the population.[70]

Barely tenable even when Allied raids were aimed at limited military objectives and caused few casualties, the policy became inoperable when the RAF commenced area bombing and the USAAF began raids on Italy. The area attacks of late October 1942 on Genoa and Milan, which together caused some 500 deaths, forced a change of strategy: unable to hide the consequences of raids, newspapers began to emphasize the enemy's cruelty, barbarism and cowardice, and the Italian people's moral resistance. *Corriere della Sera* proclaimed that 'cowardly aggressions', far from intimidating the Italians, could only generate 'our resentment'.[71] Telegrams to Mussolini from the cities' prefects, *podestà* and Fascist party heads were published, praising the civilized, dignified and fiery response of the 'Fascist' populations in the face of 'Anglo-Saxon barbarianism'. The enemy, they declared, was 'deluded' in thinking they could lower the Italian people's combative spirit. For the first time the concept of the 'open city' – widely used in the case of Rome and other cities from 1943 – was mentioned by the Italian press.[72] *Corriere* also emphasised 'city solidarity', whether within Milan or from outside: a message from the mayor of Berlin told the Milanese that these methods of war would only strengthen the fighting spirit 'of our two peoples'.[73]

A variation on the theme of defiance, favoured by well-known Fascist broadcaster Aldo Valori, was *menefreghismo* (couldn't-care-less-ness) a typical Fascist concept from its origins and, in relation to bombing, a sort of empty bravado towards British bombs and propaganda.[74] According to *La Stampa*, the population of Trapani, a Sicilian port targeted in June 1943 before the Allied landings, had reacted to a raid 'as if nothing had happened'.[75] As late as mid-July,

Palermo's daily newspaper commented approvingly that despite RAF raids, people were still going to the beach.[76]

Outrage, though, was a more frequent response to raids in the Italian press. After the raid of 20 November 1942, the Turin newspaper saluted the 'fallen': the 117 victims of the attack were compared to soldiers who had died in Africa and Russia, 'but with this difference: the latter had weapons with which to attack and defend themselves ... these people were unarmed ... protected by international conventions and by a moral law that is stronger than the written one'. These innocents, it was claimed, would be avenged 'by our children, and by our children's children, so long as Italian blood exists'.[77] Calls to revenge, however, were often blunted by military realities. *Corriere della Sera* admitted in February 1943 that retaliation against the bombing was 'not so easy'. Reiterating that the enemy 'cannot think that these barbaric methods could win them the war', however, was not the same as showing the way to an Italian victory.[78] The radio complemented press reports, warning Italians of a tough spring ahead during which they must take a combat role.[79] Valori, when not indulging in *menefreghismo*, took British propaganda's stereotypes of fearful, peace-loving Italians seriously enough to contradict them, claiming that popular morale was strengthening, not collapsing, under the bombs.[80]

Most frequently, however, Italian media responses to bombing from early 1943 were comparable to those of Vichy France: moral outrage and vilification of the Allies. The enemy, said *Corriere*, had hit 'our beautiful cities, killed innocent civilians, and destroyed centuries-old monuments', a moral and artistic heritage for the whole of humanity.[81] The choice of reports focused on the cruelty of a sadistic enemy intent on killing, maiming and terrorizing civilians, destroying homes and centuries-old monuments. Raids on military objectives received scant coverage even when many civilians died: the attack on the military port of Civitavecchia near Rome on 14 May 1943 went almost unreported despite some 300 civilian casualties. Instead, journalists were told to concentrate on smaller towns with no apparent military objective. The Tuscan city of Grosseto, for example, was bombed on 26 April; a hospital and an entertainment park were hit and at least 134 people, including many children, were killed. Ignoring the existence of a target in the nearby aerodrome, Pavolini's office alleged that 'The enemy decided to hit the civilian population on purpose, killing women and children.'[82] The historic Sardinian cathedrals of Cagliari and Alghero, a foundlings' home in Calabria, women and children working in the fields near Foggia – all, according to the Italian press, had been deliberately targeted. The accuracy of the Americans' precision instruments, *La Gazzetta del Mezzogiorno* observed, meant they had no excuses – citing Rennes in France as well as Italian cities.[83]

A counterpoint, eliciting compassion for the victims and hatred for bombers, was offered in the heroism of ordinary people. A young Fascist was given permission to enrol as a fighter pilot in order to avenge his mother and brother, both air-raid victims; a dying mother, hit with her baby in her arms as she ran to a shelter, 'begged to the heavens for the punishment of the guilty ones, who had torn her baby's body to pieces'; at Gioia Tauro in Calabria, a woman wounded during a raid just before giving birth accepted certain death on an operating table to save her child.[84]

But in the wake of the final surrender at Tunis, the regime sought something else to counter the corrosive long-term effect of Allied propaganda. The result was a rumour, spread by the press, that the enemy dropped devices in the shape of fountain pens, pencils, toys, cigarette holders, lipsticks or sweets, which exploded once civilians, and especially children, picked them up. On 8 May, for example, *Roma* reported that an 11-year-old boy, working with his parents in the fields at Carinola in Caserta province, had had his right hand blown off when he picked up a device resembling a small watch.[85] The insidious traps were described in detail, with illustrations, in a massive, continuous campaign taking in the local and national press and radio: its implicit message was that nothing dropped by Anglo-American aircraft could be trusted.[86] The campaign reached the press in neutral Switzerland even before it went nationwide in Italy.[87] The British were worried enough to plan a rebuttal.[88]

The campaign, indeed, was so effective that it spread panic and despondency across Italy, and rebounded on its authors: from 18 May 1943 ministerial directives told newspapers to drop it.[89] But the damage was done. Many people believed that the Fascists, or the Germans, had planted the objects for propaganda purposes. Suspicions that the Fascists were to blame persisted under the Salò Republic. An anonymous letter addressed to Kesselring in October 1943 claimed that if the Ministry of Popular Culture and the German occupiers were trying to ban Italians from listening to enemy radio stations, it was because the Nazi-Fascist media told lies; the sudden, and suspect, halt to the explosive-toys propaganda was cited as proof.[90]

The bombing of Rome, six days before Mussolini's fall in July 1943, offered an opportunity for a late outburst. Rome, said the well-known radio commentator Fulvio Palmieri was 'everybody's mother', and 'from the heart of the peoples, from Christianity, one voice calls today – the wounded mother'.[91] *La Gazzetta del Mezzogiorno* described the raid as a sacrilege and drew parallels with the acts of barbarian invaders of the Dark Ages. The 'new barbarians' had attempted to destroy Rome's millenarian civilization for the sake of a 'new "civilization" forged in Washington under the sign of the dollar and the star of Zion'.[92] After the June raids on Sicily, meanwhile, the Americans were accused of betraying a population whose emigrants had brought to America 'strong arms, lively and constructive intelligence, a noble capacity for work and probity of habits, which should have served as an example to the worshippers of the dollar'.[93]

Italian hopes that Allied raids would end with Mussolini's fall were disappointed. During the 45 days of Badoglio's rule, the attacks continued, with a view to bombing Italy into surrender. Italian propaganda also continued unabated. The indiscriminate bombing of Naples, on 4 August, which destroyed priceless monuments including the medieval church of Santa Chiara, and killed an estimated 700 civilians, drew a particularly fierce response. The 'merciless shower of bombs', said *Il Mattino*, was dropped with a 'bestial rage', a fury that seemed to be dictated by the enemy's failure in their attempt to subdue the Neapolitans, 'who had since then fearlessly resisted the torment'; Paolo Scarfoglio, one of Italy's most distinguished journalists, called the bombing 'the assassination of a people', for the 'pure pleasure of killing'.[94]

Any changes in the tone of Italian propaganda under the Salò Republic were, unsurprisingly, in the direction of greater ferocity. Terrorism or sadism were invoked to explain the Allies' 'deliberate' attacks on civilians. Moving individual stories of survivors who had lost everything were offered to *La Stampa*'s readers after the raid on Turin of 5 January 1944: a woman carrying a small baby and staring at her collapsed home; a man walking like a ghost in the forlorn hope of finding his wife alive; a girl in hospital who realized a dead young woman was her sister.[95] 'Before and After' illustrations of monuments were used to illustrate the criminality of the 'gangsters of the air'.[96] The bombing of Monte Cassino Abbey was a gift in this context: *La Stampa* pointed out that at the time of its foundation, by St Benedict in the sixth century, the 'semi-savage hordes who lived in the Britannic mist, from which one of the present-day belligerents is descended, did not have any clue of what civilisation was' – before promising that 'the great Abbey, tormented and trampled over, will be reborn'.[97] The bombers were also described as 'friends of Badoglio', who was accused of suggesting raids on Bologna to the Allies.[98]

The regime could no longer offer the hint of a military victory to boost popular morale. The only remaining argument to persuade Italians, living under German occupation and hoping for a speedy Allied advance to end the war, to resist became hatred for the enemy. In this, the message from Salò resembled that of Henriot's France.

Vichy France, Fascist Italy: Assessment

The two regimes' propaganda responses to Allied bombing present obvious similarities. Each portrayed the Allies as barbarians, wantonly destroying and killing to terrorize civilians, or simply for fun. Each, too, deployed images of pathos to illustrate the population's victimhood. Each tried to stave off its own downfall by mobilizing hatred of the Allies among populations eager for liberation. Each, too, used raids on the other to reinforce its case. French reports on Italy stressed human tragedies (raids on Naples, they said, had claimed 2,300 victims by mid-June 1943) and cultural vandalism, as well as describing Italy's supposed calm and resilience, and aircraft shot down by the Italians.[99] Each, too, became embroiled in the contradictions between reports of raids on national territory and raids on other countries. Italy's glorification of the Italian air force's achievements over Britain chimed badly with indignation at raids on the motherland – and some Italians noticed. French coverage of German attacks on Britain similarly presented bombing as an entirely normal way to wage war, detracting from claims that barbarism was the Allies' preserve.[100] And when Vichy reports, using despatches from the Führer's headquarters, demonstrated the effectiveness of German air defences, they invited an obvious contrast with France but without asking why the Luftwaffe was so much weaker there.[101]

The differences, however, are at least as important as the similarities. Vichy steadily built up its message over more than two years from the Billancourt raid of March 1942. Fascist Italy erred from complete denial, to attempts to avoid 'sensitization', to *menefreghismo*, to horror and indignation, and to rumours in a barely longer period. More consistent, Vichy was also more truthful. Casualties might be exaggerated in the heat of the moment: the most flagrant example was Caen, where between 8,000 and 9,000 bodies, over four times the real number of victims, were said to have been pulled from the wreckage.[102] But on the whole, as the British Political Warfare Executive (PWE) observed, 'Vichy reports of casualties and damage are not exaggerated' – or as the Free French admitted, 'It is sad to note that Henriot does not need to lie'.[103] This was his main strength: giving powerful articulation to the palpable horror of events the French could see for themselves, at first hand or on the big screen. And it drew him an attentive audience.[104] The postal censorship services in Montpellier found approval of Henriot's broadcasts exceeding hostility by six or seven to one.[105] Even if he won over few hearts and minds completely, his ability to sway waverers and to sow doubt among committed Resistance supporters caused his enemies serious concern.[106] Henriot's dark eloquence finally cost him his life when a Resistance unit assassinated him on 28 June 1944. Italian propaganda, by contrast, was mendacious as well as inconsistent, and therefore obviously less credible. Lies included the early denial of damage to Italian targets, the booby-trapped pens rumour, and the endemic exaggeration of the body count after raids late in the war in a bid to turn Italians against the enemy.[107] To these were added reports of 'secret weapons', whether German or (more rarely) Italian. A Fascist priest even promised his Genoese congregation a riposte to the bombing of their city in the form of a 'transoceanic stratospheric missile'. But this merely detracted from the regime's already threadbare credibility. As the Salò Republic's Minister of Popular Culture warned Mussolini, everyone was wondering why 'no official voice was raised to either confirm or modify news that was spread so categorically and confidently'.[108]

Both Vichy and Fascist propaganda, finally, suffered from a fundamental weakness: their inability to offer any more attractive course of action than that of rallying to a hated or discredited government in order to ensure the continued German domination of Europe. That corresponded to their adversaries' main strength.

THE ALLIES: LIMITING THE DAMAGE?

The Allied propagandists' job was the opposite of Vichy's and of Fascist Italy's: to defend the indefensible in the name of a cause – liberation – that at least by 1943–4 commanded the near-universal allegiance of the French and the Italians. Minimizing the impact of bombing on support for that cause required delicate messages – and, in the first instance, a material challenge to the two regimes' media monopolies.

Running the media blockade

The Allies' psychological war on Fascist Italy and Vichy France was conducted through the BBC and other broadcasters, and in leaflets, journals and pamphlets dropped by aircraft. A small part of this task fell to the Free French and to the Resistance in each country.[109] But the Allies were able to commit vastly greater resources, sufficient to break the Axis monopoly on information and have a serious effect on public opinion.

The first tool was leaflets, dropped by the bombers themselves. Over France, the RAF dropped over 676 million leaflets between July 1940 and September 1944, peaking in late 1943; these were chiefly though not exclusively the *Courrier de l'Air*, a four-page newsletter appearing roughly monthly. As an issue from early 1942 ('Brought by your friends of the RAF, distributed by French patriots') said, 'While we pour bombs onto Germany and on their installations, we are proud to be the link between the British people, all free peoples, and you.'[110] Leafleting operations cost 34 downed aircraft and 58 dead airmen.[111] An American counterpart, *L'Amérique en guerre*, was launched in 1942: by late April 1944, a group of just five B17s could scatter 3,360,000 leaflets in a single night over ten French towns.[112] Italy received mostly RAF leaflets till early 1943; by that August, however, American leaflets 'aimed more and more at the Italian home front' were pouring from the Psychological Warfare Branch in Tunis at a weekly rate of 7 million.[113] In July 1943 alone, 8,173,000 leaflets were dropped on Sicily, 1,871,000 on Sardinia and 8,722,000 on the Italian mainland.[114] Not all, of course, found readers: leafleting was chiefly done by trainee air crews, who might drop many miles off target, or even in the sea.

Radio propaganda was chiefly a British operation, broadly co-ordinated with leafleting (the *Courrier de l'Air*, for example, always included radio frequencies and broadcasting times). The BBC's French service broadcast 17½ hours weekly in September 1940; three years later, this had reached 39½ hours – in addition to the paltry five minutes daily allowed to de Gaulle's Free French.[115] Although broadcasts also reached France from Swiss radio, from Radio Moscow, Radio Algiers, Radio Palermo (from 6 August 1943), and from the American Broadcasting Service in Europe (ABSIE) from 1944, the BBC became the French people's staple listening and the French prefects' major propaganda worry, confirmed by regular reports across the country from 1940 on.[116] In Italy, meanwhile, as early as late June 1940, the popular appetite for war news and the low credibility of official propaganda meant that in Milan the most listened-to radio stations were the British (the BBC Italian service Radio Londra) and the Russian. Within a year the phrase 'the

British radio said it' was counted, according to Fascist informers, as proof of a statement's veracity.[117] In November–December 1943, an Allied survey of liberated Sicily showed that the most popular radio stations were Palermo and Roma for music, but Palermo and Londra (considered more truthful) for news and comment.[118]

Not surprisingly, access to foreign propaganda was discouraged in both countries. In France, leaflets were supposed to be handed in unread to the authorities and radios were confiscated in coastal areas in early 1944. By 1943, at German prompting, listening to foreign radios, and especially to the BBC, had been made punishable by death, though there is no evidence that this penalty was ever executed.[119] In Italy, listening to foreign radio was prohibited when the country entered the war, but punishments for disobedience initially remained vague: people were usually taken to a police station and 'persuaded' to abandon their habit. On 5 January 1942, however, a new decree fixed a penalty of six months' and three years' imprisonment and a fine of 6,000–40,000 lire on those who listened to enemy or neutral radio stations, and those who spread news gathered from such sources. These penalties were tightened in a law of 27 April 1942 – and failed to achieve the desired result. Italians listened to these stations mostly to know what was really going on at the fronts, and voices like that of Colonel Harold Stevens from Radio Londra became familiar. Programmes from America such as 'La voce dell'America' (which began with the *Hymn to Garibaldi*) were also listened to.[120]

Bombing to liberate: the Allied message

Allied propaganda aimed at the same purpose in both countries: to show that bombing was a painful but necessary means to the good end of liberation. France, however, was not at war with the Allies. The Italians, by contrast, had mostly accepted, over two decades, a dictatorship which had declared war on Britain after several years of anti-British propaganda.[121] The French were assumed from 1940 to be pro-British; the Italians were viewed as needing to be prised away from their Fascist loyalties and their German ally. Hence the nuances between directives emanating from the PWE. A general instruction of May 1944 for occupied territories (including France) enthusiastically envisaged that 'Just as the RAF and the USAAF complement each other in their night and day attacks so BBC and ABSIE will blanket the targets', before observing that 'We should let the facts argue our time honoured themes: (a) inevitability of Allied victory – that is a basic assumption, (b) superiority of men and machines, (c) that the peoples of Europe are on our side – resistance in Europe is now in action or at the alert, (d) that the German people know they are beaten.'[122] The 'Italian working plan for the BBC' of a year earlier – before the surrender – argued, in somewhat different terms, that:

1. Defeat is inevitable. By prolonging the war Italians will merely bring devastation to their country.
2. It is in the power of the Italians, individually and collectively, not only to get out of the war, but to shorten it through resistance to the Germans and the Fascists.
3. It is in the interest of the Italians, individually and collectively, to get out of the war.[123]

The inevitability of Allied victory might be conveyed in leafleting campaigns by general war news, covering, for example, events on the Eastern front such as the end of the siege of Leningrad, progress in the Battle of the Atlantic, and more particularly the North African and Italian campaigns. *Le Courrier de l'Air*, in line with the BBC's aspiration to objectivity, also made a point of announcing Allied defeats – the fall of Tobruk in 1942, or the defeat in the Dodecanese in 1943 – while trying to minimize them. Diplomatic news, such as the Allies' demand for the unconditional surrender of Axis powers, or the big wartime conferences, reinforced the message of victory.[124] But its inevitability was argued, above all, through triumphant coverage of the Allied bombing offensive. A special issue of *Le Courrier de l'Air* commemorated the Dam Busters' raid on the Ruhr dams in May 1943; three months later *L'Amérique en Guerre* showed the daring American raids on Ploesti; the destruction of Hamburg was celebrated by both leaflets. The following winter, the RAF boasted of dropping 'in 100 days, 100 times more bombs on Germany than the Luftwaffe dropped on Britain' while *L'Amérique en Guerre* presented its achievements for 1943 under the title 'Bombs, bombs, bombs.'[125] Both leaflets celebrated raids on Berlin in November 1943.[126] One of the last American issues featured a photograph of the new B29 Superfortress, already in operation over Japan.[127] Meanwhile a 1941 leaflet dropped over Italy explained that Italian aircraft had no chance against the 'super-fast and well-armed British fighters'.[128] Two years later the bombing of German cities was used as a threatening example: an issue of *The Soldier's News*, distributed by the RAF and the USAAF during the Badoglio interlude in August 1943, opened with the headline: 'Hamburg has become the city of death: Will it be the same in Italy?'[129]

The naked assertion of Allied might, combined (in the Italian case) with barely veiled threats, might impress but could hardly win hearts and minds. As PWE argued, care was needed to avoid implications that the raids aimed to break civilian morale or destroy Italian cities, and to ensure that bombing did not 'create a "Piave" spirit' of heroic resistance.[130] Civilians needed reassurance that (contrary to Vichy and Fascist claims) they were not the targets, and that the Allied cause was just.

Hence a typical conclusion of British leaflets dropped on Italy in 1941 was 'Italian people! … We did not want to fight you.'[131] Churchill himself was enlisted in this cause, with a message to the Italians in January 1941 that was broadcast by Radio Londra and printed on leaflets. 'We are at war with each other: strange and terrible thing', said Churchill, 'we have always been friends' – joining hands against the 'barbarian acts of the Huns' in the Risorgimento and the Great War. But now, he continued, as Italian aircraft had attempted to bomb London, the British were going to take the Italian empire to pieces. Throughout the speech, Churchill repeated, without naming Mussolini, that 'it is the fault of one man, one man alone', before concluding 'And I leave the story incomplete, until the day comes – and it will come – when the Italian nation again will begin to forge its own destiny once more.'[132] Churchill's speech was reinforced by leaflets with tear-off strips carrying the sentence: 'Greece, Taranto, Libya … "Mussolini is always right"' in black lettering superimposed on a large red question mark,[133] and by radio claims that during air raids 'Mussolini is safely sheltered in the Vatican city.'[134] Attacks on the Duce worked because they reflected feelings that Italians themselves had begun to express on the streets, on evacuation trains or in air-raid shelters. So they repeated and discussed Churchill's speech widely; in December the following year, Mussolini even felt moved to contradict it.[135]

Women were specifically targeted in this connection, to promote a general collapse of morale. A British leaflet of 1941 encouraged them to 'Go to the Fascio; scream and shout that you want an end to this war. Write on the walls that you want peace. Britain wants peace with Italy, but Mussolini is blocking the way.'[136] Again, this type of propaganda worried the Italian authorities sufficiently for Fascist counter-propaganda leaflets to be distributed to women, and Fascist women encouraged to promote a spirit of resistance to bombing among other women in air-raid shelters.[137]

Attacks on Mussolini focused above all on the alliance with Hitler – a mistake for which the population, said British propaganda, was now paying. Thanks to Mussolini, described by one Radio Londra broadcast as 'that Carnival Caesar', Italy had become a German colony.[138] Allusions to Italy's past struggles for independence pointed out that 'the House of Savoy, helped by France and Britain, kicked the Germans off Italian soil. Mussolini has called them back.'[139] The words of Garibaldi, hero of the Risorgimento and admirer of Britain as a 'friend of the oppressed', were especially helpful in this context, and were used in a leaflet of December 1940. 'If ever', Garibaldi had written in 1854, 'England … should be so circumstanced as to require the help of an ally, cursed be that Italian who would not step forward with me in her defence.'[140] By going to war against Britain, the leaflet warned, Mussolini had placed the whole of Italy under Garibaldi's curse. The curse could be lifted only if Italians got rid of the Fascists, who had dishonoured Italy's name. They should do so 'before it is too late'.[141]

In a mirror image of Fascist comments on the 'Anglo-Saxons', Allied attacks on Germany in propaganda to the Italians claimed that the Germans were the same barbarians who had invaded Italy in past centuries.[142] Today, the argument continued, the Germans had dragged Italy into a disastrous war and forced their partners into a subordinate – and dangerous – place. The 'beautiful streets of Italy' had been sold to the 'hated German', while Italian soldiers were sent to distant battlefields for the wealth and power of the Reich.[143] The Germans had ordered Italian pilots to fight superior Allied aircraft: 'Germany has ordered ... and the Italian Royal Air Force must obey!'[144] The Germans, according to a leaflet of 1941 which compared Italian and German rations, 'filled their stomachs' while Italians starved – reflecting the 'place given to Italy in the new German order'.[145] The Germans were also, finally, to be lambasted for failing to supply Italy with promised anti-aircraft guns, as local Fascist authorities had failed to provide adequate civil defence.[146] 'So long as your government is part of the Axis', said a leaflet dropped on Milan, 'there is only one way to limit the number of victims: evacuation from the cities of the non-essential population.'[147] As the Axis defeat in Tunisia brought the invasion of Italy closer, the RAF warned Italians in May 1943 that their country would become a 'no man's land'.[148] In June, leaflets over Naples and Caserta coupled warnings with the habitual argument that only the Germans and Mussolini were to blame. 'Why die for Hitler?' they asked Italians: Italy had no defences and had been left alone: 'Whose fault is it?' Again, the population was advised to leave cities and ports and encouraged to demonstrate for peace.[149]

The final, and crucial, step in this argument was that for Italians, it was 'not derogatory to their HONOUR to get out of the war'. By 1943 at least, PWE was sensitive to this issue: Allied propaganda must 'avoid any statements which offend the Italian sense of honour' – for example, by depicting Italians as 'figures of fun' or suggesting that their defeats were due to cowardice, or that Italy was a second-class power. On the contrary, blame should be placed on Fascist corruption and maladministration, and Italians told that a break from Germany would follow 'from a sense of patriotic responsibility'.[150] A concrete example was offered in July 1943 by the island of Pantelleria – described by Mussolini as Italy's most fortified bastion of the Mediterranean – which had surrendered after five days of bombing. 'There are no soldiers in the world, however heroic', said an Allied leaflet, 'who could have resisted the terrible hammering to which Pantelleria was subjected.'[151] A new leafleting campaign, following the fall of the regime on 25 July 1943 and aimed at securing an early Italian surrender, included a postcard addressed to Badoglio stating that the Italians wanted peace; only the German presence prevented the Allies from entering Italy as its friends. Finally, it told the Italians that 'You have fought with honour!', again with due regard for their pride: 'With the same honour you can obtain the peace!'[152]

Sensitivity to the Italian predicament, and to the mental and emotional strain of a national transition from Axis partner to divided and defeated nation, was strongest on the American side. Alongside British anti-German propaganda and attacks on Italian morale, the Americans projected the friendlier message that Italians could redeem themselves by collaborating with the Allies and detaching themselves from Fascism. An idealistic note from the head of the Office of Strategic Services, argued the need to 'stress the difference between this war and the nationalistic wars of the past' by emphasizing that the conflict was between 'two conflicting ideas of life': between aggressive dictators 'and the freedom-loving people who are not only defending themselves and their right to live in peace, but also the rights of Man throughout the world'.[153] The Americans could also, in an inversion of Fascist propaganda, play on the Italian-American connection. A 12-page pamphlet entitled 'Italian-American Friendship', fronted by a portrait of Garibaldi, paid tribute to the millions of Italian emigrants who had helped build America. Dropped over Sicily after the Allied landings, it insisted that Americans and Italians shared cultural and racial ties, evidenced by the way in which some American soldiers, children of Sicilian emigrants, had communicated with Sicilians in their own dialect. Sicilians were thanked for their kindness in rescuing and caring for wounded Americans.[154]

Some Allied propaganda over France paralleled the material for Italy. The regime's leaders were attacked as German agents: Allied French news greeted Laval as a 'Gauleiter' on his return to power, and Darnand as a 'bandit' on his appointment to government.[155] Efforts were made to reassure French susceptibilities, real or perceived. Eden in person addressed the French people on 14 July 1942 with a declaration that Britain wanted France to remain a great power.[156] *Le Courrier de l'Air* showed Free French forces in Damascus in 1941 and reminded readers that the British, having taken over Madagascar from Vichy in May 1942, had handed the island to the Free French; *L'Amérique en Guerre* also stressed three times, from late 1943, that the United States would never negotiate with Vichy.[157] The exploits of the internal Resistance were praised (Raymond and Lucie Aubrac appeared in March 1944) as were those of the Fighting French in the air, in North Africa, and in Italy (with discreet reminders of British and American help in arming them). One of the last *Courrier de l'Air* issues, from July 1944, featured fulsome thanks from a pilot, Eric Sprawson, to the people of Caen who had sheltered him when his Lancaster had been shot down.[158] A final issue of *Le Courrier de l'Air* showed de Gaulle visiting New York and a grateful resident lighting Churchill's cigar during his visit to liberated Cherbourg.[159] Differences between the two governments did appear in treatment of the opposition to Vichy: de Gaulle featured in *Le Courrier de l'Air* from its earliest issues, while *L'Amérique en Guerre* promoted General Giraud. These, however, had largely disappeared by early 1944.[160]

But the Allies faced a different assignment as they pitched to France: not, as with the Italians, to stretch out the hand of friendship, but to ensure that the French did not withdraw theirs. The central problem here was the bombing of France. This might, especially in the earlier years, be presented robustly, like the air offensive against Germany. *L'Amérique en Guerre* invited its readers to celebrate the US Eighth Air Force's first birthday in August 1943, apparently ignoring its numerous raids (half of total sorties) on French territory.[161] A British leaflet on the Billancourt raid of 1942 announced that 'The Renault factories were working for the German army. The Renault factories have been hit' and pointed out the likely damage to Germany's war effort against the Soviet Union; *Le Courrier de l'Air* claimed 'demonstrations of joy' in the Paris streets after the raid.[162] This upbeat line reflected Eden's similarly sanguine view that raids *improved* French morale, and his keen wish to get leaflets dropped on unoccupied France in April 1942.[163]

During 1943, however, the emphasis had shifted, largely as a function of unease at the effects of raids on France – effects that could only intensify with the bombing effort, especially from the USAAF.[164] PWE repeatedly stressed, first, the need to tell the French that 'we shall not hesitate to bomb enemy targets wherever we may find them', since German factories in France aided the Nazi war effort, and, second, the requirement 'for individual Frenchmen, obliged to remain near targets, to take all possible Air Raid Precautions' and to demand adequate shelters.[165] As the Transportation Plan got under way, however, PWE was lucidly pessimistic about the effects of bombing on France: they had been bad, 'even among our most loyal supporters', in September 1943, and 'there is little doubt that there will be a similar, if not more violent reaction now'.[166] But a propaganda effort had to be made: Churchill himself, at the War Cabinet of 2 May 1944, recommended 'an immense programme of leaflet dropping' to minimize the 'great slaughter' he anticipated from the Transportation Plan.[167] PWE also insisted that Allied propaganda should make clear that neither the current 'preparatory' nature of the bombing, nor the 'many false alarms, many feints and many dress rehearsals' (in Churchill's words) that would take place would signal an immediate invasion, still less early deliverance.[168]

Allied leaflets therefore balanced the continued assertion of the need for raids with warnings to the French of the dangers, and acknowledgement of their sacrifice. The warnings started early. The French were repeatedly told from 1942 to keep away from the coastal zones (which the Germans, conveniently, had already defined as forbidden areas for non-residents) and to take proper air-raid precautions – the latter a curious convergence with Vichy advice.[169] Late that year, *Le Courrier de l'Air* prepared for the raids on Lorient and Saint-Nazaire with a big article on German submarine bases in France, observing that in Lorient, 'the Keroman peninsula is nothing but one huge target'.[170] A year later, *L'Amérique en Guerre* warned the French to stay away from factories working for the Germans. It then, unusually, included a list of targets across France, also broadcast by radio. Some of these were bombed in November and on 31 December, though equally, some towns hit in this period (most notably Toulon and Cannes-La Bocca) were not on the list.[171] At the same time, the more successful and economical raids of Spring 1944 – on Michelin at Clermont-Ferrand, on the marshalling yards at Creil, on German airfields – were still covered; readers learnt that one Lancaster had come home with its bombload intact from a raid because its pilot could not be certain of avoiding civilian casualties. Rouen, Lyon or Marseille did not feature in these accounts.[172]

Elsewhere, the leaflets reflected the priorities set out by PWE. Churchill's phrase about false alarms appeared in *Le Courrier de l'Air* in March 1944.[173] A month later, articles from British newspapers (the *Observer*, *News Chronicle*, and *Daily Herald*) were reproduced warning of impending raids, acknowledging the

French people's suffering and appealing for their understanding.[174] *L'Amérique en Guerre*, meanwhile, warned the French about the Transportation Plan. Just as in 1914–18, it argued, occupied French territory was unavoidably hit by French shells, today French soil was receiving Allied bombs. The French should stay away if at all possible from rail centres, marshalling yards, points, locomotive depots, and rail workshops; their liberation was at stake.[175] While the Allies' propagandists sought to convert the Italians, where France was concerned they were chiefly trying to limit the damage.

CONCLUSION

By August 1943, according to the Psychological Warfare Branch of the Allies' Mediterranean command, leaflets had successfully persuaded Italians to turn against Mussolini and to welcome the Allies as liberators. Whatever their other aims, all the leaflets had stressed the overwhelming Allied military superiority, 'especially air power'. The results, it was claimed, were evident: 'on the 25th, Mussolini fell and Italian cities took on a revolutionary aspect directed against the fascists, the Germans and the war'. These historic developments were considered to be 'along the lines aimed at in the leaflets'. The leaflets 'were believed' and acted on, according to the report, rendering enemy counter-propaganda ineffective.[176] This was all the more the case as, by late 1942, Fascist Italy's propaganda effort had run out of steam, morally and materially. It could not sustain the myth of victory. It could not claim the regime was defending civilians from air raids. Thanks to disaffection with Fascism, it could hardly get the message across. The radio was not believed even when listened to; leafleting was limited to Party headquarters, or to steadily smaller and less frequent public celebrations.

The view over France on the eve of liberation, to judge from the 1944 reports from PWE and from the Free French, was much less upbeat. Certainly, the Allies had no choice but to undertake a propaganda effort to explain their air offensive and to warn potential victims. And an attentive French reader of British and American leaflets would certainly have had an idea of the Allies' burgeoning air power, of the strategic aims of raids, of their desire to limit French civilian casualties, and of what types of locality to avoid. The BBC's reputation for truthfulness contributed to the credibility of the operation; and the leaflets worried the Vichy authorities sufficiently for realistic anti-Allied spoofs ('Brought to the French people by the American Air Force with phosphorus bombs') to be distributed. As in Italy, the Allies were generally welcomed as liberators. What they had failed to do, however, was to knock out Vichy propaganda; the killing of Henriot by the Resistance was proof of how effective he had been in winning over new listeners to the regime's message.

Did it matter that the Allies appeared to have won the propaganda war over Italy but only drawn it over France? In one sense it clearly did not. No amount of Fascist propaganda made French or Italian civilians prefer the Germans to the British or the Americans or the Canadians; no quantity of Allied leaflets or broadcasts could fully prepare civilians for the violence, the scale, and the frequent inaccuracy of Allied raids, persisting in Italy nearly 20 months after the armistice. From another perspective, however, the propaganda war and its outcome counted. They helped to shape both civilians' opinions of bombing, and their willingness to be mobilized to limit some of its worst consequences.

Notes

1 B. Maida and N. Tranfaglia (eds), *Ministri e giornalisti: la guerra e il MinCulPop, 1939–1943* (Turin: Einaudi, 2005), viii–ix.

2 ASG, Prefettura, b. 275, Pavolini to all Italian newspaper directors and to prefects, 15 June 1940.

3 D. Peschanski, 'Control or Integration? Information and Propaganda under Vichy' in M. Scriven and P. Wagstaff (eds), *War and Society in Twentieth-Century France* (Oxford: Berg, 1991), 209–11.

4 AN F41/176, Consigne temporaire no. 1158, 7 April 1943, and other *consignes* in same box.

5 Peschanski, 'Control or Integration?', 214–16.

6 SHAA 3D/186, *Le Moniteur*, 15 March 1943; SHAA 3D/187, *La Montagne*, 10 April 1943; AD Morbihan 1526W/14, RG Morbihan, Vannes, to RG Rennes, 6 February 1943; AD Calvados, Prefect of Calvados to Pétain's military office, 10 April 1943.

7 Cf. for example *Il Mattino*, 23 March 1943.

8 *Corriere della Sera*, 27 October 1942.

9 *Corriere della Sera*, 2 November 1942.

10 AFM, 'Luogo sacro profanato', pamphlet, 1944.

11 *Ibid.*, 'Su loro ricade la colpa! Chi ha cominciato?', 1944.

12 *Ibid.*, 'Chi ha cominciato', 1944.

13 AN F41/301, Affichettes Bombardements, impression en deux couleurs, 250.000 ex, 11 November 1943.

14 Cf. files on *Nos Villes dans la Tourmente* in AN F41/301.

15 AFM, poster of 1944.

16 ASG, Prefettura, b. 275, Italian propaganda posters of 1944.

17 http://laureleforestier.typepad.fr/blog_de_laure_leforestier/ma_ville_sous_loccupation/, accessed 30 May 2011.

18 An excellent collection of wartime newsreel footage, including coverage of raids, is available on the website of the Institut National de l'Audiovisuel (INA), at http://www.ina.fr/.

19 The newsreels can be seen at www.archivioluce.com/archivio.

20 SHAA 3D/174, *Le Moniteur* 5 March 1942; *La Montagne*, 9 March 1942.

21 SHAA 3D/184, *La Montagne*, 22 January 1943; SHAA 3D/186, *La Montagne*, 12 March 1943; SHAA 3D/187, *La Montagne*, 9 April 1943; AD I-et-V 502W/4, *Ouest-Éclair*, 12 March 1943; Institut National de l'Audiovisuel (INA), La région Parisienne après un bombardement de forteresses volantes, 7 January 1944 (newsreel): http://www.ina.fr/histoire-et-conflits/seconde-guerre-mondiale/video/AFE86002390/bombardement-de-la-region-parisienne.fr.html : accessed 30 May 2011; AD Loire 7W/26, Ville de St-Étienne, Bombardement du 26 mai 1944, obsèques.

22 C. Baldoli, 'Bombing and Religion in Italy, 1940–1945', in Baldoli, Knapp and Overy (eds), *Bombing, States and Peoples*, 136–7.

23 ASN, Prefettura, II Versamento, Cat. 6, b. 1222, Carabinieri of Naples to Prefect, 26 July 1941.

24 R. Aron, 'Le Maréchal en zone nord: un triomphe', *Les années 40*, 62, 1980, 1723–7.

25 AM St-Étienne 5H/37, *Le Nouvelliste* (Lyon), 30 May 1944.

26 See below, p. 204–7.

27 On the status of the BBC, cf. AN F1/cIII/1192/80, Prefect's report, Somme, 31 December 1942 (for France); M. P. Caprioli, *Radio Londra, 1939–1945* (Rome-Bari: Laterza, 1979), 34, 38.

28 Peschanski, 'Control or Integration?', 214.

29 TNA AIR 40/1720, Military attaché report, Allied bombing raids over France, May 1944 (Translation of Présidence du CFLN, Note sur les répercussions des bombardements, available in TNA FO660/191 and AN F1/A/3743).

30 INA, France-Actualités, newsreel after raids on Boulogne-Billancourt, March 1942: http://www.ina.fr/economie-et-societe/vie-sociale/video/AFE85000752/obseques-des-victimes-du-bombardement-de-la-region-parisienne.fr.html. For British coverage of the same raid, cf. http://www.youtube.com/watch?v=BRKnLO-HJu8. All accessed 30 May 2011.

31 INA, France-Actualités, newsreel produced after raids on Rennes, Rouen, Amiens and Lorient, April 1943: http://www.ina.fr/histoire-et-conflits/seconde-guerre-mondiale/video/AFE86001812/suite-aux-bombardements-de-rennes-de-rouen-d-amiens-et-de-lorient.fr.html: accessed 30 May 2011.

32 INA, France-Actualités, special air raids edition, 21 April 1944: http://www.ina.fr/histoire-et-conflits/seconde-guerre-mondiale/video/AFE86002666/discours-de-philippe-henriot-apres-les-bombardements-de-paris-et-de-rouen.fr.html: accessed 30 May 2011.

33 The SIPEG train appears in a newsreel on the bombing of Le Creusot in 1943: INA, http://www.ina.fr/economie-et-societe/vie-sociale/video/AFE86001987/le-nouveau-train-d-assistance-du-sipeg.fr.html; a reportage on Nantes from September 1943 shows emergency services at work: http://www.ina.fr/histoire-et-conflits/seconde-guerre-mondiale/video/I07348915/bombardement-a-nantes.fr.html: accessed 30 May 2011.

34 INA, France-Actualités, newsreel of 2 June 1944: http://www.ina.fr/economie-et-societe/environnement-et-urbanisme/video/AFE86002729/bombardements-de-chartres-orleans-sartrouville-chambery-saint-etienne-lyon.fr.html: accessed 30 May 2011.

35 SHAA 3D/174, *Le Moniteur* 5 March 1942; *L'Action Française*, 7 March 1942.

36 INA, newsreel of 2 June 1944, accessed 30 May 2011.

37 Archives Diocésanes de Lyon, Texte de l'Appel des Cardinaux Français à l'Épiscopat de l'Empire Britannique et des Etats-Unis, 10 May 1944; Suhard to Otto Abetz, 15 May 1944. A translation of the first broadcast of the message, which did include the phrase later censored, appears in TNA, FO371/41984, dated 14 May.

38 AN F41/301, 'Une lettre de Son Excellence Monseigneur Étienne-Marie Bornet, Évêque de Saint-Étienne, mai 1944'; and Ministère de l'Information, Services Techniques de la Propagande, 'Note à Madame Poussant', 5 July 1944: 'Indications de diffusion pour 20.000 tracts "Lettre de Monseigneur Bornet"'.

39 AN F60/379, Darlan to de Brinon, 9 March 1942; SHAA 3D/174, *Le Moniteur*, 5 March 1942; *Le Figaro*, 7 March 1942.

40 SHAA 3D/186, *Le Moniteur*, 19 March 1943.

41 INA, France-Actualités newsreel, 14 April 1944: http://www.ina.fr/histoire-et-conflits/seconde-guerre-mondiale/video/AFE86002636/bombardement-de-la-region-parisienne.fr.html: accessed 30 May 2011.

42 AN F41/301, Un bilan: 30 mois de bombardements anglo-saxons.

43 SHAA 3D/187, *Le Nouvelliste*, 8 April 1943; AN F1/A/3765, GPRF, Commissariat à l'Intérieur, Communiqué à la presse sur les bombardements alliés (source: apparently Vichy, 20 April 1944).

44 SHAA 3D/174, *Le Moniteur*, 5 March 1942; SHAA 3D/187, *La Montagne*, 7 April 1943.

45 AD Morbihan 15935/235, *La Bretagne*, 23 February 1943.

46 AN F41/301, 'Diffusion: 1940–1942'; SHAA 3D/174, *Le Journal des débats*, 6 March 1942; *Le Moniteur*, 5 March 1942; 3D/186, *Le Journal des débats*, 6 March 1943.

47 SHAA 3D/187, *Le Nouvelliste*, 9 April 1943, *Le Moniteur*, 6 April 1943.

48 As late as 2010, inhabitants of Le Havre still cited the economic argument to explain the destruction of their city.

49 SHAA 3D/187, *Le Progrès de l'Allier*, 7 April 1943; *L'Avenir*, 7 April 1943; 3D/188, *Le Journal des débats*, 30 May 1943.

50 INA, France-Actualités, 21 April 1944; Olivier Dumoulin has pointed out the central symbolism of cathedrals in wartime newsreels about bombing in France (Rouen), Britain (Coventry), and Germany (Cologne). Cf. O. Dumoulin, 'A Comparative Approach to Newsreels and Bombing in the Second World War: Britain, France, Germany', in C. Baldoli, A. Knapp and R. Overy (eds), *Bombing, States and Peoples in Western Europe, 1940–1945* (London: Continuum, 2011), 298–314. Rouen cathedral caught fire but was not destroyed.

51 http://www.youtube.com/watch?v=D4Ok-RKgCHg&feature=PlayList&p=C30CFE9A9C9A840D&playnext=1&playnext_from=PL&index=41, accessed 30 May 2011.

52 AD Loire 7W/26, Alerte!, brochure, n.d. (1943?).

53 Mémorial de Caen, PA1, *L'Amérique en guerre: apporté au peuple français par l'Armée de l'air américaine avec des bombes au phosphore*, no. 75, 30 November 1943.

54 AD Seine-Maritime 51W/70, 'Ce sont toujours les petits qui payent!' Franciste brochure, 1944.

55 TNA AIR 40/1720, Allied bombing raids over France, May 1944, 11.

56 INA, France-Actualités, special air raids edition, 21 April 1944.

57 E. Lehman, *Le ali del potere. La propaganda aeronautica nell'Italia fascista* (Turin: UTET, 2010), xvi.

58 *Il Giornale di Sicilia*, 16 January 1941, 2.

59 *Aerei italiani contro navi inglesi: non si passa!*, Aerei italiani pamphlet of 1942.

60 M. Argentieri, *Il cinema in guerra. Arte, comunicazione e propaganda in Italia, 1940–1944* (Rome: Editori Riuniti, 1998), 74–8; see also P. Cavallo, *Riso amaro. Radio, teatro e propaganda nel secondo conflitto mondiale* (Rome: Bulzoni, 1994).

61 *Corriere della Sera*, 18 August 1940.

62 M. Fincardi, 'Anglo-American Air Attacks and the Rebirth of Public Opinion in Fascist Italy', in C. Baldoli, A. Knapp and R. Overy (eds), *Bombing, States and Peoples in Western Europe, 1940–1945* (London: Continuum, 2011), 246.

63 *Il Giornale di Sicilia*, 12 January 1941.

64 ASG, Prefettura, b. 275, Pavolini to all Italian newspaper directors and to the prefects, 15 June 1940.

65 This was the regime's line from the very first raid on Turin. See ASG, Prefettura, b. 275, Pavolini to all Italian newspaper directors and to prefects, 13 June 1940.

66 ASG, Prefettura, b. 275, Pavolini to all Italian newspaper directors and to the prefects, 14 June 1940.

67 C. Baldoli and M. Fincardi, 'Italian Society under Allied Bombs: Propaganda, Experience, and Legend, 1940–1945', *Historical Journal*, 52 (4), 2009, 1017–1038.

68 ACS, MI; DGPS, A5G, II Guerra Mondiale (IIGM), b. 1, Carabinieri of Tortona (Alessandria) to the Questura of Alessandria, 21 December 1940.

69 ASG, Prefettura, b. 159: letter from citizens of Genoa to the local press, 13 February 1941; letter from readers of *Il Secolo XIX* to the direction of the newspaper, 10 February 1941; letter from Genoa citizen to the direction of *Il Secolo XIX*, no date but February 1941.

70 ASG, Prefettura, b. 275, Pavolini to all Italian newspaper directors and to the prefects, 9 July, 12 July, 19 August 1941.

71 *Corriere della Sera*, 25 October 1942.

72 *Corriere della Sera*, 27 October 1942.

73 *Corriere della Sera*, 28 October 1942, 30 October 1942, 17 February 1943.

74 P. Cavallo, *Gli italiani in guerra. Sentimenti e immagini dal 1940 al 1945* (Bologna: Il Mulino, 1997), 265.

75 *La Stampa*, 19 June 1943.

76 Bulletin no. 405, and *L'Ora: Giornale del Mediterraneo*, 16 July 1943.

77 *La Stampa*, 22 November 1942.

78 *Corriere della Sera*, 17 February 1943.

79 ACS, MinCulPop, Reports, b. 35, broadcast from Radio Roma by Mario Appelius, 31 January 1943.

80 *Ibid.*, broadcast from Radio Roma by Aldo Valori, 2 February 1943.

81 *Corriere della Sera*, 17 February 1943.

82 ACS, MinCulPop, b. 143, fasc. 'Città sottoposte alle incursioni nemiche', note by Francesco De Biase for the minister, 18 May 1943.
83 *La Gazzetta del Mezzogiorno*, 20 May 1943; *ibid.*, 1 June 1943; *La Stampa*, 3 June 1943.
84 *La Gazzetta del Mezzogiorno*, 30 May 1943; *La Stampa*, 19 May 1943.
85 *Roma*, 8 May 1943.
86 Baldoli and Fincardi, 'Italian Society under Allied Bombs', 1017–38.
87 *Corriere del Ticino*, 17 April and 5 May 1943; *Libera Stampa*, 19 April 1943.
88 TNA, AIR 20/5304, Telegram, Air Ministry to Mediterranean Air Command, 3 May 1943.
89 F. Coen, *Tre anni di bugie* (Milan: Pan, 1978), 152–3.
90 ACS, MinCulPop, Reports, b. 42, anonymous letter from Rome to Kesselring, cc. to the Ministry of Popular Culture, 5 October 1943.
91 F. Palmieri, 'Radiocorriere' programme of 19 July 1943, in G. Isola, *L'ha scritto la radio. Storia e testi della radio durante il fascismo (1924–1944)* (Milan: Bruno Mondadori, 1998), 363–9.
92 *La Gazetta del Mezzogiorno*, 21 July 1943.
93 *L'Ora: Giornale del Mediterraneo*, 9 January 1943.
94 *Il Mattino*, 5 August 1943.
95 *La Stampa*, 5 January 1944.
96 M. Nezzo, 'The Defence of Works of Art from Bombing', 113.
97 *La Stampa*, 18 February 1944.
98 *Il Resto del Carlino*, 30 January 1944; *ibid.*, 13 February 1944; *ibid*, 7 July 1944.
99 SHAA 3D/182, *La Montagne*, 14 November 1942; AD SM, *Journal de Rouen*, 17 June, 6 and 14 August 1943.
100 Cf. for example a report that the Luftwaffe had hit London with new 'Super-bombs' capable of destroying anything up to 800 metres from the point of impact (AD SM, *Journal de Rouen*, 27 May 1943).
101 'On the night of Saturday to Sunday', said the *Journal de Rouen*, 'the RAF carried out an ineffectual raid on Germany. But from 4 to 11 April, it killed over 3,000 civilians in France, Belgium and Holland' (AD SM, *Journal de Rouen*, 12 April 1943).
102 INA, France-Actualités, Dans les ruines de Caen, 30 June 1944, http://www.ina.fr/economie-et-societe/environnement-et-urbanisme/video/AFE86002758/dans-les-ruines-de-caen.fr.html: accessed 31 May 2011. Cf. also A. Beevor, *D-Day: the Battle for Normandy* (London: Harmondsworth, 2009), 268–9.
103 AN F1/A/3725, Political Warfare Executive, General Directive, week beginning 27 April 1944 ; AN F1/A/3743, CFLN, Commissariat à l'Intérieur, L'opinion publique et les bombardements sur la France, 21 April 1944/3 June 1944.
104 AN F1/A/3743, Gouvernement Provisoire de la République Française (GPRF), Commissariat à l'Intérieur, Les éditoriaux d'Henriot seraient très écoutés, 4 May/7 June 1944.
105 AN F7/14932, Commission de Contrôle technique, Inspection Régionale de Montpellier, 3 June 1944.
106 This appears in numerous reports: AN F1/A/3743, Comité Français de Libération Nationale (CFLN), Commissariat à l'Intérieur, Le Moral dans la region de Clermont-Ferrand (22 March/6 May 1944); L'opinion publique et les bombardements sur la France, 21 April 1944/3 June 1944; Les réactions de l'opinion publique à l'égard des éditoriaux prononcés par Philippe Henriot, 6 May/18 May 1944; L'opinion publique en France d'après les rapports officiels de Vichy (January–March 1944/April 1944); AN F1/A/3765, CFLN, Commissariat à l'Intérieur, L'état moral de la population en France (31 March/6 May 1944); CFLN, Commissariat à l'Intérieur, Résultat des derniers bombardements sur la région parisienne, nuit du 19 avril; AN F1/A/3765, République Française, Philippe Henriot et la contre-propagande de la BBC, 3 April 1944.
107 For example, over 5,000 victims were reported killed after a raid on Treviso had left one-third that number (still a high figure) dead on 7 April 1944. *Il Resto del Carlino*, 18 April 1944 .
108 ACS, MinCulPop, Reports, b. 46, Mezzasoma to Mussolini, 11–12 November 1944.
109 See below, p. 231.
110 Mémorial de Caen, PA2, *Le Courrier de l'Air*, 3, 1942.
111 T. Brooks, *British Propaganda to France, 1940–1944: Machinery, Method and Message* (Edinburgh: Edinburgh University Press, 2007), 40–2.

112 Freeman, *Mighty Eighth War Diary*, 122, 130–1, 136, 172, 230.
113 R. T. Holt and Robert W. van de Velde, *Strategic Psychological Operations and American Foreign Policy* (Chicago: University of Chicago Press, 1967), 141.
114 NARA, RG 226, OSS, Box 7, Allied Force Headquarters, Psychological Warfare Branch, 1 August 1943.
115 Brooks, *British Propaganda to France*, 53.
116 Cf. for example AN F1/cIII/1166/51, Prefect's report, Marne, 31 October 1941; AN F1/cIII/1178/62, Prefect's report, Pas-de-Calais, 3 August 1942; http://www.ihtp.cnrs.fr/prefets/, Synthèse des rapports préfectoraux pour les deux zones, October 1943, Chapter VI, accessed 31 May 2011.
117 M. Piccialuti Caprioli, *Radio Londra, 1939–1945* (Rome-Bari: Laterza, 1979), 34, 38.
118 ACS, Comando Anglo-Americano, b. 1, 'Summary of Enquiry into Radio Listening Habits in Sicily', 15 November–15 December 1943.
119 Brooks, *British Propaganda to France*, 120.
120 G. Isola, *Abbassa la tua radio, per favore... Storia dell'ascolto radiofonico nell'Italia fascista* (Scandicci: La Nuova Italia, 1990), 243–50.
121 On Italy's foreign policy in the 1930s see E. Collotti with N. Labanca and T. Sala, *Fascismo e politica di potenza. Politica estera 1922–1939* (Milan: La Nuova Italia, 2000).
122 AN F1/A/3725, PWE, General Directive, w/b Thursday 4 May 1944.
123 TNA, FO 898/6, report by the PWE, 21 May 1943.
124 The Mémorial de Caen, cartons PA1 and PA2, contains an extensive, though not complete, collection of Allied leaflets, including *Le Courrier de l'Air* (henceforth *CA*) and *L'Amérique en Guerre* (henceforth *AG*). For the points above, cf. *CA*, no. 3, 1941, nos. 10 and 24, 1942; 25 February 1943; 25 November 1943; 27 January 1944; *AG*, 15 and 29 December 1943, 16 February 1944. In a rare respite from war news, readers were told of Princess Elizabeth's eighteenth birthday (*CA*, 27 April 1944).
125 Mémorial de Caen PA2, *CA* 20 May, 5 August, 25 November and 2 December 1943; PA1, *AG* 9 February, 11 August, 20 October 1943.
126 Mémorial de Caen PA2, *CA* 24 November 1943; PA1, *AG* 1 December 1943.
127 Mémorial de Caen PA1, *AG* 20 June 1944.
128 ASM, Prefettura, b. C254, RAF leaflet dropped on Milan, n.d. (end 1940/beginning 1941).
129 In ACS, MI, DGPS, IIGM, A5G, b. 21.
130 TNA, FO 898/6, report by the PWE, 21 May 1943.
131 ACS, MI, DGPS, IIGM, A5G, b. 20, 'La verità', 1 February 1941.
132 *Ibid.*, b. 102, Venice Questura to Interior Ministry, 13 January 1941; *Ibid.*, b. 77, leaflet dropped by the RAF on 31 December 1940, Brindisi Carabinieri to Interior Ministry, 2 January 1941.
133 *Ibid.*
134 ACS, MinCulPop, b. 122, broadcast from Radio Londra, 12 September 1941.
135 Cf. below, p. 205.
136 ACS, MI, DGPS, IIGM, A5G, b. 20, British leaflet dropped over Italian cities in 1941.
137 ACG, AC, b. 144, n.d. (1941).
138 ACS, MinCulPop, b. 122, broadcast from radio Londra, 10 June 1941.
139 ACS, MI, DGPS, IIGM, A5G, b. 20, 1 February 1941.
140 G. Garibaldi to J. Cowen, 12 April 1854, in *Autobiography of Giuseppe Garibaldi*, vol. III (London: Walter Smith and Innes, 1889), 124.
141 ASG, Prefettura, bb. 153–154, Leaflets dropped from RAF aircraft on Genoa, sent by the Prefect to Interior Ministry on 19 December 1940. The same leaflets also fetched up in Marseille, presumably due to a (fairly large) navigational error (SHAA 3D/393).
142 ACS, MI, DGPS, IIGM, A5G, b. 20, 1 February 1941.
143 ASN, Prefettura, II Versamento, Cat. 6, b. 1222, 'Bilancio del primo anno di guerra fascista: giugno 1940–giugno 1941', RAF leaflet dropped on Naples, n.d. (June 1941).
144 ASM, Prefettura, b. C254, RAF leaflet dropped on Milan, n.d. (late 1940–early 1941?).
145 ACS, MI, DGPCA, b. 104, RAF leaflet dropped on Italian cities, early 1941.
146 TNA, FO 898/6, PWE report, 21 May 1943.
147 ASM, Prefettura, b. C254, RAF leaflet dropped on Milan, n.d. (spring 1943?).

148 ASN, Prefettura, II Versamento, Cat. 6, b. 1224, RAF leaflet, May 1943.
149 ASN, Prefettura, II Versamento, Cat. 6, b. 1224, leaflets sent from the Provincial Committee of Anti-Aircraft Protection of Naples to Prefect, 22 June 1943.
150 TNA, FO 898/6, PWE report, 21 May 1943.
151 ASN, Prefettura, II Versamento, Cat. 6, b. 1226, Allied leaflets dropped on Naples during raid of 20–21 July 1943.
152 TNA, AIR 8/777, 'C.A.S. to Air Chief Marshal Tedder', 30 July 1943; ASN, Prefettura, II Versamento, Cat. 6, b. 1226, Allied leaflet, n.d. (summer 1943).
153 NARA, RG226, OSS, M-1642, roll 23, 'Memorandum for the president' from William J. Donovan, 17 April 1942.
154 In Holt and van de Velde, *Strategic Psychological Operations*, 145–6.
155 Mémorial de Caen PA2, *CA* 14, 1942; PA1, *AG* 9 February 1943.
156 TNA, FO954/23, M. Anthony Eden au people français à l'occasion de la fête nationale du 14 juillet.
157 Mémorial de Caen PA2, *CA* 13, 1941; 17 December 1942; *AG* 20 October and 3 December 1943, 9 February 1944.
158 Mémorial de Caen PA2, *CA* 12 July 1944.
159 *Ibid.*, *CA*, 10 and 12, 1942; 23 September and 28 October 1943; 30 March, 3 April and 2 August 1944; PA1, *AG* 12 May, 8 September, 15 and 29 December 1943; 16 February, 19 April, and 20 June 1944.
160 Mémorial de Caen PA2, *CA* 24, 1942, 3 June, 1 July, 5 August and 11 November 1943; PA1, *AG* 9 February 1943.
161 Mémorial de Caen PA1, *AG* 11 August 1943.
162 AD SM 51W/67, Leaflet on the Renault raid of March 1942; Mémorial de Caen PA2, *CA* 10 and 14, 1942.
163 TNA FO954/23, Eden to Sinclair, 20 April 1942. See also above, p. 24.
164 These concerns appear clearly in correspondence between Portal, Eden and Sinclair, and in orders given to Bomber Command and the US 8th Air Force, in TNA AIR19/218, 11–21 June 1943.
165 AN F1/A/3726, PWE, Directive for BBC French Service, 13–26 September and 27 September–10 October 1943.
166 AN F1/A/3725, PWE, General Directive, w/b 27 April 1944.
167 TNA CAB65/46, WM(44) 61st. War Cabinet, 2 May 1944.
168 AN F1/A/3725, PWE, General Directive, w/b 27 April 1944.
169 Mémorial de Caen PA2, *CA* 24 and 26, 1942; AN F1/A/3726, PWE, Directive for BBC French Service, 14–28 June 1942.
170 Mémorial de Caen PA2, *CA* 17 December 1942.
171 Mémorial de Caen PA1, *AG* 13 October and 24 November 1943, 6 January 1944. The list, which appeared on 24 November and was also included in *Le Courrier de l'Air*, included fairly specific targets in the Paris area (Quai de Javel, Gennevilliers, Bois-Colombes, Argenteuil, Billancourt, Ivry, Courbevoie); Metz (Woippy); Nantes (Bouquenais, Roche Maurice, Saint Joseph); Le Mans (Arnage); Limoges; Toulouse (Saint Martin du Touch, Montaudran); Lille-Fives; Denain; Strasbourg (Meinau, Molsheim); Albert; Meaulte; Lyon (Vénissieux); Bourges; and Clermont-Ferrand.
172 Mémorial de Caen PA2, *CA* 10 February, 8 and, 10 February, 8 March, and 3 April 1944.
173 *Ibid.*, *CA* 30 March 1944. PWE's warnings were not, however, systematically followed. *CA* advertised 'the final assault' months before the event on at least two occasions (Mémorial de Caen PA2, *CA* 6 January and 4 April 1944).
174 *Ibid.*, *CA* 27 April 1944.
175 Mémorial de Caen PA1, *AG* 26 April 1944.
176 NARA, RG 226, OSS, Box 7, Allied Force Headquarters, Psychological Warfare Branch, 1 August 1943.

6

Mobilization and its Limits: Evacuees, Air-Raid Wardens, Looters

One reason for the importance of the propaganda war was that bombing demanded a new relationship between states and peoples. All of the public were supposed to respect air-raid precautions; some were best moved out of harm's way; many were also required for civil defence duties. In principle, Vichy France and Fascist Italy possessed the necessary powers to compel compliance. But transporting hundreds of thousands of evacuees to distant destinations demanded trains and police in vast numbers; an unwilling civil defence corps would require full-time military discipline. In practice, with much of the adult male population at war (for Italy) or in prisoner-of-war camps, or doing forced labour in Germany (for France, then for Italy too), and with the police and paramilitary forces increasingly involved in fighting resistance movements, neither state had the resources to rely on compulsion. The only available alternative was to mobilize popular consent and participation, through the propaganda methods discussed in Chapter 5 and through presence and example on the ground.

Italy might appear to have been better equipped for this task. In the Fascist Party, the regime disposed of a tool used over two decades to mobilize the public for the government's purposes. Vichy France, by contrast, possessed no official party; the Germans would never countenance one; and the little Fascist parties of the northern zone – Marcel Déat's Rassemblement National Populaire (RNP), Jacques Doriot's Parti Populaire Français (PPF), and Marcel Bucard's Francistes – existed as much to challenge the regime as to support it. The attempt to use ex-servicemen's associations, gathered in the Légion Française des Combattants, as a moral support for the regime was a (brief) numerical success but a political failure. The Legion attracted 1.7 million members at its peak in 1941, but the Germans kept it out of the occupied northern zone of France, where the bombs were falling. It soon divided on the issue of collaboration with Germany and proved incapable of securing popular loyalty to the regime even in the south.[1] The record, however, suggests that Vichy was more successful than Fascist Italy at mobilizing people for civil defence – while neither regime managed a very effective evacuation policy.

EVACUATION: THE CHIMERA OF CONTROL

Pre-war planners had seen evacuation as a cheaper alternative to providing comprehensive shelter for city-dwellers. The plans had not worked. In May–June 1940, Fascist Italy attempted evacuation measures that could not be implemented, while the French government altogether failed to control the exodus of a quarter of the population. Evacuation policy proved scarcely less intractable thereafter.

The number of evacuees was probably greater in Italy than in France, although comprehensive figures are not available for either country. Elena Cortesi has counted a total of 2,279,104 evacuees received in Italian provinces by May 1944, but this is almost certainly an underestimate; as the situation deteriorated from early 1943, many evacuees did not officially register.[2] In France, figures for 33 of the 90 *départements*, taken from prefects' reports between late 1943 and mid-1944, show that some 655,000 people were registered as refugees.[3] These figures should also be viewed as a minimum, as most were reported before the large-scale evacuations of spring and early summer 1944; according to the Swedish paper *Morgon-Tidningen*, for example, over 50,000 women, children, and old people had been evacuated from Paris in the first ten days of May.[4]

Italy's triple U-turn

The uncertainty of evacuation policy in Italy is illustrated by the Interior Ministry's decision to withdraw its directive of 3 June 1940 on voluntary evacuations less than three weeks from the start of mobilization. On 20 June, the Air Ministry told Italy's prefects and territorial defence commanders in north-western provinces that voluntary evacuations had reached 'unjustified proportions' and must be limited immediately. Evacuees were to be persuaded home with carrots (prefects were ordered to meet costs for those in need) and sticks (state assistance would be withheld from those who refused to return).[5] Those who still decided to evacuate, said another Air Ministry order, must be told that they could only do so by their own means.[6]

No clear evacuation plan emerged in the whole period of Italy's war. This caused severe difficulties for local authorities when raids intensified from autumn 1942. Mass evacuation followed the first area-bombing attacks on northern Italy in October 1942 and provoked Mussolini to give a landmark speech on 2 December in an attempt to keep control of the process.[7] The speech was heard above all as a pressing invitation to the population to leave major cities, and mass evacuation soon extended to southern Italy and Sicily. From then until the Liberation (which came at different times in different places on the peninsula), hundreds of thousands of Italians continued to move, leaving industrial and port cities in the hope of finding refuge in nearby provinces. Once these had reached capacity, people would move on to other regions.[8]

The spontaneous evacuations from Milan after the raid of 24 October 1942 and Mussolini's speech saw 426,000 people leave, 61,000 to other parts of Milan province and 365,000 further afield. Most of those who relocated within the province were evening evacuees, who still worked in Milan during the day. A second exodus followed the raid of 14 February 1943: now 70,000 left for other parts of Milan province and 400,000 elsewhere. They included people who had returned to the city in January or early February when the schools reopened. The nearby provinces of Como, Varese, Bergamo, and Pavia constituted the main destinations and, as the prefect observed, were 'likely to continue to be the target of evacuees until they are saturated'. He believed that 'the raids will increase in number and violence', and 'as a result the number of those forced to leave the city will also increase'. Within the Interior Ministry it was stated that evacuees should go first to the provinces of Lombardy, and, when these were full, south and east to Piacenza, Parma, Verona, Vicenza, Reggio Emilia and Modena.[9]

On 4 December 1942, echoing Mussolini's speech, the Interior Ministry told prefects to encourage evacuation. Indispensable personnel could move their families to small centres in the suburbs; discounted transport tickets were to be provided for the new commuters. But arrangements for compulsory evacuation remained vague: 'from now, a complete plan needs to be organized, ready for immediate and ordered realization whenever it becomes necessary'.[10] Despite the best efforts of the Interior Ministry, the prefects and the Fascist Party to organize evacuations, when cities were heavily bombed and the surrounding areas filled up, local authorities found the situation impossible to control. The *commissario prefettizio* (who replaced a *podestà* when the latter was removed from office) of Monte di Procida wrote to the prefect of Naples on 21 December that, because of the mass evacuation from the city, his small commune had been inundated with people: 820 had arrived (for a normal population of some 7,500), 749 from Naples alone, between 8 and 20 December. The town had very few houses and resources and there was a desperate need for food and coal.[11] The next day, the *commissario prefettizio* of San Valentino Torio also wrote to the prefect stating that there were no more homes available there, but the exodus continued 'at all times of the day'.[12]

In Palermo too, Mussolini's speech, and public awareness of the city's importance as a target, had encouraged voluntary evacuations. 'So far', wrote the prefect to the Interior Ministry in January 1943, 'more than 60,000 people have evacuated to various peripheral localities of the province, without counting the number of those who moved to other provinces of the island and to the continent.' The provincial bodies responsible for dealing with this emergency sought to rein back rent and transport prices, and appealed for more frequent trains and buses to ease evening evacuations, plus extra petrol rations. These attempts achieved limited success. Palermo province was at capacity and the local authorities did not know where further evacuees could go in the event of more raids. The prefect had already asked the ministry for a list of mainland destinations for Palermo's evacuees, but had received no answer.[13]

Palermo's systems for evacuation, in fact, could not cope with the situation of winter 1942–3. In November 1942, moreover, the prefect had told *podestàs* in the province to be highly restrictive in relation to evacuees' welfare:

> Considering that evacuation is not compulsory, generally speaking no assistance is provided to the evacuees. Communal authorities will mostly have to look after the question of housing and the possibility of the evacuees finding jobs … In cases of exceptional need, the communes are authorized to grant special benefits, for a few days only … The extent of benefits must not exceed the sum presently attributed to the daily relief for soldiers' families.

The legal status of evacuees also had to be settled: they had to produce a 'declaration of evacuation' in their home city and, once relocated, to obtain a residence permit (for which citizens of Jewish origin were not eligible).[14] Therefore, if evacuation was not compulsory and the communes had to provide help (however limited, as specified above), there were no means to compel evacuees to move on from their chosen destinations, or to keep them away from any particular town. However, when the province, or even the region, of a bombed city had received too many evacuees, the ministry answered requests from prefects by sending lists of cities around Italy where people could be sent: for example, the ministry encouraged the prefect of Naples to send 5,000 evacuees to the provinces of Teramo, Ascoli Piceno, Perugia, Pescara and Pesaro.[15]

The Fascist Party was also directly involved in evacuation, that of children in particular. The evacuation of children aged 6–14 – still voluntary, at their families' request – was the responsibility of the *Gioventù Italiana del Littorio* (GIL), a Party satellite. With its summer-camp buildings (*colonie*), the GIL could put up 12,000 children, but this was no longer sufficient by the end of 1942. Other *colonie*, though managed by the GIL, were owned by others; direct arrangements had to be made with owners and requisitions organized where this did not work. In November 1942, this was done immediately for the provinces of Genoa, Turin and Milan; for other provinces it would be arranged as soon as need arose, on permission from the Interior Ministry.[16] Children could also be hosted by families, who received ten lire per day for each hosted child from the Interior Ministry via the GIL.[17]

In repeatedly bombed cities, meanwhile, evening 'commuter' evacuations were suffering, by the spring of 1943, from transport difficulties. In Milan, for example, a shortage of petrol and tyres meant that too few buses were available.[18] At the other end of the peninsula, the problem had become far more serious by June 1943: many evacuees in Palermo province had nothing to eat. Communes that could not help the high number of evacuees saw the 'sad spectacle of extremely poor people' every day: resources were needed so that they should 'not die of hunger', and the ECA did not possess them.[19] Communes continued to press the prefect with requests for petrol, money and food.[20] As elsewhere in Italy, the intensification of raids in the first half of 1943 increased problems of all types for municipalities, including water stoppages, and shortages of food or of workers to remove debris.[21]

In March 1943, a letter from the Interior Ministry following a meeting with prefects in Rome, Milan and Naples contained an order that totally contradicted Mussolini's instructions of 2 December 1942. As many areas had exhausted their receptive capacity, transport was insufficient, and industrial production had almost ground to a halt, prefects were asked to *dissuade* civilians from leaving bombed areas. 'Totalitarian evacuation', the minister concluded, 'was practically impossible.'[22] Prefects across the country proved unable to resolve the problem. Many appealed to the Interior Ministry for their province to be declared unavailable for evacuees. Some even produced circulars warning that they would have to send evacuees home. However, the ministry warned against this:

> Initiatives of this kind cannot be allowed, partly because the problem of evacuation ... needs to be disciplined from the centre with rules of a general character, inspired by the overall situation of the country and by the urgent needs of the moment ... it must be kept in mind that an organic and concrete evacuation plan cannot be prearranged in all its particulars.

The ministry appealed to a spirit of solidarity and to prefects' understanding, so they would exploit to the maximum 'any receptive capacity', if necessary by requisition. It was also important to maintain propaganda among the population, with the collaboration of the Party and the *podestà*, in order to keep alive 'feelings of brotherly solidarity among populations that have been so far saved from the hatred of the enemy'. This was necessary because the question of evacuations was having an impact on the social and political order 'especially from the point of view of the internal resistance of the country'.[23]

Friction grew between local authorities (both those sending and receiving evacuees) and the national government, which was signally failing to get a grip on the situation. In June 1943, having received negative messages from all over Italy, the prefect of Genoa compiled a list of provinces that were out of bounds to Genoese evacuees. This provoked contrary instructions from the Interior Ministry: 'According to higher orders' wrote the prefect on 12 July, 'evacuees from bombed cities must not be sent back. All communications sent earlier from individual prefectures are declared void.'[24]

New population movements were added to earlier ones following the Allied landings on 9 July 1943. Throughout the ensuing campaign, people sought to escape from the battlefront and from a continuing bombing offensive against central and northern Italian cities and communication lines. In central and northern Italy between the first half of 1943 and the advent of the Salò Republic in September, towns which had hitherto accepted evacuees either became too full to take more or were themselves bombed. Cities hitherto untouched, and considered good destinations for Genoese evacuees once the Ligurian towns were saturated, were bombed from 1944 as industry relocated to them, or simply as they became communication links. This was true of villages too, since bombing was no longer just an urban phenomenon. For example, on 25 January 1944, when Carrodano in La Spezia province was bombed, many of the 90 people made homeless had been urban evacuees.[25] In Bologna, those able to do so began moving to the countryside at the start of 1943, although the city was bombed for the first time only in July. A mass exodus followed the armistice and particularly after the raid of 25 September, which left 905 dead, 1,200 wounded, and thousands of houses damaged. However, as bombing began to hit central Italian towns, by the end of November many evacuees returned to the city.[26] A similar situation characterized population movements between cities and countryside in Tuscany from early 1944.[27]

Likewise, in Turin that January the province head told *podestàs* to house evacuees in public buildings and to invite families to demonstrate 'national solidarity'.[28] By June 1944 the situation had continued to worsen: no material was available to construct huts or to repair damaged buildings, and again the province head appealed to families whose homes were intact to host evacuees.[29] A few days later, one of the province *commissari prefettizi* replied that assistance to evacuees was also limited by lack of transport, aggravated by bomb craters on the roads.[30] In October, Interior Minister Buffarini told the Republic's province heads that 'to house *sinistrati* is simply a question of humanity which cannot and must not be limited by anything'. The concept of 'saturation point', he added, did not exist 'in an absolute sense', and had 'no value in comparison with the concept of Fascist solidarity'.[31]

Not all civilians were persuaded by claims such as Buffarini's. Those whose homes were requisitioned to house evacuees wrote letters to the prefect in the hope of reversing the decision. Some of these were evacuees themselves who had decided, as the battlefront moved, to return to their own homes, only to find them occupied by others. Other householders simply did not want to share an already crowded space with more people. In turn, evacuees who were refused accommodation wrote to the prefect claiming they had been turned away on false pretexts.[32]

While the Salò Republic authorities thus inherited this difficult situation, the state in liberated southern Italy also had to deal with problems provoked by the return of evacuees. In July 1944, damage caused by bombing, the retreating German army, and, in Naples, the eruption of Vesuvius, as well as military requisitions meant that housing was desperately short. Many evacuated families, even if housed somewhere, had no security against the return of previous occupants. This issue became acute in 1944–5, when people whom the fortunes of war had forced to move more than once might return to find their homes intact but requisitioned.[33] In the south, it was left to the Allied Control

Commission to resolve the issue.[34] To some degree, the division of the country after September 1943 merely confirmed a pre-existing situation in which Italy's central government had lost control, leaving local authorities to handle the evacuation issue as best they could.

France: three types of evacuation

In France, where ground combat lasted three months over most of the country, compared with nearly two years in Italy, the number of evacuees was considerably smaller and the problem of 'saturation' correspondingly slighter. But many of the issues were comparable. The pre-war reliance on large-scale evacuation, undermined by mid-1939 owing to uncertainties over its compulsory nature, was effectively abandoned in January 1940 because of a lack of available places in reception *départements*.[35] The chaos of May–June 1940 reinforced official scepticism towards a big evacuation policy. As Sérant, national Passive Defence Director from December 1940, wrote to the prefects in April 1941, 'The experience of war has condemned massive and widespread population movements. The organization of civil defence must therefore be conceived in expectation that the population will be stationary.'[36] Three years later, a SIPEG note stressed the 'fatal consequences' of the pre-war policy in 1940; in any case, it added, the transport shortage made mass evacuations impossible.[37] Officially, therefore, Vichy was consistently opposed to large-scale evacuation. However, this policy was repeatedly challenged by realities on the ground and, on occasion, by German demands.

In the bombed localities, Sérant's statement was belied before it was issued. By March 1941, Dunkirk's population had fallen from 90,000 to 60,000, that of Boulogne from 52,000 to 30,000, and that of Calais – bombed 62 times since the armistice of 1940 – by a similar proportion.[38] Brest, similarly, lost some 30,000 of its 68,900 inhabitants to evacuation in the early months of 1941.[39] When Jean-Pierre Ingrand, the Interior Ministry's chief delegate to the Occupied Zone, told prefects in coastal *départements* to prepare evacuation plans for vulnerable groups, he was seeking to regain control of a process already under way.[40] Two more Ingrand circulars, in July 1942 and February 1943, required contingency plans for the evacuation of threatened zones and especially coastal towns. While stressing that only the Germans could compel evacuation, he added that prefects could encourage departures, for example by closing schools – and that evacuation might need to be ordered at short notice after heavy raids.[41] Meanwhile a succession of measures progressively aligned the system of allowances for evacuees, refugees and *sinistrés* (bombed-out households).[42]

Scarcity of resources was not the only obstacle to an effective evacuation policy. Political issues were also involved. A purely rational policy would be conducted in advance of air raids and would remove so-called 'useless mouths' – children, the elderly, the sick, and anyone not gainfully employed – leaving behind the 'indispensable' group required to run essential services and production. Although Vichy had a variety of means to encourage evacuation (incentives such as flat-rate payments for removals and daily allowances for the needy, or constraining measures such as closing schools, or withholding ration tickets), it still required some public co-operation. But as a perceptive intelligence report from the Toulon Renseignements Généraux observed, where there was no immediate threat, and with looting prominent in popular memories of the 1940 exodus, few wished either to send family members away or to leave their own homes.[43] Poor parents, moreover, might be reluctant to lose the food rations to which the presence of children entitled the family.[44] Intercepted mail showed extreme reluctance to depart, even in spring 1944. 'We're advised to leave. That's fine but how, and where? The trains are non-existent and the roads are machine-gunned', wrote one correspondent in the Marseilles area. 'We wouldn't leave without it raining bombs', wrote another; 'Evacuation is planned on foot by stages – can you imagine what such an exodus would be like? You'd have to abandon everything.'[45] One really fierce raid, though, could overwhelm all hesitation and provoke a mass exodus, swamping national and local administrations and leaving a town without even its 'indispensable' inhabitants. Any large-scale evacuation, therefore, would need to be canalized and controlled.

In such a context, a degree of official hesitancy is unsurprising. In practice there were at least three distinct, though overlapping, types of evacuation taking place in France in 1941–4 – orderly, precipitate, and German.

The first of these was the removal or departure of non-essential personnel from towns suffering repeated raids – the Channel ports and Brest in the first instance, later joined by the Atlantic ports, then Toulon on the Mediterranean, and from 1944, towns seen as threatened by the Allies' offensive against rail centres. The Conference of Municipalities of Coastal Towns discussed evacuation at regular meetings held from 1941 with senior figures such as Sérant, his successor Cazes, or Lacombe, head of the SIPEG.[46] There were three spurs to such evacuation: German demands (for example, in parts of Le Havre and Toulon); Vichy encouragement; and Allied warnings (for example, to leave the 'forbidden' coastal zones, as defined by the German occupiers, from mid-1942) and raids.[47]

In the coastal zones repeated raids led many people to sleep outside town and commute by day to the more dangerous city centres.[48] The task of the authorities was to canalize the movement, bringing in compulsion as a last resort. Without a big raid, however, few heeded such encouragement and fewer went where they were told. In Saint-Nazaire, for example, the evacuation of schoolchildren was ordered on 18 November 1942, after being recommended two years earlier and attempted in spring 1941, but with little success. By late February 1943, some 6,000 people, out of a pre-war population of 43,000, had left the town.[49] Of these, most preferred to go to the nearby Brière area rather than to the designated reception zones in the Maine-et-Loire *département*.

Even in Caen, at the heart of Normandy's war zone and subjected to regular shelling and aerial bombardment from the night of 5–6 June 1944, where the mayor, the prefect and the Germans had all issued evacuation orders, some 15–18,000 people (out of a population of 60,000) remained at the liberation on 9 July.[50] In Le Havre three months later, about a quarter of the population stayed despite a German order to leave and the near-certainty of a heavy bombardment.[51] These were, it is true, extreme cases. Most of the population (especially children) had already gone, and many of those who remained feared being strafed on the open road as much as being bombed at home.[52] But their resolve to stay put still testifies to the extraordinary difficulty of getting people to move who did not wish to.

Probably the easiest form of evacuation to organize was that of schoolchildren. Although the evacuees of 1939 had soon returned, the process was relaunched from 1942 and gathered pace from 1943. School closures could hasten the process; so could bombs. In Rennes, for example, 6,741 children were officially evacuated following the American raids of 8 March and 29 May 1943.[53] By November 1943, A. Watteau, Vichy's Director for Refugees, stated that 150,000 schoolchildren had so far been evacuated, a total that rose to 215,000 early in 1944.[54] As in Italy, they were either placed in school camps, not very different from the holiday colonies they had known before the war, or with families, who were paid.[55] The *Œuvre des Petits Réfugiés*, a para-state organization linked to the Secours National but led by a representative of the Refugees Directorate, was responsible for the management of child evacuees at their destinations; over FF1.2 billion was allocated to them in the 1944 budget.[56]

The second, precipitate, type of evacuation resulted from massive raids. The prototype case is that of Lorient. Here, raids had been both experienced and expected, but a modest 1,600 people, out of a pre-war population of nearly 43,000, had left the town between April and December 1942, despite the closure of schools from November.[57] However, Bomber Command's unprecedented area offensive on Lorient from 14 January 1943, and the BBC's announcement that the plan was to destroy the town, provoked a mass evacuation.[58] On 16 January, according to the Morbihan Director for Refugees, 40,000 people left Lorient. Over the following weeks some 10,000 tons of refugees' furniture were transported.[59] Some evacuees would return, but by 3 March, after over a month of raids, 35,172 people, over three-quarters of the pre-war population, were registered as refugees; the RAF had effectively turned Lorient into a German town with a skeleton French presence to service German needs.[60] Given that the only available evacuation plan had been an incomplete study for the eventuality of an Allied landing, the evacuation of Lorient may be considered a brilliant piece of improvization, which helped ensure that the death toll by 22 February, for nearly 4,000 tons of bombs, was below 200.[61] A similar feat would be achieved at Saint-Nazaire, where an evacuation plan was placed in the newspapers on 27 February; the following night Bomber Command dropped over 1,000 tons of bombs on the port, for a modest 29 deaths.[62]

In these cases, the challenge to the municipal and prefectoral authorities, with the town hall, the sub-prefecture, and other administrative services themselves bombed out of town, was not to get people to leave but to bring them under control. As early as 21 January, press announcements ordered all Lorient men aged 21–60 to return and register details of their former occupations and places of refuge as a condition of receiving any allowances.[63] Meanwhile, both the Refugees Directorate in Paris and the prefect of Morbihan stated that refugees should be sent to the *départements* of Mayenne and Indre-et-Loire, and not allowed to stay in Brittany or to go to the Paris region.[64] Few evacuees heeded these last instructions. By mid-March, only about 7,500 had gone to Mayenne and Indre-et-Loire, despite promises of good housing; over 34,000 had stayed in Morbihan, where they had relatives and friends and might hope to check on the family property (if not destroyed), or to drift home if the threat passed. If French evacuees did travel far, moreover, the most popular, although wholly forbidden, destination was Paris, where some 300,000 evacuees were said to have gravitated in February/March 1944 – whether because provincials had relatives in the capital or because Paris, like Rome, was rumoured to be immune from bombing.[65]

The raids on Lorient, confirmed by those on Saint-Nazaire, were a landmark for civil defence policy because they showed that the Allies were both able and willing to annihilate a French town. For the public, any major raid, especially if repeated, carried with it the threat of a new Lorient, and with it the possibility of panic. This was amply demonstrated in Nantes when the heavy raid of 16 September was followed by two further attacks a week later. Between 100,000 and 120,000 Nantais – half the population – flowed away, in Caillaud's words, 'like water from a broken vase', spreading up to 40 kilometres around the city.[66] The heavy industrial sector, a major target, had lost 5,864 of its 11,627 workers to evacuation by early October.[67] The prefect and the mayor ordered road blocks placed around the city to stop essential persons from leaving and direct others to officially approved destinations.[68] Nine months later the prefecture was again encouraging the most vulnerable to leave – while at the same time setting out which categories of the public must remain.[69] Few episodes illustrate better than Nantes the difficulties of reconciling a policy intended both to move people to safety and to ensure that production continued, to the chief benefit of the occupying forces.

The third type of evacuation was dictated by the Germans, and was demanded (as in Italy) on general military grounds rather than bombing. Parts of cities such as Le Havre, Toulon, or Marseille were taken over, and in some cases destroyed, by the occupying forces between 1942 and 1944, their inhabitants summarily removed. In Italy a similar fate befell towns of central Italy and near the Gothic Line in 1944, as the German troops retreated.[70] On an altogether larger scale, however, was the demand in early 1944 for the evacuation of a 15–20 kilometre band along France's Mediterranean coastline. The Vichy government reacted, as to any other German initiative, by attempts at negotiation, followed by collaboration. Total compulsory evacuation measures were limited, following the SIPEG's conversations with the occupying authorities, to a few localities, but non-essential persons, especially children, were still to be removed. Numbers were expected to reach half a million;[71] prefects were warned that resistance would lead to tougher German demands; an emissary was despatched to persuade the Mediterranean public of need to leave; plans were made for 20 special trains a day.[72] But by late March, according to the *Petit Dauphinois*, some 270,000 people had been evacuated; only the Var, the most heavily bombed southern *département*, had exceeded projections. Instead of 20 special trains a day just 17, enough for perhaps 20,000 passengers, had been laid on altogether.[73] The rest had to take their chance with what scheduled services or road transport they could find, or go on foot.

Evacuation could be a positive experience. Some evacuees found themselves in national monuments requisitioned for the purpose, including abbeys like Fontenay in Burgundy and Royaumont east of Paris, the château of Salses near Perpignan, or even the Palace of the Popes at Avignon.[74] Children might fetch up in idyllic rural locations and enjoy more and better food than in the cities.[75] Marcel Labussière, who left Caen in June 1944, praised the hospitality of people along the Norman roads, and of rural mayors who did their best to cope with sudden influxes of refugees.[76] After the Liberation, the mayor of Saint-Étienne wrote to his rural counterpart of Tournon St-Martin, whence a group of child evacuees had just returned: all were 'magnificently healthy' and had put on weight.[77] But for many evacuees life was extremely arduous. Pierre Courant, mayor of Le Havre and president of the coastal mayors' association, told Lacombe of the SIPEG that many refugees were treated like 'tramps' by their host communities, and that tuberculosis sufferers might find themselves in hamlets with no access to medical care.[78] Individual case histories confirm Courant's report. Evacuees from Le Havre and Yvetot were accused by their 'hosts' of thieving; so were children evacuated from Brest to Lyon.[79] In Nyons in the Drôme, the sub-prefect had to defend himself against rumours that refugees from Toulon were being treated as *pestiférés* – bearers of plague.[80]

Letters intercepted in southern France in May and June 1944 showed negative opinions outnumbering satisfied ones by ten to one: selected passages included 'They make refugees pay as if they were tourists', 'We sleep like dogs', or 'Tomorrow we're off back to Marseille, we don't want to die of hunger here.'[81] From Aurillac came the remark that 'we pay 650 francs a month for two rooms – that's shameful for a village. People are about as nice as prison doors, mistrustful and very nasty.'[82] Among the worst conditions were those at Neufchâtel-en-Bray near the Channel port of Dieppe. Here, refugees were described by the sub-prefect as living in huts without drains, insulation or windproofing, with corrugated iron roofs, and stagnant water for washing and drinking; on 23 January 1943 the camp had been hit by stray bullets from an attack on a locomotive at the nearby station.[83] Nor did allowances always arrive: in December 1944, refugees in Goderville, near Le Havre, were reported as having received no payment for two months, as the refugee service in Rouen had still not recovered from the previous April's raids.[84]

Vichy's record on evacuation, like that on shelters, is therefore very patchy. It hesitated (as had pre-war governments) between compulsion and reliance on voluntary departures; it fixed destinations where refugees often had no wish to go; it mobilized insufficient transport; it failed to plan adequately for the really big raids, as at Lorient or Nantes. On the other hand, both central government and local and prefectoral authorities were operating under conditions made triply difficult by the penury of resources, the unpredictable and inconsistent demands of the Germans, and the legacy of the 1940 exodus. The low casualty rates at Lorient and Saint-Nazaire owed something to the efforts of government officials; the evacuation of hundreds of thousands of schoolchildren, though it might be criticized as too few and too late, still indicated a state capable of acting in defence of its population.

In terms of mobilizing the population or even securing its compliance, neither Vichy France nor Fascist Italy could be said to have developed a successful evacuation policy. Civilians in both countries stayed put when told to leave, flooded away even when told to stay, or made for the 'wrong' destinations. Host communities frequently shunned evacuees placed among them. The difference was that in Italy, but not in Vichy France, the policy effectively collapsed under the strain of events, with national directives being countermanded and local and regional authorities increasingly left to their own devices.

MOBILIZATION AND PASSIVE DEFENCE

Mobilization entailed not only securing the public's compliance with government measures but also enlisting their active co-operation and solidarity, whether through participation in relief work during raids or through personal or financial assistance in their aftermath. This involved, in the first place, building up adequate manpower within the state apparatus – something that had not, as Chapter 3 showed, been done when war broke out. In addition, public participation was enlisted through organizations within civil society. In Italy, the Fascist Party dominated such mobilization; Vichy France, like the French Third Republic, had recourse to a range of bodies. Few aspects of policy revealed so clearly the differences between the two regimes.

At the core of passive defence in Italy were UNPA's volunteers. Low before the war,[85] UNPA numbers dropped further from 1940. Mobilization drew away men of military age; the state offered no financial incentives to join; and the war, unpopular from the start, placed UNPA volunteers in harm's way. By 1941, UNPA counted just 70,000 volunteers: more numerous and better organized in the big cities of northern Italy, they were less so in the countryside, smaller towns, and the south.

Alongside the UNPA men were the fire brigades, and the Carabinieri to ensure public order. The Genio Civile, the civil engineers of the Ministry of

Public Works could also, on occasion, remove debris. The armed forces were called in to assist with particularly heavy raids. Emergency assistance also came from the Red Cross, with about 226,000 members across Italy before 1940; at the outbreak of war it fell under the responsibility of the War Ministry, with responsibility for tending the injured or sick in shelters and taking them to hospital where necessary. The ECAs were charged with welfare provision to bombed-out families. The Fascist Party, meanwhile, formed auxiliary fire-fighting groups (*Guardiani del fuoco*, or Fire guardians), made up of young Fascists and organized under the UNPA.

The job of co-ordinating these services in towns and cities fell to the *podestà*. Co-ordination often worked for minor raids. When Naples was attacked on 9–10 July 1941, with hits to the railway station and other parts of the city and some 15 deaths, fire services joined the Carabinieri, the Red Cross, railway workers and German soldiers to dig out the dead and wounded. With these initial operations complete, the prefect, the local Fascist Party leader and the local police chief arrived at the bombed station, which was repaired within a day.[86] Throughout that month, the ECA continued to provide support for bombed-out families, and was later reimbursed by the prefecture.[87]

Nor did larger raids provoke immediate collapse. When Milan was hit twice on 24 and 25 October 1942, the city *podestà*, at the prefect's request, ordered that all available empty and furnished properties must be reported by their owners by 12 November 1942.[88] The Fascist Institute for Popular Housing was mobilized to house bombed-out civilians. In December 1942, 65 homes belonging to it and to private owners were given to homeless families in Milan.[89] After another raid on 4 March 1943, some 953 people were housed in schools, 190 in hotels. Meanwhile the ECA provided 4,508 breakfasts and 4,129 dinners in school and factory refectories and (more rarely) in restaurants.[90]

How well these local institutions worked together varied from city to city, according to geographical and financial characteristics and the severity of the attack. But most components of the Italian array soon revealed serious deficiencies. The Fascists' *Guardiani del fuoco* were simply inhabitants of apartment blocks who had to help *capi fabbricato* fight fires: they had no training and more or less disappeared with evacuations. The Red Cross lacked money to pay for resources such as dedicated first aid posts or modern ambulances. When the alarms sounded, during the heavy raids of 1942 and 1943, Red Cross units moved to the principal public shelters, which could make them more vulnerable. In Genoa on 23 October 1942, for example, a panic at the entrance to the Porta Soprana tunnel led to 340 deaths – including two Red Cross members – before the ambulances arrived. Two weeks later Red Cross buildings were themselves hit by bombs, and some destroyed by fire.[91] A similar situation was reported in Turin in May 1943.[92]

The role of the armed forces in passive defence was highly controversial, as soldiers were needed on active service. In November 1942, the Interior

Ministry asked prefects to negotiate, with all due speed, agreements under which local Air Force units would provide resources and personnel after raids. As Buffarini wrote to the Air Force high command, 'the recent enemy raids on cities of northern Italy have made clear how precious the help of the military could be in alleviating the damage'.[93] But the armed forces did not rush to help. In Naples, Italy's most bombed city, lack of army assistance meant that early in 1943, the year of the heaviest raids, debris had to be removed with hand-carts.[94] In June, the growing number of deaths of victims buried under rubble prompted the War Ministry to agree to army assistance with clearance.[95] Three weeks later, however (and two weeks before his own fall), Mussolini intervened personally against this decision, stating that it was unacceptable to take soldiers from the front, and calling all civilians to the 'defence of the motherland'. He concluded, implicitly admitting that the regime had failed to confront the threat from the air: 'Little or nothing has been done. We are late and there is no more time to waste.'[96]

The activities of the Genio Civile, like those of the Red Cross, were useful but hampered by lack of resources and bomb damage. After heavy raids on La Spezia in February 1943, the local Genio Civile proved unable to find the 100,000 tiles it needed to patch up roofs. Lack of transport, material and workers prevented effective responses to the 600 applications for help received from bombed-out citizens.[97] In Taranto, after a major raid on the night of 26 August, the Genio Civile worked with the local fire services, as well as UNPA and groups of soldiers and sailors, to rescue the wounded and extract the living and the dead from the rubble; during 27 August and the morning of 28 August, the army sent 200 men with two lorries and 50 workers to help clear major roads and remove corpses. But two further raids on 28–29 August cut Taranto off and halted work. No one returned to the job on 30 August, and only 40 men could be found the next morning; as soon as the roads were cleared, a mass exodus of the population began.[98] With the aid of the army, as well as 100 men and four lorries, the Genio Civile undertook the tasks of ensuring basic hygiene and water and food supplies;[99] the police also patrolled destroyed or damaged houses in the old city in an attempt to control looting.[100] Any longer-term help, however, was beyond the capacities of the Genio Civile; its own reconstruction plan, dated August 1944, showed that the situation had not improved a year later.[101] Lack of resources and manpower increasingly hampered Italian efforts to cope with raids.

France did rather better: there were over a million prisoners in Germany and (from 1943) about 650,000 forced labourers, but no war to fight. The enforced shrinkage of the armed forces after 1940 offered a ready pool of recruits. Although the 1938 law and the decrees linked to it offered a legal basis for civilian conscription, the Passive Defence Directorate preferred volunteers where possible.[102] To that end, Vichy legislation offered basic accident insurance and incapacity benefit, and raised hourly pay for both volunteers and conscripts.[103] These remained, it is true, low and rather undifferentiated: from FF5 for runners, look-outs, or labourers in a town of under 10,000 inhabitants to FF10, in 1941, for a *Directeur de la défense passive* in a big city or *département*. Though they were raised, to FF7.50 and FF16 respectively, in January 1943, they meant that top personnel (typically retired officers) earned little more per hour than a Parisian metal-worker, and the lower ranks considerably less.[104]

Passive defence personnel worked as block, building and shelter wardens, auxiliary firemen, drivers, secretaries and telephonists, doctors, nurses, pharmacists, paramedics, stretcher-bearers, as well as building workers and labourers (notably for rubble clearance). Most were recruited as part-timers, committed to being available during raids and for a few hours' training.[105] Reports for 33 cities, submitted late in 1943 to the German authorities, show numbers that were variable but quite large: a total of 128,100 (a third of them in Paris), or an average of 1 in 40 of the populations concerned.[106] This was not far from the 1 in 32 represented by UK civil defence personnel in September 1939, though France certainly had fewer full-timers than the 200,000 employed in Britain.[107] Even in Gers, a rural, low-risk, south-western *département* of fewer than 200,000 inhabitants, 110 recruits received training certificates in September 1943.[108] Consistent figures for how many of these were volunteers, and how many were conscripts, are not available: in the single *département* of the Loire, 51 per cent of recruits in June 1944 were volunteers, though variations were considerable between localities.[109] In addition, a 1943 report to the German authorities claimed a *Corps des Sapeurs-Pompiers* of as many as 300,000 firemen, mostly volunteers.[110] In contrast with Italy's UNPA figures, these figures made the Défense Passive one of the largest organizations (albeit a loosely-knit one) within French civil society; much bigger, certainly, than the Milice, Vichy's paramilitary organization formed in January 1943 to destroy the Resistance, which numbered some 15,000 active members.[111]

Substantial though the numbers were, they rarely sufficed to cope with a major raid. The state had four other resources of its own to draw on. First, the SIPEG could bring in passive defence teams from neighbouring towns and *départements*. Second, the Ponts et Chaussées – the French equivalent of Italy's Genio Civile – cleared debris, in principle as soon as the passive defence teams had finished rescue operations proper.[112] Third, four mobile Passive Defence Batallions, chiefly of fire-fighters, were created in 1943 at the Germans' request and stationed in the southern towns of Lyon, Avignon, Aix-en-Provence and Montpellier. Some 1,900 strong in total, they were available to assist at prefectoral request and with SIPEG and German authorization.[113] Finally, the special SIPEG trains and their crews could sometimes provide help – notably in Le Creusot in July 1943, Le Portel and Nantes in September 1943, Toulon in February and in March 1944, and Rouen in April 1944. They could provide, in particular, vital medical aid where local hospitals had been wrecked, and could be backed up, from spring 1944, by railcars to evacuate the wounded.[114] Their usefulness, however, was increasingly limited as Allied raids targeted the rail network itself. Their vulnerability was demonstrated on 26 May 1944 when one of them was destroyed in the big raid on Lyon.[115]

The state's own personnel were joined by ancillary forces of various kinds. The technical expertise of the National Electrical Safeguard Service (which made safe and then repaired severed cables) was integrated into the passive defence system in an instruction of July 1943; specialized building workers and miners could be requisitioned under a law of 9 December 1943 setting up a Technical Assistance Service.[116] Miners were valued for their skills in rescuing people trapped under rubble.[117]

The diversity of French emergency services can be observed in the municipality of Rouen's vote of thanks to individuals and groups who had assisted during and after the raid of 18/19 April on the city and its suburb of Sotteville.[118] These included: the regional prefect and the prefect of Seine-Inférieure; the archbishop (for his spiritual comfort); the services of the state and the *département*; the local fire services; Rouen's own passive defence teams, and municipal employees; the Red Cross; the Assistantes du Devoir National, a women's volunteer group working in first-aid stations; the Sections Sanitaires Automobiles Féminines, a volunteer group of ambulance drivers linked to the Red Cross and officially dissolved in 1940[119]; the Secours National; the Comité Ouvrier de Secours Immédiat; the various relief centres which had taken in the bombed-out; a youth movement, the Équipes Nationales, and other groups of young people; the personnel of the city's hospitals; the neighbouring towns which had sent help in the form of personnel and supplies, the latter with the help of the official farm union, the Corporation Paysanne; the miners of Lens (Pas-de-Calais), who had freed trapped victims; the press, for their prompt diffusion of official communiqués; and all those individuals who had given spontaneous assistance during the raid.[120] Even allowing for the councillors' wish to be as inclusive as possible, this record suggests a significant capacity to mobilize in occupied France four months before its liberation.

The Red Cross, in France as in Italy, provided important medical support in raids, enlisting the services of over 71,000 women in the course of the war.[121] Closely linked to the state, which appointed the president and three members of its board until the Liberation, its civil defence activities were regulated by two circulars of 1943 and 1944.[122] In Lyon, for example, 210 Red Cross teams, each 12 strong and consisting of nurses, paramedics and stretcher-bearers, were available by April 1944, 40 of them for operations within a radius of 100 kilometres.[123] As in Italy, too, its members were killed and its premises hit during raids.[124] They also, however, fell foul of the Germans: a group of leading members of the French Red Cross, all women of the French establishment, were imprisoned at Fresnes early in 1944 following anti-German remarks by one of their number.[125]

Volunteer organizations provided further back-up. They included the much-loathed Milice and the three French Fascist movements (RNP, PPF and

Francistes). The Comité Ouvrier de Secours Immédiat (COSI) drew its leaders from among PPF and RNP activists and its money from the Germans. Each was the object of extreme suspicion from the wider public, which viewed their generous press coverage with scepticism.[126]

Somewhat less politicized was the Mouvement Prisonniers, an association of released prisoners of war whose participation as passive defence auxiliaries was regulated in an instruction of September 1943.[127] But perhaps the most important such group was the Équipes Nationales, set up by Vichy's Secretariat-General for Youth in 1942 but operational from spring 1943. The Équipes Nationales were intended to inculcate the values of Vichy's 'National Revolution' among French youth aged 14 to 25.[128] However, from April 1943 their 'immediate objective' became 'to organize, with all speed, the participation of young people in the protection of the population against the events of war'.[129] This language resembled that of SIPEG, and the mission was confirmed in a circular of 17 June 1943 in which Laval offered the services of young people to prefects, as volunteers or, if necessary, as conscripts.[130] Duties might include rubble clearance, stretcher-bearing, fire-fighting, first aid, assistance to refugees, help in canteens or with furniture removal, childcare, but also pall-bearing and even, for over-18s, the cleansing of the dead.[131] The Équipes' role was further formalized in spring 1944.[132] While their official Pétainism led to their dissolution on 14 September 1944, their 'abnegation and spirit of sacrifice' received official acknowledgement from the Liberation authorities in Seine-Inférieure. The suspicion with which the Germans viewed them was broadly justified: some of their leaders, in particular, were reported as active in the Resistance.[133]

How well did such groups work under the bombs with the official emergency services? Some raids, at least at first, overwhelmed both. In Lorient, the sub-prefecture was burnt out by incendiaries; so was the Maritime Prefecture, despite its 250 fully equipped firemen. Telephone lines were cut, and blocked streets prevented contact between neighbourhoods by cycle and motorcycle, or even, sometimes, by runners. After the second big raid of January 1943, again according to the prefect, the population of the Lorient area was 'seized by panic'.[134] The Rouen raid of 18–19 April 1944, which inspired the municipal vote of thanks, also saw fires burning out of control for 48 hours, water mains cut, and buildings collapsing onto cellars.[135] In the small Norman town of Condé-sur-Noireau, vain attempts to fight fires with a hand-powered pump after two raids on 6–7 June ended with a collective decision to give up and leave.[136]

More frequently, complete chaos was avoided but relief efforts suffered from a lack of resources or failures of co-ordination. Severed water mains hampered fire-fighting in towns as varied as Lorient, Le Creusot (in June 1943), and Sisteron.[137] Lack of fuel was equally widespread. In both Boulogne-Billancourt in March 1942 and Rennes a year later, ambulances failed to start because lack of petrol had prevented their use in exercises over the previous months.[138] Equipment of all kinds might also be lacking. Rennes had too few vans to transport emergency teams and helmets to protect them; Nantes was short of dump trucks (many had been hired out by owners for private removals), picks and shovels, car jacks, oxy-acetylene torches and pneumatic drills; the raid on Biarritz on 27 March 1944, which killed 105 people and left a further 100 seriously injured, led to cars with loudspeakers rushing round the town requesting vehicles for use as ambulances – while too few operating theatres were available even when the transport was.[139]

Difficulties of co-ordination were also endemic. These could result from the bombing itself, when blocked or dangerous streets prevented liaison, or when the raid killed or wounded key personnel.[140] But the problem was also one of organization. After the raids of early 1943, a blistering circular from Sérant to France's prefects complained that passive defence chiefs seemed to think that instructions, once issued, could simply be followed to the letter, regardless of developments in a real raid; first-aid teams had not been appointed or trained; measures for places of entertainment had not been drawn up, or not implemented.[141] The mayor of Rennes conceded, in the light of experience, the need for a stronger command structure. The report on the Toulon raid of 24 November criticized the ill-defined division of authority between the DDDP, the Prefecture and the local SIPEG branch; tellingly, it likened the passive defence services to an army with a mass of private soldiers, a handful of officers, and almost no NCOs; at a meeting in Marseille that December, a sector chief complained of confusion as orders flooded in from all sides.[142] Again, in June 1944, Sérant's successor Cazes complained to prefects that passive defence teams were performing poorly because of inadequate guidance from the top.[143]

One consequence was that passive defence teams and volunteers might crowd into bombed sites only to be left awaiting orders.[144] Portal, the passive defence chief for Marseille in December 1943, referred to the local Équipes Nationales as 'a mass of young people who presented no interest', and 'I had no idea how to deploy them'.[145] Young people were also misused. In Rouen, ill-shod young people burnt their feet as they picked their way through smouldering ruins; among Billancourt survivors interviewed by Dodd, boys of 15 were put to clearing rubble with their bare hands, to carrying coffins, or even to picking up body parts from the street.[146]

Expectations that passive defence teams would swing into action with military discipline were disappointed. Although many command personnel were former officers in the armed services, discipline among volunteers and passive defence personnel could never approach that of a well-trained army.[147] Records on the conduct of the police in Nantes that September show that a minority collapsed under the strain: bombed-out themselves or simply traumatised by their experiences, they went on drinking binges, commandeered food, looted, or left town to recover in their home villages.[148] In Avranches in June 1944, indiscipline led to passive defence teams being 50 per cent below strength; 'Ill-will and fear were stronger than the sense of duty', their chief wrote six months later.[149] The judgement is perhaps severe; it would have been astonishing if human weaknesses had not appeared in groups of men with little training and often unclear command structures, subjected to the extreme stress of repeated air attack.

Shortages of equipment, inadequate command and control, and poor discipline thus marred the record of French emergency services in many raids. The successes, however, were at least as important. First, numbers were rarely lacking. The morning after the raid of 16 September 1943, Nantes found 800 people – building and shipyard workers, Équipes Nationales members, and simple volunteers – available for clearance work. By 19 September, in addition to the SIPEG train, medical teams had arrived from the nearby towns of Rennes, Vannes, Angers, Cholet and Segré.[150] In Toulon, a generally critical Renseignements Généraux report still praised the spontaneous efforts of volunteers to rescue their own neighbours.[151] When 247 Lancasters bombed the northern Paris suburb of La Chapelle on 20/21 April 1944, 1,527 people helped with clearance work; some 1,000 trapped people were rescued, 250 in especially difficult conditions.[152]

Le Havre and Caen deserve particular mention because each city sustained, under siege, some of the heaviest, most destructive raids inflicted on French territory. In Le Havre, the municipal authorities, with the Town Hall destroyed on 5 September 1944, took on the task of somehow finding shelter for 12,000 bombed-out families and feeding the 35,000 remaining inhabitants; at the Liberation a week later the mayor, Pierre Courant, was carried shoulder-high by grateful supporters, before being stripped of office as a Vichy appointee.[153] The ordeal of Caen was longer, beginning on 6 June, continuing to a partial liberation (after heavy bombing) on 9 July and the complete departure of German forces ten days later, with the last German shells falling in mid-August. Most of the remaining 18,000–20,000 inhabitants congregated in a (relatively) safe haven around the lycée Malherbe, the abbey church of Saint-Étienne, and the former psychiatric hospital of Bon Sauveur. The latter had been designated and equipped from 1943 by Dr Cayla, medical chief of passive defence for the Calvados *département*, as the main hospital in the event of attack. During the siege, despite early disorganization, constant bombing and shelling, Caen's medical teams performed nearly 1,700 operations, with a survival rate of over 85 per cent, and delivered 80 babies. They lacked gas, mains electricity, and running water; thanks to prudent stocking, they never wanted for instruments, dressings, or gloves.[154] The municipality and the prefecture continued to function throughout; so, remarkably, did the post. When Prefect Michel Cacaud, in his last despatch to Vichy, wrote on 23 June that 'Administrative life continues in the *département* of Calvados, in difficult and delicate conditions, but it continues', it was not a wholly idle boast.[155]

In the Norman countryside, less accessible to prefectoral authority, mayors, charitable organizations and the public still attempted to maintain a minimum of normal life in a war zone. The head of the Secours National in Falaise, first bombed on 6 June, requested and received a delivery of food, clothes, money, and even communion wafers, which he was able to distribute to refugees housed in nearby villages and farms. A medical station was improvised at Tilly-sur-Seulles.[156] Some 20,000 refugees from Caen found refuge in the former quarries surrounding the city; these developed into emergency communities in which duties were shared, food found (from supplies in Caen, or from battle casualties among the Norman cattle) and prepared, medical care given, and church services organized.[157]

In the most elementary sense, then, France succeeded in mobilizing to face the emergency of bombing: willing personnel were rarely lacking. The armature of the emergency services lay in the official organizations. Some volunteer groups, like the Équipes Nationales, at least officially, had clear ideological links to the regime. Equally, however, French civilians proved capable, where necessary, of organizing to cope with raids quite independently of the official ideology and in contexts where the state's presence was minimal. This was achieved despite often poor equipment and mediocre organization. The record under extreme conditions contrasts with the apparent inability of the Italian emergency services to cope with major raids by mid-1943.

AS DUST SETTLED: THE BOMBED-OUT, SOLIDARITY AND ASSISTANCE

Mobilization continued, or was meant to, after the bombs had stopped falling. Both France and Italy offered official welfare benefits to civilians who had suffered materially from air raids. Both tried to supplement them by appealing to the public's solidarity. In each case there was a difficult balance to be struck. As well as serving its ostensible purpose of assistance, genuine solidarity could be instrumentalized to show the unity of people and government; pursued to excess, however, such a link, in unpopular regimes, risked discrediting the whole process.

A degree of spontaneous solidarity was certainly discernible in Italy. After the naval bombardment of Genoa in February 1941, offers of money reached the victims' families from across the country, mostly from companies and newspapers but also from private citizens. Messages came particularly from Palermo, which referred to Genoa as a 'sister city', suggesting a special solidarity between great ports.[158] People in repeatedly-bombed cities expressed anxiety and fellow-feeling for cities experiencing their first raids. Thus on 31 January 1943 the Milanese were reported to have reacted with pity and concern for the towns of Sicily and Calabria, considered to be less well defended than the industrial North.[159] Elettra Sarra, an adolescent in Trento during the war, described how Italians living in unbombed areas listened with anxiety to news about raids elsewhere during the autumn of 1942. She could still remember, she wrote years later, imagining 'the terror of those poor people' in Piedmont, Lombardy and Liguria hearing the exploding bombs and trying to escape their devastating fury. Although Trento was still untouched, sorrow had entered her household through the radio.[160] In her wartime diary from Rome in summer 1943, the writer Jolanda di Benigno noted how people switched the radio on every day 'with shaking hands and eyes fixed on the terrible question: which of our dear, illustrious, courageous cities has been violated last night?'[161]

But it was always the Fascist Party that gave a public 'frame' to such sentiments, discreetly or not. When Italian newspapers reported on 'solidarity competitions' in bombed areas, for example, the major listed donors turned out to be members of Fascist organizations.[162] Solidarity between cities – for example, the donations sent to bombed-out households in Turin from elsewhere in Piedmont, and beyond, following the December 1942 raids – was accompanied by messages expressing loyalty to Party and regime. Sums of money and messages arrived, for example, from groups of soldiers, or from the children and teachers of primary schools in Cuneo and Aosta – the latter concluding in writing 'We will win!' Workers from Biella sent a day's salary 'to those bombed out by the British barbarian acts', and sent 'Fascist greetings'. A man from Piombino wrote a long message saying that, if 'Ciurcillo [Churchill] and the other two beasts who follow him ... believe they can frighten us by bombing at night homes where children are sleeping ... they are wrong'; Italians were even closer now, he declared, to 'our Duce'. A teacher from a mountain school sent money and a message on behalf of his pupils 'to the small *camerati* of Turin hit by British ferocity, which will never bend us, but will nourish our hatred, our will to win'. In some cases children wrote the messages themselves. Children from a school in Cossato in Biella province asked the prefect to use the money they sent to buy a Christmas present for 'a small child damaged by the evil British' and to give him a kiss from them.[163]

The Fascist Party also organized public collections directly. For example, after the raids of October 1942 the Fascist women's section of Milan established a clothes collection centre. Schools were used both as channels for the appeal and as collection points.[164] On 30 October the *Corriere della Sera*, the Milan-based national newspaper, announced a 'great solidarity competition for the bombed-out', aiming to provide accommodation for all those made homeless. This was described as a Fascist action; examples of well-known Fascists – Edmondo Mazzucato and other Fascists of the 'first hour' – giving shelter to children were publicized.[165] Mussolini's paper *Il Popolo d'Italia*, also based in Milan, added next day that the names of 'the fallen' during the raid would be inscribed in a roll of honour, to be guarded by the Fasci in the 'Sacrarium of the fallen in the Revolution and the War'. Commenting on private and public offers of assistance, it concluded that 'Milan has found again the generous acts of its finest hours'.[166]

Such solidarity was, however, very much orchestrated from above. Unlike in France, where a system of 'town adoption' developed, the *podestà*s of bombed cities had to beg other *podestà*s to help them, for example by trying to persuade people to adopt air-raid orphans. A meeting after the raids of October 1942 in Milan between the prefect, the Party head, the *podestà*, a Health officer, representatives of the women's section and the GIL, expressed the hope that 'in the spirit of solidarity and human understanding' families of nearby provinces would want to adopt Milanese children, while the Commune of Milan would bear the expense. The meeting decided that the *podestà* of Milan should write to his counterparts in Venetia, Trentino, Emilia Romagna and all the nearby Lombard provinces asking them to promote solidarity and to find families willing to help. The letter was steeped in revolutionary rhetoric and appeals to Fascist solidarity and the destinies of the motherland.[167] The relatively small number of newspaper articles reporting the population's response indicates the appeal's limited success. The cases of solidarity that did occur could be distorted by the press. For example, in March 1943, *Il Mattino* declared that in the provinces of Avellino, Salerno and Benevento more than 4,000 Neapolitan children 'will find hospitality'; however, this was mostly provided by the GIL at *colonie*.[168] While towns might exchange messages of sympathy – as, for example, when the podestà of Venice told his Neapolitan counterpart that Venice was with Naples 'in its pain and pride' in December 1942 – such solidarity was often symbolic.[169]

From March 1943, the Party launched a new institution called the 'Association of the Families of the Fallen, Mutilated and Invalided by Bombing', creating centres for the assistance of these households. This had obvious 'revolutionary' overtones, with victims of bombing compared (in line with the tone of *Il Popolo d'Italia* in October 1942) with 'the fallen' of the war or of the Fascist revolution. The Neapolitan newspaper *Il Mattino* commented that the Party had replaced bureaucracy with 'generous and precise dynamism and the intelligence of revolutionary faith'.[170] The role of the Party was emphasized again with its rebirth as the Republican Fascist Party during the Salò Republic, which seemed to return it to its early revolutionary rhetoric. For example, when Alessandria's marshalling yard was bombed on 30 April and 1 May 1944, the prefect described the activity of the Fascists who went to rescue the wounded as almost heroic, and a paragon of efficiency. The idea was again that the Party, its membership now reduced to a minority of Italians, was going 'towards the people'.[171] Italy's difficulty was that a quasi-monopoly of appeals to popular solidarity was given to an institution, the Fascist Party, which was increasingly discredited with most of the population. This diminished or even choked off any genuine popular response, forcing the party back on empty rhetoric.

In France, the leading non-state channel for assistance to bombed-out households was the Secours National, a para-public organization set up in 1914 and revived under Daladier in 1939. The pre-eminence of the Secours National arose from its quasi-official status, established by a law of 4 October 1940 which placed Pétain himself at its head and gave it a monopoly on charitable donations. Although the monopoly was often breached in practice, the Secours National still commanded colossal resources. Its budget in 1941, for the Occupied zone alone, amounted to FF1.3 billion; for 1944, across France, it reached FF4.25 billion;[172] for the whole period 1939–46, it amounted to some FF36 billion. A large and growing part of this – 55 per cent for the whole period, but 65 per cent in 1943 – came from the state. The rest was drawn from donations, whether from individuals (national appeals brought in FF530 million in 1942 and FF640 million in 1943) or businesses, whose contributions were fully tax-deductible. These sums enabled the Secours National to pay 5,000 full-time staff in 1941 and 11,700 by 1 January 1944, to employ 1,000 of France's 7,500 social workers, and to pass financial help to some 12,000 other charitable organizations.[173] It also managed large-scale direct aid, chiefly in the form of food and clothing. In the wake of just two raids on the Paris region, on 18 and 20 April 1944, for example, the Secours National served 146,050 breakfasts, 207,668 lunches and 202,166 dinners, as well as distributing 69,475 articles of clothing and 8,025 pairs of shoes.[174] Overall, the number of meals distributed through the war to refugees and *sinistrés* but also to prisoners and even camp internees ran into the hundreds of millions. The ideology of the Secours National was resolutely Pétainist, its senior members distinctly bourgeois where they were not aristocrats; it preferred assistance in kind not in cash, to families rather than to individuals, churchgoers rather than the secular-minded; its model was charity to the deserving rather than aid on the basis of rights. It was unpopular among other charities, and among many local authorities, because of its size, its bureaucratization, and its tendency to behave as a 'state within the state', acting outside prefectoral control in the *départements*. But it proved indispensable enough to be renamed (as *Entr'aide française*) rather than disbanded at the Liberation, surviving till 1949.[175]

The leading competitor to the Secours National in post-raid assistance was the Comité Ouvrier de Secours Immédiat (COSI). Set up after a meeting at the German embassy in the wake of the Renault raid of March 1942, the COSI was at least partly an excrescence of the fascist parties: its president René Mesnard was a member of the RNP, Jacques Teulade, the vice-president, of the PPF, while all three fascist parties competed for position nationally and at *département* level.[176] Although COSI received some gifts in its own right – FF10 million from March to June 1942, according to its own claims – it owed its independence chiefly to German donations financed by fines imposed on French Jews. As many as five German payments of FF100 million each were made from spring 1942.[177] COSI distinguished itself from the Secours National through its 'workerist' tone, reflecting roots in a certain pacifist French syndicalism, through its willingness to hand out cash (typically FF500–FF1,500 to *sinistrés*) rather than benefits in kind, and its indifference to the moralism of Vichy's National Revolution: common-law wives who lost their partners were as much widows as if they had been married, its brochures emphasized.[178] COSI also offered legal advice, and possessed three country houses for children. By 1 October 1943 it claimed to have helped 65,000 families, distributed FF220 million (hardly a huge feat given the German donations), placed 4,000 children in families or homes, and served 200,000 food rations.[179] After the Marseille raid of 1944, it handed out FF13 million in cash.[180] These were considerable amounts, though not on the same scale as the Secours National.

The 'flexible' accounting procedures with which COSI processed its (mostly ill-gotten) money got cash to air-raid victims faster than the state.[181] But COSI was more obviously tainted in the eyes of the public and the Vichy establishment alike by the origin of its money and its fascist connections. The Bishop of Lille, for example, would have nothing to do with it; its leading figures were sometimes kept away from public ceremonies; its members, and letterboxes, attracted verbal and written insults.[182] Like the fascist parties (and like the Fascist Party in Italy), the COSI acted as a goad on the state and its local representatives. When it organized *Unions de Sinistrés*, pressure groups lobbying for better assistance to the bombed-out, which held their first national congress in October 1942, these were viewed as instrumentalizing the legitimate grievances of air-raid victims for (fascist) political purposes; in Morbihan, refugees from Lorient formed their own independent association in opposition.[183] *Unions de Sinistrés* might mutate into respectable organizations; the COSI was banned from August 1944.

A final form of mobilization lay in soliciting financial and other donations. The Secours National's own general appeals were far from the only form of this. Subscriptions were frequently opened for *sinistrés* after major raids. A month after the raid of 8 March 1943 on Rennes, gifts totalling nearly FF1.14 million had been collected at the Town Hall.[184] Over the four months following the September 1943 raids on Nantes, some FF4.2 million had been raised under a subscription started by the prefect of Brittany for the ravaged city.[185] Much of this fundraising drew on existing groups within civil society, notably the Church and business. The size of these donations suggests that Vichy was able to draw not only on individual generosity but also on a civil society which war and authoritarian rule had not wholly dislocated.

Inter-town solidarity was put on a longer-term basis by the 'adoptions' procedures organized from 1942. These had a precedent in the aftermath of World War One, when France's devastated front-line towns were adopted by more distant municipalities (Reims by Bergerac, for example). The first example under the Occupation resulted from contacts between Cardinal Gerlier, Archbishop of Lyon and Primate of France, and the Church in Brest: the municipality of Lyon adopted Brest in December 1941, voted an immediate subsidy of FF1 million and created a Comité Lyon-Brest. More cash followed, both from the municipal budget and from charity events (the first of which raised another FF1 million).[186] To the purely financial dimension, the Comité Lyon-Brest raised the profile of Brest in Lyon via activities commonly associated with modern town twinnings. The Vichy government quickly tried to generalize from this example: between January 1942 and May 1943, four circulars from the Interior Ministry to prefects first asked for information on any adoptions taking place, then increasingly centralized the process around the Ministry and (for the financial aspects) the Secours National.[187]

While the total number of adoptions was not vast (aside from Lyon, there were seven, for example, in the populous *département* of the Rhône), arrangements were quite flexible (*départements* could adopt towns; smaller municipalities could group together to undertake an adoption), and most major bombed localities had a 'godparent' by March 1944. Lorient, for example, was adopted by the *département* of Seine-et-Marne, east of Paris, and Saint-Nazaire by Angers, which sent its young people to help clear rubble after the raids of February 1943. Le Havre and Rouen, adopted respectively by Algiers and Oran in 1942, found themselves cut off from their sponsors after that November's Allied North African landings; the *départements* of Landes and Ain stepped in to replace the Algerian cities. Visits by Pétain's personal representative Colonel Bonhomme also helped give a high profile to the adoptions process.[188]

A final, and remarkable, instance of solidarity came from French prisoners of war in Germany. Isolated from the realities of the German occupation of France, and from BBC broadcasts, and a (literally) captive audience for Vichy propaganda, prisoners were often more hostile to bombing than the general French public.[189] Opinion aside, their solidarity, in 1943–4, appears remarkably unstinting, and for once the French recipients benefited from an exchange rate that transformed each Reichsmark into a generous FF20. Many gifts were specifically from Breton groups, the largest from the officers' camps, the Oflags: FF228,000 from Oflag VIIIF and FF300,000 from Oflag IVD, for example, in autumn 1943.[190] Most remarkably, FF165,000 reached the regional prefect in Rennes from Oflag VIA in January 1945, when liberated France was again at war with the Reich.[191]

The bombing of occupied France thus provoked significant expressions of solidarity among the French public right up to the Liberation in 1944. Vichy not only allowed a range of agencies to deliver assistance, but also chose to channel a large part of the aid given to *sinistrés* through the Secours National, a more flexible but also more discretionary body than the state. Groups created or revived under Vichy enjoyed the cautious respect of the Liberation authorities; the renamed Secours National survived the Liberation by five years. That suggested a distinction between the expression of civic solidarity and links to the regime. Vichy's attempts to co-ordinate the efforts of diverse groups may have helped direct resources where they were most needed, but there is little sign that they achieved their second purpose – reaping for the regime some of the benefits of solidarity existing within civil society.

SOLIDARITY AND ITS LIMITS: THE REVERSE OF THE COIN

For solidarity to involve the whole population, in a context of extreme social stress under unpopular regimes of contested legitimacy, would be an unrealistic expectation. The French, for example, often proved more willing to give money than to behave decently to refugees on their own doorsteps. In both countries, too, both passive defence and post-raid assistance were tainted by anti-Semitism. In Italy, this took the form of excluding Jews from residence permits for evacuees. In France it involved, through the COSI, using money stolen from Jews to assist air-raid victims. Moreover, in Saint-Étienne and possibly other towns, flats confiscated from Jews were offered to bombed-out families.[192] However, our research has not indicated that the systematic anti-Semitism of the German Reich, under which, for example, Jews were excluded from shelters, was reproduced in either country.[193]

In Italy, fellow-feeling between the inhabitants of bombed or endangered cities stopped at the gates of Rome. As early as February 1941 an informer reported that Milanese envied Rome, which was alleged to be well protected by the 'anti-aircraft batteries of the Vatican'. The Pope's presence, they believed, safeguarded the capital against British attack: though seen as a sign of great civility on the part of the British, this also provoked continual complaints that 'the Romans are always luckier than the Milanese'.[194] A confidential note from Lisbon dated 9 October 1941 considered that 'even if the Romans dislike the bombing, the Neapolitans, Milanese and others would rejoice, such is the inter-urban rivalry among Italians'.[195] This was at least partly accurate. In *The Watch* (1950), a novel based on his Second World War memoirs, the writer and anti-Fascist exile Carlo Levi describes how workers on a commuter train in northern Italy in 1942 fantasized, despite their fear of Fascist spies, about the bombing of Rome:

> There was always someone who said, however: 'But what are they doing here? I know where they should go and it would be over once and for all!' And someone else, more explicitly, replied with everybody's approval: 'To Rome, it's to Rome they should go. Not here ... and they shouldn't leave a stone untouched.' ... Everyone applauded and laughed, happy as they pictured Rome's destruction, and they almost forgot that only a few miles away their own houses were going up in flames. They felt safer at the idea.[196]

According to one sensitive observer, the Florentine jurist Piero Calamandrei, the view of Rome as Italy's disgrace, the capital of Mussolini's Fascist government that had taken Italy into the war and attracted enemy bombing in the first place, was widespread from 1941. His diary entry for 22 January notes: 'The Neapolitans, obsessed by air raids, say: "blessed St Gennaro, please let them [the airmen] know that *chillo fetentone* [that 'smelly man'] does not live in Naples but in Rome!"'[197] All over Italy, people began openly to wish for bombs to fall on Mussolini's city, home to those regarded as responsible for Italy's suffering. Intelligence obtained for the American secret service from Switzerland reported on 30 July 1943 that people in Turin, the most anti-Fascist city in Italy, were 'delighted to learn that the Fascist officials ... in Rome were getting their medicine at last', and northern Italian cities 'received the news of the raid on Rome with silent joy'.[198] The view from the far South was no different. In Sicily, three days after the bombing of Rome, people complained that it had occupied so much space in the press, while the hundreds of raids experienced by Sicilians seemed to count less than 'those three-hour raids' on the capital.[199] As Calamandrei noted, people commonly thought that a few bombs on Rome, after so much horror experienced by innocent civilians, 'finally touched the right place'. Many were sick of hearing about Roman ruins, and were now glad that they were finally collapsing: 'A few bombs to bring a little bit of mess among these archaeological gardens are not misplaced.'[200] There is no evidence that the French took a similar view either of Paris (which largely escaped bombing) or of Vichy (which was completely unscathed).

Solidarity might also by limited by the frequent opportunities for gain offered by the disorder surrounding bombing and evacuation. In Italy's rural and mountain areas, for example, landlords were reported to be charging exorbitant rents in Venice province from June 1940, in Naples province from winter 1942.[201] In France, all means of transport, and especially lorries, were in heavy demand during and after raids for clearance or to move personnel, bombed-out families and their property. Their availability was limited by the fact that 90 per cent of France's lorry production was destined for Germany.[202] Some owners preferred to hire lorries out to private clients than to see them requisitioned. Reports from Lorient complain at the 'ill will and bad faith' of lorry owners; just one bus out of 25 expected appeared to evacuate civilians on 9 February. In Toulon, barely half the required lorries turned up following the raid of 24 November 1943. Further west along the Mediterranean coast, by spring 1944, black-market lorries were reported to charge 22 francs per kilometre, with payment also due for the return journey. French evacuees might also find food and accommodation ruinously expensive.[203]

If profiteering was common in France, so was looting, at least on a small scale. Widespread looting during the exodus of 1940 discouraged evacuation for the rest of the war. When air raids began, some passive defence workers appear to have regarded looting as a perk of their dangerous, ill-paid job. In Le Creusot, for example, they were reported as leaving bomb sites with bags and pockets full of food and other finds; in Toulon, one was apprehended with a revolver he had taken from a desk.[204] Petty thieves in the aftermath of the Nantes raid were reported as making off with cigarettes, laundry and linen, bicycles, and even a car.[205] Thieves might also offer to help evacuees move their furniture, only to carry it off for themselves. The mayor of Rennes reported that prefabricated cabins for bombed-out households were unusable because vital components had been stolen; the first head of SIPEG warned of the need for constant surveillance of bombed buildings as looters were eager to take non-ferrous metals.[206] And in combat zones both German and Allied soldiers looted frequently.[207] In principle, as the public were warned, looters could incur the death penalty.[208] In practice, it appears to have been rare but not unknown: in Marseille, a looter who cut a dead woman's fingers off to get her rings was executed after a summary trial.[209]

By contrast, there is no evidence that even in the last weeks of Vichy the French practised on-the-spot executions on the German model.

The Italian public, too, were periodically reminded that death was the penalty for looting, under a law dated December 1942.[210] There are few official reports of looting, suggesting that the Fascist authorities did not view it as a major problem. Equally, though, looting in Italy could occur on a heroic scale. The town of Benevento, 50 kilometres north-east of Naples, was bombed in September 1943 and then systematically plundered by German troops and organized gangs of looters, who also fought one another. In the wake of the armistice, as Gribaudi observes, all civil authority had broken down there.[211] There was no equivalent to this episode in France, where the internal Resistance, the Free French, or the Allies were generally able to take over localities directly after the Germans' departure.

CONCLUSION

Vichy France and Fascist Italy suffered from severe handicaps as they tried to enlist their respective publics' co-operation and mobilization in the face of air raids. Getting hundreds of thousands of people to follow their lead, whether by evacuating, manning the emergency services, or assisting air-raid victims, was intrinsically difficult. Both regimes suffered from straitened material circumstances, and, by the time the heavy raids started in 1942, from deep unpopularity as well. At the same time, however, air raids could provoke both spontaneous evacuation and movements of solidarity among the public; the trick for governments was to canalize these.

Both France and Italy had seen their pre-war evacuation policies fail in 1940, with particularly disastrous effects in France. Both then struggled to encourage evacuation of cities at risk while seeking to restrain or channel massive departures from cities that were heavily and repeatedly bombed. In neither country were their endeavours very successful; most individuals and families preferred to choose for themselves whether to stay or to move (and *where* to move) rather than allowing the state to decide. But the French at least managed, as late as May 1944, to run an evacuation policy that took tens of thousands of schoolchildren, and other civilians, to safety. The policy was executed too slowly, and too often followed raids rather than anticipating them. Nevertheless, it compares favourably with Italy, which in 1942–3 proved incapable even of formulating a coherent policy, still less of implementing it. From the summer of 1943 on, policy was left *de facto* to prefectures and local authorities – and some evacuees in Sicily faced starvation.

In principle, Italy's means of mobilizing the population should have been more effective than those of France. For 15 years before the war, Mussolini had been engaged in 'initiatives designed to galvanize almost every aspect of Italy's moral, economic and cultural life'.[212] And the central tool of mobilization was to be the Fascist Party, instrument for the promotion of the Fascist revolution and of the cult of the Duce. With over 21 million members (including men, women and children from 6 years of age), by 1939 the party not only colonized the Italian state but spread a tentacular grip into Italian civil society too. Although it is impossible to establish the precise depth of its popular influence, its organization reached men, women and youths in town and country. However, in the second half of the 1930s, the Party had also become both hugely bureaucratized and increasingly rejected by large parts of civil society. As it became clear that the war would not be a short one, its omnipresence was ever more resented.[213] Vichy France, with its squabbling little Fascist parties and its ramshackle, divided Legion, had no established equivalent. The Secours National was run by paternalist notables; the Équipes Nationales were a newly created Pétainist replica of the (banned) French Boy Scout movement; the COSI was always suspect because of its leaders and its dependence on 'German' money.

In practice, however, Vichy France proved more effective. This is reflected for example, in the contrasting record of French and Italian emergency teams on the ground. There were manpower constraints in both countries. French local authorities, however, were able to build up passive defence teams in every locality. The teams were poorly paid, their training less than systematic. Some deserted their posts. But they were available, and could be supplemented by specialists such as miners as the raids worsened. Sheer manpower was not a major problem during raids on France. Although the authorities sometimes lost control of the situation, the state generally proved remarkably resilient, and collapse local and temporary. Italy, by contrast, appears to have suffered from a structural shortage of men, as the tussle over the use of military personnel in 1943 indicates. Moreover, some passive defence teams simply melted away in the face of repeated raids, as in Taranto in August 1943. And while both France and Italy sought to mobilize the public beyond the ranks of official state bodies, the French did so with considerably greater effect, whether it came to enlisting volunteers or attracting donations.

The clearest explanation is that by 1940, Italy's Fascist Party had become, not a spur to mobilization, but a handicap. Even in January 1939 a police informer was reporting that Italians resented the party's growing invasion of their daily lives; in January 1940, a leading industrialist observed that 'never has Fascism been held in lower esteem by the Italians'.[214] Within barely a year, Italy had been launched on what was proudly called *la guerra fascista*, only to suffer defeats in the Mediterranean, the Balkans and North Africa, signalling 'the ideological death of the regime'.[215] The loathing of the Italian public for the regime that had toppled them into war is well illustrated by their attitude towards the bombing of Rome. In such a context, and in particular in the absence of any state apparatus independent of the party, mobilization in Italy, even for the public good that passive defence was, could not be dissociated from support for a discredited regime.

The French situation was altogether more nuanced. To begin with, while the regime sank into unpopularity from 1941–2, and Laval's return to office in 1942 and open support for a German victory were widely disliked, the figurehead of Pétain retained a degree of support, if not as a policymaker then at least as a symbol.[216] His honorary presidency of the Secours National could thus remain an asset more than a handicap for the organization. Second, France's state apparatus, more robust to begin with than Italy's, sustained less damage in four years of National Revolution than Italy's in twenty years of fascism. French office-holders could not oppose the regime, and Laval demanded vigorous support for government policy from key figures like prefects; often, however, he had to settle for compliance. It was therefore easier than in Italy to dissociate acts of solidarity, even in collaboration with quasi-official organizations, from support for the regime. The presence of Resistance sympathies within the Équipes Nationales and the Red Cross, as well as the Nantes passive defence teams, is evidence of this. And where the regime itself began to lose its grip, for example in Normandy, French civil society achieved exceptional feats of organization and solidarity under the pressure of extreme events.

In Britain and Germany, mobilization for civil defence could be presented not only as a bid to safeguard lives and property, but as a patriotic duty and a contribution to victory. Such a proposition was far harder to accept in Italy, where victory appeared impossible by 1942, and in France, where the only desired victory for most people was that of the nations doing the bombing. This more complex position was reflected in the propaganda on both sides, but also in the ways in which people thought about the bombers and the raids.

Notes

1 P. Giolitto, *Histoire de la Milice* (Paris: Perrin, 2002), 26, 58–9.
2 E. Cortesi, 'Evacuation in Italy during the Second World War: Evolution and Management', in Baldoli, Knapp and Overy (eds), *Bombing, States and Peoples*, 60–6.
3 AN F1/c/III, Prefects' reports, various dates, 1943–4.
4 AN F1A/3745, *Morgon-Tidningen*, 12 May 1944. For obvious reasons, few prefectoral reports exist for the period June–August 1944.
5 ACS, MA, 1940, b. 83, fasc. 13, telegram from Interior Ministry to prefects, secretary of Fascist Party, army Stato Maggiore, territorial defence command of Turin-Genoa-Alessandria-Milan and War Ministry, 20 June 1940.
6 *Ibid.*, War Ministry to prefects and central Air Protection headquarters, 2 July 1940.
7 Mussolini's last speech to Chamber of Fasci and Corporations, 2 December 1942, broadcast on the radio and published in *Il Popolo d'Italia* on 3 December 1942. B. Mussolini, *Opera Omnia*, vol. 31, ed. E. and D. Susmel (Florence: La Fenice, 1951–1963), 118–33. See below, p. 205.
8 On phases of evacuation in Italy, see Cortesi, 'Evacuation in Italy', 60–6.
9 ACS, MI, DGPCSA, b. 106, report by prefect of Milan, 4 March 1943.
10 ASN, Prefettura II Versamento, Cat. 6, b. 1210, Interior Ministry to prefects, 4 December 1942.
11 *Ibid.*, *Commissario prefettizio* of San Valentino Torio to prefect of Naples, 21 December 1942.
12 *Ibid.*, *Commissario prefettizio* of San Valentino Torio to prefect of Naples, 22 December 1942.
13 ASP, Prefettura, b. 636, prefect of Palermo to Interior Ministry, 5 January 1943.
14 ASP, Prefettura, b. 638, prefect of Palermo to all *podestàs* of the province, 23 November 1942.
15 ASN, Prefettura II Versamento, Cat. 6, b. 1227. Telegram from Interior Ministry to prefect of

Naples, cc prefects of Teramo, Ascoli, Perugia, Pescara, Pesaro, no date but probably end 1942–early 1943.

16 ASP, Prefettura, b. 638, Interior Ministry to prefects, 24 November 1942. In the case of younger children and their mothers, the National Institution for the Protection of Maternity and Childhood took the place of the GIL (*ibid.*, President of Opera nazionale per la protezione della maternità e dell'infanzia to all prefects, 13 February 1943).

17 For details on this see Cortesi, 'Evacuation in Italy', 68.

18 ASM, Prefettura, b. C254, Commander Major of Carabinieri of Milan to prefect of Milan, 14 April 1943.

19 ASP, Prefettura, b. 638, *Podestà* of Alimena to prefect of Palermo, 1 June 1943.

20 *Ibid.*, *Podestà* of Caccamo to prefect of Palermo, 16 July 1943.

21 ASP, Prefettura, b. 636, prefect of Palermo to Interior Ministry, 2 April 1943.

22 ASTo, Prefettura, b. 521, Interior Ministry directive, 20 March 1943.

23 ASP, Prefettura, b. 638, Interior Ministry to prefects, 8 July 1943.

24 Cf. ASG, RSI, Prefettura Repubblicana di Genova, b. 30.

25 ASLS, Prefettura, b. 160, report from commune of Carrodano to province head of La Spezia, 31 January 1944.

26 A. Varni, 'La società bolognese immersa nella guerra', in C. Bersani and V. Roncuzzi Roversi Monaco, *Delenda Bononia. Immagini dei bombardamenti 1943–1945*, (Bologna: Patron, 1995), 24–6.

27 I. Tognarini, 'La popolazione toscana e i "problemi della guerra". Aspetti della vita sociale attraverso i carteggi e le relazioni pubbliche', in L. Arbizzani *Al di qua e al di là della Linea Gotica, 1944–1945. Aspetti sociali, politici e militari in Toscana e in Emilia Romagna* (Bologna-Firenze: Regioni Toscana e Emilia Romagna, 1993), 47–9.

28 ASTo, Prefettura, I Versamento, b. 521, province head of Turin to *podestàs*, 3 January 1944.

29 *Ibid.*, province head of Turin to *podestà*, 10 June 1944.

30 *Ibid.*, *Commissario prefettizio* of Sestriere to province head of Turin, 15 June 1944.

31 *Ibid.*, telegram from Interior Ministry to province heads, 18 October 1944.

32 Cf. for example many letters regarding Bologna in ASB, Prefettura, Serie I, Cat. 16, b. 1.

33 Cf. for example ASG, RSI, Prefettura repubblicana di Genova, b. 28, *Podestà* of Genoa to province head, 15 January 1945.

34 ASN, Prefettura II Versamento, Cat. 6, b. 1223, director of Ufficio Assistenza Profughi, Naples prefecture, to Col. James L. Kincaid, Commissario Provinciale di Controllo, 5 July 1944.

35 SHAT 2N/200, Réunion du 22 janvier 1940, DDP (dispersion).

36 SHAT 2P/20, Secretary of State for War (signed Sérant) to prefects, 17 April 1941.

37 SHAA 3D/44, SIPEG, Note technique sur les Évacuations, n.d. (early 1944).

38 AN F60/407, J. Marlier, Special Delegate for Refugees, to F. de Brinon, Vichy Government Delegate in Occupied Zone, 2 March 1941.

39 F. Jacquin, *Les bombardements de Brest, 1940–1944* (Brest: Éditions MEB, 1997), 74–5.

40 AD IetV 4W/8, Ingrand to prefects of coastal *départements*, 27 November 1941.

41 *Ibid.*, Ingrand to prefects in Occupied zone, 29 July 1942; Head of Government (signed Ingrand) to prefects, 4 February 1943. Localities mentioned in the latter circular were Dunkirk, Calais, Boulogne, Dieppe, Cherbourg, Le Havre, St-Malo, Brest, Lorient, St-Nazaire, La Pallice, as well as the rail centre of Lille-Fives-Hellemmes.

42 See above, p. 101.

43 AD Var 1W/22, RG Var, report for 29 February–5 March 1944. Cf. also AN F7/14904/Rouen, RG Dieppe, report for 13 February 1943; AD SM 51W/85, RG Le Havre, report for 23–29 January 1944.

44 L. Dodd, 'Children under the Allied Bombs: France 1940–1945', unpublished Ph.D. thesis, University of Reading (2011), 207; Archives de Paris 1103W/81, Bouffet, Éloignement de la région parisienne, 2.

45 AN F7/14931, Commission de contrôle technique international de Marseille, July 1944; *and* Contrôle technique Toulon, July 1944.

46 Cf. AN F1A/3745, Réunion des maires des ports français, 19 février 1944; AM Nantes 4H/103, Conférence des Municipalités des Villes Côtières, 28 février 1942.

47 Mémorial de Caen PA2, *Le Courrier de l'Air* 24 and 26 (n.d., but mid–late 1942).
48 The prefect of Seine-Inférieure reported that 10,000 people from Le Havre commuted in this way by December 1942 (AD SM 51W/Cab/2/6, Prefect of Seine- Inférieure, monthly report, 31 December 1942). Smaller numbers were doing the same around Lorient at the same period (AD Morbihan 14W/2078, Sub-prefect of Lorient to prefect of Morbihan, 15 October 1942). Dodd ('Children under the Allied Bombs', 161) also notes night commuting in Brest, Lille-Fives and Boulogne-Billancourt. According to Jacquin (*Les Bombardements de Brest*, 71), three-quarters of Brest's inhabitants slept outside the town at the height of the bombing.
49 ADLA 1694W/66, Sub-prefect of Saint-Nazaire to prefect of Loire-Inférieure, 17 March 1943.
50 AN F7/14904, Avis: Il faut partir (signed Prefect Cacaud and Mayor Detolle), Caen, 16 June 1944; A. Beevor, *D-Day: the Battle for Normandy* (London: Penguin Books, 2009), 268.
51 TNA WO223/72, Special Interrogation of Colonel E. Wildermuth, Commandant Fortress Le Havre, 12 January 1946, 5; M. Bengtsson, *Un été 44: de l'état de siege à la paix retrouvée* (2nd edition: Le Havre: Éditions-Imprimerie Grenet, 2004), 57.
52 AN F7/14904, Prefect of Calvados to heads of state and government, 23 June 1944.
53 AD IetV 4W/8, Prefect of Ille-et-Vilaine to Direction des Réfugiés, 29 April 1944.
54 AD Rhône 182W /240, Head of government (signed Watteau) to prefects, 6 November 1943; SHAA 3D/44/1, SIPEG, Note technique sur les Évacuations, n.d. (early 1944).
55 Cf. for example AN AJ41/356, Aisne, Prefectoral Report (excerpt), 3 March 1944.
56 *JO*, 1 January 1944, *États annexes*, 13a; AD Manche 2Z/106, Notice sur le placement des enfants évacués, annexe à la circulaire no. 133 du 2 avril 1943.
57 AM Lorient 5H/14, Prefect of Morbihan to regional prefect of Brittany, 11 March 1943.
58 AD Morbihan 2W/15935, Gendarmerie Nationale, Section de Lorient, Rapport 44/2 du Capitaine Salomon, 19 January 1943.
59 *Ibid.*, Report from M. Jolivel, head of Morbihan refugee services, 12 February 1943.
60 AD Morbihan 9W/38, Préfecture du Morbihan, Service des Réfugiés, Liste Numérique des Réfugiés de l'agglomération lorientaise repliés, le 4 mars 1943.
61 AD Morbihan 7W/4799, Prefect of Morbihan to de Brinon, Ingrand and Regional Prefect, Rennes, 22 February 1943.
62 ADLA 1694W/66, Sub-prefect of Saint-Nazaire to prefect of Loire-Inférieure, 17 March 1943; Middlebrook and Everitt, *The Bomber Command War Diaries*, 359.
63 AD Morbihan 2W/15935, *Le Nouvelliste de Bretagne*, 21 January 1943.
64 AD Morbihan 9W/38, Refugees Directorate, Paris, to prefect of Morbihan 26 January 1943; Prefecture du Morbihan, service des réfugiés, Instructions à suivre dans la mesure du possible pour l'évacuation de la population de Lorient, 24 January 1943.
65 AN F1/A/3745, CFLN, Commissariat à l'Intérieur, Résumé d'un exposé de Taittinger, 28 March/6 May 1944.
66 P. Caillaud, *Les Nantais sous les bombardements, 1941–1944* (Nantes: Aux Portes du Large, 1947), 74–82.
67 ADLA 1694W/64, RG Nantes to RG Vichy, 6 October 1943.
68 Caillaud, *Les Nantais*, 76–7.
69 ADLA 1694W/1, Prefect of Loire-Atlantique, Final call to the population, 9 June 1944.
70 Cf. L. Baldissara and P. Pezzino (eds), *Crimini e memorie di Guerra. Violenza contro le popolazioni e politiche del ricordo* (Naples: L'ancora del Mediterraneo, 2004), 5–58; V. Belco, *War, Massacre and Recovery in Central Italy, 1943–1948* (Toronto: University of Toronto Press, 2010), 57–102.
71 Cf. SHAT 2P/20, Conférence des Préfets sur l'évacuation de la côte méditerranéene, 27 January 1944; AN F1/A/3745, *Le Petit Dauphinois*, 27 March 1944.
72 SHAT 2P/20, Conférence des Préfets, évacuation de la côte, 27 January 1944; AN F1A/3745, Radio Paris 6.2.44 (0800).
73 AN F1/A/3745, *Le Petit Dauphinois*, 27 March 1944.
74 P. Tanchoux, 'La protection monumentale en 1939–45', unpublished paper given at the conference 'Guerres, œuvres d'art et patrimoine artistique à l'époque contemporaine', University of Picardie, 16–18 March 2011, 12. Avignon, however, was bombed on 27 May 1944.

75 This was recalled by two former evacuees interviewed by Dodd ('Children under the Allied Bombs', 213).
76 Mémorial de Caen, TE471 (Marcel Labussière).
77 AM St-Étienne 5H/29, Mayor Henri Muller of Saint-Étienne to Mayor of Tournon St-Martin (Indre), 23 October 1944.
78 AN F1/A/3745, Réunion au ministère des maires du littoral, 19 February 1944 (CFLN intercept).
79 ADSM 51W/70, Gendarmerie Nationale, 3e Légion, Compagnie de la Seine-Maritime, Rapport, juillet 1943; M. Schmiedel, 'Orchestrated Solidarity: the Allied Air War in France and the Development of Local and State-Organized Solidarity Movements', in Baldoli, Knapp and Overy (eds), *Bombing, States and Peoples*, 210.
80 AD Var 1W/22, RG Toulon report, 29 February–5 March 1944; AD BduR 76W/26, Sub-prefect of Nyons to prefect of Drôme, 20 March 1944.
81 AN F7/14932, Contrôle technique, Inspection Régionale de Montpellier, 5 July 1944.
82 AN F7/14930, Contrôle technique, Aurillac, 31 August 1944.
83 AD SM 51W/69, Sub-Prefect of Dieppe to Prefect of Seine-Inférieure, 5 February 1943.
84 AD SM 51W/250, Direction Départementale des Prisonniers de Guerre, Déportés et Réfugiés, notes of 17 December 1944 and 12 February 1945.
85 Cf. above, p. 73.
86 ASN, Prefettura, II Versamento, Cat. 6, b. 1222, Railway Militia of Naples to National Railway Militia, 10 July 1941.
87 *Ibid.*, Prefect of Naples to president of ECA, 12 July 1941. The ECA, created with the law 847 of 3 June 1937 to replace all charity organizations, became the main institution assisting the bombed-out and evacuees during the war.
88 ASM, Prefettura, b. C268, Order by *podestà* to Milan landlords, 30 October 1942.
89 *Ibid.*, Report of 9 December 1942.
90 *Ibid.*, *Podestà* of Milan to prefect of Milan, 4 March 1943.
91 ASG, Prefettura, b. 129, Red Cross of Genoa to President of Red Cross in Rome and to Prefect of Genoa, 8 December 1942. See the same file for more Red Cross reports.
92 ASTo, Prefettura, b. 519, Red Cross report, provincial zone of Turin, end May 1943.
93 ASTo, Prefettura, I Versamento, b. 527, Interior Ministry to prefects, 20 November 1942.
94 ASN, Prefettura II Versamento, Cat. 6, b. 1227, Public Works Ministry to prefect of Naples, 8 March 1943.
95 *Ibid.*, War Ministry to armed forces' headquarters, 16 June 1943.
96 ASG, Prefettura, b. 155, Mussolini to all ministries and armed forces, 9 July 1943.
97 ASLS, Prefettura, b. 159, report by Genio Civile on damage provoked by the raid of 14 February 1943.
98 ASTa, Prefettura, Cat. 6, b. 116, Engineer Director of Genio Civile of Taranto to Prefect and Public Works Ministry, 3 September 1943.
99 *Ibid.*, 6 September 1943.
100 ASTa, Prefettura, Cat. 6, b. 116, Questura of Taranto to prefect, 2 September 1943.
101 ASTa, Genio Civile, Nuovo Versamento, b. 1422, report by Ministry of Public Works, Genio Civile of Taranto, 14 August 1944.
102 Décret du 30 janvier 1939 (Organisation de la défense passive), *JO*, 1 February 1939; SHAT 2P/20, Rapport sur l'état d'avancement du programme de la Défense passive à la date du 31 décembre 1941, 14.
103 Décret portant application du décret du 30 January 1939 (*JO*, 5 September 1940); Loi du 3 juillet 1941 (Règles d'indemnisation, Défense passive, Incapacité de travail) (*JO*, 14 July 1941); Loi du 26 juillet 1941 (Pension d'invalidité, victimes civiles de la guerre (*JO*, 28 September 1941). Cf. also AD Manche 127W/1, Ministère de l'Intérieur, Répertoire des principales Notes, Instructions et Circulaires, 17–18.
104 Arrêté du 1er septembre 1941 (Relèvement du montant des vacations horaires, défense passive) *JO*, 11 October 1941; *ibid.*, 15 janvier 1943, *JO*, 21 January 1943; Sauvy, *La Vie économique*, 243.
105 AD Manche, 127W/1, Notice sur l'Organisation Générale de la Défense Passive dans le département de la Manche, n.d. (mid-1942).

106 SHAT, Vincennes, 1P/20, Notes pour le colonel Mehrhart, 9 and 25 November 1943; SHAA 3D/473, Note pour le colonel Mehrhart, 19 November 1943; AN F1/A/3780, CFLN, France-Politique, Organisation de la Défense Passive, 29 July 1943 (Paris); AD Rhône 182W/264, Organisation générale de la Défense Passive département du Rhône, September 1943 (Lyon).
107 T. H. O'Brien, *Civil Defence* (London: HMSO, 1955), 340–4.
108 SHAT 9P/104, Département du Gers, Plan de défense contre les attaques aériennes, 22 May 1944.
109 AD Loire 134W/68, Préfecture de la Loire, Défense passive, État numérique du personnel appartenant en propre au services de la défense passive, 17 June 1944. Paul Caillaud, former Directeur de la Défense Passive in Nantes, put numbers there at 2,601 in April 1944; here too, half were volunteers: P. Caillaud, *Nantes sous les bombardements: Mémorial à la Défense Passive* (Nantes: Éditions du Fleuve, 1946), 73, 93.
110 SHAA 3D/473, Note pour le Colonel von Merhart, 19 November 1943.
111 Giolitto, *Histoire de la Milice*, 157.
112 The respective responsibilities of passive-defence teams and the Ponts et Chaussées were outlined on 5 April 1944 in a joint circular (0400-I/DP) to prefects signed by Darnand for the Interior Ministry and Schwartz, Secretary General for Transport, for the Industry Ministry (AD IetV, 47/W/6).
113 AN AJ41/633, Note for Colonel von Mehrhart, 28 July 1943; AN F1A/3780, GPRF, Service Courrier, Diffusion 13.7.44, Instructions Relatives à l'Emploi des Bataillons Mobiles de Défense Passive.
114 SHAT 2P/20, Ministère de l'Intérieur, Direction Générale de la Protection Civile, Instruction Générale sur les Évacuations des blessés, 19 April 1944. Good pictorial representations of the train appear in *L'Illustration*, 26 May 1943, and in a newsreel preserved by the Institut National de l'Audiovisuel (http://www.ina.fr/recherche/recherche?search=SIPEG&vue=Video).
115 G. Chauvy, *Lyon, 1940–1947: L'Occupation, la Libération, l'Épuration* (Paris: Perrin, 2004), 239.
116 AD Morbihan 7W/4794, Ministère de l'Intérieur, DDP, Instruction Générale (Service Électrique National de Sauvegarde), 16 July 1943; Loi du 9 décembre 1943 (Service du Secours Technique), *JO*, 3 February 1944.
117 AM Nantes, 4/H/107, *L'Ouest-Éclair*, 2 October 1943; AM Lyon, 1188WP/14, Convention provisoire entre M. le Préfet du Nord et M. Defline, Président de la Chambre des Houillères du Nord et du Pas-de-Calais, 9 September 1943; AM Lyon, 1129WP/10, Ville de Lyon, Corps de Sapeurs-Pompiers, Report by Commandant Rossignol, 22 June 1943; AM Lyon, 1188WP/14, Chief City Engineer to Mayor of Lyon, 21 July 1943; AM Lyon, 1188WP/14, Comité des Houillères de la Loire to General Duplat, DDP, Prefecture of Loire, 7 October 1943.
118 Carried out by 289 aircraft of Bomber Command, this was the heaviest single raid on Rouen, leaving 850–900 dead, 344 of them in Rouen itself, where over 7,000 were left homeless. Cf. P. Le Trévier and D. Rose, *Ce qui s'est vraiment passé le 19 avril 1944: Le Martyre de Sotteville, Rouen, et la Région* (Saint-Germain-en-Laye: Comever, 2004), 96; AM Rouen 4H/5/6, Bombardements subis par la ville, n.d.
119 J.-J. Monsuez, 'Les sections sanitaires automobiles féminines', *Revue Historique des Armées*, 247 (2007), 98–113: 111. On-line version at http://rha.revues.org/index2033.html.
120 AM Rouen, 4H/27/24, Rouen, Conseil Municipal, 27 avril 1944.
121 Monsuez, 'Les sections sanitaires', 98–113.
122 J.-P. Le Crom, 'De la philanthropie à l'action humanitaire', in P.-J. Hesse and J.-P. Le Crom (eds), *La protection sociale sous Vichy* (Rennes: Presses Universitaires de Rennes, 2001) 218–19; AD Manche 127W/1, Ministère de l'Intérieur, Répertoire des principales Notes, Instructions et Circulaires, 9. Le Crom puts total Red Cross membership at perhaps a million in 1943.
123 AD Rhône 182W/66, Résumé succinct du plan d'organisation de la défense passive dans le département du Rhône, 20 April 1944.
124 AD BduR 76W/197, Croix-Rouge Française, Bulletin d'Information, 24, Septembre-Octobre 1943.
125 AN, F1/A/3778, CFLN, Arrestations parmi le haut personnel du Comité de la Croix Rouge Française, 23 March 1944, ref. WTZ/2/35900.
126 AM Nantes 4H/107, *Ouest-Éclair*, 9 October and 22 November1943; AM St-Étienne 5H/37, *Le*

Mémorial de Saint-Étienne, 1 June 1944; AM Lyon 1127WP/09, *Lyon Républicain*, 5 June 1944; AD BduR 76W/129, RG Marseille, Information, 2 June 1944; AD Loire 7W/26, RG Saint-Étienne, Information, 7 June 1944.

127 AN F7/14901, Secrétariat d'État à l'Intérieur, DDP (signed Cazes), Instruction Générale relative à la Coopération des équipes du mouvement 'Prisonniers' au service de la Défense Passive, 21 September 1943.

128 L. Yagil, '*L'homme nouveau' et la révolution nationale de Vichy, 1940–44* (Villeneuve d'Ascq: Presses Universitaires du Septentrion, 1997), 87–91; AD Morbihan, 7W/4793, Ministère de l'Éducation Nationale, Secrétariat Général à la Jeunesse, Équipes Nationales: Règlement Intérieur de la Branche Masculine, n.d. (1943?).

129 AD IetV 47W/6, Secrétariat Général à la Jeunesse, Équipes Nationales, Instruction no. 15, Délégué Régional chargé des Équipes Nationales au Délégués Régionaux, 15 April 1943.

130 AD Morbihan, 7W/4793, Head of Government to Prefects and Rectors and Inspectors of Academies, 17 June 1943. W. D. Halls, in *The Youth of Vichy France* (Oxford: Oxford University Press, 1981), 345, suggests that membership of the Équipes was compulsory for young people. In fact, while young people could be requisitioned into the Équipes after major raids, they never constituted a permanent compulsory youth organization – and it is unlikely that the Germans, who tried to ban the scout movement in France, would have tolerated one. The regional prefect of Lyon was clear, in August 1944, that large-scale requisitioning of young people should only be a last resort (AD Loire 7W/27, Regional Prefect of Lyon to prefect of Loire, 4 August 1944).

131 AD IetV 47W/6, Équipes Nationales, Note annexe à la circulaire no. 15: Services que peuvent accomplir les Jeunes.

132 SHAT 2P/20, Ministère de l'Intérieur, DDP, Instruction relative à la coopération des Équipes Nationales de la Jeunesse au Service de la Défense Passive, 23 juin 1943; SHAA 3D/44/1, Ministère de l'Intérieur, DDP, Instruction relative à l'intervention des Équipes Nationales dans les opérations de Défense Passive, 28 April 1944.

133 Yagil, '*L'homme nouveau*', 93–4; AD Manche 127W/1, Interior Ministry, DDP (signed Cazes) to prefects, 2 October 1944; AD Morbihan 2W/15921, Mayor of Vannes to Prefect of Morbihan, 26 August 1944.

134 AM Lorient, 5H/14, Prefect of Morbihan to Ambassador de Brinon, 22 February 1943.

135 Le Trévier and Rose, *Ce qui s'est vraiment passé*, 84–5.

136 F. Lefaivre ed. *J'ai vécu les bombardements à Condé-sur-Noireau* (Condé-sur-Noireau, Éditions Charles Corlet, 1994), 36.

137 AD Morbihan 7W/4799, Prefect of Morbihan, Observations ... 11 March 1943; AM Lorient 5H/14, Prefect of Morbihan to Ambassador de Brinon, 22 February 1943; AM St-Étienne 5H/66, Ville de St-Étienne, Compte-rendu sur les Renseignements recueillis au Creusot, 20 July 1943; O. Collomb and C. Bonfort, *Le Bombardement du 15 août 1944 et la reconstruction de Sisteron* (Lyon: Éditions Sup'Copy, 1994), 10.

138 AD Manche 2.Z/373, Prefect of Manche to passive-defence services, 22 March 1942; AM Rennes 6H/23, mayor of Rennes to Information Ministry, 10 December 1943.

139 AD IetV 502W/3, Rennes, Directeur urbain de la défense passive to Ille-et-Vilaine, Directeur départemental de la défense passive, 12 June 1943; SHAA 3D/406, *BIDP* no. 14, November 1943; AN, F7/14901, *BIDP* no. 19, April 1944.

140 AD Manche 127/W1, *BIDP* no. 20, May 1944; AD BduR 76W/121, Prefect of Bouches-du-Rhône to head of government, 7 June 1944. The destruction of the Marseille shelter is commemorated by a plaque in Place Léon Blum, in the city centre.

141 AM Lorient 5H/10, Laval (signed Sérant) to prefects, 6 May 1943.

142 AM Rennes 6H/23, mayor of Rennes to Information Ministry, 10 December 1943; AD BduR 76W/187, Département du Var, DDP, Compte rendu, bombardement de Toulon le 24 novembre 1943; AM Marseille 29II/4, Réunion du service de Coordination de la Protection Contre les Événements de Guerre, 11 December 1943.

143 SHAA 3D/44, *BIDP* no. 13, October 1943; AD BduR 76W/187, Département du Var, DDP, Bombardement de Toulon, le 24 novembre 1943; AD IetV 47W/6, Interior Minister (signed Cazes), to prefects, 17 June 1944.

144 SHAA 3D/406, *BIDP* no. 15, December 1943.
145 AM Marseille 29II/4, Service de Coordination de la Protection Contre les Événements de Guerre, 11 December 1943.
146 AD Calvados 9W/98, Équipes Nationales, Caen, Rapport du Chef de Ville de Caen, 24 avril 1944; Dodd, 'Children under the Allied Bombs', 185.
147 AD BduR 76W/127, Capt. Seyeux, Rapport sur l'activité de la DP pour la periode du 15 mai au 15 juillet 1944.
148 AM Lorient 5H/14, Prefect of Morbihan, Observations ..., 11 March 1943; AM St-Étienne AM5H/37, Ville de St-Étienne, Défense Passive, Rapport sur la Visite au Creusot, le 24 juillet 1943; AD LA 1623W/42 and 1623W/43, *passim.*
149 AD Manche 127W/25, Directeur de la défense passive, Arrondissement d'Avranches, to DDDP Manche, 5 December 1944.
150 SHAA 3D/406, *BIDP* no. 14, November 1943; ADLA 1694W/64, Nantes: Rapport sur l'activité des Équipes d'Urgence lors des bombardements de septembre 1943.
151 AD Var 1W/21, Renseignements Généraux (RG), Toulon, weekly report, 22–28 November 1943.
152 AD Manche 127/W1, *BIDP* no. 20, May 1944.
153 AM Havre H4/13/2, Mayor of Havre to Departmental director of Prisoners, Deportees and Refugees, 15 May 1946; J. Guillemard, *L'Enfer du Havre* (Paris: Éditions Medicis, 1948), 236.
154 Mémorial de Caen, TE193, Philippe Plichart and Odile Plichart-Pescheux, 'Un hôpital psychiatrique dans la tourmente: le Bon Sauveur de Caen (1939–1947)'; TE73, Dr Duncombe; TE82.15, Dr Raymond Villey; TE82.17, Lucienne Brée-Verrolles.
155 Mémorial de Caen, TE82.15, Dr Villey; TE74, Jacques Laberthe; TE78, Marguerite Morin; AN F7/14904, Prefect of Calvados to heads of state and government, 23 June 1944.
156 Mémorial de Caen, TE18, Raymonde and Pierre Mougin; TE52, Michelle Le Roux.
157 L. Dujardin and D. Butaeye, *Les réfugiés dans les carrières pendant la bataille de Caen, juin-juillet 1944* (Rennes: Éditions Ouest-France/Mémorial de Caen, 2009).
158 ASG, Prefettura, b. 159, 15 February 1941.
159 ACS, MI, DGPS, DPP, b. 211, fasc. 2, informer's report from Milan, 31 January 1943.
160 ADN, MG/03, Elettra Sarra, *A ritroso nel tempo*, unpublished memoir written 2000–2002, 30.
161 J. Di Benigno, *Occasioni mancate. Roma in un diario segreto, 1943–1944* (Rome: SEI, 1945), 95.
162 Cf. among many examples *La Gazzetta del Mezzogiorno*, 2 June 1943.
163 ASTo, Prefettura, I Versamento, b. 513, 'Offerte a favore dei danneggiati dalle incursioni aeree su Torino', December 1942.
164 ASM, Prefettura, b. C268, Director of schools, Milan, to school principals, 29 October 1942.
165 *Corriere della Sera*, 30 October 1942.
166 *Il Popolo d'Italia*, 31 October 1942.
167 ASM, Prefettura, b. C268, Minutes of a meeting between the prefect, the Party head, the *podestà*, the ufficiale Sanitario, the representatives of the women's section and the GIL of Milan; and letter from *podestà* of Milan to *podestàs* of Venetia, Trentino, Emilia Romagna and the other Lombard provinces. No dates but after raids of October 1942.
168 *Il Mattino*, 2 March 1943, 2.
169 *Il Mattino*, 10 December 1942, 2.
170 *Il Mattino*, 14 March 1943, 1.
171 ACS, MI, DGPCSA, b. 104, Head of Alessandria province to Mussolini and to Interior Ministry, 10 May 1944.
172 AN F1/A/3778, GPRF, service courrier, diffusion 16.6.44.
173 Le Crom, 'De la philanthropie', 184–5, 187, 202–3.
174 Mémorial de Caen, FQ72, Secours National, section parisienne, Bilan des Secours aux Sinistrés, 1943–4.
175 Le Crom, 'De la philanthropie', 201–17, 235. The confessionalism of the Secours National was, however, limited by the regime's concern that it should not be viewed as a wholly Catholic organization. Cf. the correspondence between the sub-prefect of Saint-Nazaire and the prefect of Loire-Inférieure, May–July 1943, in AD LA 1690W/146.
176 In Dieppe, the local COSI president was a member of the Légion des Volontaires Français,

who fought on the Eastern front alongside the Germans, and had personally taken German nationality (AD SM 51W/71, sub-prefect of Dieppe, report for January–February 1944).

177 Le Crom, 'De la philanthropie', 227; SHAA 3D/186, *La Montagne*, 5 March 1943; AD SM, *Journal de Rouen*, 27 September 1943.

178 AD Manche 2Z/106, COSI brochure, n.d. (mid-1942).

179 Le Crom, 'De la philanthropie', 224.

180 AD BduR 76W/121, RG Marseille, Information, le 3 juin 1944.

181 Cf. remarks by the Prefect of Bouches-du-Rhône in AM Marseille 29/II/4, Réunion du service de Coordination de la Protection Contre les Événements de Guerre, le samedi 11 décembre 1943. After the Boulogne-Billancourt raid of March 1942, COSI distributed almost as much (nearly FF9 million) as the municipality, the *département*, and the Secours National combined. Cf. L. Dodd, 'Relieving Sorrow and Misfortune? State, Charity, Ideology and Aid in Bombed-out France, 1940–1945', in Baldoli, Knapp and Overy (eds), *Bombing, States and Peoples*, 78.

182 Dodd, 'Relieving Sorrow?', 93; AD Morbihan 1526W/14, RG Morbihan, Vannes, to RG Rennes, 2 October 1943; AD BduR 76W/129, RG Marseille, Information, 2 June 1944.

183 AD Morbihan 1526W/14, RG Morbihan, Vannes, to RG Rennes, 29 October 1943.

184 AM Rennes 6H/23, Mairie de Rennes, 8e bureau, note du 8 April 1943; Ville de Rennes, Secrétaire-Général Adjoint, note to M. Piton, n.d.

185 AM Nantes 4H/107, *La Bretagne*, 19 January 1944.

186 Schmiedel, 'Orchestrated Solidarity', 206–18.

187 The circulars, officially from the Interior Minister but signed in the last three cases by G. Hilaire, the secretary general of the ministry, are dated 26 January and 16 October 1942, and 15 February and 19 May 1943 (AD Rhône 3958W/120).

188 Schmiedel, 'Orchestrated Solidarity', 213–14.

189 S. Kitson, 'Criminals or Liberators? French Public Opinion and the Allied Bombing of France, 1940–1945', in Baldoli, Knapp and Overy (eds), *Bombing, States and Peoples*, 284.

190 ADLA 1690W/128, Col. Le Bris, President of the Breton group of Oflag VIIIF, to regional prefect of Brittany, 5 December 1943; AM Nantes 4H/107, Oflag IVD groupement 'Bretagne' to Regional Prefect of Brittany, 18 November 1943.

191 ADLA 1690W/128, Commissaire Régional de la République à Rennes to Prefect of Loire-Inférieure, 14 May 1945.

192 Cf. the correspondence in AM St-Étienne 5H/79.

193 Cf. D. Süss, 'Wartime Societies and Shelter Politics in National Socialist Germany and Britain', in Baldoli, Knapp and Overy (eds), *Bombing, States and Peoples*, 30.

194 ACS, MI, DPP, b. 211, fasc. 3, informer's report from Milan, 13 February 1941.

195 TNA, FO 371/29918, Sir R. Campbell, Lisbon, to the Foreign office, 9 October 1941.

196 C. Levi, *The Watch* (London: Cassell, 1952), 205–6.

197 P. Calamandrei, *Diario, 1939–1945*, vol. I, 1939–1941, 290, entry for 22 January 1941.

198 FDRPL, Map Room files, Box 72, OSS Bulletins March–Dec 1943, report 43 from Bern office, 30 July 1943.

199 ACS, MI, DGPS, DPP, b. 239, informer's report, Rome, 22 July 1943.

200 Calamandrei, *Diario 1939–1945*, vol. II, 1942–1945, 149–50 (23 July 1943).

201 ACS, MI, DGPS, DPP, b. 210, informer's report, Venice, 16 June 1940; *Il Mattino*, 5 December 1942.

202 A. Milward, *The New Order and the French Economy* (Oxford: Oxford University Press, 1970), 132.

203 AD Morbihan 2W/15935, Note au chef de division, Vannes, 22 February 1943; AD Morbihan 7W/4799, Prefect of Morbihan to Regional Prefect, Rennes, 22 February 1943; AD BduR 76W/187, Département du Var, DDP, Bombardement de Toulon du 24 novembre 1943, 14 December 1943; AN F1/A/3743, GPRF, Commissariat à l'Intérieur, État d'esprit de la population, 5 May/26 May 1944.

204 AM St-Étienne 5H/37, Ville de Saint-Étienne, Défense Passive, Rapport sur la visite au Creusot, 24 July 1943; AD Var, 1W/64, Police Commissioner, Marseille, to Prefect of Var, 27 November 1943.

205 AM Nantes 4H/107, *Le Nouvelliste*, 2–3 October 1943.
206 AM Rennes 6H/25, Mayor Chateau to Regional Delegate for Reconstruction, 16 December 1943; AN F7/14901, Lacombe to Bousquet, 5 August 1943.
207 Boivin, *Les Manchois*, vol. v, 43. Looting by SS troops in Caen is recorded in many written testimonies (Témoignages écrits) at the Mémorial de Caen.
208 AD LA 1694W/61, Prefecture de Police, Communiqué à la Presse: actes de Pillage, 20 September 1943.
209 AM St-Étienne 5H/37, *Le Nouvelliste* (Lyon), 1 June 1944.
210 Cf. for example *La Stampa*, 3 December 1942, 4.
211 G. Gribaudi, 'The True Cause of the "Moral Collapse": People, Fascists and Authorities under the Bombs. Naples and the Countryside, 1940–1944', in Baldoli, Knapp and Overy (eds), *Bombing, States and Peoples*, 233–5.
212 C. Duggan, *The Force of Destiny: a History of Italy since 1796* (London: Allen Lane, 2007), 450–1.
213 E. Gentile, *La via italiana al totalitarismo. Il partito e lo Stato nel regime fascista* (Rome: La Nuova Italian Scientifica, 1995), 186–98.
214 E. Gentile, 'Fascism in power: the totalitarian experiment', in A. Lyttleton ed. *Liberal and Fascist Italy* (Oxford: Oxford University Press, 2002), 171–2. Cf. also S. Colarizi, *La seconda guerra mondiale e la Repubblica* (Turin: UTET, 1984), 62–70.
215 M. Knox, 'Fascism: ideology, foreign policy, and war', in Lyttleton (ed.), *Liberal and Fascist Italy*, 134–5.
216 P. Laborie, *L'opinion française sous Vichy* (Paris: Le Seuil, 1990), 255–70.

7

Societies under the Bombs

'Bombardments', as Sandro Portelli has observed, 'are impersonal; bombed people, however, die *personally*.'[1] This chapter analyses civilians' accounts of what air raids did to them, to their families and their localities, and the opinions they formed of the bombing campaign. Their reactions were complex, changeable, at times contradictory. They were shaped, not only by the raids themselves and the Allied and Vichy and Fascist propaganda spun around them, but also by constantly changing contextual elements – most obviously, attitudes towards the western Allies, the progress of the war, and the concrete experience of German occupation.

As a source for the public's views, opinion polling – in any case in its infancy, and requiring the free expression of opinion – existed in neither regime. But the authorities used very extensive covert means to satisfy their own curiosity about what people thought. In France, the division in the Prime Minister's office responsible for collating such information, the Service des Contrôles Techniques, reported the interception of 2,484,356 letters, 1,717,266 telegrams, and 279,835 telephone calls for the single, average month of February 1944.[2] These intercepts, interpreted with few illusions, were passed to the police intelligence service (the Renseignements Généraux), to the prefects, to the government – and, illicitly, to the Resistance and to the Comité Français de Libération Nationale (CFLN). In Italy, the rebirth of public opinion after 20 years of dictatorship became a major worry for the regime throughout the conflict. Fascist spies operated throughout Italy, in cafés, markets, trains, factories, churches, offices and shops. Those employed by the OVRA, the regime's political police, were particularly reliable as they were specifically required to 'say everything'.[3] In both countries, too, prefects sent their own reports to the interior ministry. While these were more likely to include expressions of confidence in the government, and especially in Pétain or Mussolini, they soon began to emphasize discontent and problems too.

Both French and Italian publics formed opinions of bombing in a complex, difficult context. In France, as Allied raids intensified from 1942, giving civilians steadily more cause to loathe their liberators, they were also given more reasons to detest the Germans and Vichy and desire a speedy liberation: these included Laval's return to power in April 1942 and his expressed desire for a German victory, and Vichy's failure, in November 1942, to defend French North Africa against the Allies or the southern zone from the Germans. The Italians, meanwhile, had to swallow a succession of military defeats and the growing domination of their country by the Germans, which reached a climax under the Salò Republic. In both countries, direct labour conscription for work in Germany, the increasingly violent persecution of Jews and of Resistance suspects, and worsening food shortages, all helped to detach peoples from regimes, discernibly from 1941 and conclusively by 1944.[4] As early as September 1942, intercepts in France were finding that the official media – written and broadcast – were viewed as 'totally in the service of the occupying power', and thus 'very discredited', a state of affairs worsened by the proliferation of 'stupid' songs on the radio. In the spring of 1943, the Contrôles Techniques reported that 'An Anglo-Saxon victory remains the only hope of salvation for the majority' and this outcome was not only desired but increasingly expected.[5] In Italy, the Allies' arrival was similarly looked forward to after the surrender of the Axis in Africa on 13 May.[6]

HORROR AND TRAUMA

Neither the context nor their hopes, however, diminished the horror, for many civilians, of the primary experience of bombing and its aftermath. This appears especially vividly in autobiographical novels in both Italy and France. In *The Skin*, Curzio Malaparte, a former Fascist journalist turned anti-Fascist, described the raid on Naples of 28 April 1943. He entered a cave, but left when it was invaded by a huge, agitated crowd. 'When crowds are fearful, they are dangerous. They will crush us', he told a Neapolitan soldier, just returned from Tobruk. By midnight, he continued, more than 400 bodies and some 100 wounded had been removed from the rubble.[7] Many were still trapped, but only one ambulance arrived. Municipal engineers engaged in rescue work told Malaparte that 'There are only twelve ambulances left in the whole of Naples' and that 'The others have been sent to Rome, where they do not need them. Poor Naples! Two raids a day, and not even ambulances. There are thousands of dead today … what can I do with twelve ambulances?'[8]

Chantal Chawaf's *Je suis née* is the story of a French girl cut from her newly-dead mother's womb during an air raid: her scene-setting exceeds in clarity and ferocity the more conventional narratives of diarists.

> In that month of September 1943, three air raids bloodied Paris and its suburbs, on the 3rd, the 9th, and the 15th, as if the bombs were taking advantage of the summer and the last long well-lit days, the last fine nights, to fracture skulls, to smash in chests, to fill the mouths of women and children with rubble, to rip off arms, to crush bodies under falling walls or collapsing floors, to blow off part of a child's head, or its thorax, to amputate a leg from a corpse, to perforate heads, to tear faces to pieces as they exploded.[9]

In official accounts, by contrast, horror appears more rarely, almost by accident. A good illustration is the dry catalogue of unidentified bodies (in numbered coffins) after the Rennes raid of 8 March 1943:

> 185: Child, 4–5 years old; 190: Well-built woman, naked, brown hair, about 40; 191: Carbonized body of a man, found at l'Économique shop; 196: Well-built elderly woman, carrying a sailor's beret as a keepsake in her corsage; 197: Woman's head, found in rue Plelo; 202: Headless man – brown corduroy trousers, light laced boots; 204: Very well-built man, almost naked, disfigured; 206: Coffin containing human remains found in rue Lucien Decombe.[10]

The medical language of surgeon Jean Perves, writing in Toulon in November 1943, is also suggestive. He noted 'the immense gravity of these wounds, caused by traumatic shock. … the magnitude of the shock in the lesions of lower limbs, and its frequent irreversibility.' Among his patients, 'Several victims arrived dying, their thorax crushed' or suffering from 'cardio-pulmonary lesions caused by blast'. Of those he could not save, he observed, 'Crushing of the thigh and knee – treatment for shock and rapid amputation – died on operating table' or 'Crushing of the right leg and open fracture of the right thigh – intensive treatment for shock – amputation – died one hour later.'[11] In Saint-Étienne six months later, Dr Jérôme Gerest recalled visiting a patient who showed him his wife's headless body, laid out in the bedroom; another who had been driven insane by the destruction of his house and the death and mutilation of his father; and a social worker who had found a young girl alone in the family flat, her mother's severed head carefully folded into her dress.[12]

Contemporary diaries and more recent memoirs (like Dr Gerest's) are also important sources. In his diary entry for 30 October 1942, Florentine anti-Fascist jurist Piero Calamandrei recorded the terror on faces in a Milan shelter six days after the first big raid on the city. The fourteen-year-old son of a lawyer friend from Genoa, he added, had had his hair turned white by the experience of running into a shelter that caught fire.[13] Calamandrei also records the writer Carlo Levi's account of the first major raids on Turin: people were still buried under rubble ten days later, some kept alive by oxygen from rubber tubes pushed through the ruins. A young woman reached Turin from the countryside to find her mother trapped inside her burning home.[14]

Socialist exile and partisan leader Pietro Nenni arrived in Milan a few days after the raid of August 1943. The train halted in the outskirts, at Rogoredo, where the station was full of families waiting for evacuation transport, and he had to continue on foot. Every step towards Milan's centre, he wrote, was 'a grief and a blow':

> In front of my dismayed eyes was an immense ruin. … One could breathe the fire brooding under the rubble. There were no trams working, no telephones. Among the destroyed houses, women, the elderly and children wandered, stupefied. In many blocks of flats they still need to begin work to remove the bodies. There is talk of people who were buried alive and died after having implored vainly for help for days.[15]

Elettra Sarra, an adolescent in Trento during the war, recalled that, despite people's previous mistrust of the shelter, they all ran there in terror when the city was eventually bombed on 2 September 1943:

> I begin to run close to the walls, with the noise of the aircraft and the roaring of the bombs and I arrive in the shelter which is full of people. Some women cry, many pull their smaller children to their breast as they cry, terrified: there are men with terror etched on their faces and others who seek to inspire courage in those who are desperately trying to find their relatives ... We hear the explosions of bombs which make the earth shake, stones and dust penetrate through the cracks in the walls and I fear that this trench we are in will bury us all.[16]

Iole Bresadola, an adolescent at Pontremoli on the north coast of Tuscany, wrote that on the night of 10 May 1944, 'two roaring blows broke the silence of the night as the siren gave a sinister howl'. All of a sudden, windows opened and people shouted and ran out. A mass of people made for the open countryside in a dramatic procession, terrified by the news of entire families buried alive under the ruins of their own homes amid the most atrocious suffering. The nearby town, Aulla, was almost destroyed on 18 May. A commonplace at the time was that whoever bombed or invaded, one side or the other, it would make no difference, 'so long as this slaughter ends'.[17]

The bombing of Treviso, near Venice, on 7 April 1944, hit a city crowded with people from surrounding areas visiting relatives, where schools were closed and churches preparing for Easter celebrations. The air-raid sirens were disregarded by inhabitants, convinced that their town was too small and too lacking in military objectives to be bombed, especially on Good Friday. Bombers had passed overhead before, apparently heading for Milan or Turin.[18] That Good Friday, however, Treviso was the target; 82.2 per cent of the town's buildings were hit, including historic neighbourhoods and several shelters; almost 1,600 civilians were killed. Witnesses described bodies loaded onto carts and covered with newspapers, the smell of bombs, of dust, of exploded drains and burned human beings. People dug among the rubble with their bare hands, shouting and praying to the saints, God and the Madonna. Bodies exploded together with stones of the cobbled streets and fell, lacerated, on the tops of trees, the roofs of houses, and under piles of bricks. The survivors, women, children, young and elderly, silently, as if 'switched off', recomposed what was left of the dead and waited to identify them officially. Others wandered around in the hope of finding relatives alive. One survivor later told of having seen 'a woman with a headless child in her arms, asking everyone if by any chance they had seen a head'.[19] Similar images were reported by survivors of the 4 December 1942 raid on Naples. One of the most common images that remained in the collective memory was that of mutilated, headless bodies still moving.[20]

In Rouen during the 'Red Week' immediately preceding the D-Day landings, victims trapped in a shelter next to a burst main watched powerless as the water rose around them.[21] Raids on Normandy following the landings produced further horrors. In the town of Valognes in the Manche, shocked survivors emerged from houses and shelters to see body parts draped over blasted trees; a visitor to the town's hospital described the faint smell of fresh blood, closely followed by the stench of two-day-old corpses.[22] South of Caen, Charles Massinot observed the remains of a neighbour, Mlle Lequesne, strewn in pieces along the main street of Saint-Martin-de-Fontenay.[23] In a ruined house at Évrecy, Robert Marie discovered David, an acquaintance one year his junior, his face 'a hideous mask, red, blue, black'. A further attack sent Marie rushing for shelter, wondering if he would soon come to resemble David.[24] The young Michèle Oudinet, in childish handwriting and dreadful spelling, gives an account of her family's flight from Caen to the quarries at Fleury, where it stops dead: 'that was where poor Maman was killed'.[25] The Normandy campaign had a terrible postscript, too, in the raids on Le Havre. On 6 September 1944, in the most dramatic episode of a week of bombing that claimed over 2,000 lives, bombs hit the Jenner tunnel, then under construction: of the 326 men, women and children sheltering there, just seven survived; the rest died of asphyxiation before they could be dug out.[26]

One raid could have a devastating effect on a small community. In the village church of Bruz, near Rennes, on 8 May 1944, a group of young people were celebrating their first communion in church when 55 Lancasters of Bomber Command struck. The raid took 183 lives out of a population of 800.[27] One of the best individual accounts of bombing, because of the clarity and variety of its impressions, is that of Charlotte Barbotin, a young Rouennaise born in 1932. Her first raid was delivered by 70 B-17 Flying Fortresses at noon on 28 March 1944:

> ... the window-panes shuddered, the plates and glasses on the table seemed to go mad, afflicted with St Vitus' Dance. With horror, I saw the ceiling break open with a sinister cracking sound. The plaster fell out, covering our heads and shoulders with a fine whitish dust ... I was paralysed, breathless. There was a last, dry sound from my parents' bedroom – it was the chandelier. Two of its three cords had gone – but the third carried its weight, miraculously. ... There was a heavy, almost palpable silence that you could have cut with a knife. My heart was pounding as if to break loose. I could barely believe that the nightmare was growing more distant and that we were still alive. The raid had only taken a few seconds, but it had seemed to last a century, during which all the devils in hell had chosen to meet in our home. 'One day this house is going to be our coffin', muttered my mother in an unsteady voice.[28]

Curiosity later leads her to the Cité des Cheminots, the railwaymen's housing estate close to the tracks in nearby Sotteville, where she learns that the remains of the local baker were now indistinguishable from those of the horse he had used for his rounds; and to a temporary morgue where 'tens upon tens' of dead bodies – men, women and children – were laid out. The family took refuge at the village of Croix-Mare, some 30 kilometres away near Yvetot, but without escaping danger: Barbotin witnessed a Mosquito attack on nearby Motteville station.[29] Back in Rouen in time for the raids of spring 1944, she again visited Sotteville. But 'I no longer recognized it. The whole neighbourhood seemed to have been ploughed up by a drunken titan, or devastated by a hurricane. There was no longer a road, everything had been turned over like a potato patch.' The obliteration of any recognizable landmark left her completely lost, and she had to be led to her father.[30] On the night of 18 April, when 273 Lancasters attacked Sotteville and Rouen, she recalls:

> In my confused thoughts, memories of the exodus [of 1940], of the raid on Rouen when my father had taken every risk to try and find me, the vision of those dozens of bodies laid out at the school turned before my eyes, telescoped in my head. I was aware that I might die at any moment, and this thought, this expectation of a catastrophe was intolerable, inhuman.[31]

Barbotin was both fascinated by the bombs – she started a collection of fragments – and traumatized, inclined to panic at the mere prospect of a raid. Her physical symptoms included jaundice, vomiting and diarrhoea, and she finally took to sleeping in the shelter every night.[32]

War trauma, of course, can resurface unexpectedly decades after the event.[33] A whole generation of French and Italian city-dwellers have carried with them more or less hidden recollections of seeing, hearing, and smelling events of a peculiar and terrible intensity. A striking example, also from the Rouen area, is given by a woman who, in middle age and after an interval of over half a century, heard a B-17 for the first time since her childhood in 1944.

> A few years ago there was an air show at Boos [Rouen airfield] and a B17, a Flying Fortress, turned up. I was weeding the garden, it was a fine June day, I was looking at the weeds not up in the air, and there was the sound of a plane and I suddenly had the impression of a shard of ice in my back. I went back into the house and my son said 'You're all white!' I had goose pimples and I said 'I've just heard a Flying Fortress.' … I live very close to the aerodrome, I hear planes all day long, but that one – well, it made an impression I'm not likely to forget in a hurry.[34]

CIVIL DEFENCE AND NON-COMPLIANCE

Horror might be all the more terrible for being unexpected. Despite the efforts of the authorities, civilians, especially in Italy, were often under-prepared for raids, and disinclined to comply with air-raid precautions.

Widespread disregard for Italy's blackout regulations is recorded throughout the war in prefects' letters, in newspaper articles and interior and air ministry reports. Major raids encouraged compliance; periods of respite undermined it. An informer from Milan noticed disrespect for air-raid precautions from the city's first alert, on 11 June 1940.[35] On 18 June, *Corriere della Sera* discussed the blackout as a curious change in city life to which people would soon get accustomed.[36] By mid-August, however, it observed that the latest RAF raid had still found many Milanese with lights on and windows open because of the summer heat.[37] Non-compliance was widespread in Italy's north and south: in Padua, people believed their town out of range of air raids; in Bari the age-old habit of sociable evenings spent on chairs in the streets continued unperturbed. [38]

The armistice with France in June had relaxed attitudes further. Some Milanese protested that without French airfields, British aircraft could not possibly fly all the way to Milan.[39] Venetians, too, kept their lights on, convinced that the bombing was over. Romans, many of whom had been fined for disregarding the blackout, thought the authorities were sounding the alarm merely to instil discipline. In Grosseto, too, people continued chatting from well-lit windows during alerts. Nor did the Carabinieri or the UNPA intervene very energetically, especially in the countryside. People driving with headlights on country roads outside Florence felt sure of impunity 'since the Carabinieri don't bother'. When Carabinieri in Lazio enforced the rules, under pressure from Rome, people complained of harassment. In Padua, clients and waiters at the famous Pedrocchi Café declared that the forthcoming total blackout was an unwarranted exaggeration: 'they may as well shut all the bars and send us home'.[40]

That summer of 1940 set the pattern for the rest of the war. The Turin Anti-aircraft Protection Committee worriedly told the prefect that the population considered civil defence precautions anachronistic since the war had moved away from the Alps; *La Stampa* admonished readers to 'create a war mentality', without which no victory was possible.[41] In Venice, accidental drownings in darkened canals were seized upon as an excuse not to observe the blackout; the Piedmontese were persuaded that the British were now too busy countering German raids on their country to bomb Italy.[42] Even state institutions were lax. In November 1940, Mussolini in person told the Air Ministry that the blackout was disregarded at Littorio airport; three days later the War ministry reported lights on in ministries in Rome.[43] Reports of non-compliance continued to reach the Interior Ministry from all over Italy.[44] In August 1942, Milanese newspapers announced serious fines for blackout infringements, while in Rome, an informant observed that 'the blackout is a myth'.[45] Remarkably, little improved even under the Salò Republic, despite the regime's greater authoritarianism and the intensity of raids. In December 1944, Turin's provincial civil defence inspector told the police chief that blackout rules would be observed only if infringements were punished with the 'necessary energy'.[46] In January 1945, the German Command in Turin told the province head that the blackout was not fully observed even in public and military buildings.[47] A week later, in Bologna, the Italian and German authorities used the local newspaper to state that any vehicle found with lights on would be requisitioned; citizens 'here and there', the article continued, were still ignoring the blackout.[48]

Though probably less widespread than in Italy, indifference to the blackout in France still provoked three attempts to tackle it by law, in 1941, 1942 and 1944, with increasingly heavy 'taxed warnings', or on-the-spot fines.[49] This did not stop German complaints. The mayor of Rennes was told his city's blackout was 'the worst in all Brittany'; the prefect of Morbihan passed on German remarks to his police superintendents in September 1942; the prefect of the Rhône and the DDP in Lyon received three admonitions in 1943, the last stating that the population had been warned 'for the last time'; Laval relayed German dissatisfaction to prefects in September 1943.[50] As in Italy, neither occupying forces nor Vichy authorities set an example. The mayor of Rennes reported the non-observance of blackout by German troops to his *Kreiskommandant* in 1942; the Germans observed that government buildings in Vichy itself were constant offenders, especially the Foreign Ministry, with its habit of well-lit balls.[51] As late as June 1944 – after that spring's murderous raids – 35 inhabitants of Saint-Étienne were fined for breaking blackout regulations.[52]

Indifference to the blackout carried over into poor shelter discipline. The public's attitude to shelters, however, was complex. There might, especially in Italy, simply be too few shelters; or else those that there were might be mistrusted as uncomfortable or dangerous. Attitudes also changed over time, too. In Italy, fear at alerts made for good shelter discipline early in the war. However, after the first raids – which led to few casualties in fewer cities – expectations of an early end to hostilities diminished civil defence concerns. In August and September 1940 informers across northern Italy noted a new expression, 'white alarms', to reflect the rarity with which raids followed alerts.[53] People began to take shelter again when raids restarted and intensified, but now complained to the authorities about their safety.

The inadequacy of shelters worried civilians even in June 1940. In Cagliari, for example, where alarms sounded 3–4 times a day, people did not know where to go, particularly in the port area.[54] In Milan, people did not trust the cellars of apartment blocks, which they feared would turn into traps if the buildings were hit. Afraid of raids, therefore, people also criticized attempts to make sheltering compulsory under such dangerous conditions.[55] Landlords, moreover, often refused to reinforce cellars.[56] As winter approached, a further worry was damp, cold, and the consequent risk of illness. In Rome that November many people considered pneumonia a greater danger than bombs. [57] At Sesto San Giovanni in Milan, an informer reported that only a third of the population headed for the shelters at night alerts; most – even *capi fabbricato* – waited to hear the anti-aircraft guns before leaving their beds. The poor condition of shelters, the lack of improvements by landlords, and the risk of disease were all cited as reasons – although Sesto's surrounding factories were obvious targets.[58] In January 1941, people in the Turin shelters were angrier at the landlords than at the British, and coined the term *cantinite* ('cellar-itis') for pulmonary diseases.[59]

Concerns about the soundness of cellars were sometimes well-founded. In Naples, the raid of 22 October 1941 destroyed a three-storey block, killing 17 of its inhabitants and wounding the others. All had remained in bed – but the civil protection inspector concluded that as the building had collapsed right down to the cellar, only a proper public shelter nearby could have saved them – but none existed. Noting that the Neapolitans were calm and disciplined, he added that behaviour might change if morale were allowed to fall. Safe shelters, he concluded, were necessary to ensure it did not.[60]

Then, in autumn 1942, came the area raids on Italy's northern cities. These clearly damaged morale as the British intended, and did nothing to increase trust in shelters. In unbombed cities, the raids were seen as proof that the regime had not provided adequate shelters. In Padua on 28 October 1942, people discussed how civilians in Milan and Turin had died in shelters, and exaggerated the death toll, claiming there were more than 1,000; a general comment was: 'I will no longer go to the shelter.' Many believed that bombproof shelters had been provided in Britain and Germany, but left to chance in Italy, reinforcing the conclusion that 'We should have not gone to war because we were not ready and never would be.'[61] The Milanese certainly used shelters when the alarms sounded, but protested to authorities and landlords alike about their poor equipment, and claimed that sirens were often sounded merely 'to keep the anti-aircraft crews awake'.[62] In Genoa, an informer observed that long nights spent in shelters and tunnels lowered morale.[63] At the other end of Italy, meanwhile, people in Bari were terrified that heavy raids like those in Genoa, if visited on them, would destroy their inadequate shelters.[64]

Perhaps the clearest illustration of inadequate shelter systems came when people died, not from bombing, but from overcrowding and suffocation. This killed 354 people in Genoa's Le Grazie tunnel in October 1942 and 286 at the Porta San Gennaro shelter in the heart of Naples the following 4 December.[65] Moreover, the condition of shelters also deteriorated as raids intensified. On the coast of Liguria, frequently bombed because of its railway line, civilians had fled their towns by spring 1944 and lived most of the time in railway tunnels.[66] Elettra Sarra from Trento found that her nearest shelter had no ventilation and that any nearby bomb would have blown the walls out. The family concluded that the only chance for Trento's inhabitants 'would be if the Allied bombers forgot about our city'.[67] Sarra's view of the shelter was confirmed in January 1945 by the municipal health officer, who warned the Prefect that Trento's public shelters risked becoming dangerously unsanitary:

> They are no longer places to stop for two or three hours a day as those who projected and constructed them perhaps originally thought, but had been transformed … into primitive permanent dwellings, unhealthy, infested by parasites, where people, especially from the lower strata of the population, camp out, spend the night on dirty couches of sorts in shameful promiscuity, in the darkness, humidity and cold.[68]

Official concerns reached higher than local health officers. In January 1943, Buffarini, Undersecretary at the Interior Ministry, told the Prefect of Turin that the population was furious that a month after the heavy raids nothing had been done to improve shelter provision. Two days earlier, in a hurried note to prefects, he had urged: 'Keyword: build shelters.'[69] Public confidence in shelters was badly damaged. Giornando Barbari, an adolescent who worked in Bologna during the war, recorded in his diary that, obeying his father's advice, he never used the shelter in a raid as he feared dying 'like a mouse'. The best plan, he believed, was to run to the fields.[70] In Palermo, the prefect reported that the lack of safe shelters, and of materials and workers to build new ones, meant that by April 1943 the inhabitants were losing their will to resist – precisely the aim of the Allies.[71]

While non-compliance was less widespread in France, army reports could still make withering comments on civilian behaviour in raids. 'One can say that nine times out of ten, the victims of an air raid are victims above all of their own ignorance, their own panic, their own indiscipline', reads one account on Toulon.[72] The report on Marseille referred to 'the insouciant character of the Marseillais population, which did not believe in the eventuality of an air attack, and accepted passive defence measures apparently with no enthusiasm', stressing that 'passive defence is above all a question of instruction and propaganda, and these two elements were, unfortunately, totally missing during the years preceding the war'.[73]

This verdict echoes Sérant's earlier complaint, as Passive Defence Director, at the French public's general ignorance of air-raid precautions, as well as two reports before the attack of November 1943 on Toulon: one from the commandant of the Italian occupying forces, who observed that the Toulonnais were 'in no condition to adopt the slightest civil defence measure', another from the police berating the population's 'total incomprehension' of passive defence following an exercise.[74]

Such insouciance had tragic results. The overflight of scores of bombers inspired curiosity and awe, but rarely fear, until the bombs started falling. 'No-one seemed to worry', recalled one witness of the Nantes raid of 16 September 1943, who had been on a stationary train when the aircraft arrived; 'on the contrary, everyone went to the window to see them better. There were so many of them, and so high, just like little points of light.'[75] Paul Caillaud, former head of passive defence in Nantes, recalled a woman who, urged to take shelter, replied that she had her umbrella.[76] In Biarritz, an estimated four-fifths of the casualties were people who had stayed outside to look.[77] In Marseille, the streets were still crowded half an hour after the sirens sounded on 27 May 1944.[78] In Condé-sur-Noireau, on the evening of 5 June 1944, Dr Laisney, one of the town's four doctors, had admired, from the comfort of a barber's chair, a squadron of B-17s flying south-west towards nearby Flers; he returned home to find his house destroyed, his pregnant wife and young son dead, their servant mortally wounded.[79]

Even under attack, people might linger at the doors of shelters, endangering themselves and everyone else,[80] or shelter only with the first bombs, and emerge after ten minutes without waiting for the all clear.[81] In Lyon, the *Journal de Genève* reported that 'the population is still incredibly daring; during the raid [of 26 May 1944, which caused over 700 deaths], hundreds of people followed operations with field-glasses'.[82] Sometimes, it is true, there were extenuating circumstances. No warning was given of the first raid on Rennes. Both Nantes and Toulon, on the other hand, had had so many false alarms that the one 'real' one was disregarded; and in Toulon, it was lunchtime.[83] But the clearest demonstration that behaviour had affected casualty levels is the comparison between first major raids and later ones. In Nantes, nearly half the total civilian deaths of the war – 850 out of 1,732 – resulted from the first big raid, on 16 September 1943. The evening raid on 23 September cost 150 dead; *no* other single raid caused even 100 fatalities. Over half of all bombs dropped on Nantes fell in 1944, a year which accounted for just 11 per cent of the deaths and 8.5 per cent of the injuries.[84] Toulon suffered nine raids, and some 640 deaths, between 24 November 1943 and 7 August 1944; the first of them alone killed 450.[85] In Marseille, the raid of 27 May 1944 claimed 1,831 lives; that of 14 August, just 34.[86] While more accurate bombing and better passive defence measures may have contributed, the consistency of the pattern, as well as contemporary assessments, indicate public behaviour as the prime reason. As the report on the second Toulon raid observed, 'The population takes shelter at each alert, whereas before 24 November, they were happy to look up in the air.'[87] Conversely, towns with early and regular experience of bombing, such as the Channel ports or Brest, were likely to use shelters more. If Le Havre, bombed over 130 times since 1940, suffered over 2,000 deaths during the final raids of September 1944, it was less the result of poor shelter discipline than of the devastating impact of 9,790 tons of bombs in a single week.

Often reluctant, until taught by terrible example, to use shelters, French city-dwellers were also, on occasion, susceptible to panic. The exodus from Nantes on 23 September is the outstanding, but not the only, example. In the northern mining and rail town of Somain, which had already attracted several raids, panic broke out after the attack of 5 May 1944, and 4,000 people out of a population of 10,000 left spontaneously.[88] In recently bombed localities as varied as Rouen, Saint-Étienne, or Toulon, an alert could provoke, not an orderly descent into shelters, but a rush to supposedly safe areas – higher ground or woods; at La Seyne near Toulon, the sound of a car backfiring at a funeral provoked the same result.[89] La Seyne also saw France's worst shelter crush, when a combination of overcrowding, shortage of air, and rumours of rising water levels caused a stampede, killing 75 people.[90]

Non-compliance with defence regulations, particularly in the first years of the war, should not be construed as resisting the war effort, let alone as an expression of pacifism or anti-Fascism. Rather, it arose from confusion and from the difficulties of adapting society to the dynamics of war, of integrating complicated new rules into a daily life already subject to numerous unaccustomed stresses. Yet there was also a political dimension to non-compliance:

it suggested lack of co-operation with and trust in the state. This was noted with some alarm by the government, especially in Italy. Another area in which people's feelings and behaviour concerned the authorities in both countries was their attitude towards the bombers.

WAITING FOR THE BOMBERS, WAITING FOR THE LIBERATORS

In both France and Italy the Allies enjoyed substantial public support, in Italy from 1943, in France from 1940. 'All hopes', said Vichy's summary of intercepted correspondence for late October, 'rest on England.'[91] Britain's success in resisting invasion was much admired and the BBC much listened to, its propaganda seen as 'very effective'.[92] The German presence, marked as early as September 1940 by 'requisitions, looting, occupations of apartments, and expulsions', was increasingly detested.[93] Anglophilia persisted despite Mers-el-Kébir, despite claims that the RAF had deserted France's armies in May 1940, and despite the Vichy government's best efforts to exploit both episodes. In Italy a broadly comparable state of mind had developed by 1943. In Rome, the British Fascist James Strachey Barnes could observe that many Italians were ready to welcome the Allies and even to blame the bombs on the Germans.[94] Allied propaganda about Italy being controlled by Germany, and portrayals of Mussolini and the Italian authorities as servants of Hitler, played on widespread anti-German sentiment, reported by prefects and informers across Italy from before June 1940 until the war's end.[95] Under the Salò Republic, with the regime's dependence on Germany even clearer, civilians absorbed more themes from Allied propaganda. Letters to the province head of Genoa, for example, asked if it was true that he needed German permission to sound the alarm. Everyone believed that the Germans 'could not care less' about alarms, which only sounded when bombs were already falling. One letter concluded that 'Radio Londra is just telling the truth ... when they say that we are not allied with, but servants of the Germans.'[96]

However, opinions of the Allies and bombing changed as the war, and the bombing campaign, progressed. While in Italy contradictory views on bombing continued to be expressed throughout the campaign, in France it is possible to distinguish three clear phases, moving from support to fierce anger at the bombers.

Come, friendly bombs: France 1940–2

The limited British raids on France early in the war were widely tolerated, even welcomed. The (probably accidental) raid on Marseille of December 1940 received favourable comment – or else was blamed on the Italians.[97] 'RAF blue' became a fashionable colour for women, a manifestation of defiance and a link with an air force that held out a chance, however remote, of deliverance.

Women wrote to the BBC (which the French could, via neutral countries) positively requesting a 'visit' from Bomber Command.[98]

The Boulogne-Billancourt raid of 3/4 March 1942 – 'a massive, continuous, bombardment, the first real one we have had' in the words of the diarist Jean Guéhenno – changed little. In Place des Fêtes, on high ground on the east of Paris, Guéhenno found that 'No-one was angry. Most had trouble hiding their jubilation.' The Germans were blamed for not sounding the alert. [99] From Montmartre, much closer to the bombs, Berthe Auroy noticed spectators applauding from their windows; it was an open secret that Renault worked for the Germans, who were rumoured to have kept workers at their posts at gunpoint.[100] Jean Grenier noted that the Paris electricity supply suddenly improved once the energy-greedy Renault plant was down, and that Vichy propaganda, accustomed to minimizing the impact of raids on Germany, was suddenly claiming huge losses in this first big raid on France.[101] Vichy's propaganda posters calling the British cowards were compared with the Germans' shooting of hostages outside Paris the same week.[102]

Official records broadly confirm these testimonies. The weekly Paris prefecture report (leaked to the Free French) observed that shock at the damage and the number of victims soon lost ground to the view that the target was legitimate and the raid a promise of liberation. The Germans were condemned for tardy air-raid precautions – but also for placing anti-aircraft guns close to factories, a step viewed as increasing the danger to them. Workers in arms factories feared further raids, and being deported to work in Germany, but were more resigned than indignant. From the southern zone, British explanations following the raid were reported to have turned initial indignation into acceptance or even support: 'the French do not like the British, but still favour them because of their hatred for the Germans'.[103] In the weeks and months after 4 March, a spate of letters to the BBC requested British leaflets, more British raids (new targets were suggested even in the free zone), British arms, and British landings. Such letter-writers were certainly a small minority, but the British propaganda ascendancy was solid and nationwide.[104] As prefect René Bouffet reported from Seine-Inférieure, 'Despite the tragic result of this raid, the British still benefit from an extreme indulgence from part of the population.'[105] Eden's view of raids as positive propaganda for the Allied cause seemed justified by events.[106] Even among prisoners of war, susceptible to Vichy propaganda, there was dissent from the official view: officers' camps (Oflags) might be vigorously anti-British, but the other ranks in the harsher regime of the Stalags were strongly anti-German and resented pressure to make donations for the victims of bombing.[107]

From support to malaise: France 1943

Within a year French civilians' support or toleration of bombing would be seriously tested. Raids intensified. The Americans, from their first sorties in August 1942, were seen as more careless of civilian life than the British. Allied victories in North Africa and Sicily, and (especially) at Stalingrad, meant that air power no longer offered the sole means to Allied victory. For the first time, the Free French made representations to the Allies about the damage they were doing to their own cause.[108]

The Lorient and Saint-Nazaire raids early in 1943, though heavy, provoked relatively little reaction. Less publicized than attacks on larger cities with less obvious targets, they occurred just as Vichy imposed the *Impôt-métal,* a household levy of non-ferrous metals, and above all the Service du Travail Obligatoire (STO). As Prefect Marage wrote in March 1943, opinion in the Morbihan *département*, though shaken by the Lorient raids, had been turned wholly against the government by the STO, and against the Germans by requisitioning.[109] Later reports stated that the Morbihan was in a state of 'latent insurrection' against the government.[110] Public opinion was more affected by the raid on Rennes on 8 March, well publicized in newsreels and the press, and above all the American daytime raid on Boulogne-Billancourt on Sunday 4 April 1943. Some American bombs hit Paris; many fell north of the target on Longchamp racecourse, during the season's first race meeting. SIPEG reported 344 lives lost.[111] Bouffet, now prefect of the Seine *département*, which included the capital, observed that the Americans' apparent indifference to civilian casualties, and the deaths of Parisians on Parisian territory, meant that while some people excused the attack, very few openly rejoiced in it as they had 13 months earlier.[112] A report for the Free French, meanwhile, said that the month's raids on the suburbs had 'sent a chill' through the Parisian public.[113]

But French opinion still did not turn against the bombing. Everyone knew why Renault was the target in April. The Germans were blamed for putting an anti-aircraft battery at the racecourse, the French authorities for allowing the races to resume. Communist support for raids remained solid. In Seine-Inférieure, prefect Pujes thought anti-Allied feeling strong but quick to dissipate.[114] The postal censors noted increasingly hostile reactions to raids, but found the population more worried by the STO, adding that 'An Anglo-Saxon victory remains the only hope of salvation for the majority.'[115] These hopes were reinforced by Allied successes in the Mediterranean – victory in North Africa, the fall of Mussolini, the Italian armistice. These moderated indignation at the summer's raids on the Le Creusot works, Villacoublay aerodrome, or industrial targets at Sochaux and Besançon: 'the bombs are feared', wrote the censors, 'but accepted with resignation as one of the painful conditions of "Liberation"'.[116] One source claimed that when local fascist groups – RNP and Francistes – offered assistance after attacks on Aulnay-sous-Bois and Drancy, near Paris, the local population treated them as 'bastards'.[117] Nantes, meanwhile, was described as 'more and more pro-British' by a CFLN correspondent; prefect Édouard Bonnefoy reported food shortages there, hostility to the government, and a general expectation of an early Allied victory.[118] Bouffet, similarly, reported early in September that the Parisians' main concern was food.[119] While little enthusiasm for raids remained by summer 1943, anger was balanced by hopes of early deliverance, ensuring a conditional acceptance of bombing.

That equation was upset by the raids of September 1943, especially those on the Paris suburbs (three times), Le Portel and Nantes. Paris, though it suffered little in comparison to many provincial cities, was hit harder than before, including in its smart western quarters.[120] The attacks on Le Portel and Nantes stood out for their destructiveness (Le Portel was annihilated, much of the centre of Nantes wrecked), their heavy loss of life (500 deaths in Le Portel, 1,400 in Nantes) and their apparent futility: Le Portel was destroyed as part of a decoy operation (codenamed Starkey), while the bombing of Nantes lacked any obvious focus on the city's industry. These raids, moreover, were followed by the first serious attacks in the south, hitting Modane, on the Italian frontier, from September; Annecy, Cannes-La Bocca, and above all Toulon in November; and Marseille, albeit on a small scale, in December, before another raid on the Paris area on New Year's Eve, which claimed 263 victims.

For these reasons, the raids of September 1943 appear as a turning point. As Bouffet observed, the raids on the Paris area of 3, 9 and 15 September damaged people's sense of security.[121] In the southern zone, Naples was cited in letters as an example of what could happen to France.[122] The cumulative effect of raids made public anger more widespread and more durable. A CFLN report observed in October that while most people had accepted bombing as a 'necessary evil' in springtime, 'Now the proportion has been reversed. Few people now accept the raids without making a few more or less barbed, critical remarks.' With so many apparently ineffective raids, the view that 'they're all the same, and none of them cares what happens to us' had gained wide acceptance.[123]

A new bitterness, too, entered comments on the bombing. In the southern zone late in September, the Allies were accused of dropping bombs at random, of going for easy French targets not tougher German ones, and of trying to wreck French industry to please the City of London – the latter a constant theme of Vichy propaganda that reappeared, enlarged to include the Americans, at the year's end.[124] In Nice, correspondents wrote that '"Liberators" is now synonymous with "murderers"', and that the Allies meant to 'afflict the population with famine as the basis for a revolution', to 'suppress French competition after the war', or to 'destroy a nation that they envy'.[125] In Nantes, the Renseignements Généraux even reported people calling for arms to defend the city against an Allied landing.[126] Resentment at the Nantes raids, moreover, had barely subsided when the attacks on the south started.[127] It was in this promising context that Philippe Henriot toured the south making speeches on the theme of 'Gentlemen, your "liberators"'.[128]

More general confidence in the western Allies diminished after the summer's optimism. According to Free French correspondents, the BBC, though still widely listened to, was accused of claiming successful, precise raids, without acknowledging that bombs sometimes missed their targets and killed civilians.[129] No longer could the anticipation of an early Allied victory sweeten the pill of bombing, as in the summer, for the Italian campaign was swiftly bogged down, likened to a race between snails and slugs. Only the USSR escaped public disillusionment with the Allies, as the Red Army advanced briskly westward. Even in conservative circles, wrote prefect Bonnefoy, even among Finance Ministry officials, said CFLN sources, few feared Communism.[130] Neither the Vichy regime nor the Germans, however, drew any benefits from disappointment with the western Allies. Bouffet, now France's most senior territorial prefect, reported 'widespread discontent' with the government in September. According to reports from Toulon in November, bombing had turned people against the Allies but Germanophobia remained undiminished and no confidence existed in the French leadership.[131]

The French in late 1943, then, could still support raids that were successful and economical of lives, but were sickened by the many that appeared to be neither, eager for liberation yet tired of waiting for it. But some 80 per cent of the air raids on France, and 70 per cent of civilian deaths, were still to come.

The breaking point: France and the Transportation Plan

The neutral and Allied press noticed the continuing shift of opinion. Eight days before D-Day the *Manchester Guardian* ran a headline: 'France and the Allies: A Critical Mood'.[132] Bombing, and especially the nearly 64,000 tons dropped on Transportation Plan targets between March and June,[133] was central to this development. 'Many people', Bouffet reported on 5 June, 'who up until the last few weeks had excused the raids, invoking military necessity, now strongly condemn them.'[134] Both the CFLN and the Vichy authorities attempted statistical analyses of developments in opinion. A CFLN report, based on information gathered early in 1944, claimed – but through no clear methodology – to represent the opinions of over 1.5 million people, and found an overwhelming majority (99.2 per cent) expecting an Allied victory. Air raids, however, were fully approved by just 22.5 per cent of the 'sample', opposed by 8.7 per cent – and approved with reservations by 68.8 per cent.[135] More revealing are the monthly rankings by Vichy's postal censors of the preoccupations of those French who wrote letters or telegrams or made telephone calls. Air raids ranked seventh in January and eighth in February – but third in April and first in May and June, before falling back to third again in July. Although many letters made no judgement on the raids, those that did were overwhelmingly negative. In January, 10,779 correspondents disapproved of the bombing against 852 who found excuses for it; by June, while 'neutral' references were in the majority, at 156,490, negative views outnumbered positive ones by 96,443 to 2,811. Of course, letter-writers' views were not necessarily representative, and they would have known that their correspondence might be opened. But self-censorship had its limits: letters did include numerous hostile references to the Germans, and expectations of an Allied victory. Less than perfectly reliable, then, the censors' summaries remain a key indicator of French opinion.[136]

Some of the commentaries selected by the censors simply indicate despair: 'I've had enough', said a resident of Amiens in June; 'Start roaming the highways of France again? I'd rather croak here', wrote one Marseillais.[137] Other quotations, especially in the southern zone, stand out for their violence. 'It is not enough to have planes and kill women and old people to win the war', and 'let those monsters land and let us shove them into the sea for once and for all', wrote two Niçois in April.[138] 'Everyone is revolted and curses the British'; and 'What bastards with their delayed-action bombs' were among comments noted in May.[139] A Marseillais in June called the Allies 'pretty poor airmen but splendid murderers'.[140] In Saint-Étienne, a correspondent in April – *before* the city had been bombed – said that he 'looked forward to the Germans' reprisals'; a letter in June rejoiced that the V1 offensive against London would 'teach the English what an air raid is really like'.[141] Other sources confirmed these views. The Renseignements Généraux claimed that after major raids Rouennais besieged the *impôt-métal* offices, eager to surrender their copper as a gesture of defiance against the Allies.[142] A CFLN correspondent in the Var reported that the Allies were considered to have no decent airmen, and that 'in every *milieu* they are given names – murderers, vandals, jailbirds from Sing-Sing, niggers' – a reproach directed at Americans more than at the 'civilized' British.[143] But the overall downturn in the Allies' standing was undeniable.

Anger also reflected disappointment when no landings followed the raids. By February 1944, a CFLN correspondent found the public disillusioned with promises of liberation; raids no longer portended an imminent landing, merely death and ruin.[144] From Rouen, Prefect Guérin of Seine-Inférieure noted that the French both feared and hoped for a landing, wishing that it would hasten the war's end.[145]

If neither the Germans (whose presence was considered the main cause of the raids) nor the regime benefited directly from disillusion with the Western allies, Vichy propaganda themes still found their way into mainstream public opinion, notably through Henriot's broadcasts. As Galtier-Boissière wrote on 5 May 1944:

> It is useless to deny the evidence. Philippe Henriot's propaganda is having a considerable effect on all those unfortunates who have suffered from the air raids. His warm, resonant voice, his impeccable diction, and the insidious skill of his arguments have reached many ordinary French people.[146]

The CFLN's reports, though more sceptical, conceded that Henriot's broadcasts had attracted listeners in unprecedented numbers, that the bombing campaign offered him excellent opportunities, and that he was capable, at least, of swaying waverers Vichy's way.[147] Probably the most successful of his claims concerned the economic motivations for the bombing.[148] CFLN reports included claims that the Americans were prolonging the war for economic reasons, that the Allies aimed to destroy France's industry and port infrastructure for their own post-war purposes, and that they were happy for French workers to be reduced to misery as this would make them less militant.[149] Suspicion of 'Anglo-Saxon' capitalism, common across the French political spectrum, added to the credibility of such reports. As Henriot was listened to more, there were also signs of scepticism about Allied propaganda. A further report from May 1944 indicated that listeners had stopped believing in any landings and positively 'resented' BBC broadcasts, especially the songs of the comedian Pierre Dac.[150] Allied propaganda for home consumption probably produced the worst effects, as when the *Daily Mail* of 21 April 1944 cheerfully announced 'Another 600 tons of bombs on France', or the *Illustrated London News* gloried in the destruction of the Creil marshalling yard a month later. When such reports reached the French, their treatment of France as a target equivalent to Germany was particularly disliked.[151]

Perhaps the most spectacular development in 1944 was the effect of air raids on those favourable to the Allied cause. One reaction was astonishment. 'Who would have thought that Montmartre would be bombed?', wrote Bernadette Auroy on 21 April.[152] With surprise went perplexity. Madeleine Raillon, a student living in the (unbombed) Latin Quarter, in a building equipped with a serviceable cellar, wrote after the same raid on La Chapelle:

> I didn't know what to think. I couldn't tolerate the Germans, but today it was the Anglo-Americans that I detested. Their planes sprinkled their target from very high and spread their engines of death across the periphery over several kilometres.[153]

Among the Allies, the Americans were most resented on the ground that their raids, conducted from altitudes of 6,000–7,000 metres, were the most indiscriminate, and effectively treated French targets like German ones. 'In general', said one report, 'the population consider American raids more deadly for the French, and less effective, than those of the RAF.'[154] The RAF could, on occasion, command respect for accurate bombing, and the raid by Free French forces on the Chevilly power plant, on 3 October 1943, was viewed as altogether superior.[155]

The Transportation Plan, therefore, achieved much of the negative impact on French opinion that Britain's War Cabinet had feared. It alienated many ordinary French civilians and shook the convictions of the Allies' committed supporters. Less certain, however, was whether this effect would be overcome by the Allied landings and liberation.

Italians and the guilt factor

The Fascist regime had prepared the Italians for war for almost two decades. By the time Italians suffered major Allied raids, the country had for years been an aggressor state, and had perpetrated crimes against civilians, including summary executions and reprisals, burning of villages, deportations and bombing, from the 'pacification' of Libya to the invasion of Ethiopia, Albania, Greece and parts of Yugoslavia. Until 1943, Italy fought the same war as Nazi Germany. The first defeats and the realization of the country's unpreparedness for war provoked criticisms of the regime and the German alliance; by January 1941, with the loss of Cyrenaica, people in the 'critical part of Italy' (the industrial north) questioned Mussolini's personal responsibility.[156] Allied messages using memories of the First World War to remind Italians of their 'eternal [German] enemy' had an early impact. But it was from autumn 1942 that civilians began to detach themselves from the Fascist war, to become receptive to Anglo-American arguments. The Allies now sought, with some effect, to persuade the Italians of their guilt for supporting Fascism.

Civilians thus began to think that the Allies would treat them according to their attitudes toward the regime and the Germans – that they might warn anti-Fascist populations before raids, but punish pro-Fascist cities with bombs. Giacomo Guglielminetti, aged 14 during the raid of 18 November 1942 on Turin, recalled Radio Londra promising a short respite to allow 'the Turin population, whose aversion to the regime was known, to abandon the city'.[157] Conversely, a woman from South Tyrol, where friendly demonstrations had greeted German troops on 4 September 1943, recorded in her diary Radio Londra's threat to 'bomb again to punish the inhabitants of Bolzano for all the flowers and apples that South Tyrolese women offered the German invaders'.[158] Attitudes towards the Germans were closely monitored by the Italian authorities. Complaints of public hostility, for example by a German soldier in the *Flakregiment* at Cornaredo near Milan in June 1942, were taken seriously, especially as the German pointed out that he was only there to 'defend the population from British air attacks'. But hostility was so widespread, extending in this case to the local priest, that the *podestà* could do little in response.[159]

One effective Allied claim was that by sending Italian aircraft to bomb southern England, Mussolini had provoked an inevitable retaliation. Fascist informers noted this argument both in working-class areas of bombed cities, such as Sesto San Giovanni in Milan, and in cities as yet untouched, like Bologna, where a local priest had delivered a sermon approving Allied retaliatory raids.[160] Civilians responded to the area raids on La Spezia in February 1943 with the resigned view that 'we too have now had our ration'.[161] Giacomo Retico, a writer from Brescia province, recalled that during a journey through the Lunigiana countryside with other children and the village priest, the priest had declared that 'we Italians are being paid back for what we did to England in the summer of 1940'.[162]

Similar feelings appeared at the other end of Italy. A handbook prepared for British soldiers before their 1943 Sicilian landing conceded that air raids had destroyed much pro-Allied feeling in Sicily, but added that Sicilians had a long-standing dislike of the Germans, which 'crystallized' when Luftwaffe personnel arrived on the island.[163] An example of the complex relationship between Sicilians and the Allies is provided by Caltagirone, a western coastal town where the Allies landed on 9 July. The heavy daytime raid preceding the landing was unexpected, as people believed that the town's anti-Fascism – its most famous son was the anti-Fascist exile Don Luigi Sturzo – would save it from raids. When the Allies appeared, many of the 300 civilians killed lay unburied and unidentified. Yet they were welcomed without resentment. A local priest remembered that 'the most logical thing to do was to applaud the arrival of the soldiers'. Greeted by an exhausted population, the Allies 'were not welcomed as liberators from the Fascist dictatorship ... but as bearers of peace'.[164]

Although Allied correspondence and reports state that most of the population welcomed them as liberators,[165] civilians' feelings were often more confused. Grazia Pagliaro, a young woman in Palermo, explained in her diary that while the Anglo-Americans claimed to be the enemies of Fascism, not of Italians, 'this does not change the fact that what is happening is terribly humiliating and keeps the memory and pain of the disasters even more alive'.[166] In southern Lazio, towns appeared to attract the bombers whether or not they contained military or communications targets. Some raids seemed entirely gratuitous, but research indicates widespread acceptance of Allied mistakes in the collective memory. At St Ambrogio sul Garigliano, a bomb hit a shelter on 2 December 1943, killing 42 people, and German soldiers helped extract the bodies and carry them to church. Even in cases like this, there was rarely any clear accusation against the Allies.[167]

The combination of anticipation and resentment of the Allies, noted among the French, also applied to Rome. Gloria Chilanti, an adolescent member of the Roman Resistance, anticipated 'happy days' after the Allies occupied Aprilia and Littoria in January 1944.[168] Corrado Di Pompeo, who worked for the Corporations Ministry in Rome, also regarded bombing as the prelude to liberation, writing in February 1944 that 'Every time American aircraft cross the sky my heart rejoices.' This was not, he specified, because he preferred the Allies to the Germans 'but because I wish everything would end'. Soon, however, he was berating the Allies for killing civilians not Germans, especially after helping with rescue work following a raid on 14 March. That evening he wrote of seeing maimed bodies, of arms and legs among the rubble, of a young child's body covered in blood, and wondered 'what do the British and Americans want from us, when they know that the majority is on their side?' Eleven days later, he observed that 'the Americans ... are only able to destroy and to kill unarmed people'.[169]

Like the French, Italians differentiated between American and British bombing – but with a north-south divide. In southern Italy the British were associated with long nights in shelters and with a sort of gentlemanly bombing, while the Americans, who arrived swiftly during the day, were blamed by Neapolitans for carpet bombing.[170] In the north this perception was inverted. Into 1943 at least, the idea persisted that the 'Americans hit roads, bridges, railways, especially factories', while the British, responsible for the autumn 1942 area raids, 'dropped bombs like rain, with no discrimination and causing many deaths among unarmed citizens'.[171]

In northern Italy the longer wait for liberation, and the relentless bombing, sharpened both anticipation and resentment. In August 1944 an informer in Genoa wrote 'even those who were not pro-British (a minority) are now waiting for the British' because they longed for the agony to end – although the latest raid on Genoa 'had all the characteristics of terrorism' and people had 'discussed the probability of falling from the frying-pan into the fire'. Crucially, however, all this was blamed on the Fascists for taking Italy to war unprepared.[172] The Germans, too, were viewed with more hostility and anxiety than the Allies. Giorgina Scatassa's family had had to abandon Anzio at the Germans' behest at the end of September 1943. Although she correctly ascribed the October raids to the Allies, in 1944 she blamed raids between the countryside of Lazio and Naples on the Germans.[173]

Negative events tended to be blamed on the Axis, allowing Allied responsibility to be expunged from memories, or even sometimes from immediate perception. The bombing of the Gorla quarter of Milan in October 1944, which killed 200 schoolchildren, was attributed in the neighbourhood to 'the Anglo-Americans' or else the British, when in fact it was a USAAF raid; elsewhere in Milan, however, the Allies escaped all responsibility for the raid for years because they were 'represented as "liberators"'. It became more 'politically correct' to remember other slaughters of Italian civilians undertaken by the Nazi-Fascists.[174]

The Church too, even when it locally accused the bombers of barbarism, stopped specifying who they were by 1944. A diocesan letter from the archbishops and bishops of Piedmont at Easter 1944, for example, expressed outrage at the 'savage air attacks ... which ruin the most populated cities, slaughter unarmed populations, destroy centuries-old monuments which had enjoyed the world's admiration'. Even Rome, centre of the Catholic world, had been 'violated in cold blood just as during the most execrable barbarian invasions'. These new barbarians, however, were not named.[175]

Italy and the 'collapse of morale'

Before September 1943, the Allies explicitly aimed to provoke a collapse of morale by bombing Italy. Evidence suggests that they did so, not by the sheer weight of bombs, but by revealing the impotence of the Italian state. In Florence, Calamandrei noticed, people suffered from a 'terrible sense of fatalism' and impotence, and fear after the autumn 1942 raids on northern Italy because their city lacked basic defences such as shelters or fire-fighting equipment. 'Our cities', Calamandrei wrote in his diary, 'the most beautiful thing we have in Italy, the only thing which, despite the humiliation, allows us to identify ourselves as Italians, will be destroyed one by one.'[176]

As prefects and informers reported from across Italy from 1942 (but earlier in cities like Genoa or Turin), the crisis of morale reflected a collapse of belief in the regime's propaganda and organizations. UNPA, for example, incurred a barrage of negative comments from 1940 on. It was a Fascist institution; its leaders were poorly trained (and so their orders could be disregarded); its personnel were old and infirm, useless in case of danger; UNPA women had loose morals; the Duce's praise for UNPA was surprising 'because the serious deficiencies of the institution are well known'.[177] This perception steadily extended to include anti-aircraft companies. At La Spezia, close to Puccini's birthplace, the anti-aircraft battery was nicknamed 'la Tosca' because, like Puccini's melodramatic heroine, 'it never harmed a living soul'.[178] Civil defence personnel, unsurprisingly, also suffered from poor morale. In Turin in 1944, *capi fabbricato* were demoralized at having no public or financial recognition despite their extra expenses, and at being forbidden to evacuate with their families.[179]

Poor alarm systems also damaged morale: the 66th raid on Naples, for example, in January 1943, occurred before the sirens sounded, leading the Naples UNPA to raise the problem with Rome.[180] More dramatic, however, was the panic provoked by certain raids (as at Nantes) and the regime's inability to repair the damage to the social tissue. In February 1943, Cagliari sustained three consecutive air attacks. The first caused 200 deaths, the second 400; many buildings were wrecked. The terrified population began to leave, when another raid struck two days later, bringing 'devastation' to the city centre and the port, and trapping hundreds of victims under rubble. What chiefly worried the prefect was the public's reactions. People decamped to shelters and never emerged, 'not even to look for food'. Company heads and employees disappeared; public administration ground to a halt; soldiers deserted, with the excuse of taking their families to safety, or refused to clear rubble because of the risk of further raids. Such a collapse in morale, confessed the prefect, 'has been a disappointment for me'.[181]

The prefect of Palermo reached similar conclusions a few months later. In October 1942, former Fascist Party chief Roberto Farinacci could celebrate the anniversary of the March on Rome in Palermo and even receive acclaim for declaring Sicily to be Italy's 'bulwark' in the Mediterranean. But by June 1943, people had lost their capacity for resistance, discipline and 'sense of responsibility'. The raids of the previous six months had caused massive damage, numerous victims (1,373 dead and 2,548 wounded since 1941), and a mass exodus – either to nearby, and already overcrowded, towns or, 'in dangerous mingling', to caves and tunnels outside the city.[182] Air attacks on Agrigento province provoked a similar mass exodus to nearby villages, leading the prefect to describe the public's behaviour as 'calm and resigned'; as elsewhere in Italy, this became a euphemism for 'depressed'.[183]

On 23 July 1943, the US Office of War Information reported 'manifestations of war weariness' in 13 urban and rural locations across Italy. These included religious processions, petitions to the Madonna, and visions supposed to foretell an 'early peace'. Significantly, 'these comments do not in any case mention pleas for victory, but only for peace'.[184] Religion grew in importance within bombed Italian communities, both institutionally (through the role of the Catholic Church and its priests) and in civilians' reliance on supernatural help through processions and pilgrimages and offers to the Madonna and local patron saints. Both were viewed by Fascist informers as potentially defeatist.[185]

The regime's inability to protect cities left a gap that the Church filled. Priests blessed shelters, placed crucifixes in them, and brought comfort to survivors. When raids on Naples intensified, some shelters came to resemble church annexes, with priests organizing activities such as collective prayer, masses, meetings of Catholic associations and catechism lessons – as well as religious assistance for the wounded and the dying. The archbishop blessed improvised altars built by the people in some shelters.[186] Sacred images – plastic representations of the local Madonna della Consolata, embellished with flowers and candles – appeared in shelters as early as November 1940 in Turin, where the prefect worried that they signified depression among the population.[187]

Such concerns were justified; Italians' reliance on the supernatural and the Church reflected a lack of faith in the regime's protection. This became particularly clear when Rome was bombed. The Pope's appearance in San Lorenzo represented a symbol of order in chaos. Even the very young Ugo Baduel, still then a supporter of Mussolini, would recall the 'angelic' vision of the Pope with his arms open among the crowd.[188] By 1944, after many attempts to make Rome an 'open city',[189] the Pope had become *the* symbol of peace and security for Romans. This became true for the rest of Italy too as the Holy See, through its bishops, tried to persuade both Allies and Germans to recognize Italian cities as 'open cities', to be spared from bombing. If the Germans agreed to demilitarize the towns, it was hoped the Allies would agree not to bomb them. The Salò Republic's refusal, on occasion, to accept the bishops' proposals reinforced the view that it was the Church not the Fascists that defended civilians. In Bologna, a city exhausted by repeated bombing throughout 1944, the Cardinal, supported by both the Vatican and the local *podestà*, began official negotiations with Kesselring in July 1944, following a similar attempt for Florence. But Interior Minister Buffarini called their initiative a 'demonstration of cowardice' and blocked it.[190]

The myth that the Pope could spare cities was widely believed – and at times frustrated by events. As early as 1942, priests in Apennine villages were asked why the Pope was not stopping the war.[191] Gloria Chilanti wrote on 11 and 12 March 1944 of expectations that the Pope would declare Rome a 'holy city', and then of 'great disappointment with the Pope's speech' when he failed to deliver.[192] But this did not last: Corrado Di Pompeo reported in his diary a month later that 'It seems that Rome will be declared an open city so that it will be illuminated at night, it will not be bombed, and the Vatican will assume responsibility for food deliveries.'[193]

People also turned to supernatural help from the winter of 1942–3. While Church authorities repeated that no peace could come without moral renewal, the Catholic masses simply hoped that the Madonna could divert bombs from their homes. Processions and offers of *ex-votos* were common all over Italy from Turin, where mass ceremonies to propitiate the Madonna of the Consolata started from June 1940, to Pompeii, where the sanctuary of the Regina became a year-round pilgrimage site for women asking for safety.[194]

Processions to do penance and propitiate the Madonna and patron saints, from Agrigento in Sicily to Garfagnana in Tuscany and to Verona, sometimes with tens of thousands of participants, worried the authorities.[195] With good reason: the belief in saints' miracles against bombs shows how the Catholic Church had come to replace the cult of the Duce by the time the regime fell. The apparition of the Virgin at Ghiaie di Bonate in Bergamo province between May and July 1944 attracted tens of thousands of visitors to the village from all over northern Italy, despite the disruption of public transport and the real danger of air raids. The Waffen-SS, again justifiably, interpreted this as a sign of defeatism.[196]

Bombing and the cult of the Duce

British propaganda attacks on Mussolini himself both reflected and reinforced feelings that Italians had begun to express. Small cracks in their faith in Mussolini appeared with the first raids, or even the first alarms. The Milanese may have received Mussolini's war declaration speech enthusiastically, an informer reported, but the ensuing alerts provoked an 'evident state of distress'.[197] As sirens sounded in Genoa, people ran for shelter in the city's tunnels only to find that they lacked lighting, water and toilets: women fainted, and people cursed 'the one who had wanted the war'.[198] In Turin the night raid of 11 June 1940 missed its target, the FIAT factories, and killed 17 people. As the first aircraft arrived, the lack of effective defence was clear and people concluded that 'we have been taken by surprise'. Italy, a police informer observed, had many 'internal enemies'. Next day, during the first alarms in working-class areas of Rome, women were heard cursing Mussolini, who they claimed was making war to please Hitler.[199]

Some early reports confirmed that the cult survived. In June 1940, for example, a police informer reported people in a shelter near Trento reciting the rosary for the Duce.[200] But continuing confidence in Mussolini was matched by a conviction that he was unaware of the inadequacies of the Fascist authorities, locally and nationally. 'We are making war without weapons', a group of soldiers told peasants at Tempio in Sardinia in July 1940: 'We are disarmed in many other things', the peasants replied: '... if Mussolini knew how we have to live here in Gallura: bread is so black that it is inedible'.[201] After the bombardment of Genoa in February 1941, a citizen wrote to the prefect: 'Are you not ashamed of what happened to Genoa? ... to let an enemy navy stroll around our gulf ...!!

You must tell the Duce.'[202] In late October, people in Bari feared that if the campaign in Greece was lost, Britain might establish air bases within range of their city; the only hope, an informer reported, was that 'Italy, under the guidance of the DUCE, will manage in a few days to ensure Greece is in no condition to do any harm.'[203] Even by February 1943 it was still possible to hear in Rome: 'The Duce is doing all he can to win this war, but those around him are mean.' Others, however, asked why he could not provide rural accommodation for evacuees.[204]

But negative comments on Italian defences in general and on Mussolini as the cause of the war progressed steadily from 1940. Churchill's message of January 1941[205] coincided with raids on port cities and the south, and helped bring enemy propaganda in line with popular perceptions. Night-time in the shelters was an ideal context to spread rumours and what prefects and informers called 'defeatist opinions'. These were often reported as if they had been uttered by someone else, generally by the Germans or by the enemy. In October 1941 an informer heard Romans in a crowded shelter attribute to a German official remarks that Italians were good at war, but very poorly led and unprotected by bad air defences. Women in particular gave vent to their feelings against Mussolini as the cause of the war.[206]

The raids of autumn 1942, and the lack of air defences and shelters, spread panic across northern Italy and dealt another blow to Mussolini's prestige. After the first big raid on Milan a crowd of 100 people watched as inhabitants tried to salvage belongings from a burning house; incited to assist, they said that the Duce, as the author of the war, should be helping. In another street, outside a second house on fire, a crowd of 50 shouted that the bombing of Rome would have been a good thing, to be finally finished with the Duce and Fascism.[207]

This crisis prompted Mussolini to break 18 months of silence, with his speech of 2 December to the Chamber of the Fasci and Corporations, broadcast to all Italians.[208] Justifying his long absence, Mussolini claimed that when 'the voice of the cannon sounds', the less one spoke the better. Now, however, he had 'the vague impression that a large part of the Italian people had the desire to hear my voice again'. The most depressing passage was the Duce's call for evacuation. He told women and children to abandon their cities; workers who could do so were to organize evening evacuations; only combatants should remain. This implicit admission that no defence, active or passive, could protect civilians from the bombs was, he conceded, the negative part of his speech. The 'positive' part was a promise that Germany was sending anti-aircraft guns to defend Italy. This too, however, was negatively received; the admission of dependence on Germany again demonstrated Italy's unpreparedness for a modern air war.[209]

Public reactions to the speech worried local authorities across Italy. Calamandrei noted that it had spread panic: 'this imbecile' Mussolini, exactly like the British, had invited the Italians to 'run away, disperse themselves and abandon their positions ... And this time the word of the Duce was not ignored: terror has spread all over Italy', not only in bombed towns but also in those still untouched. People began to leave Florence, Arezzo and Siena – while others streamed into Florence from Turin and Genoa. Italians had never shown so much cowardice, Calamandrei observed – and that after 20 years of the 'warrior regime' of Fascism. The Fascists had 'evacuated both materially and morally'.[210] The prefect of Genoa recognized that the speech had tried to counter a rising mood of depression caused by the bombing. Among all social strata, he said, there was an awareness that Mussolini had sought to summon the people to resist – but also that he had failed to explain why or how.[211] Instead, his call to evacuate provoked uncontrolled flight. In Palermo and in Taranto, for example, the population began to leave 'by any means and in any direction bringing with them anything they can'.[212] Reactions could be more moderate in unbombed towns, for example Pistoia in Tuscany, where the Duce's silence had been viewed as resulting from the 'critical moment' the war had reached, and where the (generally unexpected) speech apparently brought relief. [213]

In March, despite their belief in papal protection, Romans began to fear that bombing would reach them too. They expressed hatred for Mussolini in different ways, although not as openly as in Genoa with the riots of November 1942 or Turin with the strike of March 1943. In the capital it mostly took the form of rumours in which Mussolini was identified as the main barrier to peace, or of jokes. One was a pun involving Mussolini's latest mistress: 'the synthesis of Fascism: twenty years of hot air, and two of Petacci' (farting).[214]

In his last speech from the balcony of Piazza Venezia, on 5 May 1943, Mussolini recalled that there, seven years earlier, Italians had celebrated the conquest of the empire: now, he claimed, Italians were suffering from the *mal d'Africa*. There was only one remedy: 'to return. And we shall return.'[215] This rather by-passed the concerns of millions of Italians: fear of bombing, shortage of food and (owing to alarms) of sleep. Enemy propaganda worked better because it discussed civilians' real condition, and offered advice on how to cope. The last letters from ordinary civilians to the Duce reveal their alienation. A group of Neapolitans wrote in May 1943 to ask how, in a civilized country, people could be allowed to die without rescue after four days trapped under rubble.[216] In June, a leaflet dropped on Naples after a raid pointed out that it was futile to write to the Duce: 'Italians! You have been left alone. Whose fault is it?'[217] On 19 July, the first raid on Rome, followed by Mussolini's fall five days later, demonstrated that the Pope had replaced Mussolini in Roman hearts. The Pope's visits to bombed areas, then and after successive raids in August, were well publicized by the Vatican press.[218] The Pope's tour, an informer said, caused 'a true delirium of the people'; 'the Duce who went to war', however, was viewed as lacking the courage to visit bombed sites.[219]

In his last public speech at the Lirico theatre of Milan on 16 December 1944, Mussolini resumed his identity as a leader, but effectively addressed, not the entire nation, but the last Fascist cohorts of the German-controlled Salò Republic.[220] His main message, in a city that had suffered some of the worst raids of the war since August 1943, was the guilt of Badoglio and the King for betraying the Italian people by surrendering in September. Italy's declaration of war on Germany, Mussolini concluded, had brought, not peace, but more bombing. Nevertheless, from Milan, cradle of Fascism in 1919, a 'signal of restart' was possible. The crowd called him back on stage at the end, begging him to appear more in public.[221] But they were a minority in a shrunken territory, in a city reduced to ruins. Most Milanese were simply waiting for the war to end. A partisan poem of 1944, entitled *Mussolini's Testament*, focused blame firmly on the Duce: 'To Italy I leave dust of empires, / new ruins for her museums.'[222]

RUMOURS AND LEGENDS

Rumours are of their nature uncertain, changeable, and hard to document. They may arise from the distortion, exaggeration or diminution of factual events, whether wilfully or randomly through oral repetition. They may be planted intentionally – in this case, by the Allies or the authorities. Or they may correspond to what people want to believe, whatever the evidence to the contrary. All three origins were evident in France and Italy under the bombs, but the third, especially, was common to both.

In France, Toulon appears to have been particularly fertile in rumours. The Allies, people said after the raid of November 1943, had broken a promise to spare the city from bombing as a reward for the scuttling of the French fleet before the Germans could reach it in 1942. Reports stated that the city had been entirely razed, that dogs had been fighting over human remains, that children were playing football with severed heads, or that body parts were loaded into bags to make up a uniform weight of 60 kilograms. Aircraft had either bombed from 6,000 metres, or had descended to 1,000 metres to minimize casualties. Passive Defence teams had been heroic, or else so useless that they risked being lynched if they showed their faces in public; young people had either behaved like thugs, or had displayed the noblest altruism. The prefect concluded that the raid had provoked a sort of 'collective mythomania' among the Toulonnais.[223]

Very many French rumours, however, were in mitigation of Allied bombing. One type concerned hidden reasons for raids. Only Italian workers had been in Le Creusot during the raid of June 1943; air activity over Le Havre in November 1943 was due to drops of Allied parachutists; raids on Rouen in April and May (according to rumours in Marseille) had been reprisals for lynchings of parachutists.[224] The most common rumours, however, allowed blame to fall on the Germans. Many casualties at Billancourt in 1942, and in other raids, were blamed on the Germans preventing the sirens from sounding or workers from taking shelter.[225] The town and cathedral of Rouen had been crammed with explosives by the Germans at the time of the spring 1944 raids.[226] More destruction had been caused by anti-aircraft fire, downed aircraft, damaged aircraft jettisoning bomb loads, or German aircraft bombing their Allied enemies from above, than by intentional Allied bombing. One CFLN report, for example, stated that fragments of German bombs were found on the ground after the raids on La Chapelle in April 1944.[227] Some of these rumours were products of British black propaganda.[228] They were attractive because they appeared to resolve the jarring dissonance between what most of the French wanted – an end to the German occupation through the only means possible, an Allied victory – and the reality of their suffering at the hands of their liberators.

Few expressed this dissonance better than Jean-Paul Sartre. Young Allied pilots, he wrote, were simultaneously harbingers of freedom and messengers of death for the French; it took a huge effort of faith not to hate the Allies, but to wish, with the airmen, the destruction they wrought upon France; part of that effort lay in finding 'the most ingenious excuses' to explain the slaughter of civilians. 'What is terrible', Sartre added, 'is not to suffer or to die, but to suffer and die in *vain*.'[229]

In Italy, rumours and legends independent of state propaganda were one way in which civilians coped with the collapse of state defences and their own exhaustion. Rumours could reveal feelings of admiration for the enemy's strength, lack of trust in the state, and aspects of the complex relationship between bombed and bombers. From the spring of 1943, many of Italy's rumours were directly related to the desire for peace. In Bari, Germany and Russia were rumoured to have signed an armistice in May 1943; the news brought hundreds of women and children to demonstrate their joy in the main square. Similar events occurred in Campania.[230] Other rumours involved prophecies about when the war would end.[231] Still others, more directly related to bombing, reinforced the belief that the Italian government, rather than the Allies, was to blame. For example, in February 1943 the government supposedly turned down an Allied peace offer made at the Casablanca conference, which would have given Italy its African empire back plus Tunisia, Corsica, Nice and Savoy; after this refusal the Allies intensified the bombing, to provoke unconditional surrender or revolution. Many Romans expected to be bombed on 1 March 1943 because they heard that the Italian government had flouted a papal ultimatum; that meant that only the Duce could be blamed if the Allies hit Rome.[232]

Rumours abounded about Mussolini's role in causing unnecessary alerts, or the comfort of his place of refuge. In Rome in February 1941, the latest alert was put down to an RAF attempt to hit Mussolini's train as it returned from Bordighera. The rumour then mutated: 'the latest alarm sounded because on the Duce's arrival from Bordighera, all streets must be empty'.[233] By August 1942, repeated alerts in Rome were said to be set off whenever Mussolini left or returned to the capital.[234] Speculation early in 1943 on Mussolini's place of shelter during raids highlighted the distance between the Duce and ordinary Italians. A message from Radio Londra, which never really took root, had suggested that Mussolini found safe refuge in the Vatican City.[235] Other accounts, though, had the Duce travelling to Caprarola (in the Viterbo countryside) at night, or staying at Rocca delle Caminate, his summer residence, or even in Berlin.[236]

The most widespread rumour in Italy was more fantastic, and arose from the Italians' not always conscious attempts to resolve their ambiguous relationship (including guilt, and the need for protection) with the bombers. Particularly common under the northern Salò Republic, the legend concerned a lone pilot, almost an anthropomorphic plane, who checked on civilians' behaviour, and either photographed or bombed those who ignored air-raid precautions. It was 'as if this invisible watchman personified the collective super-ego of a society that was subjected to the mechanisms of war but felt alienated from them'.[237] Named Pippo in northern Italy, the imaginary plane acquired other nicknames in other regions, including *Ciccio 'o ferroviere* (Ciccio the railwayman).[238] Pippo appears and reappears in the memories of wartime children and adolescents who survived the bombing. For Palmira Marchioli, for example, Pippo surveyed the whole region (around Monfalcone) every night and photographed everything.[239] Two inhabitants of Prevalle, in Brescia province, remembered that 'when Pippo arrived we had to cover the windows so that no light could be seen outside', and that 'at home we covered the windows with blue paper … otherwise … Pippo would bomb'.[240]

On most accounts Pippo was an Anglo-American aircraft. Riccarda Fedriga from Rovereto recalled that Pippo was always alone and bombed wherever he saw house or car lights. Although he was 'nicer than the other bombers: indeed we waited for him in the evenings', he was also 'unnerving … and we never knew if he was British or American'.[241] For Elettra Sarra, Pippo was a British reconnaissance plane with two small bombs, which the pilot dropped if he saw any lights or any suspicious movement. In the morning, she remembered, 'Pippo's *passeggiate* in the sky' were the main subject of neighbourhood conversations.[242] Other recollections, however, do not specify a nationality, or give an ambiguous one – an Italian in enemy service, or an Italian or German plane spying on them. Paola Susini wrote that Pippo was also called 'the Badoglian, who drops hand grenades when he sees light'.[243] Franco Pogioli, a sixteen-year old who spent many nights of 1944 in a tunnel on the Ligurian coast, recorded that an isolated aircraft dropped leaflets identifying itself as an Italian plane named Pippo. Several nights without a visit from Pippo encouraged Franco to sleep at home one night; Pippo's return, however, sent him back to the tunnel.[244]

Like other rumours surrounding the bombing, Pippo personified Italians' difficulties in coping with a regime they had supported, but which had brought war to their homes, imposing oppressive rules without protecting them. It revealed their sense of guilt at not respecting those rules, as well as fears generated by bombing. But Pippo also symbolized their difficult relationship with the Allies, who sent Italians friendly messages while punishing them for their acceptance of the regime. Pippo could also, finally, represent the problematic collaboration between the Allies and those Italians who resisted German occupation. Several accounts represent Pippo supplying the partisans or dropping parachutes carrying flares. These last visits were worrisome because no-one knew which side Pippo was on. Partisans, however, put silk and cotton from the parachutes to good use.[245]

A constant threat to some, to others Pippo was a friendly counsellor, able to warn of coming danger. This contradiction reflects the uncertain but intense relationship that emerged, particularly from 1943, between the formation of a free Italian public opinion and Allied propaganda; but also the political ambivalence with which civilians in Fascist Italy, both aggressors and victims of the war, perceived Allied bombing.

CIVILIANS AND DOWNED ALLIED AIRMEN

Civilians' behaviour in encounters with Allied aircrew, often young men who had dropped bombs minutes before being shot down, might be expected to reflect the complex mixture of resentment and admiration they felt towards the bombing generally. Available accounts, however, suggest a simpler story, in which airmen were hidden, and helped to escape, by French and Italian civilians who often risked their lives.

Some, of course, were dead on reaching the ground. These received consistent respect from French civilians – and, when possible, from Italian ones too. This could be spontaneous and private: the 16-year-old Claude Métayer, coming upon remains of a Mosquito crew shot down over Rouen a few minutes earlier, recalled wishing that their parents could know that someone was watching over these corpses of their children, men barely older than him.[246] Funerals, however, offered opportunities to demonstrate pro-Allied sentiment more publicly. This was possible thanks to the attitude of the occupying Germans; especially early in the war, Allied airmen were buried in France with military honours. Odd games of cat-and-mouse could result, as three reports from Loire-Inférieure in 1941 show. On 10 May, several thousand visitors paid their respects at a Nantes cemetery to six British airmen shot down the previous day; the German authorities requested the French police to ensure that German wreaths were left intact. At nearby La Baule, a crowd of 400–500 gathered for the funeral of two British airmen; the ceremony was postponed until the following day, when just 20 mourners appeared, but wreaths dedicated 'To our Heroes', and 'To our Allies' were deposited, then removed by German soldiers. A constant procession filed past the day after. In Nantes, both official German wreaths and illicit ones from the Allies' supporters were laid at the graves of two more airmen in December; the latter were removed and the cemetery placed under continuous surveillance for 48 hours.[247]

The intensification of air raids does not appear to have altered this behaviour among the French, though the occupiers seem to have changed theirs by 1944. Late in February 1943, weeks after the destruction of Lorient, a funeral of downed airmen near Ploermel, some 40 miles distant, attracted a crowd of some 2,500 – 'a real demonstration' according to the Renseignements Généraux. The following month, when the Italians occupying south-east France denied military honours to six British airmen shot down while dropping arms to the Resistance near Annecy, the funeral still attracted a crowd of over 2,000, who sang the *Marseillaise* and *God Save the King*, and shouted *Vive de Gaulle!*[248] On 11 November 1943, Troyes cemetery was closed to anyone with flowers after 'marks of sympathy' had been shown to freshly-buried Allied airmen. The same day a group of Marseille Corsicans laid wreaths, marked 'to our liberators, the Americans' on the graves of two American airmen in the Saint-Jérôme cemetery; these were soon cut and trampled by Germans.[249] Resentment at the American style of bombing, said a CFLN report in April 1944, had not prevented the French from honouring equally the sacrifice of British and American airmen 'for the liberation of France'.[250]

Neither the Transportation Plan raids nor the fighting after D-day ended this. When two Allied airmen were shot down over Toulon during the raid of 5 July 1944, the German authorities attempted to bury them naked and without ceremony. This was the sixth of nine raids, which wrecked much of the town and killed 640 Toulonnais. Nevertheless, a crowd of over 170 protested at the treatment of the dead men, who were handed over to the municipality; two women brought sheets; and the mayor was forced to supply two coffins and make a speech, before they were buried. The graves were covered in flowers, renewed on 14 July. The incident, moreover, was reported in the local paper, *Le Petit Var*.[251] None of these accounts, of course, demonstrates that *every* dead airman was thus honoured. They do, however, show that they *could* be, right through the war, throughout France, and in circumstances where public feeling might be expected to be unsympathetic.

Such open expressions of respect for dead airmen were harder to find in Italy, an enemy until 1943. However, in post-armistice northern Italy they became more common, despite German control. In Varese in April 1945, partisans told the Swiss Allied headquarters that a Canadian airman had been brought to the mortuary at Belforte in a bag. The population protested so strongly that the authorities buried him at Belforte cemetery; the next day his grave was covered with flowers.[252]

Respecting Allied dead entailed slight risks. Not so the living. For the Allies, getting a trained airman back to operational duties was highly valuable: as Harris pointed out, it cost £10,000 to train one member of a bomber crew, 'enough to send ten men to Oxford or Cambridge for three years'.[253] Inevitably, the Germans punished anyone who helped recover such valuable assets. In Italy, rewards were publicized for the capture of Allied airmen – and death penalties for those who helped them. In France too, the death penalty for helping Allied airmen was set out in a German *ordonnance* of 14 July 1941, though a later notice specified lesser penalties for unintentional assistance.[254] Some exceptions were indeed made. In July 1943, for example, prefect Bouffet persuaded the Germans to commute the sentences of two men guilty of helping Allied aircrew.[255] The *concierge* of the Théâtre Moncey in Paris, having protected an airman who had parachuted onto the theatre roof, was released after several days' custody – owing her life, probably, to being a mother of three.[256] But the death penalty was executed in many other cases, and its principle was reaffirmed in April 1944.[257]

Notwithstanding the risk, between 2,000 and 3,000 members of Allied forces, mostly aircrew, were helped to get out of France with French assistance.[258] Similar figures exist for Italy, where almost 3,000 airmen, mostly Americans, escaped with civilian help.[259] Small compared to the 158,500 Allied airmen lost in action over Europe, these figures are still impressive in absolute terms given the difficulties involved. In a letter to Massigli, the GPRF's ambassador to London, Harris praised the assistance given to Allied airmen by

> … French people who well knew that the penalty for aiding escapers was death. They knew also that the enemy employed agents provocateurs dressed in Royal Air Force flying kit […] It was in such circumstances that these people provided safe lodgement, food when they themselves were hungry, clothing, often from a pitifully meagre store, even bicycles – their sole and irreplaceable means of transport. … Men, women and indeed sometimes even small children led our airmen from hiding place to hiding place. They tended their wounds, they bought them rail tickets, they carried them hidden in farm carts, they passed them safely through cordons and barriers, they misled and confounded the enemy's search.[260]

Aside from the overall figures above, it is hardly possible to gauge how representative such helpers were. Some contrary indications do exist. The Morbihan Renseignements Généraux reported that following the raids on Lorient, the population had withheld assistance, turning some airmen over to the Germans; again, a CFLN correspondent reported in 1944 that the French did not give help when, as at Nantes, they had been subjected to 'area bombing' without military targets being hit.[261] The Vichy press claimed in June 1944 that downed airmen had been beaten and even lynched by the French – but this information, from a German source, may be treated with scepticism.[262] There were ambiguous cases, too. Warrant Officer Albert Berry, who went missing on 8 July 1944, was first sheltered, then betrayed and captured; in 1946, he was 'still rather in a quandary' as to whether the betrayal had been calculated, or simply forced by German threats to his helper's wife.[263]

Alongside these accounts, plenty of anecdotal information confirms Harris's eulogy. René Marsollier, for example, claimed to have assisted a downed airman in the small town of Ploemeur, 6 km from Lorient, on 4 February 1943, two weeks before the Renseignements Généraux report stating that no one was giving help in this way. Sitting in a café with friends after curfew, he heard an aircraft crash on the road; opening the door to a persistent knocking, they found 'a British airman in flying kit wearing a leather-lined flying coat and fur-lined boots'. Delegated by his friends, Marsollier claimed to have taken the man home, given him fresh clothes, and bought him a rail ticket to Bayonne, on the Spanish frontier.[264]

If Marsollier's account remains unverified, the statements of Allied airmen, with no particular stake save gratitude, are more readily taken at face value. Warrant Officer Spencer, of the Royal Canadian Air Force, gave an extraordinarily vivid account of the couple who sheltered him in Alençon, south of Caen, in November 1943 – after the raids on Nantes and the Paris suburbs.

> A man came to the door and I identified myself to him. He took me through the café into the kitchen where we were joined by his wife ... The wife had very black wavy hair and was about 21 years old. She was pregnant at the time and expecting in about 6 months. The man was about 23 with straight fairish hair and of average height. They questioned me and when I satisfied them I was a Canadian they gave me warm wine and an egg with bread and butter ... The man gave me a flash-light which he went out and bought one night ... We had rabbit for one meal. In their presence I tied the rabbit foot to my clothes. I tore off the gauntlets from my flying gloves and gave the pieces of leather to them. They said they would use it to mend shoes etc. Before I left they gave me a lunch of rabbit etc. to take with me. I think the man worked in a flour mill because he came home at night with flour on his clothes. They had only one straw bed in an upstairs room and the 3 of us slept together.
>
> In conclusion I would like to state that in my opinion these people were utterly patriotic and hated the Germans. They risked their life to help me and gave me food when they didn't have enough for themselves.

The theme of personal generosity – aside from risking life and freedom – appears in a number of accounts. Flight Lieutenant S. M. Garlick, for example, recalled that his main helper 'saved my left leg from being amputated at great expense to himself, because he had to buy expensive medical supplies'. Warrant Officer Metcalfe, who bailed out over Seine-Inférieure in July 1944, stated that his helpers 'looked after him for a week, gave him a set of civilian clothes, including a pair of shoes, worth 2,000 francs' bought on the black market.[265] A CFLN correspondent reported that an escaped airman shot down after a raid on Lorient in May 1943 was hidden for two days by a farmer; no one had given him away despite the offer of a reward of FF50,000 – about four years' wages for a worker.[266]

Of Italian helpers, one British PoW, out of the 30,000 Allied prisoners who escaped from the 72 Italian prison camps, wrote that while they blamed the Allies for 'destroying Italy', they still treated them 'like sons'.[267] Downed airmen taken before the armistice escaped from the camps after 8 September 1943; many of those shot down later avoided capture by the Germans thanks to Italian help. RAF officer James Charles Cole landed by parachute at Mignano in Caserta province in autumn 1943. After three days hiding from German patrols, with scant food rations and little water, he tried moving southwards towards the Allied lines. Feeling ill and weak, he sought food and water from an

Italian family living in a cave. As he later recalled, they 'did all they could to help me'. They passed him to peasants who gave him food and shelter in their hut, and helped him evade capture by a German patrol. Thanks to assistance from more Italians, despite the dangers, he eventually reached an American sentry post.[268]

While an airman's first steps towards escape might result from a happy encounter with a civilian who, minutes earlier, might not have imagined becoming a helper, prolonged avoidance of capture, and movement through the country, depended on communities and networks – the latter often carefully nurtured by the Allies.[269] Pierre Montaz's authenticated account recalls how an Alpine Resistance network saved the whole crew of a Liberator from the US Fifteenth Air Force.[270] RAF Lieutenant A. H. Kell bailed out over Sicily on 10 July 1943, and was given water and let go by Italian soldiers who believed his claim, in broken French, to be from Vichy France. Later, however, he was captured by less credulous German soldiers, and, as he was injured, sent him as a prisoner to hospital in Lucca. Escaping a second time, he jumped off a train in the countryside, where Italians fed and sheltered him in a barn, giving him farm-labourer's clothes, food rations, and directions southward. On his way, he was helped by other farmers' families (with one of whom he listened to Radio Londra's war news), until he joined the partisans in December 1943 and went north, finally making contact with the British in Switzerland.[271] Warrant Officer Roland Hale, who bailed out over the Eure *département* in June 1943, named a dozen people who had assisted him, and recalled more 'indirect' helpers.[272] Flight Lieutenant J. J. Beaton remembered six men who gave direct assistance in Curmont, east of Troyes in the Haute-Marne, late in 1943. The mayor was one; in addition, four of the local gendarmes brought him tea, cigarettes or tobacco, and honey. Beaton eventually reached Switzerland.[273] Those who had direct contact with an airman themselves relied on the assistance or at least silence of a wider circle.

Even for those spared the death penalty, punishment was severe for helpers if discovered. Beaton stated that six weeks after his departure, his principal helper had been taken by the Gestapo and spent 18 weeks in German camps. 'He is ill still and walks with difficulty with the aid of two sticks. M. Bertrand was a robust, healthy man when we were with him.'[274] Of Roland Hale's dozen helpers, three women were sent to Ravensbrück concentration camp, where two died; a fourth woman endured forced labour in a salt mine. One of the men survived a stay at Buchenwald; two others, however, were accused of betrayal and imprisoned after the war.[275]

The available evidence suggests, then, that however heavy Allied bombing became, and however poorly aimed, there were always *some* Italians and French men and women, perhaps a majority, willing, at least, to pay their respects to dead airmen, and, at the most, to assist them at the risk of their own well-being and lives.

CONCLUSION

The narrative of bombing 'from below' (by civilians, or by the State's local authorities and informers) both explains what it meant for the population to be bombed, and serves to evaluate the impact of propaganda. While horror and trauma were described in similar ways by survivors in the two countries, people's reactions and interpretations could vary depending on location, phases of the war and performance of the defence measures. In France, the capital of sympathy commanded by the British from 1940 on, and by the Allies from 1942, was such that early raids were positively welcomed as an augury of liberation from a German occupier and a Vichy government that were both steadily more loathed. During the same period, Italy's position as anti-Allied belligerent might explain why there was no enthusiasm for the raids. In fact, as the raids were not yet very serious (with a few exceptions), the prevailing attitude was one of disregard for civil defence regulations.

In France, support for the Allies was tested to breaking-point from 1943 and especially spring 1944. Manifestations of this included increased support for the Soviet Union, the only major Allied power not involved, and an unaccustomed bitterness even among the western Allies' most fervent supporters. In France, too, the most effective of Vichy propagandists, Henriot, found a wide audience, receptive to several of his themes; Pétain was also received favourably during his personal appearances at bombed cities and, in April 1944, in Paris itself. However, French opinion under the impact of bombing did not shift massively to support for the Vichy regime, still less for the Germans; the sufferings and shortages imposed by the occupation effectively precluded that.

This attitude was even more extreme in the Italian case, where opinion turned decisively against the regime even as the Allied raids became most destructive. Italians' opinion and feelings were mixed and were, more than in France, expressed by the spreading of rumours and legend. Bombing made people indifferent to which side won the war, so long as it ended; the regime's inability to protect civilians made this worse, and the combination of the two gave a blow to the population's morale, which the British had monitored closely from early on in the war.[276] From this point of view, from autumn 1942 in particular, Allied propaganda and bombs achieved their initial aim: Italians began to think that *their* ruling class were responsible for the raids and their consequences. While the French maintained respect for Pétain (albeit qualified by an awareness of his diminishing power), the cult of the Duce fell, at least on the home front, under the impact of bombs even more than under that of military defeats. This did not mean that bombed populations became unequivocally pro-Allied. As in France, bombing was more tolerated if it could be set into a broader narrative about the liberation by friendly allies. It was thus more acceptable if its military use against Germany could be demonstrated, and if care was seen to be taken to minimize civilian casualties.

The available (and fragmentary) evidence indicates that even at the worst of the bombing, downed airmen were always met with respect if dead, and often with assistance if alive. In most cases, helpers were simply moved by an instinct of human charity (a behaviour typical, in peasant communities, of a deep-rooted Christian culture).[277] However, this phenomenon suggests widespread sympathy for the Allies, and should also be framed within the history of the Resistance, when Allied bombers collaborated with French and Italian partisans. As the next chapter will show, this too was a less than straightforward relationship.

Notes

1 S. Portelli, 'So Much Depends on a Red Bus, or Innocent Victims of the Liberating Gun', *Oral History*, 34, (2006), 30.
2 AN F7/14929, Chef du gouvernement, Service Civile des Contrôles Techniques, Synthèse mensuelle des interceptions (CTSM), February 1944.
3 M. Franzinelli, *I tentacoli dell'OVRA. Agenti, collaboratori e vittime della polizia fascista* (Turin: Bollati Boringhieri, 1999), 386–92; S. Colarizi, *L'opinione degli italiani sotto il regime, 1929–1943* (Rome-Bari: Laterza, 2000), 19–20.
4 P. Laborie, *L'opinion française sous Vichy: les Français et la crise d'identité nationale, 1936–1944* (Paris: Le Seuil, 1990), 260–70; P. Laborie, 'Solidarités et ambivalences de la France moyenne', in J.-P. Azéma and F. Bédarida (eds), *La France des années noires*, vol. II (Paris, Le Seuil, 1993), 336–7; Colarizi, *L'opinione degli italiani sotto il regime*; P. Cavallo, *Italiani in guerra. Sentimenti e immagini dal 1940 al 1945* (Bologna: Il Mulino, 1997).
5 AN F7/14929, CTSM, 10 August–10 September 1942 and 10 March–10 April 1943.
6 C. Baldoli and M. Fincardi, 'Italian Society under Allied Bombs: Propaganda, Experience, and Legend, 1940–1945', *Historical Journal*, 52 (4), 2009, 1029.
7 In fact there were 125 killed, according to Gioannini and Massobrio, (appendix to *Bombardate l'Italia*); and 106 according to the prefect's report a few days after the raid (see Gribaudi, *Guerra totale*, 130–1).
8 C. Malaparte, *The Skin* (London: Hamilton & Co. Stafford, 1964), 56–8.
9 C. Chawaf, *Je suis née* (Paris: Des Femmes-Antoinette Fouque, 2010), 31.
10 AD Ille-et-Vilaine 502W/4, Ville de Rennes, Commissariat Central, Bombardement aérien du 8 mars 1943, Liste des décédés.
11 AD Var 1W/64, J. Perves, Le bombardement de Toulon.
12 APA, Dossier 60, Dr Jérôme Gerest, 101–4.
13 P. Calamandrei, *Diario 1939–1945*, ed. G. Agosti, vol. II, *1942–1945* (Scandicci: La Nuova Italia, 1992), 75–6 (6 November 1942).
14 *Ibid.*, 95 (16 December 1942).
15 P. Nenni, *Tempo di guerra fredda. Diari 1943–1956* (Milan: Sugarco edizioni, 1981), 30 (20 August 1943).
16 ADN, MG/03, E. Sarra, *A ritroso nel tempo*, unpublished memoir written between 2000–2002, 89.
17 ADN, MG/Adn, I. Bresadola, *I nostri verdi anni*, unpublished memoir written in 1965, 39–40, 62.
18 Cited by E. Lorenzon, 'Il 7 aprile e la memoria di una città', in L. Tosi ed. *Testimoni loro malgrado. Memorie del bombardamento del 7 aprile 1944*, (2006), 9.
19 *Ibid.*, 11–18.
20 Gribaudi, *Guerra totale*, 101.
21 A. Maurois, *Rouen dévasté* (Fontaine-le-Bourg, Le Pucheux, 2004), 60–8.
22 G. Lecadet, 'Valognes: les foyers sont devenus des tombeaux', in M. Boivin, G. Bourdin, and J.

Quellien, (eds), *Villes normandes sous les bombes (juin 1944)* (Caen: Presses Universitaires de Caen/Mémorial de Caen, 1994), 219–26; Mémorial de Caen, Témoignage Écrit (TE) 111, Paul Manuelle.

23 Mémorial de Caen, TE 62, Charles Massinot.

24 *Ibid.*, TE 230, Robert Marie.

25 *Ibid.*, TE 14, Famille Oudinet.

26 M. Bengtsson, *Un été 44: de l'état de siège à la paix retrouvée* (2nd edition: Le Havre: Éditions-Imprimerie Grenet, 2004); and Institut National de l'Audiovisuel (INA), 'Le Tunnel Jenner fête ses 50 ans', http://www.ina.fr/economie-et-societe/environnement-et-urbanisme/video/HA00001399062/le-tunnel-jenner-du-havre-fete-ses-50-ans.fr.html (accessed 5 May 2011).

27 Middlebrook and Everitt, *The Bomber Command War Diaries*, 508, 577; AD Manche 127/W1, *BDIP* no. 21, June 1944; M. Coutel, *Bruz sous les bombes: un village breton dans la guerre* (Rennes: Éditions La Part Commune, 2005).

28 APA, Dossier 337, Charlotte Barbotin, 139.

29 *Ibid.*, 140–5.

30 *Ibid.*, 172.

31 *Ibid.*, 179.

32 *Ibid.*, 185.

33 Cf. for example P. Heinl, *Splintered Innocence: an Intuitive Approach to Treating War Trauma* (New York and Hove: Brunner-Routledge, 2001); C. Caruth, *Unclaimed Experience: Trauma, Narrative, and History* (Baltimore, Md., Johns Hopkins Press, 1996).

34 http://laureleforestier.typepad.fr/blog_de_laure_leforestier/grand_rouen/ accessed 5 May 2011. Originally from C. Laboubée ed. *Rouen, mémoires 44* (Ville de Rouen, 2004).

35 ACS, MI, DGPS, DPP, b. 210, informer's report, Milan, 15 June 1940.

36 *Corriere della Sera*, 18 June 1940.

37 *Ibid.*, 15 August 1940.

38 ACS, MI, DGPS, DPP, b. 210, informers' reports, Padua, 23 June 1940; Bari, 26 June 1940.

39 *Ibid.*, informers' reports, Milan, 3 and 5 July 1940. Aircraft could of course reach northern Italy from Britain, though with a reduced bombload.

40 *Ibid.*, informers' reports, Venice, 6 July 1940; Rome, 5, 6 and 9 July 1940; Grosseto, 27 July 1940; Florence, 7 August 1940; Rome, 3 August 1940; Padua, 7 August 1940.

41 ASTo, Prefettura, b. 513, Committee of Anti-Aircraft Protection of Turin to Prefect, 2 August 1940; *La Stampa*, 15 August 1940.

42 ACS, MI, DPP, b. 211, fasc.1, informers' reports, Vicenza, 30 September 1940; Milan, 15 October 1940.

43 ACS, MA, b. 82, Mussolini's secretary to Air Ministry, 16 November 1940; Ministry of War to all ministers, 19 November 1940; cited in R. Overy, 'Introduction', in Baldoli, Knapp and Overy (eds), *Bombing, States and Peoples*, 6.

44 Cf. for example ACS, MI, DGPS, DPP, b. 211, fasc. 3, informer's report, Genoa, 29 May; Bari, 1 June; Brescia 12 September 1941.

45 *Ibid.*, fasc. 2. Informer's report, Rome, 14 August 1942.

46 ASTo, Prefettura, I Versamento, b. 524, Provincial Inspector of Anti-Aircraft Defence to the Police Chief of Turin, 8 December 1944.

47 *Ibid.*, Platz Kommandantur to the Province Head of Turin, 5 January 1945.

48 *Il Resto del Carlino*, 11 January 1945.

49 Loi du 5 août 1941 portant modification à la réglementation générale sur la défense passive, *JO*, 6 August 1941; Loi du 16 avril 1942 (Réglementation générale, défense passive), *JO*, 23 April 1942; Loi du 23 février 1944 (Réglementation générale, défense passive), *JO*, 24 February 1944.

50 AD Rhône 182W/262, Kommandatur Lyon to Prefect of Rhône, 20 April 1943; AD Rhône 182W/263, État-Major Lyon (1A) to Prefect of Lyon, 13 August 1943; *ibid.*, Kommandatur Lyon to DDP Lyon, n.d. (August 1943?); SHAA 3D/44/1, Laval to prefects, 21 September 1943.

51 AM Rennes 6H/22, Mayor of Rennes to Kreiskommandant, 2 April 1942; SHAT 1P/20, General von Neubronn to General Bridoux, Secrétaire d'État à la Défense, 30 July 1943; Secrétariat d'État à la Défense, Note pour Cabinet défense terrestre, 4 August 1943.

52 AD Loire 112W/72, Commissariat Central to Bureau du Commandant des Gardiens de la paix, 28 June 1944.
53 ACS, MI, DGPS, DPP, b. 210, informers' reports, Genoa, 13 August 1940; Turin, 21 August; Milan, 21 August and 23 September; Trento, 17 August 1940; Verona, 24 September.
54 *Ibid.*, b. 229, police report from Cagliari to Chief of Police, 18 June 1940.
55 *Ibid.*, b. 210, informer's report, Milan, 19 June 1940.
56 ASTo, Prefettura, I Versamento, b. 524, National Fascist Landlords' Federation to Fascist Union of Industrialists, 8 August 1940.
57 ACS, MI, DGPS, DPP, b. 211, fasc. 1, informer's report, Rome, 14 November 1940.
58 *Ibid.*, informer's report, Sesto San Giovanni, 15 November 1940.
59 ASTo, Prefettura, I Versamento, b. 524, intercepted telephone call between inhabitants of Turin. War Ministry to Prefect of Turin, 20 January 1941.
60 ACS, MI, DGPCSA, b. 106, General Direction of Anti-Aircraft Services to Interior Ministry, 28 October 1941.
61 ACS, MI, DGPS, DPP, b. 211, fasc. 2, informer's report, Padua, 29 October 1942.
62 *Ibid.*, informer's report, Milan, 3 November 1942.
63 *Ibid.*, informer's report, Genoa, 2 December 1942.
64 *Ibid.*, informer's report, Bari, 15 December 1942.
65 On Genoa, see above, p. 155; on Naples, see Gribaudi, *Guerra totale*, 95. In 1943 London suffered a comparable tragedy at Bethnal Green, which took 173 lives. Cf. J. Gardiner, *The Blitz: the British under Attack* (London: Collins, 2010), 82.
66 ASG, RSI, Prefettura, b. 27, Commissario prefettizio of Recco to the Prefect of Genoa, 21 June 1944.
67 ADN MG/03, Sarra, *A ritroso nel tempo*, 51.
68 Report from Health Officer, Trento to Prefect, January 1945, in P. Pedron and N. Pontalti, *Uomini e donne in guerra. Trentino, 1940–1945* (Trento: Museo Storico, 2001), 41.
69 ASTo, Prefettura, I Versamento, b. 524, Buffarini to prefect of Turin, 15 January 1943; Buffarini to prefects, 13 January 1943.
70 ADN MP/02, G. Barbari, *Miriam l'ebrea* (Bologna: Comune di San Benedetto Val Sambro, 2002), 96.
71 ASP, Prefettura, b. 636, Prefect of Palermo to Interior Ministry, 2 April 1943.
72 SHAA 3D/321/1, Rapport sur les bombardements aériens en territoire français (1944): Toulon.
73 *Ibid.*, Marseille.
74 AM Lorient 5H/10, Laval (signed Sérant) to prefects, 6 May 1943; AD Var 3W/59, Col. Farina to sub-Prefect, 25 March 1943; Sûreté, Information, 12 August 1943.
75 AD Loire-Atlantique 27J/13, Bombardement du 16 septembre, souvenirs.
76 P. Caillaud, *Les Nantais sous les bombardements, 1941–1944* (Nantes: Aux Portes du Large, 1947), 27ff. This contrasts with the wiser frivolity of an experienced shelter-goer in Toulon, who always took with her a whistle to call for help, a small bottle of crème de menthe, and a tube of lipstick (AD Var 1W/65, *Le Petit Var*, 30 May 1944).
77 AN F7/14901, *BIDP* no. 19, April 1944.
78 AD BduR 76W/121, Rapport du Capt. Saunois, Directeur des Services, Marins-Pompiers Marseille, 16 June 1944.
79 F. Lefaivre ed. *J'ai vécu les bombardements à Condé-sur-Noireau* (Condé-sur-Noireau: Éditions Charles Corlet, 1994), 106–8.
80 Caillaud, *Nantais*, 155–6; AM Rennes 6H/22, Chef d'Escadrons Vaylac (DDP for occupied zone) to Prefects, 2 February 1943.
81 AD Ille-et-Vilaine 502W/3, *BIDP* no. 12, 30 September 1943.
82 AN F60/1690, *News Digest*, 6 June 1944, from *Journal de Genève*, 6 June 1944.
83 AM Rennes 6H/23, Mayor of Rennes to Technical Services Director, Information Ministry, 18 December 1943; AD Var 1W/21, RG Toulon, Bulletin hebdomadaire, 22–28 November 1943.
84 AN AJ41/356, Délégation du gouvernement français dans les territoires occupés, Extrait du compte-rendu des secrétaires-généraux du 7 octobre 1943; P. Caillaud, *Nantes sous les bombardements: Mémorial à la Défense Passive* (Nantes: Éditions du Fleuve, 1946), 32; Caillaud, *Nantais*, 47; R. Freeman, *Mighty Eighth War Diary* (London: Jane's, 1981), 112, 115, 260.

85 AD Var 1W/64, Prefect of Var to head of government, 4 January, 10 March, 13 March, 3 May 1944, 5 July 1944, 13 July 1944, 7 August 1944; Département du Var, Rapport succinct au sujet du bombardement du 4 février 1944, 7 February 1944.
86 AD BduR 76W129, RG Marseille, État d'esprit de la population à Marseille, 21 June 1944; AD BduR 76W121, *Marseille-Matin*, 15–16 August 1944.
87 AD Var 1W/64, Département du Var, Rapport succinct, 7 February 1944.
88 AD Manche 127/W1, *BIDP* no. 21, June 1944.
89 AN F1/cIII/1188, Prefectoral report, Seine-Maritime, 30 April 1943; AD Loire 7W/25, RG to Prefect, 1 June 1944; AD BduR 76W/26, Prefect of Var to head of government, 3 May 1944.
90 *Ibid*., Report by General Guichard, SIPEG representative, Toulon, 22 July 1944.
91 AN AJ41/25, Contrôles Techniques, weekly summary, 18–24 October 1940.
92 *Ibid*., Contrôles Techniques, weekly summaries, 11–17 October, 25 November–4 December 1940, 6–20 February 1941.
93 *Ibid*., Contrôles Techniques, weekly summaries, 6–12 September and 11–17 October 1940.
94 ACS, Archivi di Famiglie e Persone, Barnes, b. 4, *Diary of 1943: 'Flight from Rome'*, 25 and 28 September 1943.
95 Cf. for example: ASG, Prefettura, b. 156, Commander, Difesa Territoriale of Genoa, to 15th Army Commander and prefect of Genoa, 5 September 1939; ACS, MI, DPP, b. 210, informer's report, Milan, 18 June 1940; ACS, MI, DPP, b. 239, informer's report, Rome, 23 February 1943; *ibid*., informer's report, Rome, 6 April 1943; ASTa, Prefettura, Cat. 6, b. 116, Manifesto signed by *podestà* of Laterza, 15 September 1943; ASM, Prefettura, b. C401, Head of Milan Province to the Duce, 13 October 1944.
96 ASG, RSI, Prefettura Repubblicana di Genova, b. 28, from a Genoese citizen to Province head, 10 May 1944.
97 AN AJ41/25, Contrôles Techniques, 25 November–4 December 1940.
98 S. Kitson, 'Criminals or Liberators? French Public Opinion and the Allied Bombing of France, 1940–1945', in Baldoli, Knapp and Overy (eds), *Bombing, States and Peoples*, 281–3.
99 J. Guéhenno, *Journal des années noires, 1940–1944* (Paris: Gallimard, 2002 (1st edn. 1947)), 244.
100 B. Auroy, *Jours de guerre: Ma vie sous l'Occupation* (Montrouge: Bayard, 2008), 212–14.
101 J. Grenier, *Sous l'Occupation* (Paris: Éditions Claire Paulhan, 1997), 249.
102 Guéhenno, *Journal*, 244.
103 AN AJ41/24, Synthèse des Rapports mensuels des Commandants des Légions de Gendarmerie de la Zone Libre, mars 1942.
104 AN F7/14929, CTSM, 10 April–10 May 1942; AN AJ41/25, Contrôles Techniques, 10 July–10 August, 10 August–10 September, and 10 September–10 October 1942.
105 AN F1/c/III/1188, Prefectoral report, René Bouffet, Seine-Inférieure, 2 April 1942.
106 See above, p. 24.
107 AN AJ41/25 and AN F7/14929, CTSM, 10 May–10 June 1942: Annexes prisonniers de guerre.
108 See below, p. 235.
109 AN F1/c/III/1156, Prefectoral report (P. Marage), Morbihan, 31 March 1943.
110 AN 3AG/2/333.069, État d'esprit dans la région sud du Finistère, 20 May 1943; AN F1/A/3745, CFLN, diffusion 11 October 1943: Informations sur le Morbihan par un chargé de mission 'gouvernemental', Vichy, 16 July 1943; AN F1/A/3743, CFLN, France-Politique, État d'esprit de la population: Lorient (6 April/11 May 1943). AN 3AG/2/333.077, CFLN, France-Politique, Rapport Général sur la Bretagne, August 1943.
111 AN AJ41/356, SIPEG, Sommaire des bombardements survenus pendant la période du 29 mars au 5 avril 1943. Eddy Florentin, in *Quand les Alliés bombardaient la France* (Paris: Perrin, 1997: 113) puts the death toll at 291. The diarist Jean Galtier-Boissière wrote that the race meeting continued once the bodies had been removed (J. Galtier-Boissière, *Journal 1940–1950* (Paris: Quai Voltaire, 1992), 143).
112 AN F1/c/III/1187, Seine, Prefectoral report (René Bouffet), 5 May 1943.
113 AN 3AG/2/333, France Libre, France-Politique, État d'esprit de la population, April 1943.
114 *Ibid*., France Libre, France-Politique, État d'esprit de la population, April 1943; AN F1/c/III/1187, Seine, Prefectoral report (René Bouffet), 5 May 1943.
115 AN F7/14929, CTSM, 10 March–10 April 1943.

116 *Ibid.*, CTSM, 10 May–10 June, 10 June –10 July 1943.
117 AN 3AG/2/333, CFLN, Après les bombardements d'Aulnay, Drancy etc. – de source collaborationiste, 31 July 1943.
118 AN F1/A/3743.164, CFLN, France-Politique, Rapport Général sur la Bretagne, August–September 1943; AN F1/c/III/1162, Prefectoral report, Loire-Inférieure (Édouard Bonnefoy), 1 July–2 September 1943.
119 AN F1/c/III/1187, Prefectoral report, Seine (René Bouffet) 5 September 1943.
120 Galtier-Boissière, *Journal 1940–1950*, 155.
121 AN F1/c/III/1187, Prefectoral report, Seine (René Bouffet), 5 October 1943.
122 AN F7/14930, Contrôle Postal, 31 October 1943.
123 AN F1/A/3743, CFLN, France-Politique, L'opinion publique: la réaction en face de bombardements alliés (September/October 1943).
124 AN F7/14930, Contrôle Postal, 30 September 1943; AN F1/A/3744, CFLN, Commissariat à l'Intérieur, État d'esprit de la population, Contrôle postal de Haute-Savoie, November–December 1943; AN F1/A/3743, CFLN, Commissariat à l'Intérieur, L'état d'esprit de la population, Allier, December 1943–January 1944.
125 AN F1/A/3744, CFLN, Commissariat à l'Intérieur, Situation politique générale, Contrôle postal de Nice, 9 December 1943/9 February 1944.
126 AN F7/14901, RG, Note de renseignements, Situation générale à Nantes, 28 September 1943.
127 AN F7/14930, Contrôle Postal, 30 November 1943.
128 AN F1/A/3744, CFLN, Commissariat à l'Intérieur, État d'esprit de la population, 18 December 1943.
129 AN F1/A/3743, CFLN, France-Politique, État d'esprit en Bretagne, 17 July 1943; État d'esprit de la population dans la région du Cantal, September/November 1943.
130 AN F7/14930, Contrôle Postal, 31 October 1943; AN 3AG/2/333, CFLN, France-Politique, La vie et l'opinion des Parisiens en 1943; AN F1/A/3744, CFLN, Commissariat à l'Intérieur, État d'esprit de la population, Contrôle postal de Haute-Savoie, November/December 1943; AN F1/c/III/1162, Prefectoral report, Loire-Inférieure (Bonnefoy), 3 September–4 November 1943; AN F1/A/3743, CFLN, Commissariat à l'Intérieur, Réaction de l'opinion publique française en regard de bombardements anglo-américains, n.d. (December? 1943).
131 AN F1/c/III/1187, Prefectoral report, Seine (Bouffet), 5 October 1943; AD Var 1W/21, RG reports, Var, 15–21 November, 22–28 November and 29 November–5 December 1943.
132 AN F60/1690, *Manchester Guardian*, 29 May 1944. Cf. also *La Gazette de Lausanne*, 25 February 1944; *News Digest 1456*, from *St Galler Tagblatt*, 19 May 1944.
133 See above, p. 29.
134 AN F1/c/III/1187.75, Prefectoral report, Seine (René Bouffet), 5 June 1944.
135 AN F1/A/3743, CFLN, Enquête sur l'opinion française au début de l'année 1944, May 1944.
136 AN F7/14992, Rapports Statistiques, Interceptions Postales, January–July 1944.
137 AN 3AG/2/333, Post and telegraph censorship, Captured enemy mail (France), 5 June 1944, 'Air Raid Damage in Amiens, Low Morale due to Allied Bombing'; AN F1/A/3744, CFLN, Commissariat à l'Intérieur, État d'esprit de la population, Contrôle postal Inspection Régionale de Marseille, région Sud et Sud-Ouest, spring 1944; AN F7/14931 IC Marseille, Contrôle technique international de Marseille, July 1944.
138 AN F1/A/3744, CFLN, Commissariat à l'Intérieur, État d'esprit de la population, Contrôle postal de Nice, 17 April/2 May 1944.
139 AN F7/14929, CTSM, May 1944.
140 AN F7/14931, Contrôle technique international de Marseille, July 1944.
141 *Ibid.*, Contrôle Technique, St-Étienne, April and June 1944.
142 AN F1/A/3744, Commissariat à l'Intérieur, L'état d'esprit de la population rouennaise, June 1944 /16 July 1944.
143 AN F1/A/3743, CFLN, Commissariat à l'Intérieur, État d'esprit et réactions aux bombardements de la population varoise (24 February/6 July 1944).
144 *Ibid.*, Commissariat à l'Intérieur, L'état d'esprit de la population, 9 February 1944/21 February 1944.
145 AN F1/c/III/1188, Prefectoral report, Seine-Inférieure (Pierre Guérin), 5 March 1944.

146 Galtier-Boissière, *Journal 1940–1950*, 177.
147 AN F1/A/3743, CFLN, Commissariat à l'Intérieur, L'opinion publique en France d'après les rapports officiels de Vichy, January–March 1944/April 1944; CFLN, Commissariat à l'Intérieur, Les réactions de l'opinion publique à l'égard des éditoriaux prononcés par Philippe Henriot', 6 May/18 May 1944; GPRF, Commissariat à l'Intérieur, Les éditoriaux d'Henriot seraient très écoutés, 4 May/7 June 1944.
148 Cf. above, p. 195.
149 AN F1/A/3743, CFLN, Commissariat à l'Intérieur, Moral et ambiance de la population en France, January 1944/11 April 1944; AN F1/A/3765, CFLN, Commissariat à l'Intérieur, Les Bombardements de l'aviation anglo-américaine et les réactions de l'opinion française, 15 May/5 June 1944.
150 AN F1/A/3743, GPRF, Commissariat à l'Intérieur, Aperçu d'ensemble sur le moral de la population en France, 21 May/7 June 1944.
151 TNA AIR40/1720, Military attaché report, Allied bombing raids over France, Annexe II; SHAA, 3D/321/3, Documentation d'origine britannique, *Illustrated London News*, 27 May 1944.
152 B. Auroy, *Jours de guerre: Ma vie sous l'Occupation* (Montrouge: Bayard, 2008), 300.
153 APA, 1795, Madeleine Raillon, '1944–1945, "ma liberation" de Paris', 15–16.
154 AN F1/A/3743, CFLN, France-Politique, La situation en France, 13 November 1943; *ibid.*, Commissariat à l'Intérieur, L'état d'esprit de la population, Allier, December 1943–January 1944;
155 TNA AIR40/1720, Military attaché report, Allied bombing raids over France, 30 May 1944, 16–17. French original (Note sur les répercussions des bombardements anglo-américains sur le moral des populations en France, signed col. Jousse) available in TNA FO371/41984 and FO660/191, and in AN F1/A/3743.
156 A. M. Imbriani, *Gli italiani e il Duce: il mito e l'immagine di Mussolini negli ultimi anni del fascismo, 1938–1943* (Naples: Liguori, 1992), 121–2.
157 ADN MG/02, G. Guglielminetti, *Cronache di un'adolescenza di guerra*, unpublished memoir, 1.
158 ADN DG/06, A. Vita (born Milan, 1924), *Il mio segreto diario di guerra*, unpublished diary, 24 (4 September 1943).
159 ASM, Prefettura, b. 267, Generale di Corpo d'Armata, Commander A. Canale, Comitato Difesa Territoriale di Milano, to prefect of Milan, 4 March 1943.
160 M. Fincardi, 'Anglo-American Air Attacks and the Rebirth of Public Opinion in Fascist Italy', in Baldoli, Knapp and Overy (eds), *Bombing, States and Peoples*, 241–55; ACS, MI, DGPS, DPP, b. 238, Fascist informer from Sesto San Giovanni, 26 January 1943, cited in S. Colarizi, *La Seconda Guerra Mondiale e la Repubblica* (Turin: UTET, 1984), 180; ACS, MI, DGPS, DAGR, IIGM, A5G, b. 27, Prefect of Bologna to Interior Ministry, 3 April 1943.
161 U. Burla, *La Spezia nel ventennio. Dal 1922 al 1943* (La Spezia: Luna Editore, 2008), 137.
162 G. S. Retico, *Paura oltre la Cisa* (Brescia: Toroselle, 2008), 127.
163 UK Foreign Office, *Sicily Zone Handbook 1943*, ed. R. Mangiameli (Caltanissetta-Rome: Salvatore Sciascia Editore, 1994), 45.
164 R. Mangiameli and F. Nicastro (eds), *Arrivano … gli americani a Vittoria nell'estate del '43* (Vittoria: Comune di Vittoria, 2004), 21, 197, 233, 237–8.
165 N. Gallerano, 'L'arrivo degli alleati', in M. Isnenghi, ed., *I luoghi della memoria. Strutture ed eventi dell'Italia unita* (Rome-Bari, 1997), 459.
166 G. Pagliaro, *Giorni di guerra in Sicilia. Diario per la nonna, 9 maggio–8 agosto 1943* (Palermo, 1993), 53 (30 July 1943).
167 T. Baris, *Tra due fuochi. Esperienza e memoria della guerra lungo la linea Gustav* (Rome-Bari: Laterza, 2003), 58–71.
168 G. Chilanti, *Bandiera rossa e borsa nera. La resistenza di una adolescente* (Milan: Mursia, 1998), 34 (23 January 1944).
169 C. Di Pompeo, *Più della fame e più dei bombardamenti. Diario dell'occupazione di Roma* (Bologna: Il Mulino, 2009), 48 (22 November 1943; 54 (28 November 1943); 107 (25 February 1944); 111 (7 March 1944), 115 (14 March 1944); 121 (25 March 1944).
170 Gribaudi, *Guerra totale*, 93.

171 ADN MG/03, Sarra, *A ritroso nel tempo*, 43.
172 ASG, RSI, Prefettura di Genova, b. 30, sub-file on 'Public Spirit', informer's report to the police chief of Genoa, 20 August 1944.
173 G. Scatassa, 'Diario di una ragazza di Anzio', in P. Colantuono, *Lo sbarco e la battaglia di Anzio. Immagini e testimonianze* (Anzio: Tipografia Marina, 2009), 64 (3 March 1944); 65 (2–3 April 1944).
174 A. Rastelli, *Bombe sulla città. Gli attacchi aerei alleati: le vittime civili a Milano* (Milan: Mursia, 2000), 147, 217, 229.
175 'Lettera degli arcivescovi e vescovi della Regione Piemontese al Clero e al Popolo nella Pasqua 1944', *Bollettino Mensile della Parrocchia di S. Giulia*, Torino, June–July 1944, no. 6–7, 1.
176 Calamandrei, *Diario 1939–1945*, vol. 2. *1942–1945*, 83–4 (25 November 1942).
177 ACS, MI, DPP, b. 211, informers' reports, Varese, 15 July 1940; Brindisi, 12 July 1940; Genoa, 5 July 1940; *ibid.*, b. 210, informer's report, Naples, 27 August 1940.
178 Retico, *Paura oltre la Cisa*, 23.
179 ASTo, Prefettura, I Versamento, b. 519, UNPA Provincial Command of Turin to the Province Head, 5 August 1944.
180 ACS, MI, DGPCSA, b. 106, UNPA Provincial Command, Naples to UNPA General Command, Rome, 29 January 1943.
181 *Ibid.*, b. 104, Prefect of Cagliari to Interior Minister, 4 March 1943.
182 ASP, Prefettura, Gabinetto 1941–5, b. 636, Prefect of Palermo to the Ministry of Interior, 4 November 1942; Prefect of Palermo to the Ministry of Interior, 10 June 1943.
183 See for example ACS, MI, DGPCSA, b. 104, Prefect of Agrigento to the Ministry of Interior, 4 June 1943.
184 NARA, RG 208, box 329, Office of Overseas War Information, Bureau of Research Analysis, 23 July 1943.
185 G. Vecchio, *Lombardia 1940–1945. Vescovi, preti e società alla prova della guerra* (Brescia: Morcelliana, 2005), 144.
186 A. Caserta, *Il clero di Napoli durante la guerra e la resistenza (1940–1943)* (Naples: Luciano Editore, 1995), 4–5.
187 ASTo, Prefettura, b. 524, Prefect of Turin to Ministry of Interior, 29 November 1940.
188 U. Baduel, *L'elmetto inglese* (Palermo: Sellerio, 1993), 107.
189 M. Carli and U. G. Silveri, *Bombardare Roma: gli alleati e la città aperta, 1940–1944* (Bologna: Il Mulino, 2007).
190 F. Manaresi, 'Bologna città aperta', in C. Bersani and V. Roncuzzi Roversi Monaco, *Delenda Bononia. Immagini dei bombardamenti, 1943–1945* (Bologna: Patron, 1995), 57–74.
191 D. Gagliani, 'La guerra in periferia. Cittadini e poteri in un comune appenninico', in Annali della Fondazione Micheletti, *L'Italia in guerra, 1940–1943*, vol. 5 (Brescia: Fondazione Micheletti, 1991), 911.
192 G. Chilanti, *Bandiera rossa e borsa nera*, 43 (11 and 12 March 1944). Pietro Nenni also noticed disillusionment with the Pope's speech: cf. Nenni, *Tempo di guerra fredda*, 47 (12 March 1944).
193 C. Di Pompeo, *Più della fame*, 130 (11 April 1944).
194 For details, cf. C. Baldoli, 'Religion and Bombing in Italy, 1940–1945', in Baldoli, Knapp and Overy (eds), *Bombing, States and Peoples*, 136–53.
195 ACS, Ministero dell'Interno, A5G Seconda Guerra Mondiale, b. 27, prefect of Verona to Ministry of Interior, 12 April 1943.
196 Baldoli, 'Religion and Bombing', 149.
197 ACS, MI, DGPS, DPP, b. 211, fasc. 1, informer's report, Milan, 12 June 1940.
198 *Ibid.*, b. 210, confidential note, Genoa, 13 June 1940.
199 *Ibid.*, informer's reports, Turin, 16 June 1940; Rome, 17 June 1940.
200 *Ibid.*, informer's report, Trento, 19 June 1940.
201 *Ibid.*, b. 229, informer's report, Cagliari, 10 August 1940.
202 ASG, Prefettura, b. 159, letter from a citizen of Genoa to the prefect, n.d. (February 1941).
203 ACS, MI, DGPS, DPP, b. 211, fasc. 1, informer's report, Bari, 30 October 1940.
204 *Ibid.*, b. 239, informer's report, Rome, 15 February 1943.

205 ACS, MI, DGPS, DAGR, IIGM, A5G, b. 102, from Questura of Venice to Interior Ministry, 13 January 1941. See above, p. 000.
206 ACS, MI, DGPS, DPP, b. 211, fasc. 2, informer's report, Rome, 26 October 1941.
207 ASM, Prefettura, b. C268, Commander of the 24th Legion of the Carabinieri to the prefect of Milan, 26 October 1942.
208 Cf. above, p. 144.
209 Mussolini, *Opera Omnia*, vol. 31, (Florence: La Fenice, 1951–1963), 118–33.
210 Calamandrei, *Diario 1939–1945*, vol. II, 87–9 (12 December 1942). See also Imbriani, *Gli italiani e il Duce*, 174–6.
211 ASG, Prefettura, b. 157, Commander of Genoa Carabinieri to prefect of Genoa, 3 December 1942.
212 ASP, Prefettura, b. 636, citizen of Palermo to Mussolini and to the prefect, 5 December 1942; ACS, MI, DGPS, DAGR, IIGM, A5G, b. 61, report of the Questura of Taranto, 13 December 1942.
213 ACS, MI, DGPS, DPP, b. 211, fasc. 2, informer's report, Pistoia, 8 December 1942.
214 *Ibid.*, b. 239, informer's report, Rome, 2 March 1943.
215 *Il Popolo d'Italia*, 6 May 1943; Mussolini, *Opera Omnia*, vol. 31, 178.
216 ASN, Prefettura, II Versamento, Cat. 6, b. 1224, Neapolitan citizens to Mussolini, 23 May 1943.
217 *Ibid.*, Carabinieri of Naples to prefect, 17 June 1943.
218 *L'Osservatore Romano*, 21 July 1943; *L'Osservatore Romano*, 14 August 1943; *L'Osservatore Romano*, 15 August 1943.
219 ACS, MI, DGPS, DPP, b. 239, informer's report, Rome, 24 July 1943.
220 M. Isnenghi, *Le guerre degli italiani. Parole, immagini, ricordi: 1848–1945* (Bologna: Il Mulino, 2005), 62–3.
221 *Corriere della Sera* on 17 December 1944; Mussolini, *Opera Omnia*, vol. 32, 126–39.
222 INSMLI, Corpo Volontari della Libertà, b. 479, fasc. 'Canzoni e poesie', *Il testamento di Mussolini*, 1944.
223 AD Var 1W/64, Prefect of Var to Head of Government, 13 December 1943.
224 AN 3AG/2/333, CFLN, Tour d'horizon politique, June 1943; AD BduR 76W/129, RG Marseille, Information, 5 June 1944.
225 AN F7/14901, RG Bordeaux, note du 2 juin 1943; AM Rennes 6H/26, anonymous flyer, copied by Central Police Commissariat, 27 March 1943; AN F1/A/3765, GPRF, Commissariat à l'Intérieur, Les agissements odieux des Allemands pendant les bombardements, 18 May/7 June 1944.
226 AN F7/14931, Contrôle technique, Digne, June 1944.
227 AD SM 51W/86, RG Rouen, Rapport, 29 August–4 September 1943; AN F7/14901, Sondage de l'Opinion au lendemain du bombardement de Paris, September 1943; AN F7/14901, RG IetV to Prefect of IetV, 8 June 1943; TNA AIR40/1720, Military attaché report, Allied bombing raids over France, Annexe III; AN F1/A/3765, GPRF, Commissariat à l'Intérieur, Les agissements odieux des Allemands pendant les bombardements, 18 May/7 June 1944.
228 T. Brooks, *British Propaganda to France, 1940–1944: Machinery, Method and Message* (Edinburgh: Edinburgh University Press, 2007), 152–3.
229 J.-P. Sartre, *Situations, III* (Paris: Gallimard, 1949), 30–1.
230 ACS, MI, DGPS, IIGM, A5G, b. 60, 'Promemoria per il Duce', 17 May 1943.
231 Cf. in particolar documents in ACS, MI, DGPS, IIGM, A5G, b. 1.
232 *Ibid.*, Fascist informers, Rome, 5 and 7 March 1943.
233 ACS, MI, DGPS, DPP, b. 211, fasc. 3, informer's report, Rome, 18 February 1941.
234 *Ibid.*, fasc. 2, informer's report, 19 August 1942.
235 ACS, MinCulPop, b. 122, 12 September 1941.
236 ACS, MI, DGPS, DPP, b. 239, Fascist informers, Rome, 23 and 26 February 1943.
237 Baldoli and Fincardi, 'Italian Society under Allied Bombs', 1,031.
238 G. Chianese, *'Quando uscimmo dai rifugi'. Il Mezzogiorno tra guerra e dopoguerra (1943–46)* (Rome: Carocci, 2004), 39.
239 ADN A/Adn2, Palmira Marchioli, *Ricordi*, unpublished memoir written in 1970, 10.

240 Testimonies collected in Comune di Prevalle, *Ricordi Ninetta... Uomini e donne di Prevalle si raccontano* (Brescia: Liberedizioni, 2008), 55; 71.
241 Report from the Health Officer of Trento to the Prefect, January 1945, in Pedron and Pontalti, *Uomini e donne in guerra*, 41.
242 ADN MG/03, Sarra, *A ritroso nel tempo*, 138.
243 ADN DG/04, P. Susini, *Diario agosto 1944–agosto 1946*, unpublished diary, 4 (19 September 1944.
244 ADN DG/89, F. Pogioli, *Il bidone in cima a un palo*, unpublished diary, 35, 38, (2 and 9 September 1944).
245 M. Carazzolo, *Più forte della paura. Diario di guerra e dopoguerra (1938–1947)* (Sommacampagna: Cierre, 2007), 204; 250–1; ADN MG/Adn, Iole Bresadola, *I nostri verdi anni*, unpublished memoir written in 1965, 96, event undated but probably February 1945; ADN MG/04, Ada Carrara, *La mia guerra*, unpublished memoir written in 1990, 17. The event occurred in summer 1944.
246 Mémorial de Caen, TE696, Claude Métayer, 5.
247 ADLA 1623W/2, Commissaire de Police, Nantes, to Prefect of Loire-Inférieure, 12 May 1941; ADLA 1694W/61, Commissaire de Police, La Baule, to sub-prefect of Saint-Nazaire, 21 July 1941; AM Nantes 4H/103, Commissaire Central, Nantes, to Prefect of Loire-Inférieure, 5 December 1941.
248 AD Morbihan 1526W/14, RG Vannes to RG Rennes 28 February 1943; AN.F1A3743, CFLN, France-Politique, État d'esprit en Bretagne, 17 July/22 July 1943; AN F1/A/3765, République Française, BCRA, Informations diverses: avion anglais abattu et funérailles d'aviateurs, October 1943.
249 AN F1/A/3743, CFLN, Commissariat à l'Intérieur, L'état d'esprit de la population, December 1943–January 1944/11 April 1944: Secteur 9, B du Rh, Groupe Marseille Duguesclin, 30 December 1943; AN.F1A3765, CFLN, Commissariat à l'Intérieur, La Résistance en France, November 1943/17 February 1944: note of 15 November 1943.
250 AN F1/A/3744, CFLN, Commissariat à l'Intérieur, L'opinion française (Île de France): un historique depuis juin 1940 (16 March/13 April 1944).
251 AN F1/A/3765, GPRF, Commissariat à l'Intérieur, Compte-rendu des obsèques de deux aviateurs alliés, 31 August 1944; B. Gautier, 'À travers les années quarante', (Toulon: Les Presses du Midi, 2001), 103.
252 INSMLI, CVL, Fasc. 44, partisans from Varese to the Allied Swiss headquarters, 1 April 1945.
253 Harris, *Bomber Offensive*, 98.
254 ADLA 1694W/1, Prefecture of Loire-Inférieure, press release, 7 August 1941; SHAA 3D/48, Rundstedt (CinC West) HQ to French Govt., 9 September 1943.
255 ADSM 51W/86, RG Rouen, report for 25–31 July 1943.
256 AN F1/A/3765, GPRF, Commissariat à l'Intérieur, Les populations françaises et les prisonniers alliés, July/ 8 August 1944. The story is reminiscent of an early episode in *La Grande Vadrouille*, the 1966 comic film starring Bourvil and Terry-Thomas about the escapades of three Allied airmen who bail out over Paris.
257 AN F1/A/3765, CFLN, Commissariat à l'Intérieur, Avis allemand concernant les avions étrangers ayant parus dans le 'Progrès de Saône et Loire', 17 April/4 May 1944.
258 Kitson, 'Criminals or Liberators?', 282; J. M. Langley, *Fight Another Day* (London: Collins, 1974), 251.
259 TNA, AIR 40/1897, Air Intelligence, Chart of Escapers and Evaders, n.d. (1945).
260 TNA AIR 14/1021, Harris to Massigli, 18 October 1944.
261 AD Morbihan 1526W/14, RG Morbihan, Vannes, to RG Rennes, 20 February 1943; AN F1/A/3765.026, CFLN, Commissariat à l'Intérieur, Bombardements de l'aviation anglo-américaine, réactions de l'opinion française, 15 May/5 June 1944.
262 AM St-Étienne 5H/37, *Le Mémorial de Saint-Étienne*, 1 June 1944; AN F1/A/3765, GPRF, Commissariat à l'Intérieur, Ces bons Allemands! (À propos des aviateurs alliés parachutés), 2 June/11 July 1944. The latter report refers to articles that appeared in the *Réveil du Nord* and the *Grand Écho du Nord*. It adds that the Germans failed to state that four weeks previously, near Arras, they had killed a parachuted British airman, and kicked and trampled the body.

263 TNA AIR 20/8911, Air Ministry, A.I.1(a)P/W, to I.S.9(AB), Paris, 21 February 1946. Ref. 10087/A.I.1(a)P/W/136.
264 *Ibid.*, René Marsollier, Quimperlé, 'To the Director', 2 June 1945 (translation, A.I.1, 14 February 1946).
265 *Ibid.*, Air Ministry, A.I.1(a)P/W, to I.S.9(AB), Paris, 13 February 1946 (ref. 10087/A.I.1(a) P/W/119) and 21 February 1946 (ref. 10087/A.I.1(a)P/W/140).
266 AN F1/A/3743, CFLN, France-Politique, État d'esprit de la population: Morbihan (30 May/17 July 1943).
267 In R. Absalom, *Strange Alliance: Aspects of Escape and Survival in Italy, 1943–1945* (Florence: Olschki, 1991), 151.
268 TNA, AIR 40/2467, Air Intelligence, Evasion report by RAF Officer James Charles Cole of 55 Squadron, Bomber Command, n.d. (1945).
269 Cf. Langley, *Fight Another Day*, 129–230.
270 P. Montaz, *Onze Américains tombés du ciel sauvés par des maquis français* (Hauteville (Savoie, France): author, 1994).
271 TNA, AIR 40/2467, Air Intelligence, Capture, evasion and escape report by RAF Lieutenant A. H. Kell of 142 Squadron, Middle East Command, n.d. (1945); cf. also WO 208/3343-3345, and WO208/5393-5404 for similar accounts.
272 TNA AIR 20/8911, Warrant Officer Roland H. Hale to I.S.9(AB), 21 January 1946.
273 *Ibid.*, Air Ministry, A.I.1(a)P/W, to I.S.9(AB), Paris, 25 February 1946. Ref. 10087/A.I.1(a) P/W/144.
274 *Ibid.*, Air Ministry, A.I.1(a)P/W, to I.S.9(AB), Paris, 25 February 1946. Ref. 10087/A.I.1(a) P/W/144.
275 *Ibid.*, Warrant Officer Roland H. Hale to I.S.9(AB), 21 January 1946.
276 Cf. above, p. 000.
277 R. Absalom, 'Hiding history: the Allies, the Resistance and the others in occupied Italy 1943–1945', *Historical Journal*, 38 (1995), 111–31.

8

Resistance, Bombing, Liberation

By 1944 the Allies had established official or quasi-official relations with resistance movements in both France and Italy. The those with the French, inevitably, were older. De Gaulle had maintained quasi-official, albeit stormy, relations with the British from June 1940. His Free French movement progressively won the conditional loyalty of France's internal Resistance from 1942; consolidated into the Comité Français de Libération Nationale (CFLN) in Algiers in 1943, it received British representatives of ministerial rank (Harold Macmillan, then Alfred Duff Cooper), and less elevated envoys from the more sceptical Americans. As for Italy, although the Allies had not expected the formation of partisan brigades, they found them useful, and established official links from spring 1944.[1] An article in *The Stars and Stripes*, the newspaper of the US Armed Forces in Europe, the Mediterranean and north Africa, praised the prowess of Italy's partisans in their 'fluid, roving type of mountain warfare':

> Many tiny mountain hamlets ... are Allied outposts by virtue of the fact that partisans live in them. Italian bands have been helpful in getting our forces out of serious trouble ... Security obviously forbids in going into details in how partisans aid in gathering information about the enemy, in sabotaging enemy lines of communication, in sheltering escaped Allied prisoners and shot-down flyers, and in encouraging desertion among Italian Fascist troops.[2]

But Allied bombing was a growing embarrassment to resistance organizations in both countries. In public, they blamed it on the Germans, or simply maintained silence on the issue unless challenged. Towards Allied authorities, however, while accepting the need for air raids, they repeatedly asked for better accuracy and for a better integration of locally organized sabotage into Allied strategy. The limited success of such appeals caused disappointment and bitterness among anti-Fascists risking their lives for an Allied victory in both France and Italy.

The relationship between resistance, bombing, and liberation was a complex and contrasted one in each country. France's long bombing campaign was largely (though not wholly) dissociated from the struggles of the Resistance. It was followed by a 3–4-month ground war backed by air power, and liberation of most of the country by mid-September 1944; in many, though certainly not all, French localities, the experience of liberation swiftly eclipsed that of air raids. Italy, by contrast, sustained both area bombing in 1942–3 and a 21-month ground war backed by air power, with air raids dragging well into 1945. And above all, the bombing of northern Italy was intimately bound up with the development of the anti-Fascist resistance.

BOMBING, STRIKES AND RESISTANCE

Northern Italy experienced three major waves of bombing: the area attacks on industrial cities (chiefly Milan, Turin and Genoa) in October–November 1942, the raids that followed the fall of Mussolini in summer 1943, and finally the much longer bombing campaign lasting from the armistice of September 1943 to April 1945. Each was associated with a phase in the development of Italy's anti-Fascist movement.

At the end of October 1942, a Milanese informer reported, 'the fury of the enemy air attack had precipitated an atmosphere of irritation against the government and Fascism'.[3] This proved to be an understatement. Over five months from December 1942, northern Italy experienced a wave of industrial unrest without precedent under Fascism. This took three forms. The first was absenteeism, running at some 20 per cent among FIAT workers at the end of 1942, not least due to evacuation.[4] The second consisted of protests about pay and conditions. In January Mussolini received a letter signed 'FIAT workers', warning that even if the British had not turned workers against the regime by bombing, FIAT's own inhumane treatment of its workers was about to achieve the same end. Copies were sent to the prefect and the Party secretary of Turin, FIAT owner Giovanni Agnelli and FIAT director Vittorio Valletta.[5] Third and most importantly, workers went on strike. Piedmont saw 21 strikes between August 1942 and February 1943 (16 between December and February), and in Lombardy there were 15 (10 between November and February).[6] Strikes might start small – a few dozen workers stopping work for an hour or less, as at FIAT's Ferriere and Spa plants in January 1943.[7] But the movement grew. A strike at FIAT's Mirafiori plants, starting on 5 March 1943, spread within days to all the main factories in Turin and then to other industrial centres in Piedmont. It reached Milan at the end of March and the rest of Lombardy in April.[8] Key plants included Italy's main steelworks, Falk at Sesto San Giovanni, with 7,000 workers; Pirelli in Milan; Bicocca near Sesto; and the aeronautic firm Caproni at Taliedo with its 6,000 workers.[9] Even when northern Italy returned to work, after almost a month of near-paralysis, there were still shorter stoppages as well as passive resistance, such as refusals to work overtime, and rising absenteeism among workers who commuted.

The strikes were related to bombing in two ways. Materially, they raised new issues between workers, employers and the state. These involved, for example, special payments for workers who had had to evacuate their families, or who had lost their homes and had to commute; or the payment of workers laid off when bombing disrupted production (FIAT at Lingotto tried to withhold wages during such a stoppage).[10] It was this type of issue that typically triggered strikes, and both management and the state, concerned by low morale among workers, made some attempts to buy them off; Valletta, for example, decided on 15 March to pay an advance of 300 lire to all FIAT workers who would remain disciplined.[11] In addition, the raids convinced workers that the Axis was losing the war. In this context, the strikes of March 1943 revealed the depth of the regime's crisis.[12] In Genoa, for example, a city where thousands of people had been bombed out and almost 500 killed between October and November 1942, anger at the regime and defeatism were still strong enough for workers at the Ansaldo factory to be overheard saying 'it would be good if the British came and destroyed everything'.[13] Despite an effective press blackout, news of the strikes spread through the country, dealing another heavy blow to the image of a regime already suffering from military defeats and bombing.

Fascists from Mussolini down recognized that the protests were political, not merely economic.[14] Mussolini acknowledged the links between Allied raids, civilian defeatism and strikes at a national Fascist Party meeting on 11 March 1943, warning that Turin must not set 'the same example in this war as it gave in the last one, in 1917'. To prevent this, Mussolini urged, 'It is necessary that both during and immediately after the raids the Party be present . . . so that moral and material support is provided with no delay'.[15]

Conversely, anti-Fascists politicized material demands. The Ministry of Corporations had agreed in February 1943 that workers forced to commute because their families had been bombed out and evacuated would receive an indemnity corresponding to 192 hours of work. But many could not evacuate, or chose not to, as travelling in precarious conditions after a 10–12 hour shift was hard.[16] Workers therefore demanded that the '192 hour' allowance be extended to all, evacuees or not.[17] The issue of the 192 hours, directly related to bombing, became the common cause on which a renascent (and still clandestine) Partito Comunista Italiano (PCI) was able to mobilize workers – and a far more effective lever than appeals to pre-Fascist traditions of mobilization, however strong in Turin.[18] In 1945, the Communist organisers of the FIAT strikes, Umberto Massola and Girolamo Li Causi, would claim that the movement had represented the Italian people's first contribution to the war of liberation.[19]

After Mussolini's fall in July 1943, strikes again broke out in Turin and again spread through Italy. In Bologna, on 27 July, after two days of anti-Fascist demonstrations, workers left their factories. Despite arrests, many stayed out on 28 July. Leaflets were signed by the reborn political parties, and the police feared 'Communist infiltrations'.[20] In Milan the second strike wave, after the repression of March 1943, followed the devastating raids of 8 and 17 August 1943; by 17 August, 65,000 workers were out in Milan and its province, demanding peace above all. In Turin and elsewhere in Piedmont soldiers were ordered to use live rounds to force workers back to work – and did so at Grandi Motori in Turin on 17 August, killing one and injuring seven.[21] Unchecked by the repression, the protest spread to factories in Piedmont, Emilia, Umbria, Tuscany, Liguria and

Lombardy. According to *L'Unità* on 22 August, workers had stockpiled weapons in readiness for fighting the Germans.[22] This second wave of strikes again corresponded to a period of area bombing, and to ensuing propaganda designed to persuade Italians to pressure Badoglio to sue for peace.

The third period, corresponding to the Salò Republic, was the longest and most complex. North Italian industry was increasingly mobilized for the German war effort. This produced a convergence between the Allies' aims, no longer targeting Italian morale but German war production and communication lines, and those of the Resistance, organizing workers to sabotage the Republic's industry. The German occupiers responded to constant bombing and endemic strikes with a range of strategies, most of which increased worker militancy. At the same time the human and material impact of bombing strained the anti-Fascists' propaganda resources to the limit.

A strike in Turin in November 1943, the fruit of the PCI's co-ordination of action between partisans and workers, started at Grandi Motori before extending across all the FIAT factories; there followed a one-week general strike in Milan in December, a three-day strike in Genoa in January 1944, and many smaller strikes across the region, culminating in a general strike across most of northern Italy in March 1944. Two of the organizers cited as reasons for the strikes hatred of the Germans, who were getting Italian workers to produce for them, and the terrifying impact of the raids of August 1943, which could only end when the Germans left.[23] Meanwhile every organ of the Salò Republic noticed and acted on the convergence between strikers, partisans, and Allies. On 3 March 1944 Fascist trade unions called on workers to end strikes which they said merely followed the enemy's political directives.[24] The Interior Ministry published a statement in *Corriere della Sera* qualifying the general strike as a 'genuine and classic example of complicity with the enemy'.[25] The Milan prefecture reported insurrection attempts taking place 'according to orders given by enemy propaganda'.[26] A further report in July stated that while workers in Milan were apparently quiet, new 'terrorist' raids were likely to bring on a new strike wave.[27]

The Germans too tried to end labour unrest. A poster displayed in Genoa, signed by SS Brigadeführer Paul Zimmermann, presented the German armed forces as bearers of security, giving Italy's population a chance to wipe clear the 'betrayal of 8 September'. The Germans, it claimed, had already granted better working conditions, food and pay, in Milan and Turin, and would do the same for Genoese workers if they collaborated; those who deserted the workplace, by contrast, would face harsh treatment.[28] Zimmermann's actions, however, corresponded more to the mailed fist than to the outstretched hand. Sent by Hitler to 'pacify the city and province' of Turin, Zimmermann had already crushed protests there by shooting the leaders, arresting workers, and sending almost 1,000 to Germany. These actions further widened the gulf between the working class and the Salò Republic.[29]

The Germans also attempted measures to maintain production despite the bombing campaign. Most provoked further unrest. When the US 15th Air Force bombed the Dalmine steel works in Bergamo province on 6 July 1944, the Germans delayed sounding the alarm; they had noticed that workers, not trusting their shelters, moved well away from factories during alerts. Some 200 workers were killed, triggering a strike in Dalmine.[30]

An equally provocative German tactic was dispersal. FIAT machinery in particular moved to the area around Lake Garda. On 20 June 1944, 12,000 workers at Mirafiori responded by striking, followed by another 50,000 workers at FIAT and Lancia the next day, after a petition to Agnelli had brought no results. Although the Germans still began the moving operation on 22 June, 'timely Allied bombing' delayed it, as the Committee for the Liberation of Northern Italy reported.[31] Then the workers went on strike again. With 40,000 employees out over the following ten days, Fascist police reports suggested a link between FIAT strikes and the enemy air forces.[32] A big strike had also hit OM in Brescia in July, and the Fascist and German authorities had to confess that they were 'impotent in the face of such a vast workers' movement'. Attempts to relocate industry were resisted even by the industrialists.[33] An attempt in late 1944 to move part of FIAT's aero-engine department from Turin to the road tunnels running between Gargnano in Brescia province and Riva in Trento province had to be scaled back as only some 200 of the 2,000 workers needed could be found in Turin. Only a fraction of the tunnels was eventually occupied.[34]

Removal to Germany was also tried, but even where it happened, workers rarely followed plant. When the Germans dismantled the Pignone metallurgical factory in Florence in late June 1944, only 150 out of the 10,000 employees volunteered to go, and they soon changed their minds and disappeared, with the others. In Genoa, of 14,000 workers required for Germany, only 2,000 could be rounded up and sent.[35] The strike movement, meanwhile, continued. In December 1944, workers from Milan's 23 main factories began a strike against the relocation of industry which took on huge proportions.

The Allies recognized the importance of Italian Resistance activity. An American report on production at FIAT found that, alongside the impact of Fifteenth Air Force raids between 29 March 1944 and 22 January 1945, several factories in Turin working for the Reich, such as Lingotto, Grandi Motori, Mirafiori and Lancia, were producing at 'a greatly reduced rate'. This was a result, not only of the raw materials shortage, but also of sabotage and strikes.[36] At a meeting of the US Office of Strategic Services in June 1944, Resistance groups in Italy were praised for having 'done quite a bit of demolitions' and 'exceeded … expectations in this matter'.[37]

Allied leaflets to Italians reflected the new relationship with the Resistance and began to resemble those dropped on France:[38] Italians were now on the Allied side, waiting to be liberated. The Allies reported military victories over the Germans in Italy, with Italian anti-Fascists fighting alongside the Allies;[39]

Churchill promised 'weapons and political solidarity to anti-Fascist Italy';[40] a leaflet entitled *Italia combatte* ('Italy fights on') featured successful attacks on German communication lines by Allied bombers and partisan sabotage.[41]

There remained the question of bombing, which was also approached in terms comparable to those of Allied leaflets destined for France. In February 1945 (when the weakness of Axis air defences might have been expected to improve Allied bombing accuracy), General Mark Clark told the northern Italian population that as the Allies had to bomb lines of communication, civilians should move away from roads, marshalling yards, bridges and industrial objectives; Clark also encouraged civilians to help the Allies in the fight against the Nazi-Fascist oppressors, who were held solely to blame for the Italian people's suffering.[42]

Italy's anti-Fascists told a similar story to the Allies. Posters were found at Cernusco sul Naviglio near Milan in October 1943, one stating that the Germans were being beaten by the Russians and 'were dominated in the skies by Anglo-American air power'. The other, ignoring the fact that the Allies had done the most damage to Italian cities, exhorted citizens to 'defend our homes from the merciless enemy who, in the last moment of his retreat, will not hesitate to bring ... destruction'.[43] A leaflet from the Piedmont Liberation Committee dated February 1944 explained that more bombing was likely because the Germans and the Fascists were forcing workers to produce for their war. This, said the leaflet, echoing Allied propaganda, workers should refuse to do.[44] A CLN leaflet in Milan recalled the city's glorious battle against the Austrians in 1848 at the dawn of the Risorgimento: 'The city of the Five Days ... will soon see its streets and squares covered with barricades.'[45] After the raid of 20 October 1944, which killed more than 600 civilians, a poster appeared on Milanese walls blaming the Salò Republic and pointing out that the government had failed to organize any form of assistance; survivors were left to their fate, homeless and with nothing to eat. It concluded: 'if the authorities do not help, you can act yourself'. The poster was signed by a 'Workers' Committee'.[46] Every effort was made, therefore, to turn Allied bombing into an anti-Fascist issue.

In France, Resistance activity was much less closely related to Allied bombing than in Italy, though Resistance movements could hardly fail to show awareness of air raids. After the Boulogne-Billancourt raid of 3/4 March 1942, the leading Free French broadcaster Maurice Schumann told his compatriots that the civilian victims 'fell on the same field of honour as all the French dead of two wars, and as their British comrades by their thousands in the ruins of Coventry or Bristol'. Vichy was to blame, having 'knowingly turned [France] into a huge military target, a battlefield, as they harnessed her economy to the enemy's'.[47] Schumann's message, for all its rhetorical qualities, was not calculated to bring lasting comfort to the victims of bombing; later Gaullist broadcasts tended to stay off the subject.

There were, it is true, some parallels with Italy, notably in the behaviour of the banned French Communist Party (PCF). Like its Italian counterpart, the

PCF tried to mobilize on the issue of indemnities for workers in danger zones, introduced by Vichy in 1942 but regarded as insufficient.[48] The PCF also gave Allied raids, from Boulogne-Billancourt onwards, its full support, stressing that they helped the Soviet war effort and referring to the dead as victims of Nazism, not of the British. Again like the Italians, the PCF encouraged workers to slow down production and to demand good shelters.[49] After the raid on Toulon in November 1943, the PCF's Var section berated the 'Vichy scum' as solely responsible for raids; to avoid being bombed, it continued, workers should sabotage their own machines; air-raid victims, meanwhile, should organize and press their demands for proper shelters, decent replacement housing, clothing, bedding, furniture and allowances. Or, as a PCF flyer in Marseille put it simply in July 1944, 'To avoid air raids, put the Boche to flight.'[50]

As in Italy, too, the Resistance was capable of getting London to recognize its efforts at sabotage. The Peugeot plant at Sochaux near Montbéliard was spared raids in December 1943 on precisely this ground.[51] So, apparently, was the rail centre at Ambérieu-en-Bugey, east of Lyons: after 7 June 1944, when the Resistance destroyed 52 locomotives as well as machine-tools and other station equipment, there were no further raids.[52]

The difference with Italy in both of these areas, however, was one of scope. There is little evidence that the PCF's efforts to mobilize on issues related to bombing bore fruit outside the ranks of the Resistance itself. A Renseignements généraux report following the Toulon raid claimed that, whatever the official Party line, Communist workers had been loudest in condemning the Allies.[53] The biggest French strikes of the war, in the coalfields of Nord-Pas de Calais in 1941, were unrelated to bombing. The raid on Marseille of 27 May 1944 effectively *halted* a general strike led by transport workers.[54] Similarly, while the Allies supplied explosives and other sabotage equipment to the French Resistance, they held off from bombing only in a few individual cases, despite the best efforts of the Algiers-based CFLN. Inevitably this generated tensions, in France as in Italy, between the Allies and the Resistance.

A DIFFICULT RELATIONSHIP: RESISTANCE MOVEMENTS AND ALLIED BOMBING IN FRANCE AND ITALY

Resentment at the Allied bombing of France was communicated up to the CFLN from the internal Resistance from early 1943. Indeed, Resistance views of the bombing followed the same evolution as those of the wider population, though always more positively, with criticism focusing on the techniques more than the principle. In mid-1943, for example, a message from Brest asked 'Why do they say on the radio that Brest docks were successfully bombed on 6 March, when the bombs fell 2 km away – and why must the Americans bomb from so high up?'[55] Late that year, a wide-ranging CFLN report claimed that the French were not just tolerant but fiercely enthusiastic towards even the bloodiest sacrifices if they hit the enemy. That was true of the first Billancourt raid – and even, once it became clear that Renault was the target, of the second; in Lorient, people were demanding that the British finish off the arsenal and the submarine base. Equally, however, a commentator on the successful US Eighth Air Force attack on the Rennes naval depot of 23 August 1943 stated that 'the Rennais are unanimous in declaring that this was fine work, and the same question is always asked: why hasn't it always been done like this?'[56]

An obvious reason for resentment at the raids was their sheer intensity. The CFLN's agent Coridon, who had joined the Gaullists in 1940, reported:

> One thing is certain, the raid on La Chapelle [an RAF attack of 20/21 April 1944 on marshalling yards, which spread into northern Paris] must have been frightful. I was several kilometres away ... but still, despite my experiences as a Londoner in 1940/41, I got a very unpleasant impression, much stronger than the heaviest raids on London. Besides, the figures speak for themselves: a thousand tons are more impressive than three hundred.

Coridon observed some accurate raids but also many that were not. Delayed-action bombs were particularly resented because they hampered effective rescue operations; the argument that they gave people time to escape before they exploded only held if *only* such bombs were used, which was never the case.[57] Again, for Coridon in April:

> the British and the Americans must get it into their heads that their best friends cannot understand them in France, as long as real landings do not follow immediately upon the raids on the railways. This is so much the general opinion that while the earlier raids were accepted as a near-certain sign of an imminent landing, and then nothing happened, the more recent raids have been much less well tolerated and the criticisms increase every day, along with a certain resentment.[58]

Many CFLN correspondents echoed these views. 'The clumsiness and brutality of American airmen', said a report in mid-May 1944, 'have done more to sow doubt and scepticism in French hearts than three years of propaganda from Berlin and Vichy'.[59] Another report, from April, observed that 'Listeners to the BBC, hitherto fervent, have begun to wonder whether the weight of the German occupation is not being greatly surpassed by the disastrous cost of an eventual Allied landing.'[60] A despatch from the southern town of Nîmes observed that while, thanks to the activities of the Milice, 'Hatred of the Boche and their hired assassins is unanimous', many Resistance comrades had lost family members in recent ill-aimed raids on the marshalling yards, resulting in many defections and 'an immense lassitude' in the region's Resistance groups. 'Total war?', it concluded. 'Fine! But let the airmen bomb strictly military targets, rather than giving the impression of seeking to make war with the skins of the French

Resistance.'[61] The theme of discouragement among Resistance groups was taken up by a Paris correspondent, who wrote that:

> Most of our reliable informers do not dare to take a view, and I personally would hesitate to indicate or facilitate any future raids, if so many innocent people must pay with their lives for so tiny a drop of water that such an enterprise represents.[62]

For some CFLN correspondents, finally, surprise, perplexity, moral questioning and frustration found expression in unbridled outrage.

> On several occasions, and notably since the raids on Nantes, I have spoken out against the criminal imbecility of certain raids by Allied aircraft which exterminate the French in their hundreds without even hitting any military objectives. … One must conclude that the heads of these air forces attach little importance to the views of their best informers, for we have seen, for some time now, an orgy of raids for which the 'terrorist' label used by the German press actually fits very well. The centre of Lyon is annihilated with no valid reason, the old town of Rouen is pulverized … Better still: inoffensive French shopkeepers going about their business in cars are attacked on the road by 'Allied' aircraft. It takes you back to the good old days of 1940 when Italian planes attacked civilians on the open road. At least they had the (relative) excuse of considering that the French were their enemies. But the British! The Americans! These people seem afflicted with a destructive fury bordering on the most stupid hysteria. … In these conditions, I have the honour to inform you that as of today, I categorically refuse to indicate *any* target, as it does not suit me to assume, even despite myself, any share of responsibility for such criminal operations. … Let it not be claimed that these destructions, most frequently spread across a radius of several kilometres, are inevitable. They would be avoided if the Allied aircrews were more skilled and, above all, braver. If they do not know their job they should go back to school. And if they lack the nerve to dive onto their targets to save French lives, allow me to say that for people who call themselves 'sporting' they are pretty gutless.[63]

Among the Allies, the Soviet Union probably benefited from the bombing. This did not result so much from Communist propaganda within France as from the prestige of the Red Army and the Soviet Union more generally. After the raid of 27 May 1944, the people of Marseille (who had seen the Wehrmacht destroy the Vieux-Port 17 months earlier) claimed that the Germans were 'more legal' in their military operations, and the Russians 'more humane'; in June, Stalin himself was said to have made an 'energetic protest' against the bombing of Marseille, successfully preventing any further raids.[64] Strong in the south-east, pro-Soviet feeling spread across the country: as a CFLN report noted, 'the Russian army is the object of general admiration' – especially compared to the slow Italian campaign, viewed, by spring 1944, as 'risible'.[65]

Views from agents on the ground found their way to the top of the CFLN and thence to London. The first representations to the Allies on bombing date from

May 1943, when the CFLN's foreign affairs spokesman, René Massigli, wrote to Eden about the recent raids on Rennes and on the Paris suburbs. Arguing that the French, though still favourable to the RAF, had turned against the American air forces, Massigli suggested that the Americans 'learn the methods of our British friends' and in the meantime stopped trying 'precision' raids on France. Eden's reassuring reply, followed by an attempt to secure agreement to Massigli's proposals, was swiftly overruled in the name of what would become the *Pointblank* directive of June 1943.[66]

Further notes followed in spring 1944. A CFLN report based on data from the previous winter claimed that while 70 French locomotives were being hit each month by bombing, 40 were wrecked, often more durably, by sabotage. As sabotage was vastly more economical of explosives and above all of French lives, the report continued, more substantial aid to the Resistance might generate better results than the air offensive.[67] Repeated appeals on these lines followed. Just as the British were debating the Transportation Plan, on 5 April 1944, Massigli handed a memorandum to Duff Cooper; a brochure dated 25 April on the effects of bombing on French morale, and a detailed survey of the same issue dated 17 May, listing both successful and bungled raids, also reached London that spring.[68] Each message stressed that the French approved of precision attacks on legitimate targets but deplored apparently indiscriminate high-altitude bombing, typically associated with the Americans, and the use of delayed-action bombs. Bombing, the CFLN went on, was handing golden opportunities to Vichy propagandists; the Allies', and especially the Americans', standing with the French was suffering daily damage. Sabotage was proposed as a way of achieving better results with fewer casualties, and Massigli requested that the Free French be consulted over target selection.[69]

These interventions had a negligible effect on Allied policy. Even the CFLN's own military representatives in London undermined them. General Marie-Pierre Koenig, CFLN representative to SHAEF from March 1944, told Eisenhower's Chief of Staff Walter Bedell Smith that 'we would take twice the losses to be rid of the Germans'. Air Marshal Vallin, Commander of Free French air forces in Britain, broadcast his robust support for the raids in response to the recent appeal from the French cardinals.[70] Massigli's proposal of French involvement in targeting was transmitted from the British Foreign Office (which viewed it sympathetically), to Churchill; on 7 May it reached Roosevelt, who in turn referred it, with the Transportation Plan itself, to the military commanders.[71] Britain's Chiefs of Staff thought it was too late. Unlike the Foreign Office, they saw no reason to associate a Frenchman with plans entailing high French casualties. And the Allied military seldom viewed sabotage, which could not be organized systematically from London, as more than a complement to regular bombing – not as a substitute.[72] Churchill, despite his reservations about the Transportation Plan, backed the Chiefs of Staff. 'A suggestion to de Gaulle of this kind', said the Prime Minister, 'would only give him another opportunity of obtruding himself.'[73]

De Gaulle himself, swift to condemn the Allies' encroachments on the prerogatives of France, appears less resentful of the sufferings they inflicted on the French. Allusions to air raids in his contemporary speeches and messages are rare and oblique.[74] In his memoirs, bombing is mentioned, but as the product of an impersonal agency – the war – rather than of Allied decisions.[75] To do more, publicly rather than via Massigli, would have placed the General in the position either of unsuccessful supplicant or of co-organizer of bombing – neither of them likely to reinforce his still delicate position with the French. More surprisingly, perhaps, the Allies still froze out the French even after the Allies officially recognized France's Provisional Government on 23 October 1944; protests that month from General Bouscat, Chief of the French Air Staff, against the bombing of rail targets in Strasbourg and Colmar were effectively ignored.[76]

In Italy the relationship between Resistance forces and the bombers was if anything more difficult and complex. As partisan Antonio Pesenti wrote in 1944, as Italy had been an enemy of the Allies until very recently, it was inevitable that the Allied war brought destruction on Italian cities: it was the price to be paid for liberation – a liberation to which Italians had also to contribute.[77] Like the Allies, the anti-Fascists distinguished between Fascism and Italy, and were aware that a mere change of sides would not suffice to remove the stains on Italy's national identity; they knew, as an Allied leaflet dropped in November 1943 argued, that 'those who remain inactive at home do not deserve a place next to the victor'.[78] Collaboration between partisans and Allies became particularly evident from early summer 1944, when the Resistance in the Po Valley established stable and efficient links with the Allies through the military delegation of Lugano.[79] However, even though strikers, partisans and Allies were aiming for the same results, Allied bombing often caused friction and hostility, and many reactions closely resembled those in France. Partisans' reports from Lombardy, Piedmont and Liguria included severe criticism of how raids were carried out. One, from the end of 1943, included 'grave remarks on the latest raids on Italy', which appeared 'more pertinent to the inhuman spirit of the Germans than to the military criteria of the United Nations, as they hit civilian populations carelessly and atrociously'. The partisans feared this was 'very useful to enemy propaganda'. They also specified that in Val Polcevera, northwest of Genoa, around 300 civilians had been killed; the town of Recco in Genoa province, a target because of its viaduct, had lost 90 per cent of its buildings and 127 inhabitants; in Turin an entire residential area was destroyed killing 100 people, despite the lack of any military objective; in Ancona, while the station and the port barely suffered, nearby areas ('all anti-Fascist') saw destruction and civilian deaths; at Padua the Allies, aiming at the station area, had hit a train full of commuters from Bologna. These actions, the partisans concluded, seemed to have been carried out by irresponsible people; they alienated many workers who were otherwise ready to embrace the Resistance.[80]

Some letters from partisans contained lists of pointless carnage caused by the bombers: 300 civilian deaths in Parma ('an anti-Fascist town, [which] has helped prisoners of war who managed to escape from the camps') in April 1944 to cut a railway line for 20 hours; incalculable artistic damage to Padua, Arezzo, Siena and Pistoia. As some raids on marshalling yards had been precise, the partisans wondered 'why is the same care not always applied?' It was crucial to prevent anti-Allied feelings developing in Italy: as Action Party leader Ferruccio Parri put it, 'if the Allies don't change tactics, they'll win the war, but in Italy they'll lose the peace'.[81] After raids on railways lines in Friuli and on Porto Marghera, a typed list of material damage and civilian deaths was followed by a hand-written note: 'why, with criminal carelessness, are populations who risked being shot to assist Allied prisoners assassinated?'[82]

At the end of 1944, the Socialist partisan Pietro Nenni wrote to the Allied Mediterranean Command that the 'latest imprecise mass raids with incendiary bombs' on major towns in the Venetia had caused huge damage to civilians and destroyed monuments 'known to any civilized human being', inflicting no damage on Germans, hitting no military objectives, and assisting Fascist propaganda. 'Please', he implored, 'consider the tragic situation of the population after a year and a half fighting the Germans, and do not make it harder without having ascertained clear military reasons.' Nenni added that downed airmen were always rescued and hidden by the population.[83] Parri, his co-partisan, later explained the Allied methods by the existence of 'a grave sediment of national rancour' provoked by Mussolini's aggression, particularly among the British. Despite their propaganda, they would therefore 'destroy peoples together with their governments'.[84]

If anything more bitter was Cristoforo Moscioni Negri, a lieutenant of the Alpini who returned from the Russian campaign and became a partisan in the Marche Apennine after the armistice of September 1943. Too often, he wrote, enemy aircraft hit 'families of evacuees in the countryside in their tents, believing that they were soldiers'; small villages had been destroyed 'with no reason, perhaps just because ... the streets, from the air, appeared black, crowded'. Partisans could have organized an information system for the Allies to avoid useless slaughter. Instead, they were accused of bloodshed because their actions against Germans provoked retaliation against civilians. Victims of retaliation, he argued, besides being inevitable in war, were 'always far fewer than those killed by an aircraft which misses a bridge and destroys nearby homes. Moreover, if the pilot bails out, they make him a prisoner. We get hanged.'[85]

Railway and factory workers, often anti-Fascists, were both particularly vulnerable and vocal. Attacks on railways linking Liguria, Piedmont and Lombardy in July 1944 provoked complaints from railway workers, almost all of whom worked with the partisans, requesting sufficient warnings before raids. The high percentage of the Allies' supporters among the victims, a partisan note concluded, 'is depressing their morale'. One railwayman acting as an informer for the partisans, like some of his French counterparts, decided to stop giving information to the partisans and the Allies 'until this uncivilized system of massacring the real patriots changes'.[86] This followed an attack on a workers' train on the Pavia-Codogno line on 24 July which killed some of his best friends who worked with the partisans. The same month, factory workers at Brescia went on strike after a raid had left its target, the OM factory, untouched but wrecked parts of the city centre and killed 800 people, according to partisan claims.[87] While their ostensible demand was for air-raid compensation, they also believed that holding up production would help prevent more bombing.[88]

The Allies had anticipated such reactions in September 1943, when a report by the British Political Warfare Executive (PWE) stressed that the bombing of industrial cities in northern Italy during the Badoglio period had hit the 'hotbed of anti-Fascism in Italy'. Bombing areas that hosted workers' unions and anti-Fascist organizations not only threatened 'to destroy the pro-Allied sympathies of these people', but also 'ran the risk of turning many of them toward Russia'.[89] Subsequent events confirmed PWE's forecasts.

Inevitably, letters from the 'base' were reflected in positions of the partisan leadership. One partisan request was that factories should be hit during strikes, without causing casualties. In October 1944, at a meeting with British representatives in Lugano, Italian partisans asked for criteria for undertaking raids on northern factories, especially when production was slowed down to a minimum by the workers. As the Allies justified their raids by the need to prevent the German export of machinery, the partisans requested warnings to avoid unnecessary casualties among the workers, and better co-ordination between bombing and workers' strikes.[90]

Workers' and partisans' mistrust of the Allies was evident in the organization of the insurrection from September 1944, when the Regional Military Command of Piedmont stressed that Turin 'must not be given to us by the Allies but must be conquered by the arms and hearts of the Piedmontese'.[91] The relationship between bombers and partisans was made even more complex by the fact that many of the strikes at FIAT had been organized by the PCI. If the Allies, from late 1942, had hoped to provoke a workers' rebellion by bombing, they had not meant to cause Communist-led strikes – as alarmed intelligence reports observed two years later. In April 1944, intelligence from Vichy informed the Southern Department that Russian prestige in northern Italy was 'growing rapidly'.[92] In November, a British intelligence report considered the PCI 'by far the most powerful and best organized political force in Turin, drawing their adherents from the majority of the industrial workers'.[93] This, another report explained, was partly based on Turin's experiences in 1919–20, and to Antonio Gramsci's following among workers there. But the Communist ascendancy, said the report, also owed much to the return of Communist organizers from exile in early 1943, and to their key role in preparing for that spring's strikes. These were now considered 'probably one of the contributory causes to the fall of Fascism', and an estimated '50% of the politically minded people' in Turin were Communists by 1944. The dispersal of factories elsewhere in Italy, moreover, had helped spread Communist ideas.[94] A memorandum for General Marshall of November 1944 warned of the tragic situation in northern Italy, where populations found themselves caught between Allied bombs, fear of German retaliation for partisan sabotage, and lack of food, and without hope of any early liberation. 'The danger of Communism in the industrial areas of Northern Italy', the memo concluded, in a close parallel to Eden's fears about the impact of the Transportation Plan raids in France, 'is a real one' – and Allied bombing had contributed to it.[95]

BOMBING AND LIBERATION

Reactions to bombing of the Allies' natural supporters, the French Resistance and the Italian anti-Fascist movement, were strikingly similar. Before a ferocious and apparently indiscriminate onslaught from the air, both expressed bewilderment, anger and disgust; both appealed, largely in vain, for a more reasoned policy. Yet the political relationship between bombing and liberation in the two countries was very different. In France, at least from 1943 onwards, the Allies were out to limit the political damage caused by bombing; in Italy, bombing can be said to have made a political contribution to the liberation, albeit not always as the Allies expected.

Churchill, though intensely concerned at the possible effects on French opinion of the Transportation Plan, was less worried about air attacks carried out after D-Day. This was not because of any easing-off of the bombing; between June and September 1944, Bomber Command alone dropped over 180,000 tons on enemy-occupied territory, and more than 20,000 French civilians died. Rather, Churchill believed that greater allowances would be made for bombing 'in the hot blood of battle', when Allied troops were fighting and dying on French soil.[96] And by mid-September 1944, a little over three months from the Allied landings on 6 June, over 90 per cent of French territory was liberated.

One correspondent for de Gaulle's provisional government, the former CFLN, broadly confirmed the Prime Minister's expectations after a visit to a group of seven north-central *départements* in June. Bombed once and machine-gunned three times in a single 40-mile journey from Orléans to Gien, the correspondent still reported 'the *sang-froid* and the good spirits of the rural population of this area'. The public, he claimed, 'now understands the military value of the air raids of these last weeks'; criticisms had 'totally ceased' and 'raids that must ease the Allied advance are passively accepted'.[97]

Few accounts are quite so optimistic. None of the censors' reports indicates such a speedy turnaround of opinion; in July as in April, May and June, the proportion of letters condemning air raids remained vastly greater than supportive accounts. In Toulouse, hostile reports in June outnumbered sympathetic ones by 15 to 1; in Montpellier, by 60 to 1.[98] What did alter, however, was the salience of raids. In May and June they were the leading concern in French telephone conversations and letters; in July, they dropped to third place, behind material worries and general fatigue. Out of 2,254,203 items examined in July, 246,909 mentioned air raids, against 329,297 in June; the equivalent figure for food supplies rose from 284,010 to 520,939 in the same period.[99] Even in Marseille, despite the violence of the raid of 27 May, the Renseignements Généraux pointed out that bombing had fallen back among the public's concerns.[100] Less spectacular than the transformation of opinion claimed by the Provisional Government's correspondent, this ebbing of the tide of resentment at bombing, even as the campaign continued, was still promising for the Allies.

The experience of liberation was highly varied across France. In some localities, especially in the south-west, the Resistance simply moved in as the Germans withdrew; others saw fierce battles between Resistance forces and Germans; most were liberated by Allied troops after more or less fighting. Bombing tempered euphoria in many but not all French localities. Caen and Le Havre, 30 miles apart in Normandy, were extreme cases in this respect, but the contrast between them is sufficiently illustrative to deserve detailed attention. Each suffered very heavy bombing (2,276 tons of bombs on Caen during the single day of 7 July 1944; 9,790 tons on Le Havre from 5–11 September), levels of destruction in excess of 70 per cent, and over 2,000 deaths. Each town's suffering was recognized by a collective award of the Légion d'Honneur and the Croix de Guerre. In both cases bombing preceded liberation by hours, not days or weeks; the two were seamlessly linked. Yet public reactions, both at the moment of liberation and in the longer term, were very different.

There was certainly some resentment of the bombing in Caen. Geneviève Vion wrote scornfully of attempts to bomb the Pont de l'Arquette from a height of 4,000 metres, and of the bombing of the University, which wrecked not only a centre of learning but also painfully accumulated civilian supplies of petrol, clothes, aprons, mattresses and equipment to re-sole old shoes.[101] People sheltering at Saint-Sauveur recalled that while the inhabitants of some quarters brought roses and cherries to the arriving troops, others threw stones.[102] Franck Duncombe, a Caennais with a British father, described the welcome given to French Canadian troops as warm and dignified rather than lively.[103] British war correspondents, too, were more or less appalled by what they saw. As the *Daily Mail* reported on 28 July:

> One must drive through Caen every time one goes to or from the Orne front and it's still a horrible and rather shaming thing. The people of Caen will never quite understand why we had to do anything so awful to them. Still, day by day, the bodies of their fellow-citizens are being dug out of the ruins.

Yet the strongest sentiment among the press corps that rolled into Caen after its partial liberation on 9 July was astonishment at the friendliness of the welcome. 'I couldn't have believed', wrote Christopher Buckley in the *Daily*

Telegraph, 'in the ghastly cemetery of town into which I penetrated yesterday that so many civilians would be alive, that so many who've suffered night and day under bombing and shellfire could have received us with such enthusiasm.' According to Alan Moorehead in the *Daily Express*, 'French doctors . . . came up with their bags full of instruments wanting to treat British wounded and under mortar fire they got to work at once.'[104] They were echoed by army officers: 'I spoke to very many people, not just one or two, and they were much more anxious to point out collaborators and treat the troops to wine and fruit than to moan about the bombardment' recalled Captain Dishington of the King's Own Scottish Borderers; 'Our welcome from those who had suffered so much, was overwhelming', stated Major L. J. Massey.[105] Caen later embraced its status as a city whose sufferings made possible the liberation of France and, more generally, the defeat of Fascism. Streets are named after Eisenhower and a clutch of British commanders – Montgomery, Dempsey, Mountbatten, and even Harris; the Caen Memorial stands as permanent testimony to the city's role in the liberation of Europe.[106]

The reaction in Le Havre was more sombre. After entering the city on 12 September, Major Martin Lindsay of the Gordon Highlanders observed that:

> All the restaurants and cafés are closed and I cannot help feeling that the French are rather wet; we should never have allowed bombing of one part of a town to have closed down all life in the rest of it. It has made us highly unpopular. We have had none of the rapturous welcome here that we have received elsewhere, and when Ewen made a few tentative enquiries about getting up an officers' dance he was told that the whole town is in mourning and they would have nothing to do with it. [107]

Lindsay's impressions, insensitively expressed, were accurate. 'We awaited you with joy, we greet you in mourning', announced the city's first post-liberation newspaper on 13 September. The flags put out on the streets were dressed with black crepe, the crowds – if they appeared at all – largely silent. The only individual treated as a hero was the mayor, Pierre Courant, who had remained at his post and organized relief work; though immediately relieved of his duties as a Vichy appointee, he founded his longer-term political career on his wartime record.[108] 'We had passed into another world', said one Havrais at a later anniversary; 'we were orphans of our town.'[109] An account written four years later claimed that any Allied airmen who had appeared at the city's liberation would have been 'stoned to death in a few minutes', and that 'the Allied air forces used Le Havre as an experiment in controlled total destruction to see what could be done in Germany'.[110] The longest account of the operation ends with a chapter entitled 'What liberation of Le Havre?'[111] The Allied commanders themselves had misgivings, Harris referring to the bombardment as a 'mistake'; none is commemorated by a street name.[112] In the autumn of 1944 Helga Holbek, a Swedish Quaker visiting Le Havre, wrote of intense material hardship, and of fierce resentment at the bombing. Whereas the previous 136 raids had been accepted, she said, as resulting from military necessity, the September attacks were too massive and, because they fell in areas free of Germans, too inexplicable. Worse, the Havrais were being treated as inferiors by the Americans now operating the port. They had requisitioned the best of the remaining buildings, seemed indifferent to the welfare of the population, and were increasingly referred to as 'the occupying troops'.[113] Successive commemorations were tinged with bitterness and, above all, with incomprehension; there is no equivalent to the Mémorial de Caen.[114]

Three elements help explain the difference. The first was the course of the battle. In Caen, despite the bombing, Allied troops visibly had to fight their way into the city. The Germans both resisted fiercely and mistreated the civilian population. Franck Duncombe recalls Waffen-SS troops shooting a Resistance suspect on an operating table; the *Times* correspondent, confirmed by local testimony, stated that many Germans 'lived in a drunken orgy, and before they left yesterday they went round the streets turning people out of their houses and pillaging everything they could lay their hands on'. After retreating, moreover, the Germans continued to shell the city.[115] No such conditions prevailed in Le Havre. Once the bombing was over, British and Canadian troops took the city within 24 hours, suffering fewer than 500 casualties and taking 11,000 German prisoners. German resistance was limited, and German troops – many of them older men and none from the SS – behaved with more restraint than at Caen. The Allies gave the impression of having sacrificed the town and 2,000 of its people to win an easy victory on the ground.

The second distinction is one of context. The liberation of Caen attracted the Western world's media as a crucial moment in the battle for France. Le Havre, by contrast, was a sideshow; the battle for Normandy was (and still is) widely considered as over before the end of August; Paris and even Antwerp were already in Allied hands by 12 September; when Allied troops took Le Havre, the press did not follow. The sufferings of Le Havre, at least as great as those of Caen, are denied their symbolic significance.

Third, Caen's greater salience in the narrative of liberation brought benefits both tangible and symbolic. Five days after the arrival of Allied troops in the west of the city, the Lord Provost of Edinburgh, prompted by the local branch of the Franco-Scottish Society, proposed a link that would become the Edinburgh-Caen Fellowship; by January, 160 cases of relief material had been sent; the minister of Wilton Church, Hawick, built of Caen stone, despatched a hamper packed by his congregation; the University gave 1,000 books to start its counterpart's new library. As Maurice Legrand, Calvados representative of the Entr'aide pour la Libération (successor organization to the Secours National) wrote, 'You are bringing us not only material help, so important in itself, but also your moral support, and that means a great deal for this brave old country of ours.'[116] No such speedy gesture reached Le Havre. From French territory, the city received the support of neighbouring towns, and of its two 'godparents' – the city of Algiers and the *département* of Landes; Algiers sent FF500,000 in February 1945; the mayor of Southampton asked his counterpart of Le Havre to visit that January; the Lord Provost of Aberdeen, invited by the French Health Minister to support the city, wrote a somewhat nonplussed letter to the mayor of Le Havre offering general sympathy; the *département* of Hérault sent a lorryload of relief supplies in early March.[117] But to a greater extent than those of Caen, the people of Le Havre were left to their own devices during that first post-bombing winter. Churchill's forecast that bombing would do limited political damage once the ground battle had been joined was broadly correct in France as a whole. But in Le Havre, and a number of other localities, the scars of the experience ran deep.

To a greater extent than in France, the liberation of northern Italy owed something not only to the military effects of bombing but also to its psychological and even political impact. When the Allies entered Turin on 3 May 1945, they found a city liberated by partisans and FIAT workers five days earlier, following a general strike on 18 April involving some 18,000 workers, the subsequent occupation of the factories and fighting with the Germans.[118] This was the culmination of a process that had begun in the autumn of 1942. From the very start of their bombing campaign on northern Italy, the British had assessed the possibility of detaching the Italian home front from the regime. By autumn 1942, the raids were no longer limited to military objectives but aimed at workers' houses and morale. Asked to comment on the effects of the bombing of northern Italy's industry in 1942–3, German informants told the Allies in July 1945 that it had brought about the 'absolute disorganization of Italian labour': workers 'just ran away and even the provision of organized shelter accommodation inside the plant could not get [them] inside the factory'. The Germans at the time were Italy's ally, and 'could not take force measures against the workers'. This, the informants thought, was 'probably aimed at by the British'.[119]

What the Allies had not expected, however, was the mass strikes which would contribute to the fall of the regime and, later, to the anti-German insurrection in co-ordination with partisan bands. While some reasons for the strikes were economic, they should be understood in the wider context of Italy at war. Workers initially went on strike because their families were bombed out, because their wages were falling behind rising prices, and because women were protesting against a regime that had not provided shelters. The strikes of 1944–5 took the shape of co-ordinated action with Allied raids: despite deep contradictions, both had the same aim of sabotaging war production. Both stages of the strikes were in part, and in different ways, responses to the Allied bombing campaign.

Against the Western Allies' preferences, both France and Italy ended the war with strong Communist parties, for broadly similar reasons. The prestige of the Soviet Union was at its peak, its wartime sacrifices more than compensating for the shame of the 1939 Nazi-Soviet Pact; Communists had played a leading role in the resistance in both countries, in France from 1941, in Italy from 1943.

Both PCF and PCI contributed ministers to post-Liberation governments. Removed from office at the start of the Cold War, in May 1947, the two parties remained crucial players in French and Italian politics, with strong organizations and between 20 and 30 per cent of the popular vote, till the 1980s. One of many ironies of the Cold War was that these two parties, vigorous defenders of the Allied bombing campaign (in public) during the war years, were not above using it later as a propaganda tool against the United States. French Communists exaggerated the death toll in Caen, placing it at 10,000;[120] in Le Havre during the 1953 municipal election campaign, the destruction of the city, though carried out by RAF Bomber Command, was presented as an example of American bellicosity.[121] The PCI was more discreet. Without blaming the Allies directly, Italy's Communist press simply pointed out that the Russians, alone among the belligerents, had not bombed enemy cities.[122]

Notes

1 See, among other works, S. Peli, *Storia della Resistenza in Italia* (Turin: Einaudi, 2006), 41–55.
2 *The Stars and Stripes*, 25 February 1945.
3 ACS, MI, DGPS, DPP, b. 211, fasc. 2, informer's report, Milan, 30 October 1942.
4 ASTo, Prefettura, Gabinetto, b. 514, Confederazione Fascista dei Lavoratori dell'Industria, provincial Union of Turin, to prefect of Turin, 30 December 1942.
5 ASTo, Prefettura, Gabinetto, b. 250, anonymous from FIAT workers to Mussolini, n.d. (early January 1943).
6 U. Massola, 'Gli scioperi del marzo 1943', in F. Antonicelli (ed.), *Dall'Antifascismo alla Resistenza: trent'anni di storia italiana (1915–1945)* (Turin: Einaudi, 1961), 43.
7 ASTo, Prefettura, Gabinetto, b. 516, Confederazione Fascista dei Lavoratori dell'Industria, provincial Union of Turin, to Confederazione in Rome and to prefect of Turin, 16 January 1943; in the same file, see the directive of the Ministry of Corporation, 13 January 1943.
8 *Ibid.*; U. Massola, *Gli scioperi del '43. Marzo-aprile: le fabbriche contro il fascismo* (Rome: Editori Riuniti, 1973); V. Castronovo, *FIAT, 1899–1999: un secolo di storia italiana* (Milan: Rizzoli, 1999), 613–14.
9 L. Ganapini, *Una città, la guerra: lotte di classe, ideologie e forze politiche a Milano, 1939–1951* (Milan: Angeli, 1988), 45–7.
10 ASTo, Prefettura, Gabinetto, b. 250, Questura of Turin to the prefect, 17 January 1943.
11 Castronovo, *FIAT, 1899–1999*, 598–601, 615–16.
12 G. Oliva, *La Resistenza alle porte di Torino* (Milan: Franco Angeli, 1989), 44–5.
13 ASG, Prefettura, Gabinetto, b. 157, Command of Genoa Carabinieri to prefect and Interior Ministry, 5 May 1943.
14 C. Senise, *Quando ero capo della polizia, 1940–1943* (Rome: Ruffolo, 1946); F. W. Deakin, *The Brutal Friendship: Mussolini, Hitler, and the Fall of Italian Fascism* (London: Weidenfeld and Nicolson, 1962), 226–8.
15 B. Mussolini, 'Al Direttorio Nazionale del PNF', 11 March 1943, in Mussolini *Opera Omnia*, 159–68.
16 CGIL (ed.), *Torino marzo '43. Scioperano 100,000 operai contro la guerra* (Turin: CGIL, 1993), 4–5.
17 P. Spriano, *Storia del Partito Comunista Italiano*, vol. 5. *I fronti popolari, Stalin, la guerra* (Rome: L'Unità, 1990), 182.
18 L. Passerini, *Fascism in Popular Memory: the Cultural Experience of the Turin Working Class* (Cambridge: Cambridge University Press, 1987), 67–74, 122–6; Luigi Ganapini, *Una città, la guerra*, 41.
19 U. Massola, Girolamo Li Causi, *Gli scioperi 1943–1944. La classe operaia in lotta contro il fascismo e l'occupante* (Rome: L'Unità, 1945), 9.

20 ACS, MI, DGPS, A5G, IIGM, b. 77, Police chief of Bologna to Head of Police Senise, 28 July 1943.

21 ACS, MinCulPop, Reports, b. 42, fasc. 130. Comando Difesa Territoriale of Turin to the Military Zone Command of Turin and Novara, the Carabinieri, the Questura and the prefect of Turin, 29 July 1943.

22 Ganapini, *Una città, la guerra*, 55–6.

23 Massola and Li Causi, *Gli scioperi 1943–1944*, 12.

24 'Manifesto agli scioperanti – Parole chiare ai lavoratori', 3 March 1943, in Mussolini, *Opera Omnia*, vol. 31, 56–61.

25 *Corriere della Sera*, 8 March 1944.

26 ACS, MinCulPop, Reports, b. 46, Republican Prefecture of Milan, monthly situation report (May), 3 June 1944.

27 *Ibid.*, Republican Prefecture of Milan, monthly situation report (July), 8 August 1944.

28 ASG, Prefettura, Gabinetto, b. 275, poster of 19 December 1943.

29 G. Bocca, *Storia dell'Italia partigiana, settembre 1943–maggio 1945* (Milan: Mondadori, 1995), 140.

30 ACS, MI, DGPCSA, b. 106, Provincial Committee for Anti-Aircraft Protection of the Republican Prefecture of Milan to Province Head, 4 August 1944; Province Head of Bergamo to Interior Ministry, 7 July 1944.

31 INSMLI, CVL, 'Delegazione Svizzera', Fasc. 44, 'Notizie industriali di fine giugno', June 1944. For details of the attack, in which the 15th US Air Force hit successfully the FIAT aero-engine factory at Mirafiori, see the report by the Ministry of Home Security in TNA, AIR 20/5988.

32 Deakin, *The Brutal Friendship*, 702.

33 INSMLI, CVL, Fasc. 44, documents of the Allied Swiss delegation, summer 1944.

34 NARA, RG 243, box 158, OSS London, report from Switzerland, information date December 1944, report date 10 February 1945.

35 INSMLI, Fasc. 44, documents from the CVL to the Swiss delegation, 'Notizie industriali di fine giugno', end of June 1944.

36 NARA, RG 243, box 158, 'Fiat Aero Engine Factory', report of 9 April 1945.

37 NARA, RG 226, Caserta files, box 88, folder 5, Headquarters 2677th regiment, OSS, US Army, Lt Colonel Edward Gamble to Colonel E. Glavin, 'Special Operations Meeting', 20 June 1944.

38 See above, p. 134.

39 *Rassegna della stampa libera*, 8 April 1944.

40 ACS, MI, DGPS, RSI, b. 23, *Foglio Volante*, 8 May 1944.

41 *Ibid.*, *Italia Combatte*, 5 July 1944; *Italia Combatte*, 7 July 1944, dropped on Cremona province on 11 July, from Province Head of Cremona to Head of Police, 15 July 1944.

42 ACS, MI, DGPS, RSI, b. 23, 'Al popolo dell'Italia settentrionale: Avvertimento', from General Clark to the Italian people, 16 February 1945.

43 ASM, Prefettura, b. C254, Carabinieri of Milan to Prefecture of Milan, 4 October 1943.

44 INSMLI, Fondo 'Mucchi Gabriele', fasc. 43, Leaflet of 10 February 1944.

45 INSMLI, CVL, Fasc. 43, 'Volantini', CLN leaflet, n.d. (1944).

46 ASM, b. C254, leaflet by the Workers' Committee to the Milanese population.

47 M. Schumann, *La voix du couvre-feu: cent allocutions de celui qui fut le porte-parole du général de Gaulle, 1940–1944* (Paris: Plon, 1964), 149–52 (5 March 1942).

48 On the 'Indemnité de bombardement', established by an *Arrêté Interministériel* of 9 January 1942 and a law of 20 January 1942, cf. notably AN F60/407, Darlan to Finance Minister Yves Bouthillier, 27 December 1941, and ADSM 51W/67, Mémoire sur l'application des texts réglementant l'indemnité exceptionnelle aux salaries travaillant dans les lieux exposés, Le Havre, n.d. (1942).

49 AN 3AG/2/333, Paris, Préfecture de Police, weekly report, 9 March 1942, in France Libre, État-Major particulier du Général de Gaulle, Opinion Publique, received 27 April 1942.

50 AD BduR 76W/187 25 and AD Var 1W/64, Après le bombardement de Toulon: Les responsables sont à Vichy. Copy of PCF leaflet, December 1943; AD Var 1W/64, *Rouge-Midi*, Organ of the Var region of the PCF, December 1943; AD BduR 76W/157, RG Marseille, Information, 29 July 1944.

51 TNA AIR 20/3248, Air Ministry to Bomber Command, 4 December 1943. In this case management as well as workers were responsible for sabotage activity.

52 G. Martin, *Ambérieu, la rebelle* (Bourg-en-Bresse: Musnier-Gilbert Éditions, 2002), 63. In addition, Chawaf claims, on the basis of uncited archival sources, that Resistance members in the municipal council of Boulogne-Billancourt secured, in return for intelligence work, a promise from the Allies to stop the bombing, and there were no raids after 1943. Cf. C. Chawaf, *Je suis née*, 87.

53 AD Var 1W/21, RG Toulon, 22–28 November 1943.

54 N. Ciravegna, 'Le printemps et l'été 1944', *Marseille* (revue), 172 (1994), 13; J. Jackson, *France: the Dark Years, 1940–1944* (Oxford: Oxford University Press, 2001), 558.

55 AN F1/A/3743, CFLN, France-Politique, État d'esprit en Bretagne, 17 July/22 July 1943.

56 *Ibid.*, Commissariat à l'Intérieur, Réaction de l'opinion publique française en regard de bombardements anglo-américains, n.d. (December?) 1943.

57 AN F1/A/3765, GPRF, Commissariat à l'Intérieur, Bombardements, Extraits de documents, various dates (spring 1944): Rapport Coridon. Delayed-action bombs were introduced to prevent smoke from fires obscuring marker flares. 'Their possible effect on rescue action had been overlooked', and in early May 1944 there were not enough delayed-action fuses available to switch to a policy of using *only* this type. Cf. TNA CAB69/6, Sir Charles Portal to Defence Committee (Operations), 3 May 1944.

58 AN F1/A/3765, GPRF, Commissariat à l'Intérieur, Bombardements, Extraits de documents, n.d. (spring 1944): Rapport Coridon.

59 AN F1/A/3765, CFLN, Commissariat à l'Intérieur, Les Bombardements de l'aviation anglo-américaine et les réactions de l'opinion française, 15 May/5 June 1944.

60 AN F1/A/3743, CFLN, Commissariat à l'Intérieur, L'opinion publique et les bombardements sur la France, 21 April 1944/3 June 1944.

61 AN F1/A/3743, GPRF, Commissariat à l'Intérieur, La terreur nazi-milicienne et l'état d'esprit de la population dans le midi – fin mai 1944.

62 AN F1/A/3765, CFLN, Commissariat à l'Intérieur, Résultat des derniers bombardements sur la région parisienne, nuit du 19 avril, 26 April/6 May 1944.

63 AN 3AG/2/333, Valmy à Londres, 29 mai 1944.

64 AD BduR 76W/129, RG Marseille, daily report, 1st June 1944; RG Marseille, État d'esprit de la population à Marseille, 21 June 1944.

65 AN F1/A/3743, CFLN, Enquête sur l'opinion française au début de l'année 1944; AN F1/A/3765, CFLN, Commissariat à l'Intérieur, L'état moral de la population en France, 31 March/6 May 1944.

66 TNA AIR 19/218, Massigli to Eden, 16 April 1943; Eden to Sinclair, 25 April 1943; Eden to Massigli, 24 May 1943; Sinclair to Eden, 5 June 1943.

67 AN F1/A/3765, CFLN, Commissariat à l'Intérieur, Les Bombardements de l'aviation anglo-américaine et les réactions de l'opinion française, 15 May/5 June 1944.

68 TNA FO 371/41984: Duff Cooper to Foreign Office, 5 April 1944; CFLN, Commissariat aux Affaires Étrangères, Memorandum, 5 May 1944; CFLN, Direction Technique des Services Spéciaux, Les bombardements alliés et leurs répercussions sur le moral des Français, 25 April 1944; AIR 40/1720, Military attaché report, Allied bombing raids over France.

69 TNA, FO 371/41984, Duff Cooper to Foreign Office, 5 April 1944; minute by Mack, 7 May 1944.

70 Koenig's comment, on 16 May 1944, is quoted in R. S. Davis, *Carl A. Spaatz and the Air War in Europe* (Washington D.C.: Center for Air Force, 1993), 408, quoted in V. Orange, *Tedder: Quietly in Command* (London: Frank Cass, 2004), 261); Vallin's broadcast is in NA, FO 371/41984, French Air Marshal Replies to French Clergy on Bombings, 18 May 1944. For Free French *participation* in raids on France, cf. Florentin, *Quand les alliés*, 185–208.

71 TNA, FO 371/41984: Duff Cooper to Foreign Office, 5 April 1944; minute by Mack, 7 May 1944; Churchill to Roosevelt, 7 May 1944; Roosevelt to Churchill, 11 May 1944.

72 M. R. D. Foot, *SOE in France: An Account of the Work of the British Special Operations Executive in France 1940–1944* (London: Frank Cass, 2004), 383–4.

73 TNA, AIR 19/218: extract from COS (44) 155, 12 May 1944; Churchill to Ismay, 16 May 1944.

74 Cf. C. de Gaulle, *Discours et Messages*, vol. I (Paris: Plon, 1970), and *Lettres, Notes et Carnets* (Paris: Plon, 1983).
75 C. de Gaulle, *Mémoires de guerre*, vol. II (Paris: Plon, 1956), 203; vol. III (Paris: Plon, 1958), 8.
76 TNA, AIR 37/1034: Bouscat to Forbes (SHAEF mission to French government), 26 October 1944; Leslie Scarman to Forbes, 1 November 1944.
77 Pamphlet by A. Pesenti, *Noi e gli alleati* (A.P.E., 1944), 3.
78 C. Pavone, *Una guerra civile. Saggio sulla moralità nella Resistenza* (Turin: Bollati Boringhieri, 1991), 190.
79 T. Piffer, *Gli Alleati e la Resistenza italiana* (Bologna: Il Mulino, 2010), 82–9.
80 Report on the situation in northern Italy by Action Party partisan Alberto Damiani, 30 December 1943, in P. Secchia and F. Frassati, *La Resistenza e gli Alleati* (Milan: Feltrinelli, 1962), 57–8.
81 INSMLI, CVL, 'Delegazione Svizzera', Fasc. 44, 1944, 'Notizie e considerazioni sui recenti bombardamenti alleati in Italia'.
82 *Ibid.*, letter from partisans to the Allied Swiss Delegation, May 1944.
83 Pietro Nenni to the Allied Headquarters, no date but end 1944, in A. Celeghin ed. *Bombardamenti aerei sulla città di Padova e provincia, 1943–1945* (Padua: Tempio-Museo dell'Internato Ignoto, 2005), 32.
84 Maurizio [F. Parri], 'Il Movimento di liberazione e gli alleati', in *Il Movimento di liberazione in Italia*, 1, July 1949, 18.
85 C. Moscioni Negri, *Linea Gotica* (Bologna: Il Mulino, 2006), 78; 38.
86 INSMLI, CVL, Fasc. 44, letters of 8 May 1944 and of 31 August 1944.
87 *Ibid.*, letter of July 1944, on the raid on Brescia of 13 July 1944, which in fact killed 200 people.
88 NARA, RG 208, box 328, Office of Overseas War Information, Weekly Intelligence Summary, Italy, 14th August 1944.
89 TNA, FO898/60, Captain Skeaping to Mr Delmer, 'Report on Italian stations', 7 September 1943.
90 In Secchia and Frassati, *La Resistenza e gli Alleati*, 105.
91 INSMLI, CVL, 'Attività clandestina ed insurrezionale', fasc. 174, Piedmontese Regional Military Command to the Committee for the Liberation of Piedmont, 15 September 1944.
92 TNA, HW1/2250, 'Northern Italy – A Vichy intelligence report', translation of document dated 19 March 1944, 27 April 1944.
93 TNA, WO204/6249, Intelligence 'D' section to Mr John Rayner, 10 November 1944.
94 *Ibid.*, PWB Italian Theatre Headquarters, 'The Development of Communism in Italy', 14 December 1944.
95 NARA, RG 165, box 937, section 2, Memorandum for General Marshall, 29 November 1944. For Eden, see above, p. 36.
96 TNA, CAB 69/6, Churchill at Defence Committee (Operations), 5 April and 26 April 1944.
97 AN F60/1690 02, GPRF, Commissariat à l'Intérieur, L'état d'esprit des populations après le débarquement, 11 June/11 July 1944.
98 AN F7/14932, Commission de Contrôle technique, Inspection Régionale de Toulouse, 4 July 1944 and Inspection Régionale de Montpellier, 5 July 1944.
99 AN F7/14929, Direction CT Vichy, monthly report, June–July 1944.
100 AD BduR 76W/129, RG Marseille, État d'esprit de la population à Marseille, 21 June 1944.
101 Mémorial de Caen, TE546, Geneviève Vion. According to the *Times* (19 July 1944), about 163,000 books and 116,000 other academic publications were destroyed with the University library.
102 Mémorial de Caen FN60, Éclats de mémoire: Témoignages inédits sur la bataille de Caen, 17.
103 Mémorial de Caen TE73, Franck Duncan.
104 University of Edinburgh, Orr archive (Gen 868), Télégrammes de presse, Alger, Brazzaville, 11 July 1944.
105 Edinburgh, Orr archive, Captain E. M. Dishington, 19 September 1944; Mémorial de Caen TE 167, Major L. J. Massey.
106 Cf. http://www.memorial-caen.fr/portailgb/
107 M. Lindsay, *So Few Got Through* (London: Collins, 1946), 74, 86. Lindsay was not the only

Allied officer guilty of crass insensitivity. Anthony Beevor recounts a Canadian captain arriving in Caen and asking where he could find a good restaurant (A. Beevor, *D-Day: the Battle for Normandy* (London: Penguin Books, 2009), 272).

108 *Le Havre Matin*, 13 September 1944. Courant's temporary ineligibility did not prevent him from founding a political career on his wartime role; leader of Le Havre's conservatives till his death in 1965, he was mayor from 1947–54 and a government minister from 1951–3.

109 *Paris-Normandie*, 12 September 1984.

110 J. Guillemard, *L'Enfer du Havre* (Paris: Éditions Medicis, 1948), 220, 224.

111 E. Florentin, *Le Havre 44 à feu et à sang*, 2nd edn. (Paris: Presses de la Cité, 1985), 595.

112 TNA WO233/29, D.CIGS to D.Air, loose minute, 8 November 1944; AIR 37/1034, pp.45A: Telephone message for Air Chief Marshal Tedder from Air Vice Marshal Saunby [*sic*], RAF Bomber Command, 29 October 1944.

113 TNA FO371/49071, Conditions in Normandy: Quaker's observations on relief measures, 29 November 1944.

114 Cf. for example C. Zarifian, *Table Rase: 5 septembre 1944, Le Havre, Ville Assassinée* (Le Havre: Les Films Seine-Océan, 1988 (video)).

115 Mémorial de Caen TE73, Franck Duncan; TE7, Méligne; APA 459, Thérèse Robineau, 'Journal du débarquement et de l'exode 1944'; *The Times*, 12 July 1944.

116 *The Scotsman*, 20 October 1944. Records of the Edinburgh-Caen Fellowship come from University of Edinburgh, Orr archive (Gen 868). Professor John Orr was a leading member of the Fellowship.

117 Archives Municipales du Havre, H/4/13/4, Prefect of Landes to Mayor of Le Havre, 8 November 1944; Lord Provost of Aberdeen to Mayor of Le Havre, 23 January 1945; Mayor of Southampton to Mayor of Le Havre, 29 January 1945; Dr Murat (Algiers) to Mayor of Le Havre, 5 February 1945; Sub-Prefect of Le Havre to Mayor of Le Havre, 1 March 1945.

118 TNA, HW1/3713, 'CX/MSS/T526/11- General strike (80,000 strikers) in TURIN on 18th April. Attack on the City by rebels expected', Top Secret Ultra, Air Intelligence message, 18 April 1945. See also L. Boccalatte, A. D'Arrigo and B. Maida (eds), *38/45 Luoghi della guerra e della resistenza nella provincia di Torino* (Turin: Blu Edizioni, 2006), 123–35.

119 TNA, AIR 14/2839, 'Notes of a discussion with Major von Reichel and Dr Smend of the effects of bombing in Northern Italy', 3 July 1945.

120 A. Beevor, *D-Day*, 269.

121 AM Le Havre, Dossier élections municipales 1953, *Lettre à tous les Havrais*.

122 In Pavone, *Una guerra civile*, 200–1.

9

Conclusion

France and Italy, we have suggested, deserve greater attention in the history of the bombing war. And bombing deserves a greater place in the wartime history of France and Italy. Part of the reason is quantitative: the two countries accounted for some 34.3 per cent of Allied bombs dropped in the West, compared to 51.1 per cent for Germany;[1] bombing accounted for nearly 120,000 deaths across France and Italy. But the reasons are also qualitative. They concern, first, the moral ambiguities involved in bombing, for a just cause, countries whose populations are considered friendly, or which have surrendered. Second, they concern the record of relatively weak states and peoples, among the European powers, as they struggled to survive. This concluding chapter explores both of these aspects.

BOMBING, LEGALITY, AND MORALITY

Discussion of the morality and legality of bombing in World War Two has typically focused on the sufferings of Germany.[2] The Allied bombing of France and Italy lacked the scope and the brutality of the strategic offensive against the Reich. However, it was still significant in purely numerical terms. And there is at least an argument that in twenty-first century terms, these attacks would count as war crimes.

Such a case can be based on the Geneva Conventions of 1949, and more particularly the First Additional Protocol to the Geneva Conventions, signed in 1977, and the Rome Statute of the International Criminal Court signed in 1998. These rules effectively place area bombing, which makes no effective distinction between the civilian population and combatants and is not directed against a specific military objective, beyond the limits of acceptable warfare. Thus Article 48 of the First 1977 Protocol specifically requires parties to a conflict to 'distinguish between the civilian population and combatants and between civilian objects and military objectives and accordingly [to] direct their operations only against military objectives'. Article 51.2 states that 'The civilian population as such, as well as individual civilians, shall not be the object of attack.'[3] Consistently with this, the war crimes listed under Article 8.2(b) of the Rome Statute of 1998 include 'Intentionally directing attacks against the civilian population as such or against individual civilians not taking direct part in hostilities.'[4] The attacks on Italian cities before the armistice of September 1943 were certainly small-scale relative to other strategic bombing offensives;

their contribution to the fall of Fascism was arguably very economical.[5] There is little doubt, however, that they constituted area bombing; as Bufton's note of 22 September 1943 showed, the question for Bomber Command after that month's armistice was simply whether to stop it.[6] As such, they fall into the category of war crimes as presently defined.

By contrast, all of the Allied raids on France, and all of the post-armistice Allied raids on Italy, were aimed, in principle, at specific industrial, communications, and military targets linked to the enemy's war effort. Civilian deaths were foreseen – most explicitly, in the debate on the Transportation Plan – but not intended. In contemporary parlance, civilians were collateral damage. The case against these raids, therefore, is more complex. It is, first, that under the terms of Article 51.4 of the First 1977 Protocol, they were 'indiscriminate' attacks, defined as:

> (a) those which are not directed at a specific military objective; (b) those which employ a method or means of combat which cannot be directed at a specific military objective; … and consequently, in each such case, are of a nature to strike military objectives and civilians or civilian objects without distinction.[7]

Second and most importantly, Article 8 of the 1998 Rome Statute defines as a war crime:

> Intentionally launching an attack in the knowledge that such attack will cause incidental loss of life or injury to civilians or damage to civilian objects or widespread, long-term and severe damage to the natural environment which would be clearly excessive in relation to the concrete and direct overall military advantage anticipated.[8]

The element of proportionality introduced by the term 'excessive' clearly invites subjective interpretation of each attack. Some well-planned, well-executed Allied raids on France and Italy did not fall into this category. Allied commanders showed sensitivity to civilian lives (and, in Italy, to historic buildings) that was largely absent from their treatment of Germany. This is reflected, for example, in Eisenhower's instructions to Allied air forces of 2 June 1944:

> It is essential to remember that much of the air fighting will take place over the heads of friendly people, who have endured the savagery of the Germans for years. Humanity and the principles for which we fight demand from our pilots scrupulous care to avoid any but military targets. … The Air Forces of the United Nations are privileged to be the spearhead of the forces fighting for freedom and the herald to the oppressed peoples of EUROPE of our approach. Be careful that nothing is done to betray this trust or to prejudice our good name in the eyes of our friends still dominated by the Nazi tyranny.[9]

There are other indications, too, that France and Italy were 'better' treated than Germany. The death toll per ton of bombs dropped there was lower than in the

Reich, despite a comparatively rudimentary level of shelter provision; a body count of 2,000 in a single raid, no more than unusual over Germany, was exceptional for Italy, unknown (just) in France. Warnings were given, some of which (as over Lorient in January 1943) saved lives. Italian cities of particular cultural importance were treated – not always successfully – with special care. The proportion of incendiaries – essential for the 'area' strategy of burning German cities – was smaller: 7.34 per cent for Bomber Command raids between April and June 1944, when raids on France were at their heaviest, against 45.77 per cent from April 1942 to March 1944.[10] In other respects, however, the Allies failed to meet the standards they had set for themselves. Neither high-altitude daytime bombing using 'boxes' on the American model, nor Bomber Command's mixture of short-fuse and delayed-action bombs, were conducive to saving civilian lives; they were techniques used over Germany, France and Italy alike. For those under it, the concrete experience of a heavy 'precision' raid appears to have been comparable to those of all but the most devastating area attacks. Raids such as those on Marseille on 27 May 1944 or Le Havre on 5 September, or, in Italy, on the cities and towns along the Gustav Line between October 1943 and March 1944, caused major damage to civilian lives and property to no discernible military advantage. Harris's statement on the bombing of a 'reported concentration of enemy motor transport and troops' at Aunay-sur-Odon in Normandy is indicative of a casual attitude to the principle of discrimination: when Bomber Command dropped 1,168 tons on the night of 14/15 June 1944, 'The road junction, the village, and anything of military importance which it may have contained, were entirely obliterated.' The mayor of Aunay-sur-Odon subsequently stated that no German troops were present.[11]

Two further lines of argument can be offered in the Allies' defence. The first is that they faced, in Nazi Germany, an enemy that was both exceptionally wicked – entirely willing, for example, to commit atrocities against both French and Italian civilians – and exceptionally tenacious. It followed that the defeat of such a foe was of inestimable benefit to human civilization. In relation to this end, the precise military advantage to be gained from an individual operation could not be meaningfully calculated in advance; it was their cumulative effect that mattered. Wrecking the Renault works – temporarily – was just one small contribution to a vast effort to curb Germany's war economy. Bombing Milan or Turin, even after the surrender, was part of a larger struggle that forced Germany to commit seven divisions to her southern defences. The Transportation Plan against French rail targets, however ill-conceived some individual raids, slowed the flow of vital German reinforcements into Normandy at the crucial moment. Some victories, moreover, would be won at the margins, and it made sense for the Allies to use every possible advantage they possessed; or, as Eisenhower wrote to Churchill in May 1944:

> The 'OVERLORD' concept was based on the assumption that our overwhelming Air power would be able to prepare the way for the assault. If its hands are to be tied, the perils of an already hazardous undertaking will be greatly enhanced.[12]

A failure of Overlord, in particular, could have prolonged the war for years. Eisenhower considered it his duty to minimize every risk he could. Whatever the tragedy of individual raids, the argument may run, the overall damage to civilian lives and property was not 'excessive' in relation to the military advantage achieved.

This defence may be answered in reference to the jus ad bellum/jus in bellum distinction: that the justice of the Allies' cause does not absolve them from the obligation to wage war according to commonly accepted standards.[13] With significant or complete air superiority over France and Italy for much of their bombing campaigns, the Allies possessed the means to measure military necessity against the cost of their attacks in civilian lives and property; they did not always take sufficient care in doing so. It could further be suggested that the Allies were under an obligation to explore other ways, less harmful to civilians, of achieving the same ends. They did this, by arming Resistance groups and refraining from attacks on targets successfully sabotaged by them – a technique that proved much more accurate and more economical than bombing. But the Allies trusted to sabotage to an extremely limited extent, because of its comparative complexity and unreliability, and (especially in Italy) because of anxieties about communist sympathies of many resisters. Resistance groups, especially in urban areas, could also be fragmented and small, so that the Allies usually found it simpler to use their overwhelming air power and order a raid – despite the mediocre precision achieved by their air forces.

A broader legal defence of the Allies is simply that the accusation of war crimes, especially in relation to France and Italy, is anachronistic or irrelevant. No generally agreed body of international law governed aerial warfare in 1939. The Hague Convention of 1907 brought it under the rules of land warfare, which were inapplicable or irrelevant to the case. The 1922–3 Hague Commission of Jurists proposed a ban on targeting civilians and on indiscriminate raids, but its findings were never ratified. At the International Disarmament Conference at Geneva in 1932, all states accepted the principle of a total ban on aerial bombing – except for the British, who wished to retain it as an option for colonial policing operations; there was no agreement before Hitler took Germany out of the conference. What existed in 1939, therefore, was what Ward Thomas has called a 'weak ethical norm' against bombing civilians, contingent on a mutual restraint which broke down in the skies of Britain and Germany in summer 1940.[14] Any legal basis for a claim against the Allies relies on the exceedingly imprecise 'Martens proviso' in the 1907 Hague convention, a general statement that for cases not covered by its regulations, the contracting parties 'deem it expedient' to rely on 'the usages established among civilized peoples, [...] the laws of humanity, and the dictates of the public conscience'. But the inclusion of this provision in the preamble not the body of the text, indicating a declaration of intent not a binding agreement, and its great imprecision, make it a weak basis indeed.[15] As to the Geneva conventions, the 1977 protocols, and the 1998

Rome Statute of the ICC, they are post-war constructs, the last two of which have never been ratified by the United States.

The war crimes case against the Allies in respect of France and Italy therefore depends almost entirely on transposing the norms of the late twentieth century into World War Two. Clear in relation to the (small-scale) area bombing of Italian cities, it is arguable but not conclusive in relation to the raids on France and on post-armistice Italy. This judgement, it may be noted, ignores the distinction between the civilians of France and post-armistice Italy and those of the Axis powers proper. The distinction was significant for the Allied policy-makers themselves: Churchill and Harris, all but merciless towards German civilians, hesitated to bomb French ones. It was also important for the civilians concerned: the French felt a particular sense of injustice at being bombed as if they were Germans; the Italians had hoped the armistice would end the raids. But it has no relevance in the moral and legal discussions of bombing, where civilians are civilians, of whatever nationality.

COMPARING VICHY FRANCE AND FASCIST ITALY

Deeply unprepossessing defenders 'protected' the civilians of France and Italy against the Allied onslaught. Some of Vichy's most abhorrent figures – Laval, Bousquet and Darnand – signed many of France's passive defence circulars. Italy's passive defence authorities were led by the Fascists who had casually led their country into a wholly irresponsible war of aggression. Fascist Italy and Vichy France had much in common as they faced attack from the air. Neither was adequately prepared, despite the expectations of war and the measures taken during the 1930s. Both, by 1942, were deeply unpopular. The rulers of both were aware that they had to be seen to be acting to protect their populations. Neither proved able to do so adequately. We have shown, however, that similarities in the responses to bombing by state and people were matched by at least equally significant points of distinction.

It is a central contention of this book that the reactions to bombing of state and people in France were more effective than those in Italy. A simple measure of this may be found in the number of deaths per ton of bombs dropped in the two countries: 0.100 in France, 0.158 – two-thirds higher – in Italy.[16] Put another way, if France had experienced the same death rate per ton as Italy, over 90,000 French civilians, more than 33,000 more than the actual total, would have died; if Italy had limited its rate to French levels, about 36,000 Italians would have died, and at least 24,000 lives of the actual total would have been saved. To ascribe this difference solely to the responses of states and peoples is perhaps an oversimplification; Italy, unlike France, experienced area bombing. But this was a limited part of the Allied offensive. Most of the time, France and Italy suffered the same type of imprecise 'precision' raids.

How did responses differ? Both states, to begin with, reformed their structures to improve co-ordination of the civil defence effort, attempted to improve civilian protection against bombing, and offered social assistance to bombed-out households. France, though, was more successful at all three. Information about raids was reliably gathered, diffused, and used; SIPEG offered a degree of co-ordination between different services (as well as its trains); the chain from government to prefects to mayors remained reasonably intact; and as the relative continuity of personnel shows, passive defence remained one of the less politicized of Vichy's services. The shelter-building programme was insufficient, owing above all to raw materials shortages, but French towns and cities were better (if still inadequately) provided for as the war progressed and lessons were drawn from raids. Social assistance received substantial and growing budgetary allocations, and measures were taken to ensure money usually reached those who needed it. In Italy, by contrast, though efforts at co-ordination were made, they appear to have broken down by spring 1943; information processing was weak; and local and regional authorities were increasingly left to their own devices. This was reflected in the provision of shelters, where piecemeal efforts at local level partly palliated the absence of a national policy, and of social assistance, where local authorities could not meet demand.

Perhaps more surprising, Vichy France also proved better at communicating with the population. Vichy propaganda, though based on impossibly shaky premises (support for a German victory) and tending to the mawkish, had its own coherence and reflected part of what the French were actually experiencing; Henriot was convincing enough to worry both Allies and Free French in 1944. The message from Fascist Italy, by contrast, moved from triumphalism over the very rare raids on Britain, to denial of any successful attacks on Italy, to mendacious claims that the Italians were indifferent to bombing, to miserabilism on the Vichy model. Its inconsistency, and the fact that Italy had attacked British towns earlier, robbed it of all credibility.

Neither regime succeeded, through propaganda related to air raids, in reinforcing public loyalty to itself. In France, Henriot sowed doubts about the Allies but could not win positive support for Vichy; indeed, there is little sign that bombing made any significant difference to the regime's general unpopularity. In Italy, by contrast, raids increased an already widespread sentiment that the Fascists had drawn the country into a disastrous and irresponsible war, and thus widened the gap between the regime and the people.

More importantly, Vichy proved more effective at mobilizing the population in response to air raids. Neither regime, it is true, had great success in applying an evacuation policy, and Italy, with the long months of ground combat, faced the harder task. But the limited achievement of France in getting over 200,000 schoolchildren to safety contrasts with the incoherence of Italy's policy, already flagrant in the wake of Mussolini's speech of December 1942. Unlike Italy, France also managed to rally, from diverse sources, numerically adequate passive defence teams – though problems of command and control often limited their effectiveness. Fascist Italy regularly lacked manpower for passive defence. In the wake of air raids, the same diversity of French organizations – the state, but also newspaper subscriptions, town adoptions, and the Secours National, for example – brought assistance, albeit at a very basic level, to the victims of bombing; in Italy, mobilization of this kind was framed by the Fascist party, which by 1942 at latest was a handicap.

If the state proved less effective in Italy than in France at protecting the public, and at mobilizing the public to protect themselves, it is not surprising that Italian and French citizens responded differently in some respects to the experience of bombing. Both, it is true, tended to ignore basic air-raid precautions until they were bombed. In both countries, raids could also cause panic. Looting, common in France though usually on a small scale, appears more rarely in the Italian records – but where it does, is clearly systematic and corresponds to a breakdown in society. That breakdown appears to have occurred after the worst raids in Italy and reflected growing evidence of social protest. French civilians faced with the most extreme destruction, as for example in Caen, achieved considerable feats of mutual assistance.

Different reactions towards the regime were reflected in the two publics' opinions of the Western Allies. The French moved, broadly, from welcoming the raids till the end of 1942 to a more equivocal attitude in 1943 and general condemnation in the months before D-Day. Then, their general sympathy for the Allies, and particularly the Americans, was severely tested; Vichy propaganda scored some clear hits, particularly with claims that the raids were motivated by a hidden economic agenda. Even in 1944, however, the French sought excuses for the raids; and their salience diminished, as the Allies had hoped it would, with the Normandy landings. In Italy, public reactions had more complex motivations, which included guilt at the bombing of Britain and a range of rumours more bizarre than anything seen in France. Public opinion was slower to condemn the Allies for the bombing, and readier to accept that bombing could bring the day of liberation closer.

It is among members of the public who had broken links with the regime that behaviour in France and Italy appears to have been closest. In both countries, downed aircrew appear to have been assisted wherever possible by ordinary citizens and resistance networks, the larger numbers in France reflecting above all the larger number of aircraft over French soil. Remarkably, collaboration between the Resistance movement and the Allies to substitute sabotage and works stoppages for bombing was more intense and more effective in northern Italy under the Salò Republic than in occupied France.

What explains the differences in responses of states and peoples to bombing in the two countries? Pre-war preparations offer some explanation. Neither France nor Italy, it is true, had achieved an adequate level of preparation on the ground by 1939. But some credit is due to France's administrative preparations under the Third Republic; mayors, prefects, ministerial field services and municipal departments had at least engaged with the issues of passive defence by the outbreak of war. There is no evidence of an equivalent commitment in Italy. Another contributing factor was certainly different levels of economic development; France had better resources. Comparing Italy and Germany, MacGregor Knox has observed that Italian industrialization by 1939 was some 30–50 years behind her northern neighbour's, and her industrial potential slightly over a fifth of Germany's. France, it is true, was certainly closer to a peasant society than Germany, but on some measures – for example motor vehicle ownership – was ahead of both countries.[17] Italy's regime, Knox continues, 'scarcely even dared to tax its subjects': tax receipts actually fell 20 per cent in the first three years of the war.[18] In France, by contrast, they were set to rise by 58 per cent between 1941 and 1944.[19] Out of this, France, it is true, had to pay enormous 'occupation costs' to Germany; but Fascist Italy was still fighting a war.

The differing ability to tax reflects a wider difference in the relationship between state and people in the two countries. In France, the record of responses to bombing under Vichy tends to challenge some aspects of narratives of the Occupation. Put most simply, the Vichy state in 1944 was still able to make things happen and mobilize people, rather than merely repressing them, even though public support for the regime was threadbare to non-existent. The French population, meanwhile, variously portrayed as heroic *résistants*, odious collaborators, or grubby profiteers, as *attentistes* waiting to see which way the wind blew, or as the passive victims of multiple shortages and multiple forms of violence, appear under the bombs – at least some of the time – as capable of considerable acts of solidarity, sometimes at risk of their lives, and of mutual self-help, with rather little reference to the growing armed conflict between the regime and its opponents. From this perspective, the French state retained a notable capacity to enlist public co-operation even as the regime was widely loathed. French civil society, moreover, even under the extreme strain of war, appears both as more vibrant than students of Tocqueville would credit, and less torn apart than sometimes supposed by the conflict between Vichy and the Resistance. By contrast, responses in Italy largely confirm accounts of a society detaching itself from Fascism without getting its bearings anywhere else. Fascism, indeed, played a wholly negative role in the Italian response: having contaminated the political system sufficiently to destroy the Italian state's capacity for independent action, the Fascist Party was too weak, by 1942, to command the loyalty of more than a small minority of the population. Only among sections of the population – the Resistance – loyal to neither state nor party did the Italian capacity for mobilization equal that of the French.

LOOKING BACK, LOOKING FORWARD

One of the most fascinating aspects of the bombing campaign is what it tells us about the nature of historical memory. In the United Kingdom, the central position of the Blitz in the national identity rests not only on the fact of the bombing and the memories of individuals but on a copious literature (fiction and non-fiction), as well as films, documentaries, and education in schools. The level of cultural production continues to grow as the number of survivors diminishes. France and Italy received many more bombs than the UK; comparable numbers of civilians died in each country; French cemeteries hold the graves of Allied airmen, French and Italian towns and villages have monuments to air-raid victims. As Évelyne Py notes, the older generation in bombed localities get talkative when air raids are mentioned.[20] Yet however remembered locally, bombing has not been underpinned by any cultural production comparable to Britain's, and has been marginalized from official memories of the war nationally. Episodes in which the liberators took lives and the oppressors attempted, with greater or lesser success, to save them do not slide easily into the broad narrative of World War Two. Most monuments do not point blame at the Allies directly, but are simply memorials to the victims of bombing.[21]

In a continent at peace – with the important exception of former Yugoslavia – for nearly seven decades, the destruction by liberal democracies of tens of thousands of 'friendly' lives may appear impossibly remote. It should not. Between 1962 and 1973 South Vietnam received as many as 4 million tons of bombs from the aircraft of its ally the United States.[22] Subsequent wars have also seen the United States (and, on occasion, its European partners) bomb objectives on the territory of allies (Afghanistan or Pakistan). Alternatively, bombing in liberal interventionist wars of liberation (Iraq or Libya) has invariably been accompanied by declarations that the target is the government not the people. Such claims have been facilitated by the 'precision revolution', begun late in Vietnam and greatly accelerated since, which has given the air forces of developed countries, especially the United States, a level of accuracy unimaginable in World War Two.[23] This has encouraged some airpower specialists to argue strongly in favour of bombing: Phillip Meilinger, for example, writes that 'Aerospace power should therefore be our weapon of first resort, because it is the most discriminate, prudent and risk-free weapon in our arsenal.'[24]

Such a recommendation is imprudent. As Clodfelter observes, 'smart munitions still do not guarantee zero collateral damage'.[25] Repeated experience has shown that 'smart' weapons may fail through faulty programming or execution, or hit the wrong target through faulty intelligence. Moreover, the political liabilities attached to bombing civilians have at least kept pace with precision. The parallel technological development of the world's media has made concealment from a global public very difficult. The multiplication of political fora – particularly the United Nations – that are not necessarily sympathetic to the bombers allows worldwide condemnation to be aired. The destruction of civilian targets such as the Al Firdos bunker in the first Gulf war of 1991, or the Chinese embassy in Belgrade in the Kosovo War of 1999, as well as the regular civilian deaths from drone attacks in Afghanistan and Pakistan, all constitute relatively minor incidents by World War Two standards. But they entailed significant political costs for their authors.[26]

To forget the enormous costs paid by the citizens of occupied territories for their own liberation is to risk smoothing out the jagged history of World War Two into an oversimplified story of good and evil. The acceptance of those who lived through these raids, and the assistance they gave to the airmen who bombed them, deserve our respect. Other survivors of 'friendly' bombing may be less forbearing.

Notes

1 Cf. Table 1.1, p. 2.
2 Cf. for example A. C. Grayling, *Among the Dead Cities: Is the Targeting of Civilians in War Ever Justified?* (London: Bloomsbury, 2007).
3 Protocol Additional to the Geneva Conventions of 12 August 1949, and relating to the Protection of Victims of International Armed Conflicts (Protocol I), 8 June 1977, on http://www.icrc.org/ihl.nsf/FULL/470?OpenDocument.
4 Article 8, Rome Statute of the International Criminal Court, 1998, from http://www.icc-cpi.int/Menus/ICC/Legal+Texts+and+Tools/.
5 From October 1942 to August 1943, Bomber Command dropped 9,073 tons on Italy, compared with 26,348 on enemy-occupied territory, chiefly France, and 123,570 on Germany in the same period – though this does not include (mostly American) raids on the south launched from Mediterranean bases (Sir Arthur Harris, *Despatch on War Operations, 23rd February, 1942 to 8th May, 1945* (London: Frank Cass, 1995), 44). In the same document (p. 22) Harris claims, without supporting evidence, that bombing 'was the principal factor contributing to the downfall of Mussolini's regime'.
6 See above, p. 34.
7 Article 51.4, Protocol I, 8 June 1977, on http://www.icrc.org/ihl.nsf/FULL/470?OpenDocument.
8 Article 8.2(b)(iv), Rome Statute of the International Criminal Court, 1998, from http://www.icc-cpi.int/Menus/ICC/Legal+Texts+and+Tools/.
9 TNA AIR 37/1012, Eisenhower to Air Commander-in-Chief, AEAF, Air Officer Commanding-in-Chief, Bomber Command, and Commanding General, USSTAF, 2 June 1944.
10 Calculated from Harris, *Despatch*, 47. These figures should be treated with caution in relation to Italy, however; Italian cities, with their low proportion of wood in the overall construction, burned less well, as Bomber Command studies showed, than German ones, and were thus more readily destroyed by high explosive than by incendiaries.
11 Harris, *Despatch*, 26; TNA FO371/49203, Mayor N. Lacaine of Aunay-sur-Odon to British Ambassador, Paris, 19 March 1945.
12 TNA AIR 37/1116, Eisenhower to Churchill, 2 May 1944.
13 C. A. J. Coady, 'Bombing and the Morality of War', in Y. Tanaka and M. B. Young (eds), *Bombing Civilians: a Twentieth-Century History* (New York: The New Press, 2009), 192; T. L. H. McCormack and H. Durham, 'Aerial Bombardment of Civilians: the Current International Legal Framework', in Tanaka and Young (eds), *Bombing Civilians*, 218.
14 Cf. W. Thomas, *The Ethics of Destruction: Norms and Force in International Relations* (Ithaca, NY: Cornell University Press, 2001), 103–30.
15 Convention (IV) respecting the Laws and Customs of War on Land and its annex: Regulations concerning the Laws and Customs of War on Land, The Hague, 18 October 1907, http://www.

icrc.org/ihl.nsf/FULL/195?OpenDocument; H. Boog, 'Harris – a German View', in Harris, *Despatch*, xliv–xlv.

16 Cf. above, p. 16.

17 M. Knox, *Common Destiny: Dictatorship, Foreign Policy, and War in Fascist Italy and Nazi Germany* (Cambridge: Cambridge University Press, 2009), 148, 151.

18 *Ibid.*, 149.

19 *Journal Officiel de l'État Français*, 1 January 1942, 3; 1 January 1944, États annexes, 49a.

20 Cf. C. Morin, *La Touraine sous les bombes* (Chambray-lès-Tours: CLD Éditions, 2000), 243; E. Py, *Un été sous les bombes: Givors, Grigny, Chasse, 1944* (Saint-Cyr-sur-Loire: Éditions Alan Sutton, 2004), 7.

21 Cf. L. Paggi, *Il 'popolo dei morti'. La repubblica italiana nata dalla guerra (1940–1946)* (Bologna: Il Mulino, 2009), 83–9.

22 Another 3 million tons were dropped on Laos, 1 million on North Vietnam, and nearly 500,000 on Cambodia. Vietnamese casualties from the war reached a total of some 2 million. Cf. D. L. Anderson, 'Introduction: The Vietnam War and its Enduring Historical Relevance', in D. L. Anderson ed., *The Columbia History of the Vietnam War* (New York: Columbia University Press, 2011), 48, 65.

23 Cf. M. R. Rip and J. M. Hasik, *The Precision Revolution: GPS and the Future of Aerial Warfare* (Annapolis, Maryland, USA: Naval Institute Press, 2002), 35, 245.

24 P. S. Meilinger, *Airwar: Theory and Practice* (London: Frank Cass, 2003), 196.

25 M. Clodfelter, *The Limits of Air Power: the American Bombing of North Vietnam* (2nd edition: Lincoln, Nebraska, USA: University of Nebraska Press, 2006), xi.

26 Thomas, *Ethics of Destruction*, 159–60, 167, 171.

Appendix: The Death Toll

The precise number of victims of bombing in France and Italy will never be known. Three main types of obstacle lie in the way of an accurate estimate.

The way bombing killed presents a first set of difficulties. Some victims were intact but unrecognizable; others were blown apart. Burial lists in Rennes and other French towns include both unidentified corpses and a (generally small) number of coffins filled with body parts.[1] Where air attacks supported ground operations, as in Normandy or in much of Italy, deaths from bombing could be indistinguishable from those from shelling. Again, the time needed to clear rubble inevitably made early body counts incomplete: in Toulon, for example, trapped bodies were still being disinterred four weeks after the big raid of 23 November 1943.[2] Bombing often killed instantly and directly, but not always. Deaths from wounds could take weeks or even months; in Naples, bombing claimed indirect victims who died from diseases contracted in air-raid shelters.[3] A simple body count in the immediate aftermath of a raid could not, therefore, offer a complete record.

A second category of difficulties is administrative. They arose, first, from the fragmentation of local government, in France (where 38,000 municipalities recorded births, deaths and marriages) but also in Italy, where registration had a patchy record even in peacetime.[4] Deaths of individuals killed outside their home towns or villages might be recorded once, or twice, or not at all. This was compounded by the circumstances of war. Evacuation and labour conscription, plus the fact that many raids hit railway targets, and thus travellers likely to be distant from home, further complicated the record. There was also the issue of who to include. In France, dead civilians might be foreign forced labourers building the Atlantic Wall as well as the French population; equally, some French prisoners of war or forced labourers died from Allied bombing in their German camps. Either, or neither, might have a claim to be included in a final total. Inevitably, too, bombing could cause a breakdown in administration. Decomposing bodies might be buried hastily without registration, especially in hot weather. Archives and registries were destroyed, archivists and registrars themselves killed, wounded, or called from their normal duties to more pressing tasks.

Given these ambiguities, it is unsurprising that a third source of uncertainty was political. During the war, regimes sensitive to the charge that they had not protected their populations might seek to minimize casualties or even, for a time at least, organize news blackouts of raids. Equally, however, casualties could be inflated to fuel anti-Allied propaganda. In the early reconstruction period, local authorities also had incentives to maximize both casualties and material damage in bids for central government funding; the emotion of the time might also encourage exaggeration.

The resulting estimates vary spectacularly. In France, the Entr'aide française, the main post-war organization for aid to war victims, gave an estimate of 300,000 French deaths through bombing from September 1939 to early 1945, adding that it was probably below the true level.[5] The French Veterans' Ministry arrived at an overall death toll from bombing of 117,473.[6] A ministerial statement to parliament in 1948 cited 56,896 civilian deaths through bombing, but also mentioned 26,294 civilian dead through undefined 'other' war-related causes, and a further 7,773 still under enquiry.[7] The only comprehensive published study of the Allied bombing of France suggests one figure of 47,771 but quotes another of 67,078 twenty pages later.[8] In Italy, the Italian institute for statistics (ISTAT) puts deaths from bombing at 64,354, of whom 4,558 were military casualties, plus a further 6,237 dead caused by other types of bombardment, bringing the total to 70,591. Local official estimates, on the other hand, would probably add up to 120–130,000.[9] One publication from 1968 claimed 20,000 victims for Naples alone; a comparable estimate was made by Foggia city council in a bid for a gold medal for civil valour.[10]

An exhaustive scrutiny of local registers of deaths across the two countries would require a large team of researchers and is beyond the scope of this study. The best available results appear contrasted between France and Italy. The French figures in Table 1.2, derived from the contemporary *Bulletin d'Information de la Défense Passive*, remain reasonably credible for several reasons. They were compiled systematically from reports sent by municipalities to prefects and by prefects to the Interior Ministry. They were confidential, not used for propaganda, and taken over intact from Vichy by the Liberation authorities, which completed the series in 1945. Each issue of the *Bulletin* included revised figures for the previous issue on the basis of complementary reports. And when figures are considered unreliable, as for September 1944, the *Bulletin* issues a caveat (the *Bulletin*'s numbers for this month have therefore been complemented by local statistics). While the *Bulletin* insists, in the final table of its last issue, that its figures should be viewed as minima, the detailed regional research that has been undertaken, especially in Normandy, indicates a death toll significantly lower than previously thought.[11] This suggests that the *Bulletin*'s figures, while incomplete, are not hopelessly low, and that a total in the region of 60,000 is not unrealistic. The *Bulletin* also supplies the only available year-on-year figures for the whole of France.

In Italy, on the other hand, recent detailed research indicates that official national figures should be revised upwards. Achille Rastelli's work on Milan published the city council's figure of 1,208 victims (for the city only, without its suburbs), but he concluded from his own research that the real number was closer to 2,000.[12] Gabriella Gribaudi's study of Naples also disputes the official sources, which claim a total of 3,100 dead in the province of Naples up to 21 September 1943 (ten days before the Allies took the city), to which we should add the 470 victims of subsequent German bombing: her work in the registries of each of the Neapolitan city boroughs concluded that in 1943 alone, the most tragic year for Naples, the dead numbered 6,097.[13] At national level, Massobrio and Gioannini, after a city-by-city work of reconstruction (still leaving out rural areas), consider the best estimate as lying somewhere between the 60,000 claimed by ISTAT in 1957 and the 120–130,000 that would result from adding up local official estimates, and suggest a figure of about 80,000.[14]

Notes

1 Cf. for example AM Rennes 1048/W/11.
2 AD Var 1/W/64, General Guichard to Prefect of Var, 20 December 1943.
3 Gribaudi, *Guerra totale*, 161.
4 Gioannini and Massobrio, *Bombardate l'Italia*, 491.
5 AD Ille-et-Vilaine 502/W/39, Entr'Aide Française, *Renseignements sur la France après 4 ans d'occupation ennemie*, January/February 1945, 87.
6 Ministère de la Défense, Service Historique de la Défense, Bureau des archives des victimes des conflits contemporains, Caen.
7 *Journal Officiel de la République Française: Assemblée Nationale, 2e séance du 25 mai 1948*, 26 May 1948, 2938.
8 Florentin, *Quand les alliés*, 426, 446.
9 Gioannini and Massobrio, *Bombardate l'Italia*, 492.
10 A. Stefanile, *I cento bombardamenti di Napoli* (Naples: Marotta, 1968) does not provide evidence for the claim of 20,000 dead. On the similar claim for the bombing of Foggia, see M. Gismondi, *Foggia: la tragica estate; Taranto: la notte più lunga* (Bari: Dedalo, 1968).
11 Prime, 'Les bombardements', 31–47. Prime reaches a total of 19,890 civilian deaths in the battle of Normandy, including the bombing of Le Havre in September. The studies from which Prime draws his figures are unanimous on the relatively low level of losses that their research revealed: cf. M. Dandel, G. Duboc, A. Kitts, and E. Lapersonne, *Les Victimes Civiles des Bombardements en Haute-Normandie* (Caen: CRHQ-RED, La Mandragore, 1997), 111; J. Quellien, B. Garnier, and Université Inter-Âges, *Les Victimes civiles du Calvados dans la bataille de Normandie, 1er mars 1944 – 31 décembre 1945* (Caen: Éditions-Diffusion du Lys, 1995), pp. 5, 13; M. Boivin, G. Bourdin, B. Garnier, and J. Quellien, *Les victimes civiles de Basse-Normandie dans la Bataille de Normandie* (Caen: Éditions du Lys, 1996), v, xii.
12 Rastelli, *Bombe sulla città*, 183–5.
13 Gribaudi, *Guerra totale*, 161.
14 Gioannini and Massobrio, *Bombardate l'Italia*, 492.

List of Primary Sources Consulted

UNITED KINGDOM

The National Archives of the United Kingdom, Kew, London

UNITED STATES OF AMERICA

Franklin D. Roosevelt Presidential Library, New York
Library of Congress, Washington DC
National Archives and Records Administration, Washington DC

FRANCE

Archives Nationales, Paris
Service Historique de l'Armée de l'Air, Vincennes
Service Historique de l'Armée de Terre, Vincennes
Archives Départementales des Bouches-du-Rhône, Marseille
Archives Départementales du Calvados, Caen
Archives Départementales d'Ille-et-Vilaine, Rennes
Archives Départementales de la Loire, Saint-Étienne
Archives Départementales de la Loire-Atlantique, Nantes
Archives Départementales de la Manche, Saint-Lô
Archives Départementales du Morbihan, Vannes
Archives Départementales du Rhône
Archives Départementales de la Seine-Maritime
Archives Départementales du Var
Archives de Paris
Archives Municipales de Boulogne-Billancourt
Archives Municipales et Communautaires de Brest
Archives Municipales du Havre
Archives Municipales de Lorient
Archives Municipales de Lyon

Archives Municipales de Marseille
Archives Municipales de Nantes
Archives Municipales de Rennes
Archives Municipales de Rouen
Archives Municipales de Saint-Étienne
Archives Municipales de Toulon
Archives Diocésanes de Lyon
Association pour l'Autobiographie, Ambérieu-en-Bugey
Mémorial de Caen, Caen

Bulletin d'Information de la Défense Passive
Most copies of the *Bulletin* are available, bound and unavailable for photocopying or photographing, in the Bibliothèque Nationale François Mitterrand, Paris.

More accessible copies of various numbers are available as follows.
1–3, 5–7, 9–12: Archives Départementales de l'Ille-et-Vilaine, 502W/3
4, 19: Archives Nationales, Paris, F17/14901
8: Archives Nationales, Paris, AJ41/356
13: Service Historique de l'Armée de l'Air, Vincennes, 3D/44
14, 15: Service Historique de l'Armée de l'Air, Vincennes, 3D/406
17, 27: Archives Départementales du Morbihan, 7W/4794
20: Archives Départementales de la Manche, AD127/W/1
16, 18, 21–26: (none detected outside Bibliothèque Nationale François Mitterrand, Paris)

ITALY

Archivio Centrale dello Stato, Rome
Archivio Comunale, Genoa
Archivio di Stato, Bologna
Archivio di Stato, Genoa
Archivio di Stato, La Spezia
Archivio di Stato, Milan
Archivio di Stato, Naples
Archivio di Stato, Palermo
Archivio di Stato, Taranto
Archivio di Stato, Turin
Archivio Diaristico Nazionale, Pieve Santo Stefano
Archivio Fondazione Micheletti, Brescia
Archivio Fotografico del Comune, Genoa
Archivio Storico Città di Torino
Archivio Storico del Santuario, Pompeii
Archivio Storico Diocesano, Naples

Archivio Storico Diocesano, Taranto
Istituto Nazionale per la Storia del Movimento di Liberazione in Italia, Milan
Istituto Piemontese per la Storia della Resistenza e della Società Contemporanea, Turin
Istituto Storico della Resistenza in Toscana, Florence
Istituto Storico Parri Emilia Romagna, Bologna

National and local newspapers have been consulted in a number of city libraries and at the Biblioteca del Senato G. Spadolini, Rome. Some of the archives listed above were consulted for images on the bombing of Italy which can be found in the web exhibition of the project 'Bombing, States and Peoples in Western Europe, (http://centres.exeter.ac.uk/wss/bombing/index.htm).

Bibliography

GENERAL AND COMPARATIVE WORKS

Air Ministry (United Kingdom), *The Rise and Fall of the German Air Force* (Air Ministry Pamphlet, London, 1948; reissued, London: Public Record Office, 2001).

Alanbrooke, Field Marshal Lord, *War Diaries 1939–1945* ed. Alex Danchev and Daniel Tudman (London: Weidenfeld and Nicolson, 2001).

Anderson, David L., 'Introduction: The Vietnam War and its Enduring Historical Relevance', in David L. Anderson ed., *The Columbia History of the Vietnam War* (New York: Columbia University Press, 2011).

Baldoli, Claudia, Knapp, Andrew, and Overy, Richard (eds), *Bombing, States and Peoples in Western Europe, 1940–1945* (London: Continuum, 2011).

Boog, Horst, 'The Strategic Air War in Europe and Air Defence of the Reich', in Horst Boog, Gerhard Krebs, and Detlef Vogel, *Germany and the Second World War*, vol. vii (Oxford: Oxford University Press, 2006), 7–458.

Calder, Angus, *The Myth of the Blitz* (London: Jonathan Cape, 1991).

Caruth, Cathy, *Unclaimed Experience: Trauma, Narrative, and History* (Baltimore, Md.: Johns Hopkins Press, 1996).

Clodfelter, Mark, *The Limits of Air Power: the American Bombing of North Vietnam* (2nd edition: Lincoln, Nebraska, USA: University of Nebraska Press, 2006).

Corum, James S., 'The Myth of Air Control: Reassessing the History', *Air and Space Power Journal*, vol. XIV no. 4 (Winter 2000), 61–77.

Craven, W. F. and Cate, J. L. (eds), *The Army Air Forces in World War II*, 3 vols. (Washington DC: Office of Air Force History, 1983 (1st edn. 1976)).

Davis, Richard G., *Carl A. Spaatz and the Air War in Europe* (Washington, D.C.: Centre for Air Force History, 1993).

Douhet, Giulio, *The Command of the Air* (Washington, D.C.: Office of Air Force History, 1983 (1st Italian edn., 1921)).

Dumoulin, Olivier, 'A Comparative Approach to Newsreels and Bombing in the Second World War: Britain, France, Germany', in Claudia Baldoli, Andrew Knapp and Richard Overy (eds), *Bombing, States and Peoples in Western Europe, 1940–1945* (London: Continuum, 2011), 298–314.

Freeman, Roger A., *Mighty Eighth War Diary* (London: Jane's, 1981).

Friedrich, Jörg, *The Fire: The Bombing of Germany, 1940–1945* (New York: Columbia University Press, 2006)

Gardiner, Juliet, *The Blitz: the British under Attack* (London: HarperCollins, 2010).

Gooderson, Ian, *Air Power at the Battlefront: Allied Close Air Support in Europe, 1943–45* (London: Frank Cass, 1998).
Grayling, A. C., *Among the Dead Cities: Is the Targeting of Civilians in War Ever Justified?* (London: Bloomsbury, 2007).
Harris, Sir Arthur, *Bomber Offensive*, revised edn. (London: Greenhill Books, 1990 (1st edn. London: Collins, 1947)).
—*Despatch on War Operations, 23rd February, 1942 to 8th May, 1945* (London: Frank Cass, 1995; also in The National Archives, Kew, London, AIR 14/4465).
Hastings, M., *Bomber Command* (London: Michael Joseph, 1979).
Heinl, Peter, *Splintered Innocence: an Intuitive Approach to Treating War Trauma* (New York and Hove: Brunner-Routledge, 2001).
Hitchcock, William I., *Liberation: the Bitter Road to Freedom, Europe 1944–1945* (London: Faber and Faber, 2008).
Holt, Robert T. and van de Velde, Robert W., *Strategic Psychological Operations and American Foreign Policy* (Chicago: University of Chicago Press, 1967 (1st edn. 1960)).
Knell, Hermann, *To Destroy a City: Strategic Bombing and its Human Consequences in World War II* (Cambridge, Mass.: Da Capo Press, 2003).
Kreis, John F., *Piercing the Fog: Intelligence and Army Air Forces Operations in World War II* (Washington D.C.: Air Force History and Museums Program, 1996).
Lacey-Johnson, Lionel, *Pointblank and Beyond* (Shrewsbury: Airlife Publishing, 1991).
Meilinger, Phillip S., *Airwar: Theory and Practice* (London: Frank Cass, 2003).
—ed. *The Paths of Heaven: the Evolution of Airpower Theory* (Maxwell Air Force Base, Alabama, USA: Air University Press, 1997).
Mets, David R., *Master of Airpower: Carl A. Spaatz* (Novato CA: Presidio Press, 1998).
Mortimer, Gavin, *The Longest Night* (London: Orion Books, 2005).
O'Brien, Terence H., *Civil Defence* (London: HMSO, 1955).
Orange, Vincent, *Tedder: Quietly in Command* (London: Frank Cass, 2004).
Overy, Richard, *The Air War, 1939–1945* (Washington, D.C.: Potomac Books, 2005 (1st edn. 1980)).
—'Introduction', in Claudia Baldoli, Andrew Knapp and Richard Overy (eds), *Bombing, States and Peoples in Western Europe, 1940–1945* (London: Continuum, 2011), 1–20.
Overy, Richard, with Andrew Wheatcroft, *The Road to War*, 3rd edn. (London: Vintage Books, 2009).
Richards, Denis, *RAF Bomber Command in the Second World War: the Hardest Victory* (London: Penguin, 2001 (first edition: W. W. Norton, USA, 1995)).
Richards, Denis, and Saunders, Hilary St George, *The Royal Air Force 1939–45*, 3 vols. (London: HMSO, 1974–5).
Rip, Michael Russell, and Hasik, James M., *The Precision Revolution: GPS and the Future of Aerial Warfare* (Annapolis, Maryland, USA: Naval Institute Press, 2002).

Roskill, Stephen, *The War at Sea*, vol. I (London: HMSO, 1954).
Schaffer, Ronald, *Wings of Judgment: American Bombing in World War II* (Oxford: Oxford University Press, 1985).
Süss, Dietmar, 'Wartime Societies and Shelter Politics in National Socialist Germany and Britain' in Claudia Baldoli, Andrew Knapp and Richard Overy (eds), *Bombing, States and Peoples in Western Europe, 1940–1945* (London: Continuum, 2011), 23–42.
Tanaka, Yuki, and Young, Marilyn B. (eds), *Bombing Civilians: a Twentieth-Century History* (New York: The New Press, 2009).
Tedder, Arthur, *With Prejudice: The War Memoirs of Marshal of the Royal Air Force Lord Tedder, GCB* (London: Cassell, 1966).
Thomas, Ward, *The Ethics of Destruction: Norms and Force in International Relations* (Ithaca, NY: Cornell University Press, 2001).
Titmuss, Richard M., *Problems of Social Policy* (London: HMSO, 1950).
United States Strategic Bombing Survey, Overall report (European War), Washington DC, 30 September 1945, on http://wwiiarchives.net/servlet/document/113/1/0.
Webster, Sir Charles, and Frankland, Noble, *The Strategic Air Offensive Against Germany, 1939–1945*, 4 vols. (London: HMSO, 1961).
Zuckerman, Solly, *From Apes to Warlords: The Autobiography (1904–46) of Solly Zuckerman* (London: Hamish Hamilton, 1978).

FRANCE

Adamthwaite, Anthony, *France and the Coming of the Second World War* (London: Frank Cass, 1977).
Alary, Éric, with Bénédicte Vergez-Chaignon and Gilles Cauvin, *Les Français au Quotidien 1939–1949* (Paris: Perrin, 2006).
Aron, Robert, 'Le Maréchal en zone nord: un triomphe', *Les années 40*, 62, 1980, 1723–7.
Auroy, Berthe, *Jours de guerre: Ma vie sous l'Occupation* (Montrouge: Bayard, 2008).
Azéma, Jean-Pierre, and Bédarida, François (eds), *La France des années noires*, 2 vols. (Paris: Le Seuil, 1993).
—(eds), *Vichy et les Français* (Paris: Fayard, 1992).
Baruch, Marc Olivier, *Servir l'État français. L'administration en France de 1940 à 1944* (Paris: Fayard, 1997).
Battesti, Michèle, and Facon, Patrick (eds), *Les Bombardements Alliés sur la France durant la Seconde Guerre Mondiale: Stratégies, Bilans Matériaux et Humains* (Paris: Ministère de la Défense (Cahiers du Centre d'Etudes d'Histoire de la Défense, no. 37), 2009).
Beevor, Anthony, *D-Day: the Battle for Normandy* (London: Penguin Books, 2009).
Bengtsson, Max, *Un été 44: de l'état de siège à la paix retrouvée* (2nd edition: Le Havre: Éditions-Imprimerie Grenet, 2004).

Boivin, Michel, *Les Manchois dans la tourmente de la seconde guerre mondiale, 1939–1945*, 6 vols. (Marigny (Manche): Éditions Eurocibles, 2004).

Boivin, Michel, Bourdin, Gérard, Garnier, Bernard, and Quellien, Jean, *Les victimes civiles de Basse-Normandie dans la Bataille de Normandie* (Caen: Éditions du Lys, 1996).

Boivin, Michel, Bourdin, Gérard, and Quellien, Jean (eds), *Villes normandes sous les bombes (juin 1944)*, Caen, Presses Universitaires de Caen/Mémorial de Caen, 1994.

Brickhill, Paul, *The Dam Busters* (Basingstoke: Pan Macmillan, 1983).

Brooks, Tim, *British Propaganda to France, 1940–1944: Machinery, Method and Message* (Edinburgh: Edinburgh University Press, 2007).

Burrin, Philippe, *La France à l'heure allemande* (Paris: Éditions du Seuil, 1997).

Caillaud, Paul, *Nantes sous les bombardements: Mémorial à la Défense Passive* (Nantes: Éditions du Fleuve, 1946).

—*Les Nantais sous les bombardements, 1941–1944* (Nantes: Aux Portes du Large, 1947).

Castellano, Philippe, *Chronique d'un bombardement manqué aux conséquences tragiques: attaque de la gare de triage de Cannes-La Bocca fin de soirée du 11 novembre 1943* (Ollioules (Var, France): Éditions de la Nerthe, 2000).

Chauvy, Gérard, *Lyon, 1940–1947: L'Occupation, la Libération, l'Épuration* (Paris: Perrin, 2004).

Chawaf, Chantal, *Je suis née* (Paris: Des Femmes-Antoinette Fouque, 2010).

Ciravegna, Nicole, 'Le printemps et l'été 1944', *Marseille* (revue), 172 (1994), 13.

Collomb, Olivier, and Bonfort, Christian, *Le Bombardement du 15 août 1944 et la reconstruction de Sisteron* (Lyon: Éditions Sup'Copy, 1994).

Courant, Pierre, *Au Havre pendant le Siège. Souvenirs du 1er au 12 septembre 1944* (Paris: Fayard, 1946).

Coutel, Marguerite, *Bruz sous les bombes: un village breton dans la guerre* (Rennes: Éditions La Part Commune, 2005).

Cumming, Michael, *The Starkey Sacrifice: the Allied Bombing of Le Portel, 1943* (Stroud (Gloucestershire): Alan Sutton, 1996).

d'Abzac-Epezy, Claude, 'Le Secrétariat général de la Défense aérienne (1943–1944), une "armée nouvelle" dans la France occupée', *Revue Historique des Armées*, 188, September 1992, 79–89.

Dandel, Michel, Duboc, Grégory, Kitts, Anthony, and Lapersonne, Éric, *Les Victimes Civiles des Bombardements en Haute-Normandie, 1er janvier 1944 – 12 septembre 1944* (Caen: CRHQ-RED, La Mandragore, 1997).

Darlow, Steve, *Sledgehammers for Tintacks: Bomber Command Confronts the V-1 Menace, 1843–1944* (London: Grub Street, 2002).

de Gaulle, Charles, *Mémoires de guerre* (3 vols., Paris: Plon, 1954–1959).

—*Discours et Messages*, vol. I (Paris: Plon, 1970).

—*Lettres, Notes et Carnets* (Paris: Plon, 1983).

de la Porte, Gilles ed. *Le Havre, Volonté et modernité* (Le Havre: Éditions La Galerne, 1992).

Diamond, Hannah, *Fleeing Hitler: France 1940* (Oxford: Oxford University Press, 2007).

Dodd, Lindsey, 'Are we defended? Conflicting representations of war in pre-war France', *University of Sussex Journal of Contemporary History*, 12, 2008, on http://www.sussex.ac.uk/history/1-4-1-1.html.

—'"Partez partez", again and again: the efficacy of evacuation as a means of protecting children from bombing in France, 1939–44', *Children in War*, 6.1, February 2009, 7–20.

—'Children under the Allied Bombs: France 1940–1945', unpublished Ph.D. thesis, University of Reading, 2011.

—'"Relieving Sorrow and Misfortune"? State, Charity, Ideology and Aid in Bombed-out France, 1940–1945', in Claudia Baldoli, Andrew Knapp and Richard Overy (eds), *Bombing, States and Peoples in Western Europe, 1940–1945* (London: Continuum, 2011), 75–97.

Dodd, Lindsey and Knapp, Andrew, '"How many Frenchmen did you kill?" British Bombing Policy Towards France, 1940–1945', *French History*, 22(4), 2008, 469–92.

Dujardin, Laurent and Butaeye, Damien, *Les réfugiés dans les carrières pendant la bataille de Caen, juin-juillet 1944* (Rennes: Éditions Ouest-France/Mémorial de Caen, 2009).

Florentin, Eddy, *Le Havre 44 à feu et à sang*, 2nd edn. (Paris: Presses de la Cité, 1985).

—*Quand les alliés bombardaient la France, 1940–45* (Paris: Perrin, 1997).

Foot, M. R. D., *SOE in France: An Account of the Work of the British Special Operations Executive in France 1940–1944* (revised edn.: London: Frank Cass, 2004).

France, État-Major de l'Armée, *Les Bombardements aériens des chemins de fer français de janvier à août 1944* (Paris: Bureau Scientifique de l'Armée, 1945) (in Service Historique de la Défense, Vincennes, ref. G1309).

Gaignebet, Jean-Baptiste, 'Incertitudes de la paix, cruautés de la guerre (1929–1944)', in Maurice Agulhon ed., *Histoire de Toulon* (Paris: Privat, 1980), 343–56.

Galtier-Boissière, Jean, *Journal 1940–1950* (Paris: Quai Voltaire, 1992).

Garnier, Bernard, and Pigenet, M., *Les victimes civiles des bombardements en Normandie* (Caen: La Mandragore, 1997).

Garnier, Bernard, Leleu, Jean-Luc, Passera, Françoise, and Quellien, Jean (eds), *Les Populations civiles face au débarquement et à la bataille de Normandie* (Caen: CRHQ, CNRS-Université de Caen and Mémorial pour la Paix, 2005).

Gervereau, Laurent and Peschanski, Denis (eds), *La propagande sous Vichy, 1940–1944* (Paris: Bibliothèque de Documentation Internationale Contemporaine, 1990).

Gildea, Robert, *Marianne in Chains: Daily Life in the Heart of France during the German Occupation* (London: Macmillan, 2002).

Giolitto, Pierre, *Histoire de la Milice* (Paris: Perrin, 2002).

Girault, Jacques, 'Le Syndicat des instituteurs', in René Rémond et Janine Bourdin (eds), *La France et les Français en 1938 et 1939* (Paris: Presses de la Fondation Nationale des Sciences Politiques, 1978), 189–221.

Grenier, Jean, *Sous l'Occupation* (Paris: Éditions Claire Paulhan, 1997).

Guéhenno, Jean, *Journal des années noires, 1940–1944* (Paris: Gallimard, 2002 (1st edn. 1947)).

Guillemard, Julien, *L'Enfer du Havre* (Paris: Éditions Medicis, 1948).

Halls, W. D., *The Youth of Vichy France* (Oxford: Oxford University Press, 1981).

—*Politics, Society and Christianity in Vichy France* (Oxford: Berg, 1995).

Hardy, Antoine, 'La défense passive à Rouen et dans son agglomération', mémoire de Master d'Histoire Contemporaine, préparé sous la direction de Jean-Claude Vimont et de Olivier Feiertag, Université de Rouen, Département d'Histoire, année 2005–6.

—'La défense passive à Rouen', *Études Normandes*, 57.1, 2008, 61–70.

Hesse, Philippe-Jean and Le Crom, Jean-Pierre (eds), *La protection sociale sous Vichy* (Rennes: Presses Universitaires de Rennes, 2001).

Hoffmann, Stanley, 'The Vichy circle of French conservatives' in Stanley Hoffmann, *Decline or renewal? France since the 1930s* (New York: The Viking Press, 1974), pp. 3–25.

Horne, Alistair, *To Lose a Battle: France 1940* (London: Macmillan, 1969).

Jackson, Julian, *France: the Dark Years 1940–1944* (Oxford: Oxford University Press, 2001).

Jacquin, Frédéric, *Les bombardements de Brest, 1940–1944* (Brest: Éditions MEB, 1997).

Johnson, Douglas, 'Churchill and France', in Robert Blake and William Roger Louis (eds), *Churchill* (Oxford: Oxford University Press, 1993), 41–55.

Karlsgodt, Elizabeth Campbell, *Defending National Treasures: French Art and Heritage under Vichy* (Stanford, Ca.: Stanford University Press, 2011).

Kiesling, Eugenia C., *Arming against Hitler: France and the Limits of Military Planning* (Lawrence, Kansas: University Press of Kansas, 1996).

Knapp, Andrew, 'The Destruction and Liberation of Le Havre in Modern Memory', *War in History* 14.4 (2007), 476–99.

Kitson, Simon, 'Criminals or Liberators? French Public Opinion and the Allied Bombing of France, 1940–1945', in Claudia Baldoli, Andrew Knapp and Richard Overy (eds), *Bombing, States and Peoples in Western Europe, 1940–1945* (London: Continuum, 2011), 279–97.

Kulok, Jan, 'Trait d'union: The history of the French relief organisation Secours national/Entr'aide francaise under the Third Republic, the Vichy regime and the early Fourth Republic 1939–1949', D. Phil. thesis, University of Oxford, 2003.

Laborie, Pierre, *L'opinion française sous Vichy: les Français et la crise d'identité nationale, 1936–1944* (Paris: Le Seuil, 1990).

Langley, J. M., *Fight Another Day* (London: Collins, 1974).

Lantier, Maurice, *Saint-Lô au bûcher* (Condé-sur-Vire: Imprimerie Corbrion, 1993).

—ed. *Renaissance et reconstruction de Saint-Lô (Manche), 1944–1964* (Saint-Lô: Université Inter-âges, 2000).

Larès-Yoël, Micheline, *France 40–44: Expérience d'une persécution* (Paris: L'Harmattan, 1996).

Latrille, Pierre, *Le Havre pendant l'occupation allemande* (Le Havre: author, 1944: in Archives Municipales de la Ville du Havre, GUE 002).

Le Boterf, Hervé, *La Bretagne dans la guerre* (Paris: Éditions France-Empire, 2000).

Le Marec, Gérard, *Lyon sous l'occupation* (Rennes: Ouest-France, 1984).

Le Melledo, Paul, *Lorient sous les bombes. Itinéraire d'un Gavroche lorientais* (Le Faouet: Liv'éditions, 2003).

Le Roc'h Morgère, Louis, and Quellien, Jean (eds), *L'Été 1944: les Normands dans la bataille* (3 volumes: Caen: Conseil Général du Calvados, Direction des Archives Départementales, 1998, 1999 and 2000).

Le Trévier, Paul, *Objectif Rouen: 1er raid américain sur l'Europe* (St-Germain-en-Laye: Comever, 2005).

Le Trévier, Paul, and Rose, Daniel, *Ce qui s'est vraiment passé le 19 avril 1944: Le Martyre de Sotteville, Rouen, et la Région* (Saint-Germain-en-Laye: Comever, 2004).

Lecadet, G., 'Valognes: les foyers sont devenus des tombeaux', in Michel Boivin, Gérard Bourdin, and Jean Quellien, (eds), *Villes normandes sous les bombes (juin 1944)* (Caen: Presses Universitaires de Caen/Mémorial de Caen, 1994), 219–26.

Lecup, Albert, *Arras sous les bombardements de 1944* (Arras: Imprimerie Centrale de l'Artois, 1979).

Lefaivre, François ed., *J'ai vécu les bombardements à Condé-sur-Noireau* (Condé-sur-Noireau: Éditions Charles Corlet, 1994).

Legrand, Jacqueline, *Courageuse Abbeville, 3 septembre 1939 – 3 septembre 1944* (Abbeville: Imprimerie F. Paillart, 1990).

Lévy, Claude, 'La Propagande' in Jean-Pierre Azéma and François Bédarida, *La France des années noires*, vol. 2 (Paris: Seuil, 2000), 57–76.

Lindsay, Martin, *So Few Got Through* (London: Collins, 1946).

Lucas Phillips, C. E., *The Greatest Raid of All* (London: Pan Books, 2000 (1st edn. London, Heinemann, 1958)).

Machefert-Tassin, Yves, 'Le bilan des bombardements aériens des installations ferroviaires en France', in Marie-Noëlle Polino ed., *Une Entreprise publique dans la guerre: la SNCF, 1939–1945* (Paris: Presses Universitaires de France, 2001), pp. 219–40. On-line version on *http://www.ahicf.com/ww2/actes.htm*

Martin, Georges, *Ambérieu, la rebelle* (Bourg-en-Bresse: Musnier-Gilbert Éditions, 2002).

Maurois, André, *Rouen dévasté*, (Fontaine-le-Bourg: Le Pucheux, 2004 (1st edn. Paris: Nagel, 1948)).

Mazey, Sonia, and Wright, Vincent, 'Les préfets', in Jean-Pierre Azéma and François Bédarida (eds), *Vichy et les Français* (Paris: Fayard, 1992), 267–86.

Mendès-France, Pierre, 'Roissy-en-France: l'attaque de Chevilly-Larue par le groupe Lorraine, le 3 octobre 1943', *Forces aériennes françaises*, 73, October 1952, 5–25.

Middlebrook, Martin, and Everitt, Chris, *The Bomber Command War Diaries, 1939–1945* (Leicester: Midland Publishing, 2000 (1st edn. London, Viking, 1985)).

Milward, Alan, *The New Order and the French Economy* (Oxford: Oxford University Press, 1970).

Mitchell, Allan, *Nazi Paris: the History of an Occupation, 1940–1944* (Oxford and New York: Berghahn, 2008).

Monsuez, Jean-Jacques, 'Les sections sanitaires automobiles féminines', *Revue Historique des Armées*, 247 (2007), 98–113. On-line version at *http://rha.revues.org/index2033.html.*

Montaz, Pierre, *Onze Américains tombés du ciel sauvés par des maquis français* (Hauteville (Savoie, France): author, 1994).

Morin, Claude, *La Touraine sous les bombes 1940–1944* (Chambray-lès-Tours: CLD Éditions, 2000).

Nobécourt, R. G., *Rouen désolée, 1939–1944* (Paris: Éditions Médicis, 1949).

Ory, P., *Les collaborateurs, 1940–1945* (Paris: Seuil, 1976).

Ousby, Ian, *Occupation*, (London: Pimlico, 1999).

Paxton, Robert O., *Vichy France: Old Guard and New Order 1940–1944* (New York: Alfred Knopf, 1972).

Péron, François, *Brest sous l'occupation* (Rennes: Ouest-France, 1981).

Pétain, Philippe, *Discours aux Français, 17 juin 1940 – 20 août 1944* (Paris: Albin Michel, 1989).

Prime, Christophe, 'Les bombardements du jour J et de la bataille de Normandie', in Bernard Garnier, Jean-Luc Leleu, Françoise Passera, and Jean Quellien (eds), *Les Populations civiles face au débarquement et à la bataille de Normandie* (Caen: CRHQ, CNRS-Université de Caen and Mémorial pour la Paix, 2005), 31–47.

Probert, Henry, *Bomber Harris: His Life and Times* (London: Greenhill Books, 2001).

Py, Évelyne, *Un été sous les bombes: Givors-Grigny-Chasse, 1944* (Saint-Cyr-sur-Loire: Éditions Alan Sutton, 2004).

Quellien, Jean, Garnier, Bernard, and Université Inter-Âges, *Les Victimes civiles du Calvados dans la bataille de Normandie, 1er mars 1944 – 31 décembre 1945* (Caen: Éditions-Diffusion du Lys, 1995).

Ribeill, Georges, 'Aux prises avec les voies ferrées: Bombarder ou saboter? Un dilemme revisité', in Michèle Battesti and Patrick Facon (eds), *Les Bombardements Alliés sur la France durant la Seconde Guerre Mondiale:*

Stratégies, Bilans Matériaux et Humains (Paris: Ministère de la Défense, 2009), 135–61.

Sainclivier, Jacqueline, *La Bretagne dans la guerre, 1939–1945* (Rennes: Éditions Ouest–France/Mémorial de Caen, 1994).

Sainte-Péreuse, Lt-Col., 'Le bombardement de la région parisienne, le 3 juin 1940', *Forces Aériennes Françaises*, 72, September 1952, 737–62.

Sartre, Jean-Paul, *Situations, III* (Paris: Gallimard, 1949).

Sauvy, Alfred, *La Vie économique des Français de 1939 à 1945* (Paris : Flammarion, 1978).

Schmiedel, Michael, 'Orchestrated Solidarity: the Allied Air War in France and the Development of Local and State-Organized Solidarity Movements', in Claudia Baldoli, Andrew Knapp and Richard Overy (eds), *Bombing, States and Peoples in Western Europe, 1940–1945* (London: Continuum, 2011), 206–18.

Schumann, Maurice, *La voix du couvre-feu: cent allocutions de celui qui fut le porte-parole du général de Gaulle, 1940–1944* (Paris: Plon, 1964).

Scriven, Michael and Wagstaff, Peter (eds), *War and Society in Twentieth-Century France* (Oxford: Berg, 1991).

Swanson, Marc, *Le bombardement de Saint-Étienne, pourquoi? 26 mai 1944* (*Saint-Étienne*: Actes Graphiques, 2004).

Tanchoux, Philippe, 'La protection monumentale en 1939–45: l'action du service des monuments historiques en temps de guerre', unpublished paper given at the conference 'Guerres, œuvres d'art et patrimoine artistique à l'époque contemporaine', University of Picardie, 16–18 March 2011.

Thomas, R. T., *Britain and Vichy: the Dilemma of Anglo-French Relations 1940–42* (London: Macmillan, 1979).

Veillon, Dominique, *Vivre et survivre en France, 1939–1947* (Paris: Payot, 1995).

Vidalenc, Jean, *L'Exode de mai-juin 1940* (Paris: Presses Universitaires de France, 1957).

Voldman, Danièle, *La Reconstruction des villes françaises de 1940 à 1954: histoire d'une politique* (Paris: L'Harmattan, 1997).

Weiss, Louise, *Mémoires d'une Européenne* (3 vols.: Paris: Payot, 1970).

Wieviorka, Olivier, *Histoire du débarquement en Normandie* (Paris: Le Seuil, 2007).

Wouters, Nico, 'Municipal government during the Occupation (1940–45): a comparative model of Belgium, the Netherlands and France', *European History Quarterly*, 36/2 (2006), 221–46.

Yagil, Limore, '*L'homme nouveau' et la révolution nationale de Vichy, 1940–44* (Villeneuve d'Ascq: Presses Universitaires du Septentrion, 1997).

Young, Robert J., 'The Strategic Dream: French Air Doctrine in the Inter-War Period, 1919–39', *Journal of Contemporary History*, Vol. 9, No. 4 (Oct. 1974), 57–76.

—*In Command of France: French Foreign Policy and Military Planning, 1933–1940* (Cambridge, Mass.: Harvard University Press, 1978).

Zarifian, Christian, *Table Rase: 5 septembre 1944, Le Havre, Ville Assassinée* (Le Havre: Les Films Seine-Océan, 1988 (video)).

FRANCE: WEB SOURCES

Boulogne-Billancourt, British propaganda footage on raid of March 1942, *http://www.youtube.com/watch?v=BRKnLO-HJu8*, accessed 30 May 2011.

France-Actualités, newsreel on the role of the SIPEG train after the bombing of Le Creusot, 25 June 1943, *http://www.ina.fr/economie-et-societe/vie-sociale/video/AFE86001987/le-nouveau-train-d-assistance-du-sipeg.fr.html*, accessed 11 July 2010.

France-Actualités, newsreel, Commentary by Philippe Henriot after raids on Paris and Rouen, 21 April 1944, *http://www.ina.fr/histoire-et-conflits/seconde-guerre-mondiale/video/AFE86002666/discours-de-philippe-henriot-apres-les-bombardements-de-paris-et-de-rouen.fr.html*, accessed 11 July 2010.

http://laureleforestier.typepad.fr/blog_de_laure_leforestier/ma_ville_sous_loccupation/, accessed 30 May 2011.

http://www.youtube.com/watch?v=D4Ok-RKgCHg&feature=PlayList&p=C30CFE9A9C9A840D&playnext=1&playnext_from=PL&index=41, accessed 30 May 2011.

Institut National de l'Audiovisuel (INA), at *http://www.ina.fr/*.

Institut National de l'Audiovisuel (INA), *http://www.ina.fr/histoire-et-conflits/seconde-guerre-mondiale/video/AFE86002390/bombardement-de-la-region-parisienne.fr.html*

ITALY

Absalom, Roger, *Strange Alliance: Aspects of Escape and Survival in Italy, 1943–1945* (Florence: Olschki, 1991).

—'Hiding history: the Allies, the Resistance and the others in occupied Italy 1943–1945', *Historical Journal*, 38 (1995), 111–31.

Agarossi, Elena, *A Nation Collapses: The Italian Surrender of September 1943* (Cambridge: Cambridge University Press, 1999).

Albergoni, Attilio, *Racconti palermitani del 1943, ovvero quando cadevano bombe a 'strafuttiri'* (Palermo: Anteprima, 1999).

Ambrose, Stephen, *Wild Blue* (London: Simon and Schuster, 2001).

Antonicelli, Franco ed. *Dall'Antifascismo alla Resistenza: trent'anni di storia italiana (1915–1945)* (Turin: Einaudi, 1961).

Aquarone, Alberto, *L'organizzazione dello stato totalitario* (Turin: Einaudi, 1995 (1st edn. 1965)).

Arbizzani, Luigi ed. *Al di qua e al di là della Linea Gotica, 1944–1945. Aspetti sociali, politici e militari in Toscana e in Emilia Romagna*, (Bologna-Firenze: Regioni Toscana e Emilia Romagna, 1993).

Arena, Nino, *La Regia Aeronautica, 1939–1943*, vol. 1 (Rome: Stato Maggiore Aeronautica, 1981).

Argentieri, Mimmo, *Il cinema in guerra. Arte, comunicazione e propaganda in Italia, 1940–1944* (Rome: Editori Riuniti, 1998).

Baduel, Ugo, *L'elmetto inglese* (Palermo: Sellerio, 1993 (1st edn. 1992)).

Baldissara, Luca and Pezzino, Paolo (eds), *Crimini e memorie di guerra. Violenza contro le popolazioni e politiche del ricordo* (Naples: L'ancora del Mediterraneo, 2004).

Baldoli, Claudia, 'I bombardamenti sull'Italia nella Seconda Guerra Mondiale. Strategia anglo-americana e propaganda rivolta alla popolazione civile', *Deportate, Esuli, Profughe*, 13–14, 2010, 34–49.

—'Religion and Bombing in Italy, 1940–1945', in Claudia Baldoli, Andrew Knapp and Richard Overy (eds), *Bombing, States and Peoples in Western Europe, 1940–1945* (London: Continuum, 2011), 136–53.

Baldoli, Claudia and Fincardi, Marco, 'Italian Society under Allied Bombs: Propaganda, Experience, and Legend, 1940–1945', *Historical Journal*, 52 (4), 2009, 1017–38.

Baris, Tommaso, *Tra due fuochi. Esperienza e memoria della guerra lungo la linea Gustav* (Rome-Bari: Laterza, 2003).

Belco, Victoria, *War, Massacre and Recovery in Central Italy, 1943–1948* (Toronto: University of Toronto Press, 2010).

Bermani, Cesare, *Spegni la luce che passa Pippo. Voci, leggende e miti della storia contemporanea* (Rome: Odradek, 1996).

Berneri, Marie Louise and Brittain, Vera, *Il Seme del Caos. Scritti sui bombardamenti di massa*, ed. Claudia Baldoli (Caserta: Spartaco, 2004).

Bersani, Cristina and Roncuzzi Roversi Monaco, Valeria, *Delenda Bononia. Immagini dei bombardamenti 1943–1945* (Bologna: Patron, 1995).

Bocca, Giorgio, *Storia dell'Italia partigiana, settembre 1943–maggio 1945* (Milan: Mondadori, 1995).

Boccalatte, Luciano, D'Arrigo, Andrea and Maida, Bruno (eds), *38/45 Luoghi della guerra e della resistenza nella provincia di Torino* (Turin: Blu Edizioni, 2006).

Bonacina, Giorgio, *Obiettivo: Italia. I bombardamenti aerei delle città italiane dal 1940 al 1945* (Milan: Mursia, 2005 (1st edn. 1970)).

Bongiovanni, Corrado, *Corso di chimica e di mineralogia per gli Istituti Magistrali* (Rimini: Stabilimento Tipografico Garattoni, 1935).

Brigaglia, Manlio and Podda, Giuseppe, *Sardegna 1940–1945. La guerra, le bombe, la libertà. I drammi e le speranze nel racconto di chi c'era* (Cagliari: Tema, 1994).

British Foreign Office, *Sicily Zone Handbook 1943*, ed. Rosario Mangiameli (Caltanissetta-Rome: Salvatore Sciascia Editore, 1994).

Bronzuoli, Anacleto, *La protezione antiaerea delle popolazioni civili* (Naples: Editrice Rispoli Anonima, 1940).

Burla, Umberto, *La Spezia nel ventennio. Dal 1922 al 1943* (La Spezia: Luna Editore, 2008).

Caglini, Camillo, *Bombardamenti su Ancona e provincia, 1943–44* (Ancona: Cassa di Risparmio, 1983).

Calamandrei, Piero, *Diario, 1939–1945*, ed. Giorgio Agosti (Scandicci: La Nuova Italia, 1992).

Callegari, Paola and Curzi, Valter (eds), *Venezia: la tutela per immagini. Un caso esemplare dagli archivi della Fototeca Nazionale* (Bologna: Bononia University Press, 2005).

Calvino, Italo, 'Le notti dell'UNPA', in 'L'entrata in guerra', *Romanzi e racconti*, vol. 1 (Milan: Mondadori, 1991).

Carazzolo, Maria, *Più forte della paura. Diario di guerra e dopoguerra (1938–1947)* (Sommacampagna: Cierre, 2007).

Carli, Maddalena and Gentiloni Silveri, Umberto, *Bombardare Roma. Gli Alleati e la 'città aperta' (1940–1944)* (Bologna: Il Mulino, 2007).

Casella, Luciano, *The European War of Liberation: Tuscany and the Gothic Line* (Florence: La Nuova Europa, 1993).

Caserta, Aldo, *Il clero di Napoli durante la guerra e la resistenza (1940–1943)* (Napoli: Luciano Editore, 1995).

Castronovo, Valerio, *FIAT, 1899–1999: un secolo di storia italiana* (Milan: Rizzoli, 1999).

Cavallo, Pietro, *Riso amaro. Radio, teatro e propaganda nel secondo conflitto mondiale* (Rome: Bulzoni, 1994).

—*Gli italiani in guerra. Sentimenti e immagini dal 1940 al 1945* (Bologna: Il Mulino, 1997).

Cavazzoli, Luigi, *La gente e la guerra. La vita quotidiana del fronte interno: Mantova, 1940–1945* (Milan: Angeli, 1989).

Celeghin, Alberto (ed.), *Bombardamenti aerei sulla città di Padova e provincia, 1943–1945* (Padua: Tempio-Museo dell'Internato Ignoto, 2005).

CGIL ed. *Torino marzo '43. Scioperano 100,000 operai contro la guerra* (Turin: CGIL, 1993).

Chianese, Gloria, *'Quando uscimmo dai rifugi'. Il Mezzogiorno tra guerra e dopoguerra (1943–46)* (Rome: Carocci, 2004).

Chilanti, Gloria, *Bandiera rossa e borsa nera. La resistenza di una adolescente* (Milan: Mursia, 1998).

Chiodi, Cesare and Mariani, Francesco, *Relazione sulle visite ad alcuni impianti di protezione antiaerea in Germania* (Milan: Industrie Grafiche Italiane Stucchi, 1938).

Colantuono, Patrizio, *Lo sbarco e la battaglia di Anzio. Immagini e testimonianze* (Anzio: Tipografia Marina, 2009).

Colarizi, Simona, *La seconda guerra mondiale e la Repubblica* (Turin: UTET, 1984).

—*L'opinione degli italiani sotto il regime, 1929–1943* (Rome-Bari: Laterza, 2000 (1st edn. 1991)).

Collotti, Enzo with Labanca, Nicola and Sala, Teodoro, *Fascismo e politica di potenza. Politica estera 1922–1939* (Milan: La Nuova Italia, 2000).

Comune di Prevalle, *Ricordi Ninetta... Uomini e donne di Prevalle si raccontano* (Brescia: Liberedizioni, 2008)

Cortesi, Elena, *L'odissea degli sfollati. Il Forlivese, il Riminese e il Cesenate di fronte allo sfollamento di massa* (Cesena: Il Ponte Vecchio, 2003).

—'Evacuation in Italy during the Second World War: Evolution and Management', in Claudia Baldoli, Andrew Knapp and Richard Overy (eds), *Bombing, States and Peoples in Western Europe, 1940–1945* (London: Continuum, 2011), 59–74.

Curami, Andrea, Ferrari, Paolo and Rastelli, Achille, *Breda. Alle origini della meccanica bresciana* (Brescia: Fondazione Negri, 2009).

Dalla Casa, Brunella and Preti, Alberto, *Bologna in guerra, 1940–1945* (Milan: Franco Angeli, 1995).

Deakin, Frederick, *The Brutal Friendship: Mussolini, Hitler, and the Fall of Italian Fascism* (London: Weidenfeld and Nicolson, 1962).

Del Boca, Angelo, Legnani, Massimo and Rossi, Mario G., *Il regime fascista. Storia e storiografia* (Rome-Bari: Laterza, 1995).

Della Volpe, Nicola, *Difesa del territorio e protezione antiaerea, 1915–1943* (Rome: Ufficio Storico dello Stato Maggiore dell'Esercito, 1986).

De Simone, Cesare, *Venti angeli sopra Roma. I bombardamenti aerei sulla Città Eterna, 19 luglio e 13 agosto 1943* (Milan: Mursia, 1993).

Di Benigno, Jolanda, *Occasioni mancate. Roma in un diario segreto, 1943–1944* (Rome: SEI, 1945).

Di Giovanni, Marco, *Scienza e potenza. Miti della guerra moderna, istituzioni scientifiche e politica di massa nell'Italia fascista* (Turin: Zamorani, 2005).

Di Nolfo, Ennio, *Le paure e le speranze degli italiani* (Milan: Mondadori, 1986).

Di Nolfo, Ennio, Rainero, Romain and Vigezzi, Brunello (eds), *L'Italia e la politica di potenza in Europa, 1938–1940* (Milan: Marzorati, 1985).

Di Pompeo, Corrado, *Più della fame e più dei bombardamenti. Diario dell'occupazione di Roma* (Bologna: Il Mulino, 2009).

Duggan, Christopher, *The Force of Destiny: a History of Italy since 1796* (London: Allen Lane, 2007).

Ellwood, David, *Italy 1943–1945* (Leicester: Leicester University Press, 1985).

Ellwood, David, Pezzino, Paolo, et al., 'The Never-Ending Liberation', monographic issue of *Journal of Modern Italian Studies*, 4 (2005).

Ferratini Tosi, Francesca, Grassi, Gaetano and Legnani, Massimo, *L'Italia nella Seconda Guerra Mondiale e nella Resistenza* (Milan: Angeli, 1988).

Ferrari, Paolo ed. *L'aeronautica italiana: una storia del Novecento* (Milan: Angeli, 2004)

Fincardi, Mario, 'Anglo-American Air Attacks and the Rebirth of Public Opinion in Fascist Italy', in Claudia Baldoli, Andrew Knapp and Richard

Overy (eds), *Bombing, States and Peoples in Western Europe, 1940–1945* (London: Continuum, 2011), 241–55.

Fondazione Micheletti, *Annali. 5. L'Italia in guerra, 1940–1943* (Brescia: Fondazione Micheletti, 1991).

Franzinelli, Mimmo, *I tentacoli dell'OVRA. Agenti, collaboratori e vittime della polizia fascista* (Turin: Bollati Boringhieri, 1999).

Gallerano, Nicola ed. *L'altro dopoguerra. Roma e il Sud, 1943–1945* (Milan: Angeli, 1985).

Ganapini, Luigi, *Una città, la guerra. Lotte di classe, ideologie e forze politiche a Milano, 1939–1951* (Milan: Angeli, 1988).

—*La Repubblica delle camicie nere* (Milan: Garzanti 2010 (1st edn. 2000)).

Garibaldi, Giuseppe, *Autobiography of Giuseppe Garibaldi* trans. A. Werner, vol. III (London: Walter Smith and Innes, 1889).

Gentile, Emilio, *La via italiana al totalitarismo. Il partito e lo Stato nel regime fascista* (Rome: Carocci, 2008 (1st edn. 1995)).

Giannuzzi Savelli, Alfredo, *Conferenza di propaganda per la protezione antiaerea del territorio nazionale e della popolazione civile - Anno 1931-X* (Rome: Istituto Poligrafico dello Stato, 1934).

—*Offesa aerea. Mezzi di difesa e protezione* (Milan: Martucci, 1936).

Giannuzzi Savelli, Alfredo and Stellingwerf, Giuseppe, *Protezione antiaerea di Roma* (Rome: Istituto di Studi Romani, 1938).

Gioannini, Marco and Massobrio, Giulio, *Bombardate l'Italia. Storia della guerra di distruzione aerea, 1940–45* (Milan: Rizzoli, 2007).

Gismondi, Mario, *Foggia: la tragica estate; Taranto: la notte più lunga* (Bari: Dedalo, 1968).

Glenny, Arthur W. F., *Mediterranean Air Power and the Second Front* (London: The Conrad Press, 1944).

Gleria, Franco and Radacich, Maurizio, *Il terrore viene dal cielo. Trieste, 1944–1945* (Trieste: Italo Svevo Edizioni, 2007).

Gooch, John, *Mussolini and his Generals: The Armed Forces and Fascist Foreign Policy, 1922–1940* (Cambridge: Cambridge University Press, 2007).

Gribaudi, Gabriella, *Guerra totale. Tra bombe alleate e violenze naziste: Napoli e il fronte meridionale, 1940–1944* (Turin: Bollati Boringhieri, 2005).

—'The True Cause of the "Moral Collapse": People, Fascists and Authorities under the Bombs. Naples and the Countryside, 1940–1944', in Claudia Baldoli, Andrew Knapp and Richard Overy (eds), *Bombing, States and Peoples in Western Europe, 1940–1945* (London: Continuum, 2011), 219–38.

Gribaudi, Gabriella (ed.), *Terra bruciata. Le stragi naziste sul fronte meridionale: per un atlante delle stragi naziste in Italia* (Naples: L'Ancora del Mediterraneo, 2003).

Gribaudi, Gabriella ed. *Le guerre del Novecento* (Naples: L'Ancora del Mediterraneo, 2007).

Guerrieri, Antonio, *La città spezzata. Foggia, quei giorni del '43* (Bari: Edipuglia, 1996).

Harvey, Stephen, 'The Italian War Effort and the Strategic Bombing of Italy', *History*, 70, 1985, 32–45.

Holt, Robert T. and Van de Velde, Robert W., *Strategic Psychological Operations and American Foreign Policy* (Chicago: University of Chicago Press, 1967 (1st edn. 1960)).

Imbriani, Angelo Michele, *Gli italiani e il Duce: il mito e l'immagine di Mussolini negli ultimi anni del fascismo, 1938–1943* (Naples: Liguori, 1992).

Infield, Glenn, *Disaster at Bari* (London: New English library, 1976 (1st edn. 1971)).

Isnenghi, Mario, *Le guerre degli italiani. Parole, immagini, ricordi: 1848–1945* (Bologna: Il Mulino, 2005).

—ed. *I luoghi della memoria. Strutture ed eventi dell'Italia unita* (Rome-Bari: Laterza, 1997).

Isola, Gianni, *Abbassa la tua radio, per favore... Storia dell'ascolto radiofonico nell'Italia fascista* (Scandicci: La Nuova Italia, 1990).

—*L'ha scritto la radio. Storia e testi della radio durante il fascismo (1924–1944)* (Milan: Bruno Mondadori, 1998).

Klinkhammer, Lutz, *L'occupazione tedesca in Italia, 1943–1945* (Turin: Bollati Boringhieri, 2007 (1st edn. 1993)).

Knox, MacGregor, *Hitler's Italian Allies: Royal Armed Forces, Fascist Regime, and the War of 1940–1943* (Cambridge: Cambridge University Press, 2000).

—*Common Destiny: Dictatorship, Foreign Policy, and War in Fascist Italy and Nazi Germany* (Cambridge: Cambridge University Press, 2009).

Labanca, Nicola, *Quando le nostre città erano macerie. Immagini e documenti sulle distruzioni belliche in provincia di Arezzo, 1943–1944* (Montepulciano: Editori Del Grifo, 1988).

Lehman, Eric, *Le ali del potere. La propaganda aeronautica nell'Italia fascista* (Turin: UTET, 2010).

Leoni, Diego and Marchesoni, Patrizia (eds), *Le ali maligne, le meridiane di morte. Trento 1943–1945* (Trento: Temi, 1995).

Leoni, Diego and Rasera, Fabrizio, *Rovereto 1940–1945. Frammenti di un'autobiografia della città* (Rovereto: Materiali di Lavoro, 1993).

Lepre, Aurelio, *Le illusioni, la paura, la rabbia. Il fronte interno italiano, 1940–1943* (Naples: Edizioni Scientifiche Italiane, 1989).

Levi, Carlo, *The Watch* (London: Cassell, 1952).

Lewis, Norman, *Naples '44* (London: Eland, 2002 (1st edn. 1978)).

Lucioli, Roberto, 'Sfollamento, mobilità sociale e sfaldamento delle istituzioni nella provincia di Ancona', *Storia e problemi contemporanei*, 15, April 1995.

Lupo, Salvatore, *Il fascismo. La politica in un regime totalitario* (Rome: Donzelli, 2000).

Lyttleton, Adrian ed. *Liberal and Fascist Italy* (Oxford: Oxford University Press, 2002).

Maida, Bruno ed. *Guerra e società nella provincia di Torino, 1940–1945* (Turin: Blu Edizioni, 2007).

Maida, Bruno and Tranfaglia, Nicola (eds), *Ministri e giornalisti: la guerra e il MinCulPop, 1939–1943* (Turin: Einaudi, 2005).

Malaparte, Curzio, *The Skin* (Hamilton & Co. Stafford: London, 1964).

Mangiameli, Rosario, *Memorie della Seconda Guerra Mondiale in Sicilia* (Catania: CUECM, 2003).

Mangiameli, Rosario and Nicastro, Franco (eds), *Arrivano … gli americani a Vittoria nell'estate del '43* (Vittoria: Comune di Vittoria, 2004 (1st edn. 2003)).

Marsetič, Raul, *I bombardamenti alleati su Pola, 1944–1945. Vittime, danni, rifugi, disposizioni delle autorità e ricostruzione* (Rovigno-Trieste: Centro Ricerche Storiche di Rovigno, 2004).

Martinelli, Franco, *Città italiana in tempo di guerra. La Spezia, 1940–1945* (Naples: Liguori, 2003).

Massola, Umberto, *Gli scioperi del '43. Marzo-aprile: le fabbriche contro il fascismo* (Rome: Editori Riuniti, 1973).

Massola, Umberto and Li Causi, Girolamo, *Gli scioperi 1943–1944. La classe operaia in lotta contro il fascismo e l'occupante* (Rome: L'Unità, 1945).

Mercuri, Lamberto, *La 'quarta arma'. 1942–1950: propaganda psicologica degli Alleati in Italia* (Milan: Mursia, 1998).

Morgan, Philip, *The Fall of Mussolini: Italy, the Italians, and the Second World War* (Oxford: Oxford University Press, 2007).

Moscioni Negri, Cristoforo, *Linea Gotica* (Bologna: Il Mulino, 2006).

Mussolini, Benito, *Opera Omnia di Benito Mussolini*, 31 vols., ed. Edoardo and Duilio Susmel (Florence: La Fenice, 1951–63).

Nenni, Pietro, *Tempo di guerra fredda. Diari 1943–1956* (Milan: Sugarco, 1981).

Nicholas, Lynn H., *The Rape of Europa. The Fate of Europe's Treasures in the Third Reich and the Second World War* (London: Macmillan, 1994).

Nezzo, Marta, 'The Defence of Works of Art Against Bombing in Italy During the Second World War', in Claudia Baldoli, Andrew Knapp and Richard Overy (eds), *Bombing, States and Peoples in Western Europe, 1940–1945* (London: Continuum, 2011), 101–20.

Oliva, Gianni, *La Resistenza alle porte di Torino* (Milan: Franco Angeli, 1989).

—*La Repubblica di Salò* (Florence: Giunti, 1997).

Origo, Iris, *War in val D'Orcia. An Italian War Diary, 1943–1944* (London: Alison and Busby, 2005 (1st edn. 1947)).

Ortoleva, Peppino and Ottaviano, Chiara (eds), *Guerra e mass media. Strumenti e modi della comunicazione in contesto bellico* (Naples: Liguori, 1994).

Paggi, Leonardo, *Stragi tedesche e bombardamenti alleati. L'esperienza della guerra e la nuova democrazia a San Miniato (Pisa): la memoria e la ricerca storica* (Rome: Carocci, 2005).

—*Il 'popolo dei morti'. La repubblica italiana nata dalla guerra (1940–1946)* (Bologna: Il Mulino, 2009).

Pagliaro, Grazia, *Giorni di guerra in Sicilia. Diario per la nonna, 9 maggio-8 agosto 1943* (Palermo: Sellerio, 1993).

Palla, Marco, 'Il passaggio del fronte nell'Italia del 1943–45', monographic issue of *Storia e problemi contemporanei*, 1–2, 1988.

Parri, Ferruccio, 'Il Movimento di Liberazione e gli alleati', *Il Movimento di Liberazione in Italia*, 1, July 1949, 8–27.

Passerini, Luisa, *Fascism in Popular Memory: the Cultural Experience of the Turin Working Class* (Cambridge: Cambridge University Press, 1987).

Pavone, Claudio, *Una guerra civile. Saggio sulla moralità nella Resistenza* (Turin: Bollati Boringhieri, 1991).

Pedron, Pina and Pontalti, Nicoletta, *Uomini e donne in guerra. Trentino, 1940–1945* (Trento: Museo Storico, 2001).

Peli, Santo, *Storia della Resistenza in Italia* (Turin: Einaudi, 2006).

Perry, Alan, 'Pippo: an Italian Folklore Mystery of World War II', *Journal of Folklore Research*, 40, 2003, 115–48.

Pesenti, Antonio, *Noi e gli alleati* (A.P.E., 1944).

Piccialuti Caprioli, Maria, *Radio Londra, 1939–1945* (Rome-Bari: Laterza, 1979).

Picciaredda, Stefano, *Diplomazia umanitaria. La Croce Rossa nella Seconda Guerra Mondiale* (Bologna: Il Mulino, 2003).

Piccioni, Lidia ed. 'Roma in guerra, 1940–1943', monographic issue of *Roma moderna e contemporanea*, 3, 2003.

Piffer, Tommaso, *Gli Alleati e la Resistenza italiana* (Bologna: Il Mulino, 2010).

Pivato, Stefano, *Sentimenti e quotidianità in una provincia in guerra. Rimini, 1940–1944* (Rimini: Maggioli, 1995).

Pizarroso Quintero, Alejandro, *Stampa, radio e propaganda. Gli Alleati in Italia, 1943–1946* (Milan: Angeli, 1989).

Porta, Gianfranco ed. *Alle origini della Repubblica. L'Italia tra guerra, resistenza, ricostruzione* (Brescia: Grafo, 1998).

Portelli, Sandro, 'So Much Depends on a Red Bus, or Innocent Victims of the Liberating Gun', *Oral History*, 34, 2006, 29–43.

Rastelli, Achille, *Bombe sulla città. Gli attacchi aerei alleati: le vittime civili a Milano* (Milan: Mursia, 2000).

Retico, Giacomo Sebastiano, *Paura oltre la Cisa* (Brescia: Toroselle, 2008).

Rochat, Giorgio, *Italo Balbo. Lo squadrista, l'aviatore, il gerarca* (Turin: UTET, 2003 (1st edn. 1986)).

—*Le guerre italiane, 1935–1943. Dall'impero d'Etiopia alla disfatta* (Turin: Einaudi, 2005).

Rochat, Giorgio, Santarelli, Enzo and Sorcinelli, Paolo (eds), *Linea Gotica 1944. Eserciti, popolazioni, partigiani* (Milan: Angeli, 1987 (1st edn. 1986)).

Rossi, Andrea, *La guerra delle camicie nere. La milizia fascista dalla guerra mondiale alla guerra civile* (Pisa: Franco Serantini, 2004).

Schofield, Brian B., *La notte di Taranto: 11 novembre 1940* (Milan: Mursia, 2005 (1st edn. 1974)).

Secchia, Pietro and Frassati, Filippo, *La Resistenza e gli Alleati* (Milan: Feltrinelli, 1962).

Senise, Carmine, *Quando ero capo della polizia, 1940–1943* (Rome: Ruffolo, 1946).

Spriano, Paolo, *Storia del Partito Comunista Italiano*, (Rome: L'Unità, 1990 (1st edn. 1970)).

Stefanile, Aldo, *I cento bombardamenti di Napoli* (Naples: Marotta, 1968).

Tonizzi, Elisabetta (ed.), 'Genova nella guerra, 1940–1945', monographic issue of *Storia e Memoria*, 1, 1993.

Tosi, Luisa ed. *Testimoni loro malgrado. Memorie del bombardamento del 7 aprile 1944* (Treviso: Istresco, 2006 (1st edn. 2005)).

Vecchio, Giorgio, *Lombardia 1940–1945. Vescovi, preti e società alla prova della guerra* (Brescia: Morcelliana, 2005).

Villa, Andrea, *Guerra aerea sull'Italia (1943–1945)* (Milan: Guerini e Associati, 2010).

Zamagni, Vera, *Dalla periferia al centro. La seconda rinascita economica dell'Italia (1861–1990)* (Bologna: Il Mulino, 1993).

Zamagni, Vera, ed. *Come perdere la guerra e vincere la pace. L'economia italiana tra guerra e dopoguerra, 1938–1947* (Bologna: Il Mulino, 1997).

Index

Printed in Great Britain
by Amazon

42181962R00179